Political Psychology

Political Psychology
Cultural and Crosscultural Foundations

Edited by
Stanley A. Renshon
and
John Duckitt

NEW YORK UNIVERSITY PRESS
Washington Square, New York

First published in the U.S.A. in 2000 by
NEW YORK UNIVERSITY PRESS
Washington Square
New York, N.Y. 10003

This book is printed on paper suitable for recycling and
made from fully managed and sustained forest sources.

Library of Congress Cataloging-in-Publication Data
Political psychology : cultural and crosscultural foundations /
edited by Stanley Renshon and John Duckitt.
p.   cm.
Includes bibliographical references and index.
ISBN 0–8147–7536–5 (cloth). — ISBN 0–8147–7537–3 (pbk.)
1. Political psychology Cross-cultural studies.   I. Renshon,
Stanley Allen.   II. Duckitt, J. H.
JA74.5.P367   2000
320'.01'9—dc21   99–26248
                                                           CIP

Printed in Great Britain

Contents

List of Tables and Figures   vii

Preface   ix

Notes on the Contributors   xiii

Part I   Foundations of Crosscultural Political Psychology

1 Cultural and Crosscultural Political Psychology: 3
   Revitalizing a Founding Tradition for a New Subfield
   Stanley A. Renshon and John Duckitt

2 The Elusive Concept of Culture and the Vivid Reality   18
   of Personality
   Lucian W. Pye

3 The Relevance of Culture for the Study of Political   33
   Psychology
   Marc Howard Ross

4 Taboo Trade Offs: Constitutive Prerequisites for   47
   Political and Social Life
   Alan Page Fiske and Philip E. Tetlock

5 Substance and Method in Cultural and Crosscultural   66
   Political Psychology
   Stanley A. Renshon and John Duckitt: with contributions by
   Marc Howard Ross, Ofer Feldman, Fathali M. Moghaddam,
   George A. De Vos, Walter G. Stephan and Kwok Leung

Part II   Culture, Psychology and Political Conflict

6 Culture, Personality and Prejudice   89
   John Duckitt

7 The Political Culture of State Authoritarianism   108
   Jos D. Meloen

8 Conflict and Injustice in Intercultural Relations:
   Insights from the Arab–Israeli and Sino–British Disputes   128
   Kwok Leung and Walter G. Stephan

9 Culture and Ethnic Conflict   146
   Marc Howard Ross

Part III The Political Psychology of Change in Cultural Regions

10 The Political Unconscious: Stories and Politics in Two South American Cultures 159
Allen Johnson

11 Cultural Nationalism and Beyond: Crosscultural Political Psychology in Japan 182
Ofer Feldman

12 Change, Continuity and Culture: The Case of Power Relations in Iran and Japan 201
Fathali M. Moghaddam and David Crystal

13 Value Adaptation to the Imposition and Collapse of Communist Regimes in East-Central Europe 217
Shalom H. Schwartz, Anat Bardi and Gabriel Bianchi

Part IV Political Psychology and the Dilemmas of Multiculturalism

14 Social Authority and Minority Status: Problems of Internalization and Alienation Among Japanese and Koreans in Diverse Cultural Settings 241
George A. De Vos

15 Multicultural Policy and Social Psychology: The Canadian Experience 263
J. W. Berry and Rudolf Kalin

16 American Character and National Identity: The Dilemmas of Cultural Diversity 285
Stanley A. Renshon

Index 311

List of Tables and Figures

Tables

6.1   Two sets of psychocultural dimensions underlying
prejudice and ethnocentrism   100

10.1   Incidence of emotions and emotionally-charged outcomes
in 29 Matsigenka folktales   162

13.1   Definitions of the value types and the single items used to
index them   221

13.2   Mean ratings of values for sets of East-Central as compared
to West European samples   226

13.3   Mean ratings of values for subsets of East-central as
compared to West European samples studied at both T1
and T2   233

15.1   Descriptive statistics for five multicultural attitudes in 1974
and 1991 surveys   271

15.2   Attitude scale means by ethnic origin, inside and outside
Québec (1991 survey)   273

15.3   Self-identity (per cent) of respondents in two national
surveys by ethnic origin   275

15.4   Self-identity (per cent) by ethnic origin, inside and outside
Québec (1991 survey)   276

15.5   Mean strength of identification with three self-identities by
region and ethnic origin (1991) survey   276

Figures

6.1   A casual model of the impact of personality and worldview
on the two social attitude dimensions, RWA and SDO, and
on prejudice and ethnocentrism   102

6.2   Personality, social attitudes and prejudice: LISREL
standardized maximum likelihood coefficients   102

7.1   State authoritarianism (early 1990s, 133 countries)   114

7.2   Model state authoritarianism   122

10.1   Common form of the Matsigenka emotion-story   163

10.2   Common emotion story in rural northeastern Brazil   169

10.3   The later Freudian unconscious   176

10.4   The 'angler's float': a psychoanalytic folk tale of the
unconscious   177

14.1   Summary comparison of Card 1: Los Angeles Koreans and
Korean Japanese   252

14.2   Summary comparison of Card 17: Loss Angeles Koreans
       and Korean Japanese   254
14.3   Summary comparison of Card 7: Loss Angeles Koreans and
       Korean Japanese   255
15.1   Mean comfort levels with ethnic groups, by ethnic origin
       of respondents in the national sample (1991 survey)   274
15.2   Distribution of mean scores on Canadianism, by ethnic
       origin and region of residence of respondents (1991 survey) 278
15.3   Distribution of mean scores on security, by ethnic origin
       and region of residence of respondents (1991 survey)   279

Preface

This book represents a crosscultural, crossdisciplinary collaboration between two political psychologists with a deep interest in culture's consequences. One comes to this interest via social psychology, the other via political science and psychoanalytic theory. Both share the conviction that the lost legacy of culture in the field of political psychology can be reclaimed, and that the field of political psychology will be better for having done so.

This collaboration began with planning for a special issue of *Political Psychology* (vol. 18, no. 2). It became clear during that process that a good deal of work being done by psychological anthropologists, political scientists and crosscultural psychologists could usefully be organized and developed as an important subfield of political psychology. Yet nowhere had this been done, and the substantial historical legacy of early cultural anthropologists and political psychologists who built on their work was in danger of being lost.

Political Psychology: Cultural and Crosscultural Foundations is an effort to rescue and revitalize the cultural tradition in political psychology. Our strategy is to bring together work from these three disciplines to illustrate the relevance of the cultural dimension for a deeper understanding of critical substantive and theoretical issues in political psychology and to facilitate crossfertilization. Our approach in creating this book was straightforward. Individually, and together, we developed a list of scholars whose work drew on training and research in at least two of the three major disciplines from which this book draws. We then wrote to each describing the book's focus and inviting their possible contribution. It is from that process that this book emerged.

In keeping with the diverse training, perspectives and interests of our contributors, we neither aspired to, nor tried to impose, any artificial or premature uniformity of view. We did however require of each chapter that it make clear and explicit its understanding of culture and psychology, the operational manifestations of these terms, and their implications for political life. The unifying focus throughout, therefore, is on cultural psychology's consequences for political life. As expected in a book with the phrase crosscultural in its title, we do so in different geographical settings. However, our focus throughout is on the conceptual and empirical clarification of culture's impact, not on cultural geography, *per se*.

The book is subdivided into four major parts: Foundations of Crosscultural Political Psychology; Culture, Psychology and Political Conflict; The Political Psychology of Change in Cultural Regions; and Political Psychology and the Dilemmas of Multiculturalism. The first part, Foundations of Crosscultural

Political Psychology, begins with an introductory essay by the editors outlining the important substantive questions raised by early work in the field. Although infrequently drawn upon, these early traditions have much to teach us, but have also left us much to examine and further explain. Lucian Pye then takes up the nature of the elusive, but indispensable, concept of culture and analyzes why it is both. In doing so, he traces the historical and disciplinary development of the concept and its relationship to personal psychology, providing an essential understanding for any work in the field. Marc Ross begins where Pye ends and examines alternative understandings of culture and its relationships to political life. He examines the role culture plays in explanations of matters of critical interest to political psychology, and provides excellent theoretical and practical reasons for paying more attention. In the next chapter, Allan Fiske and Phil Tetlock suggest that in every culture four basic forms of social relations can be identified: communal sharing, authority ranking, equality ranking and market sharing. They examine each of these for their roles in generating normative cultural understandings, and ask how individuals within each culture address inconsistencies and violations of them. This part's last chapter deals conceptually with the realtionship of substance to method in cultural and crosscultural political psychology. Rather than a homogenized survey, we invited several contributors to respond briefly and directly to several pointed questions that we posed. Their answers make good use of the contributors' long and varied experience in conducting substantive cultural and crosscultural political psychology research.

The second part, Culture, Psychology and Political Conflict, focuses on the theoretical lenses through which the intersections of cultural psychology on the one hand, and real-world political conflict and its amelioration on the other, may profitably be viewed. John Duckitt's chapter explores one of the most, if not the most, explosive contemporary domestic and international issues, the cultural bases of prejudice and ethnocentrism. He identifies two basic cognitive-cultural understandings, one focused on threat control, the other on inequality and dominance. Both arise out of basic human dispositions and experience, and are expressed in cultural values, social attitudes and political ideologies, and underlie and determine prejudice and ethnocentrism in cultures, societies and individuals. Jos Meloen's chapter continues this line of inquiry and asks a basic and provocative question: Are there political cultures which lend themselves to dictatorship? Using a unique database of over 174 countries, he has been able to develop a model which helps to answer a very important set of questions: What role do psychological, social, cultural and political expectations and customs play in the development of the political culture of state authoritarianism. Kwok Leung and Walter Stephan next examine the role of culture in key elements of international conflict: understandings of fairness, deservingness, desired outcomes and significance. Drawing on several longstanding international disputes, they argue that when cultures differ in preferences for allocation rules, techniques of achieving procedural justice, styles of conflict resolution, and approaches to retribution, conflict is likely to arise. Finally, Marc Ross takes up the explosive contemporary issue of ethnic conflict. He details how culture is both at the root of such conflicts and, as well, why it is also at the core of their solution. In short, he makes abundantly clear why a culturally focused political psychology is absolutely essential to understanding such conficts.

Part III, The Political Psychology of Change in Cultural Regions, explores the intersection of culture, psychology and political change within and across culturally distinctive geographical areas. Allen Johnson begins by drawing on his extensive fieldwork to explore how unarticulated cultural and emotional conflicts shape the political realities of two South American communities, one egalitarian, the other stratified. Both must contend with similar issues, but their different economic and social circumstances help account for the ways their cultural psychology has evolved in relation to their politics. Ofer Feldman then examines the paradox of Japanese cultural psychology and politics. Japanese people are among the most cohesive and insulated people, yet their traditional cultural orientation to leaders and politics is, in many respects, 'becoming modern'. Fathali Moghaddam and David Crystal examine power relations and inequalities in two cultures undergoing social and political change, Iran and Japan. They focus on the changing status of women and the ways in which the fit, or lack of it, between cultural and political process may either retard or facilitate inequalities. Shalom Schwartz and his colleagues make use of a naturally occurring 'experiment' which occurred when Eastern Europe emerged from decades of communist domination of its society by the Soviet Union, to ask whether cultures really do change, and if so how. They find dramatic evidence that political structures can shape political cultures, but that new political cultures may also become rooted during periods of social and political change.

Part IV focuses on the dilemmas of multicultural societies, as increasing immigration and migration raise fundamental questions of national and ethnic group identity and political integration and separation. George DeVos begins by examining the continuing impact of cultural psychology through periods of immigration and assimilation. Focusing on the Japanese and Korean experience in Japan, Brazil and the United States, he shows the ways in which culture continues to mediate group status and performance even in vastly diverse political and social circumstances. J. W. Berry and Rudolf Kalin examine the relationship among the cultural features of national societies, the policies and politics of cultural diversity issues, and individual beliefs and attitudes in Canada. They find both congruence and conflict in the continuing efforts of the government to both foster diversity and national integration. Finally, Stanley Renshon examines these same dilemmas in the United States. He argues that fundamental cultural orientations underlie inter- and intra-ethnic group tensions and in the end are more important that either race or ethnicity.

*   *   *

Words of thanks are due to many who helped bring this project to fruition. The contributors to this volume, all distinguished scholars, graciously considered the views of two editors, not just one, and almost always more than once. They did so patiently, thoughtfully and responsively, and for this we are both most appreciative. We also appreciate the interest and support the Publishing Director at Macmillan, T. M. Farmiloe and the Director of New York University Press, Niko Pfund. Sunder Katwala and Alison Howson, our editors at Macmillan, were informative, responsive and helpful – traits that every scholar values. Keith Povey provided excellent copy-editing.

Finally, we would like to offer an appreciation of our own collaboration. In this book, two scholars from different backgrounds and theoretical perspectives, but with similar work habits and expectations, came together to further a substantive area to which they were both deeply connected. In the process they were able to truly rely on each other's judgement at many crucial spots along the way, and in the process learned much from each other.

We hope you, the readers, are as substantively stimulated by the results of our collective efforts as we are hopeful that you will find them informative and useful.

STANLEY A. RENSHON
JOHN DUCKITT

Notes on the Contributors

Anat Bardi is a PhD candidate on a Doctoral Fellowship from the Israel Foundation Trustees. Her dissertation examines relations between people's basic values and their everyday behavior, and she is seeking to identify both cognitive and personality processes that account for the link between values and everyday behavior. She has published a paper on the ways people prepare to receive invalid information in the *Journal of Experimental Social Psychology*, and two papers in *Political Psychology* on the influences of the political atmosphere in East Europe on personal values.

J. W. Berry is Professor of Psychology at Queen's University. He received his PhD from the University of Edinburgh in 1966, and specializes in the areas of crosscultural, multicultural, social and cognitive psychology. He has served as consultant to the Economic Council of Canada on the social and psychological costs and benefits of multiculturalism, as consultant to the Canadian Forces on issues of diversity and equity, and as consultant to the World Health Organization on issues of immigrants' and refugees' and indigenous peoples' health. Among his many books are: *Handbook of Cross-Cultural Psychology* (3 vols, 1977), *Ethnicity and Culture in Canada* (1994, University of Toronto Press), *Indigenous Psychologies* (Sage, 1993), and *Cross Cultural Psychology: Research and Applications* (Cambridge University Press). In addition, since 1996 he has published 22 book chapters, 17 journal articles and six major technical reports for various government agencies – all in the fields of cultural diversity.

Ganriel Bianchi received his MA in psychology at Comenius University, Bratislava, in 1978 and his CSc degree (PhD equivalent), in social psychology. He is affiliated with the Department of Social and Biological Communication, Slovak Academy of Sciences, Bratislava. He has conducted research on pro-social behaviour in children (1980–84), in cognitive psychology (1984–90), in environmental education and environmental psychology (since 1988), and in social and behavioural aspects of HIV/AIDS and sexual health (since 1993). In 1991 started Slovak participation in the international cross-cultural research project on values coordinated by Shalom Schwartz, Hebrew University of Jerusalem. He is an elected member of the first democratic (post-totalitarian) City Council in Bratislava, Capital of Slovakia, and since 1995 trainer, facilitator and consultant at Partners for Democratic Change Slovakia.

David Crystal is Assistant Professor in the Psychology Department of Georgetown University. His PhD research (University of Michigan) focused on culture and social development, with specific focus on Japanese society. His most recent work explores cultural variations in reactions to deviance, particularly comparing US and Japanese youth.

George A. De Vos received his PhD from the University of Chicago and is Professor of Psychological Anthropology in the Anthropology Department of the University of Calfornia, Berkeley, and a research member of the Center For Japanese Studies, Institute of Human Development, and the Institute for Personality Assessment and Research. His Japanese and Korean research has focused on family life and religion, and the achievement motivation, social internalization and psycho-cultural comparisons between Japanese and American society on social problems, including crime and delinquency, alienation and suicide, discrimination and minority status. He has published over 20 books and over 180 articles including *Japan's Invisible Race*; *Socialization for Achievement*; *Religion and the Family in East Asia*; *Ethnic Identity*; *Heritage of Endurance*; *Koreans in Japan*; *Symbolic Analysis Cross Culturally*; *Status Inequality: The Self in Culture*; *Social Cohesion and Alienation: The United States and Japan*.

John Duckitt is a Senior Lecturer in the Department of Psychology at the University of Auckland in New Zealand, where he teaches courses in social psychology with a focus on intergroup behavior and crosscultural issues. He received his PhD from the University of the Witwatersrand in Johannesburg, South Africa with doctoral research that examined white racial prejudice in South Africa. Dr Duckitt has published widely in the fields of social psychology with a particular focus on issues of prejudice, racial and ethnic attitudes, and intergroup behavior. He is the author of *The Social Psychology of Prejudice* (Preager) and numerous other articles in major journals, including the *Journal of Social Psychology*, *Political Psychology*, *American Psychologist*, the *Journal of Personality and Social Psychology*, and the *Journal of Clinical Psychology*. He serves, or has served, on the editorial boards of *Political Psychology*, the *Journal of Social Psychology*, *Politics, Groups and the Individual*, and the *South African Journal of Psychology*.

Alan Page Fiske is Associate Professor in the Department of Anthropology, University of California, Los Angeles. He received his PhD from the Committee on Human Development (Department of Behavioral Sciences), University of Chicago, in 1985. He served in the Peace Corps in Africa from 1968 to 1972, and 1977 to 1979. He is the author of *Structures of Social Life: The Four Elementary Forms of Human Relations* (Free Press). He has published numerous articles on social cognition and social theory; he has also written on methodology, on obsessive-compulsive disorder and cultural rituals, and on personality disorders. He is co-author of the chapter on Culture in the *Handbook of Social Psychology*, 4th edn (McGraw Hill). He is currently writing a book analyzing sex and food taboos as meta-relational models, and exploring the larger question of 'syntaxes' for combining social relationships.

Ofer Feldman is Associate Professor at Naruto University of Education in Japan. He received his PhD in Social Psychology from the University of Tokyo. In 1993 the International Society of Political Psychology awarded him the Erik H. Erikson Award for Distinguished Early Career Contribution to Political Psychology. He is the author of numerous publications in the fields of political psychology and communication studies. In addition, he is the author of *Politics and the News Media in Japan* (University of Michigan Press), *The Political Personality of Japan* (Macmillan), and two books in Japanese on political behavior. He is co-editor of a book entitled, *Politically Speaking: A Worldwide Examination of Language Used in the Political Sphere* (Praeger), and the editor of *Political Psychology in Japan* (Nova Science Publications).

Allen Johnson is Professor in the Departments of Anthropology and Psychiatry, and Chair of the Latin American Studies Program, at the University of California, Los Angeles. He has a PhD in anthropology from Stanford University (1968) and a PhD in psychoanalysis from the Southern California Psychoanalytic Institute (1992). His latest book, *Oedipus Ubiquitous* (co-authored with Douglass Price-Williams, Stanford University Press) received the 1997 Boyer Prize for outstanding contribution to psychoanalytic anthropology from the Society for Psychological Anthropology. Other recent works include 'Psychoanalysis and Materialism: Do They Mix?' (in D. Spain, ed., *Psychoanalytic Anthropology After Freud,* Psyche Press), 'Anthropology and Psychoanalysis: Bridging Science and the Humanities' (in L. Adams and J. Szaluta, eds, *Psychoanalysis and the Humanities,* Brunner/Mazel), and 'The Psychology of Dependence Between Landlord and Sharecropper in Northeastern Brazil' on *Political Psychology.* He has done ethnographic field research in Mexico, Brazil and Peru.

Rudolf Kalin is Professor and Head of the Department of Psychology at Queen's University at Kingston. He has been working on multicultural issues with a focus on ethnic attitudes and ethnic identity. He has co-authored (with J. W. Berry and D. M. Taylor) *Multiculturalism and Ethnic Attitudes in Canada,* co-edited (with R. C. Gardner) *A Canadian Social Psychology of Ethnic Relations,* and has published numerous articles on ethnic attitudes, ethnic identity and evaluative reactions to accented speech.

Kwok Leung is Professor and Chairman of the Department of Psychology at the Chinese University of Hong Kong. He received his PhD from the University of Illinois with research interests in justice and conflict resolution, crosscultural psychology, and crosscultural research methodology.

Dr Leung has published numerous articles in the field of crosscultural psychology, and in addition has co-edited *Innovations in Cross-Cultural Psychology* (Swets and Zeitlinger), *Progress in Asian Social Psychology, vol. 1* (Wiley), and co-authored *Methods and Data Analysis for Cross-Cultural Research* (Sage). He is currently co-editing a book on conflict management in the Pacific Rim, to be published by Wiley. He was also an associate editor of the *Journal of Cross-Cultural Psychology*, and is currently an associate editor of the *Asian Journal of Social Psychology*. He is also the current President of the Asian Association of Social Psychology.

Jos D. Meloen is Senior Researcher at the Department of Public Administration (Sociology) of the University of Leiden, The Netherlands. He received his PhD in social science from The City University of Amsterdam. He was Social Science Researcher and Project Leader at the Universities of Leiden (LISWO) and Rotterdam (ISEO) and conducted a series of studies and wrote some books on ethnic minorities and discrimination, and on crosscultural surveys. He has published some 50 articles on authoritarianism, democracy, multiculturalism, extremism, prejudice and antisemitism, machiavellism and obedience in numerous national and international journals. His work has also appeared in a number of books including, Wm. Stone *et al.*, *Strength and Weakness: The Authoritarian Personality Today* (Springer) and R. Farnen. *Nationalism, Ethnicity, and Identity: Cross-National and Comparative Perspectives* (Transaction). He has also co-edited *Political Psychology in the Netherlands* (Molla Russa).

Fathali M. Moghaddam is an Iranian-born, British-educated psychologist who moved from McGill University, Montreal, Canada, to Georgetown University, Washington D.C., in 1990, where he is currently Professor of Psychology. His most recent books are *Social Psychology: Exploring Universals Across Cultures* (W. H. Freeman) and *The Specialized Society: The Plight of the Individual in an Age of Individualism* (Praeger). His numerous research articles have appeared in American, European and international journals. Dr Moghaddam has done field research in various Western and non-Western societies; and within North America he has conducted studies with women and men participants from many cultural groups, including white, African-American, Hispanic, Jewish, Arab, Chinese, Greek, Iranian and Haitian populations. He has worked on United Nations national development projects in areas such as refugee resettlement, health and technical training before taking up his academic appointments.

Lucian W. Pye received his PhD from Yale University and is Ford Professor Emeritus of Political Science at the Massachusetts Institute of Technology. He is also a leading specialist in comparative politics and political culture and psychology, with special emphasis upon Asia and more particularly

China. He is a past President of the American Political Science Association, former Chairman of the Comparative Politics Committee of the Social Science Research Council, a former Director of the Council on Foreign Relations in New York, former Governor of the East–West Center in Honolulu, and currently a trustee of the Asia Foundation and vice-Chairman of the National Committee on US–China Relations. He is the author/co-author/editor of 27 books and more than 250 articles and chapters in edited books.

Stanley A. Renshon is Professor of Political Science and Coordinator of the Interdisciplinary Program in the Psychology of Political Behavior at the CUNY Graduate Center. He is also a certified psychoanalyst and senior clinical faculty member at the Training and Research Institute for Self-Psychology in New York City. He received his PhD from the University of Pennsylvania in 1972, and was a Post-doctoral Fellow in Psychology and Politics at Yale University. He is the author of numerous articles and six books in the field of political psychology. His *High Hopes: The Clinton Presidency and the Politics of Ambition* (New York University Press/paperback edition Routledge Press) won the American Political Science Association's Richard E. Neustadt Award for the best book on the presidency, and the National Association of the Advancement of Psychoanalysis' Gradiva award for the best psychoanalytic biography.

Marc Howard Ross is William R. Kenan, Jr. Professor of Political Science, Bryn Mawr College. He received his PhD from Northwestern University in 1968, and his main research interest is in the comparative analysis of social science theories of conflict and conflict management. He has focused on questions of ethnic conflict and peacemaking crossculturally, paying particular attention to deeply divided societies such as Northern Ireland, South Africa, Israel and Sri Lanka, as well as understanding communities which have somewhat successfully developed institutions and practices to facilitate peaceful intergroup relations. Dr Ross has written or edited six books and several dozen articles which include: *The Culture of Conflict: Interpretations and Interests in Comparative Perspective (Yale); The Management of Conflict: Interpretations* (Yale); *Interests in Comparative Perspective* (Yale); (with Roger Cobb) *Cultural Strategies of Agenda Denial: Avoidance, Attack and Redefinition* (University of Kansas Press); (with Ray Rothman) *Theory and Practice in Ethnic Conflict Management: Conceptualizing Success and Failure* (Macmillan); *Grass Roots in an African City: Political Behavior in Nairobi* (MIT); and *The Political Integration of Urban Squatters* (Northwestern University Press).

Walter G. Stephan is Professor of Psychology at New Mexico State University. He received his PhD in psychology from the University of Minnesota in 1971, and has served as associate editor of the *Review of*

Personality and Social Psychology, and on the editorial boards of the *Journal of Personality and Social Psychology*, the *Journal of Experimental Social Psychology*, and the *International Journal of Intercultural Relations*. He has written widely in the area of crosscultural psychology and intergroup relationships including (with C. W. Stephan) *Intergroup Relations* Boulder, CO: Westview Press; with (J.R. Feagin) *Desegregation: Past, Present and Future*. New York: Plenum Press; (with C.W. Stephan). *Two Social Psychologies*, 2nd edn Belmont, CA: Wadsworth; and (with T.F. Pettigrew and C.W. Stephan) *The Future of Social Psychology: Defining the Relationships Between Sociology and Psychology*. New York: Springer-Verlag, and *Reducing Prejudice and Stereotyping in the Schools (Teacher's College Press)* In 1996, he won (with Marina Abalakina-Paap) the Klineberg award in intercultural relations given by SPSSI for the best article of 1996.

Shalom H. Schwartz is the Leon and Clara Sznajderman Professor of Psychology at the Hebrew University of Jerusalem. He received his PhD in social psychology from the University of Michigan in 1967 and he holds masters degrees from Columbia University and from the Jewish Theological Seminary of America in New York. Dr Schwartz is co-author of a text in Social Psychology and author of nearly 100 articles and chapters in psychology, sociology and political science, including *Advances in Experimental Social Psychology*, *The Handbook of Cross-Cultural Psychology*, the *Ontario Symposium*, the *Journal of Cross-Cultural Psychology*, the *Journal of Personality and Social Psychology*, and *World Psychology*. He is a Fellow of the American Psychological Association; member of the Executive Council of the International Association of Cross-Cultural Psychology; and a past President of the Israel Association for Social Psychology. He is a member of numerous editorial boards and also a member of the Steering Committee for the European Social Survey of the European Science Foundation.

Philip E. Tetlock is the Harold Burtt Professor of Psychology and Political Science at The Ohio State University. He received his PhD in psychology from Yale University in 1979 and served on the faculty of the University of California Berkeley for 16 years where he rose to the rank of Distinguished Professor and Director of the Institute of Personality and Social Research. He has written well over 100 articles in professional journals and books and has co-authored or co-edited nine books, including *Counterfactual Thought Experiments in World Politics* (Princeton University Press), *Behavior, Society, International Conflict* (Oxford University Press), *Psychology and Social Advocacy* (Hemisphere), and *Reasoning and Choice: Explorations in Political Psychology* (Cambridge University Press). Professor Tetlock has received the following professional awards: the Distinguished Scientific Award for Early Career Contribution in social psychology (1986), the Behavioral Science Research Prize from the American Association for the Advancement of

Science (1988), the Woodrow Wilson Book Award from the American Political Science Association, and the Nevitt Sanford Award for Professional Contributions to Political Psychology from the International Society of Political Psychology (1997).

Part I

Foundations of Crosscultural Political Psychology

1

Cultural and Crosscultural Political Psychology: Revitalizing a Founding Tradition for a New Subfield

Stanley A. Renshon and John Duckitt

The relationships between political and psychological process are the defining core of political psychology. Yet each alone, and both collectively, are embedded in numerous cultural contexts. We can simply, and provisionally, define culture as the shared range of acquired conscious and unconscious understandings, and their associated feelings, that are embedded in the individuals' interior psychology, the cultural group's societal (social, economic and political) institutions, and its public practices and products.[1] Thus defined, its relevance for the concerns of political psychology would seem to be reasonably self-evident.

Yet, paradoxically, while political psychology has made substantial substantive and institutional progress in the past three decades, little of the field's theory and less of its research has examined culture explicitly. This wasn't always the case.

The mixed legacy of cultural anthropology

Early studies exploring the intersection of psychology, culture and politics were strongly influenced by cultural anthropology (cf., Linton, 1930, 1945; see also Kardiner, 1939) and more specifically by the 'culture and personality' work associated with Ruth Benedict (1934), Margaret Mead (1939), Kluckholm and Murray (1953) and others.[2] Those pioneers studied relatively small, homogeneous and slowly evolving societies to chart the links among culture, socialization and personality on the one hand, and the continuity of societal conventions (embedded in political, economic, religious and social institutions) on the other. Perhaps not surprisingly, given the kinds of societies they studied, the links appeared solid. However, those who studied large, heterogeneous and rapidly changing societies were certainly justified in asking what useful implications this genre held for them.

Moreover, members of the early cultural-and-personality school often wrote as if personality were culture writ large,[3] and viewed the former through the powerful, but scarcely refined, lens of early psychoanalytic theory. Those uncomfortable with a view of internal psychology as little more than a barely contained caldron of urges set for life in instinctual concrete, and culture as a defense against them, had legitimate questions to ask. As a result, the culture-and-personality paradigm seemed ill-suited for answering the questions growing out of the intersection of culture, psychology and politics in the societies studied by most political psychologists, and in important ways it was.

Still, that early paradigm contained an important set of understandings about culture and its influences on social practices. It is worthwhile to recall these because they provide a basis for exploring culture's impact on the psychology and political practices of larger, culturally heterogeneous societies.

Understanding culture

A primary legacy of that early work is that culture is, first and foremost, human made, and its practices highly diverse. While culture is a constant across human groupings, its content in any particular group is variable. Therefore, culture in any group must be learned and its impact on that group's practices will be related to its content. Documenting and comparing cultural organization and understandings in an attempt to trace their impact on the psychology of group members and their interpersonal and social practices was *the* fundamental rationale for the field. That basic set of questions, however, soon led to more specific ones.

On what basis did cultures develop? Benedict (1934, 42) believed that cultures developed around one dominant, or a few central concerns. Linton (see Kardiner and Linton, 1939, viii) criticized that view arguing that 'cultures are not dominated by an *idée fixe.*' Yet, early cultural anthropologists were united in their view that culture arose as a response to environmental circumstances. In other words, culture was a solution to the problem of how groups might live in the physical and psychological circumstances in which they found themselves.[4] Early cultural anthropologists were also united in their view that cultural practices served adaptive functions. A culture's practices might seem odd, even bizarre, to an outsider. Yet, from the point of view of those inside the culture it could be seen to serve some purpose.

An underappreciated corollary to this perspective is that the early cultural anthropologists were remarkably open and non-judgmental about a wide array of cultural practices. Margaret Mead's classic study of sex and temperament (1935) in several New Guinea societies documented the cultural variability associated with their expression and relationship. Benedict (1934, 262–4) matter-of-factly noted the range of reactions, including acceptance and in some cases special acclaim, given to homosexuals in some societies at the same time that her's branded them psychiatrically.

Certainly, governmental, religious and economic organizations motivated to justify their exploitation or cultural intervention emphasized the difference between 'civilized' and 'primitive' cultures. However, they received no support from major figures in the field either substantively[5] or politically.[6] For the culture and personality anthropologists, unlike some modern multi-culturalists, culture always trumped race as an explanation of cognitive and behavioral practices.[7]

Culture's consequences: psychology

While 'functionalist' anthropologists insisted that specific, discrete cultural traits of behavior always served some purpose, the culture and personality anthropologists went further. They argued that cultures were best understood as integrated patterns of thought and behavior (Benedict, 1934, 42), and that cultural institutions both reflected and reinforced them. The reason for this, according to Kardiner and Linton (1939, viii), was that individuals growing up in them had common experiences resulting in similar understandings and even common psychological tendencies.

Building on early psychoanalytic theory, culture and personality anthropologists sought to document culture's role in producing basic personality structures, modal personality structures and national characters.[8] In retrospect, it is easy to see the limits of these frameworks. Relying on the unconscious to anchor these frameworks made them methodologically vulnerable and risked slighting the importance of purposeful adaptation. Moreover, identical socialization experiences could not be assumed even in small, contained cultural groups. Even if it could, variations in family dynamics and individual temperament would make the process unlikely to produce uniform results. And, even if they did, the similar results they might produce were more likely to manifest themselves in a range than a mode. Finally, it was not clear how representative any individual could be of the range of national character traits associated with large nation-states, especially as many became more culturally diverse.

Culture's consequences: understandings and practices

Early cultural anthropologists were united in the view that culture had very practical consequences. Its effects are found in the most common and ordinary social practices and, as well, in the larger basic understandings that shape community life. These 'cultural truths' are 'self-evident', often not fully explicit or articulated understandings which shape individual and cultural life. Thus Kardiner (1939, 361) argued that for members of the Tanala in Madagascar, 'the pattern of love and security in return for obedience is the most prominent pattern of adaptation for the greatest number of people in the society'. A more contemporary illustration of 'cultural truth' can be found in the beliefs associated with the work ethic in westernized societies, essentially the 'Protestant ethic' minus the religious element.

Culture's consequences could be seen as well in the regulation of expression. Some cultures prize excess in personal expression, others moderation (cf., Benedict's 'Apollonian' and 'Dionysian' cultures, 1934). In some cultures laughter covers over embarrassment, in others it reflects a sense of humor. In some cultures looking at someone directly is a sign of respect, in others not looking at them directly is respectful. Finally, culture's consequences can be seen in the ways in which elements of interior and interpersonal psychology are combined. For example, the Japanese term *giri* is ordinarily translated as 'repayment', as for a social obligation. However, it also covers gratitude and revenge. As Benedict (1946, 146) notes,

> A good man feels as strongly about insults as he does about the benefits he receives. Either way it is virtuous to repay. He does not separate the two, as we do, and call one aggression and one non-aggression, because so long as one is maintaining giri and clearing one's name of slurs, one is not guilty of aggression.

It is worth noting that the actual feelings remain constant across cultures in this example. Yet, because the feelings are put into different categories of understanding, they carry with them different prescriptions for action. Different moral calculations follow as well.

Culture's consequences: continuity and change

Early cultural anthropologists were not blind to the fact that change occurred naturally *within* cultural traditions. But they were particularly interested in cultural change brought about by forced contact with disparate cultures. This had the effect of focusing attention away from cultural evolution and towards cultural conflict.

Understandings of modern intercultural exchange represent a hybrid of these two sources of cultural change. Certainly, in an increasingly interconnected world, the avoidance of cultural contact is not a realistic option. Therefore attention to change resulting from cultural intrusion is worth continued attention. However, concerns about cultural 'imperialism' and its post-modern successor, hegemonic design, give less credit to the staying power of the 'traditional' cultures in whose name they say they speak. The ability of strong cultural traditions to repress, restrict, or even to moderate, modify, revise and transform other's traditions to their own uses is a second important focus of this book. It is also another key element of a modern cultural and crosscultural political psychology.

Culture's consequences: policy

The early theoretical development of culture and personality anthropology preceded the onset of World War II by only a few years. As early as 1939, the Committee for National Morale drew on psychologists and anthropologists to study the maintenance of morale during wartime. After Pearl Harbor, developing and applying psychologist cultural anthropology became a matter of military urgency as well as of academic theory. Ruth Benedict, Clyde Kluckhohn and others moved to Washington to help in war-related research and planning. Japanese, German and Nazi (and latter, Soviet) culture were scoured by the Allies for understanding and advantage.

Ultimately, of course, military power, not the political uses of cultural psychology, proved decisive. But it is worth noting that while the former won the war, the peace could not have been secured without the latter. Allied occupational authorities were not simply content to administer the defeated countries, but to change them. To accomplish this they attempted to transform two culturally distinct societies from totalitarian to democratic. That seminal historic event remains to be fully explored, but its enormous consequences underscore the critical role that culture plays in the intersection between psychology and politics.

But there is another, equally if not more critical, set of culturally framed policy questions unfolding. Inglehart (1997) has demonstrated that there are empirically distinct cultural regions in the world, and Huntington (1996, 310) has argued that the reassuring view that modernization and the Western values with which it became associated would trump other cultures' core values is, in his view, 'false, immoral, and dangerous'. Rather, he has argued (1996, 20), 'cultural and cultural identities, which at the broadest level are civilization identities, are shaping the patterns of cohesion, disintegration, and conflict in the post-Cold War world'. The high-rise buildings of New York and Beijing may look the same, but the core cultural values and views of those who inhabilt them are not necessarily parallel.

The fact that culture and psychology intersect so directly with political and social practices helps make this field inherently controversial to some. Drawing little distinction between analysis and judgment, 'deconstructions' and 'post-modernists' ask whether scholarship can ever trump personal values, and answer that it cannot. However, as Pye points out (this volume), these 'critical' theorists are more than willing to use the concept of culture for their own decidedly political purposes, itself a blatant manifestation of the criticisms they level at others. The same inconsistency may be seen among some multiculturalists who insist on the psychological importance and political primacy of racial or ethnic identities, while disavowing any less desirable group tendencies that derive from these same powerful currents. In the United States, 'culture of poverty' analyses elicited loud protests that such theories blamed, vilified and further marginalized the victims. As a result, ameliorative social policy was hobbled. Now, several decades later, research by a distinguished African-American sociologist (Wilson, 1996; see also Sowell, 1994, 14–28) has demonstrated that the poor underclass are indeed different in terms of their experiences and outlooks, and, equally importantly, on those practices concerned with the work ethic. That work ethic and associated cultural beliefs are, to some (cf.,

Landes, 1996), central to explaining larger macro-political and economic developments in and between nations has also been proposed.

Clearly, an appreciation of culture and psychology has an important role to play in designing policy, especially in multi-cultural countries. However, those who wish to utilize its insights must be prepared to defend their substantive insights, not only intellectually, but politically.

Building on a legacy: modern cultural and crosscultural political psychology

As Pye points out (this volume), the concept of culture is 'elusive, but indispensable' in the social sciences and political psychology. Its persistence, in spite of its elusiveness, supports his point. Already in the late 1940s, Leites (1948) was reformulating the psychoanalytic approach to examining culture's impact on the psychology of political practices. The culmination of his efforts was his now-classic work on operational codes (1951), a concept explicated by George (1969).[9]

In Leites' classic revision, the foundation of political practices were not to be found in the cultural expression of universal unconscious principles. Rather it was to be found in the internalization and operation of core beliefs, which infused experience with meaning. The intersection of culture, psychology and politics was no longer primarily a matter of affective conflicts, but as well of assumptions and the strategies of life and work that followed from them. Nor were the origins of political practices necessarily found in childhood. Rather, culture's impact on political psychology was to be found at the intersection of the cultural group's actual historical and psychological experience. Members of the Soviet Politburo did not act as they did solely, and perhaps even primarily, as a result of harsh fathers or distant mothers. Rather, it was that their childhoods had prepared them all too well to view the political world through the powerful prism of their own ruthless and conspirational personal and political histories.

The next logical step in the development of culture as belief in relation to political practice was Almond and Verba's (1963) landmark five-nation study of political culture. It is arguably one of the most influential political science books of that decade. They relied on national surveys and focused on culture as embedded in the beliefs and attitudes that support different political practices. Building on the culture and personality school, they viewed political culture as the result of a set of interrelated personal, institutional and historical experiences. 'Subject' and 'participant' political cultures differed because in each family, school, social and later political experience shaped, then reinforced a particular view of one's self in the world. In short, congruence and coherence were still the foundations of culture's impact on psychology and the political practices they shaped.

Inglehart's (1990, 1997) influential studies approached political culture and its implications from another perspective. He views culture as embedded in values, which are, in turn, a reflection of the level of need satisfaction that a society has achieved. Building on Maslow's (1954) need theory of personality and psychological development, Inglehart argues that the satisfaction of more basic human needs (physiological, safety, esteem and belonging needs) free up individuals and societies to be concerned with other, postmaterial, concerns. One of Inglehart's contributions is his use of a wholistic, but not psychoanalytic, theory of personality as the basis of understanding culture's impact on psychology and political practices and concerns. However, he also makes another contribution – his insight that different historical generations, within the same culture, can have vastly different psychological experiences. In his work, culture's impact on the psychology of political views and practices is no longer a function solely of family, institutional or political experience, but of the historical circumstances during which it unfolds. Thus does the modern sometimes reaffirm the traditional, albeit in new ways, as Ingelhart's use of generational analysis recaptures and updates Benedict's (1934, 232) insistence on the importance of history to cultural psychology analysis.

Cultural anthropologists, political scientists and psychologists are not the only ones to explore the intersections of psychology, culture and politics. Crosscultural psychologists have undertaken comparative research that highlights the intersection of cultural and political practices (Segall, Lonner and Berry, 1998). They, too, are a crucial element of constructing a modern, revitalized new subfield of cultural and crosscultural political psychology.

Spurred by the development of a psychological anthropology that focuses on cognition[10] (sometimes to the exclusion of understanding and affect), this research has examined the relationship of social cognition to group and intergroup processes (Bond, 1988; Smith and Bond, 1993). These studies have important implications for political psychology, as well as providing promising new approaches to conceptualizing and studying variation in cultural systems (Hofstede, 1980; Schwartz, 1992; Triandis, Bontempo and Villareal, 1988).[11] Examples are differences in the nature of group membership and identification, conflict management, conformity, norms of distributive justice, negotiation behaviors and style, competitive versus cooperative orientations to others, interpersonal communication styles, and leadership (Gudykunst, 1988; Mann, 1988; Smith and Bond, 1993). In many cases, of course, these differences are complex, context-dependent, and their exact nature and ramifications have not yet been clearly mapped by research (cf. the review by Smith and Bond, 1993).

Smith and Bond (1993; see also Triandis, Bontempo and Villareal, 1988), for example, have focused on the individualism vs collectivism distinction as a basic dimension of cultural differentiation. They explore the convergence hypothesis – that is, the idea that with industrialization and economic development traditional societies will converge towards modernity and individualism. Paralleling Inglehart's work, but adding a distinct frame of analysis, research now suggests that convergence in certain values may coexist with continuing differentiation on other values (Yang, 1988). The similarities and differences in political culture and practice between Japan and the West noted in Feldman's chapter illustrate this pattern, and indicate that differences in fundamental value systems can persist in characterizing political cultures over long trajectories of social, historical and political development.

A powerful correlation between individualism/collectivism and the even more politically relevant power–distance dimension of cultural variation has also been established (Hofstede, 1980). More recently Meloen (this volume) has also reported evidence from an major crossnational survey suggesting that the cultural value systems of collectivism and power distance are strongly associated with support for state authoritarianism. Findings such as Meloen's seem to have several broader implications for the study of political psychology. First, they suggest that a more systematic approach to the study of systems of cultural variation – that is, culture as the independent variable of inquiry, as pioneered by Hofstede (1990) – may be fruitful. Second, they also seem to indicate that the links between such basic dimensions of cultural variation and political culture need to be explored much more systematically. More specifically, if Meloen's findings are valid, the question arises of how exactly certain basic cultural value orientations, such as collectivism, power distance, masculinity and uncertainty avoidance, might underpin and coalesce into authoritarian political cultures.

Hofstede's four value dimensions of cultural variation, and particularly the individualism–collectivism dimension, have been extremely influential in contemporary crosscultural psychology. However, other dimensions with potential relevance for political psychology have also been proposed, such as tightness versus looseness (Peabody, 1985), cultural complexity (Lomax and Berkowitz, 1972), and modernity versus traditionalism (Yang, 1988). Schwartz (this volume) uses value dimensions for comparative purposes that have impressive empirical evidence of etic validity and provide a framework for conceptualizing cultural variation. His framework has some interesting similarities to Hofstede's dimensions (cf., Smith and Bond, 1993), but seems more comprehensive.

Old answers, newer questions

These core elements of culture's consequences are worth noting not because they produced ideal societies,[12] but rather because they produced coherent and integrated ones. How then did cultural anthropologists understand the means by which culture produces the consequences of culture? First, culture's influence was to be found within the boundaries of shared experience. The smaller cultural units that early anthropologists studied were united, psychologically and culturally, by the accumulated weight of the common experience. Second, culture's impact was to be found in the shared perception of that experience. Common frames of reference and understanding, whether in the form of cultural narratives or practices, help to insure that accumulated cultural history was not only broadly experienced, but widely shared. Third, the integrating effects of common experience and understanding were instrumental in forging an individual identity linked to common group identity. No group members searched for their identity, or constructed it, they simply assumed it.

Few, if any, of the features that aided early cultural anthropologists develop their theories characterize the societies of interest to contemporary cultural and crosscultural political psychology. The societies of most contemporary interest are large and diverse: populated by disparate cultural groups, it is increasingly difficult to assume common socialization practices, a common psychology, or even common understandings. The results are evident worldwide. An essential question, therefore, for any modern cultural and crosscultural political psychology, and one that is central to this book, is how diverse cultural traditions can be integrated into political units that transcend them. This is the fundamental dilemma of the modern multi-ethnic, multicultural states. But there are other and related important questions as well.

Early cultural anthropologists viewed cultures as integrated units whose parts made adaptive and functional sense. It is highly questionable whether this conceptualization remains wholly useful. The problem is not only of strong, diverse cultural traditions leading in different directions, although that is certainly true. The problem, as Bell (1954) pointed out in his seminal book, *The Cultural Contradictions of Capitalism*, is that some deeply rooted cultural practices can, in the absence of binding, limiting cultural or political frameworks, undermine their own foundations. Early cultural anthropologists also viewed cultural change as evolutionary, not revolutionary. Cultural contacts in the societies they studied were sporadic, limited and, even when forced, filtered through a solid and widely shared foundation of cultural experience. One reason was that the culture and its people largely stayed in place, retaining ties to their historical cultural experience. Modern 'cultural contact' appears, in important respects, quite different. The reasons are not solely a function of the world as 'global village', and the cultural interpenetration facilitated by modern communications.

An unprecedented amount of modern intercultural contact is brought about by migration and immigration. This in turn has resulted in some wholly new questions, or at least questions needing to be addressed on a wholly different, larger scale than previously. What happens to a group's cultural foundation when it gets transplanted to a new substantially different cultural setting? What happens to predominant cultural traditions when they try to integrate diverse and perhaps incompatible foreign cultural traditions? Is there a difference between shallow and deep cultural integration?[13] What is the process of cultural and intercultural change in circumstances where two or more major cultural traditions share the same physical and political space? What conceptual models help us to understand the processes of cultural assimilation, interdependence or autonomy?

The major figures in early cultural anthropology, seeing the unity of the cultures they studied, drew no conclusions about the relative merit of cultural practices. There is an echo of this *laissez faire* tradition in the modern insistence that all cultural practices be accorded equal respect and honor, even when they violate deep cultural understandings and traditions (Pangle, 1988, 176). How cultures can honor, even embrace, traditions wholly at variance with their own cultural foundations is a question of no small import in modern multicultural democracies. Stanley Fish's complaint (1988, 60) that American culture professes tolerance, 'but resists the force of the appreciated culture at precisely the point at which it matters most to its strongly committed members' is precisely right. But the question is whether it can be otherwise. Can a democracy embrace and honor an anti-democratic cultural tradition and remain democratic?

Are all cultural traditions equally deserving of respect and accommodation? As Sowell (1994, 5) points out, even the dominant Roman imperial culture adopted Arabic numerals over their own more clumsy counterparts because they were functionally superior. In our own culture, the devastating consequences of divorce on children have been well-documented, as has the generally positive experience of growing up in a warm supportive, intact family. Must we really conclude that the former is preferable for raising children, if we respect the need for choice in making and keeping marital commitments? Finally, there are questions of identity with which modern cultural and crosscultural political psychology must grapple. Erikson's defining insight was that identity must be twice fitted: it must fit the individual's interior psychology – his ambitions, skills, ideals and relations with others – but it must also find a comfortable fit in the array of places that every culture makes available to its members.

For obvious reasons, the development of a psychologically robust and socially supported identity, whether it is called that or not, is an aspect of socialization in every viable culture. Identity provides a strategic, reciprocal relationship for the individual and culture. A fitting identity provides the individual with a sense of place and purpose, but it also serves larger cultural and social functions. Individuals with an identity that fits, buttresses their culture – its understandings, institutions and practices, as well as themselves. The early cultural anthropologists studied cultures in which the understanding of who individuals were, and how they fit in, were not matters of debate or wide personal choice. The exact opposite is true in contemporary societies. The array and mix of biological, psychological, racial, ethnic, religious, political, national and professional identities present in increasingly heterogeneous societies provides unprecedented opportunities for choice, conflict and confusion.

Identity has made more progress as a political slogan than as a substantive term. The political uses (Norton, 1998) and abuses (Schlesinger, 1996) of identity politics have become clearer in the past two decades, however the development of comparative psychological theories of identity formation and consolidation have lagged far behind. Is it possible, for example, to forge a new New Zealand national identity at the same time that its major non-English group, the Maoris, are in the midst of a cultural revival and in the process of consolidating a transition from tribal to Maori identity (Durie, 1998, 55)? What are the consequences for national identities when various ethnic groups insist on their cultural and political autonomy? Can a homosexual man, whose identity is primarily defined by his sexual orientation, be patriotic in a country which continues to deny him the opportunity of a legally sanctioned marriage, or even the ability to serve in its armed forces if he publicly expresses his identity preferences? Must identities primarily defined by race be nationally divisive? Are such identities necessarily 'racist?' When individuals define their identities primarily in racial (or ethnic, gender or other non-inclusive) frames, how are other possible identifications organized psychologically?

These are not idle questions; their answers have substantial implications for individuals and the societies of which they are a part. However, as yet, we have little substantive basis on which to resolve them.

Conclusion

The chapters herein, individually and cumulatively, build on the substantial legacy bequeathed to us by the field's pioneers. However, they are also meant to provide a more nuanced, modern and therefore useful theoretical map of the relationships among culture, psychology and political practices in nation-state settings.

Our purpose is to demonstrate that a fuller understanding of culture, and its links to interior, interpersonal and social psychology, can reaffirm and strengthen its enduring relevance for political life. We seek to make a plausible, perhaps even a persuasive, case that advances in theory, method and, above all, perspective have the capacity to make culture less elusive and even more indispensable to the study of political psychology. In doing so, we hope to provide a secure conceptual foundation for a modern cultural and crosscultural political psychology.

Notes

1. Compare this with Linton's (1945, 22) definition of culture as 'the configuration of learned behavior and results of behavior whose component elements are shared and transmitted by the members of a particular society'. Also relevant is Eckstein's (1997, 26) more recent definition of culture as 'the variable and cumulatively learned patterns of orientations to action in societies'.

2. Bock (1988, 42; see also Barnouw, 1963, 3–27) divides the 'culture and personality' school into four related, but distinguishable approaches: configurationalist, basic and modal personality, national character and crosscultural. He associates these approaches respectively with the work of Benedict (1934), DuBois (1944), Kluckhohn (1957), and Whiting and Child (1953). One can gain a more detailed perspective on the development of the field by examining Inkeles and Levinson (1954–69), and more recently, Inkeles (1990–91).

3. Spiro (1972, 582–7), argues that because of its very success, 'culture and personality' anthropology can, and should, reorient its focus more towards socio-cultural systems.

4. Benedict (1934) argued, however, that even cultures organized around the same general themes, like the aggressive cultural stance of the Dobu Islanders in Melanesia and the Kwakiutl Indians of British Columbia, might develop different cultural configurations. The particular ways in which culture was organized was always an empirical, not an *a priori* theoretical, matter.

5. As early as 1911 in his book, *The Mind of Primitive Man*, Boas (1939, v) stated categorically, 'there is no fundamental difference in the ways of thinking between primitive and civilized man'. He further added (1939, 130) that the view that different races of man stand on distinct stages of the evolutionary stage 'cannot be maintained'.

6. When Canadian officials outlawed the Kwakiutl potlatch in British Columbia, Franz Boas was at the forefront of those trying to get the authorities to reconsider their ban.

7. For example, in the first chapter of the classic book, *Patterns of Culture*, Benedict points out that on the basis of field research, cultural theories of group differences have a much stronger evidentiary basis than racial ones. For a survey of some contemporary views that begin with, and reach, opposite assumptions see Pangle (1998).

8. The first conceptualized as the common denominators of the personalities passing through a uniform set of child-rearing experiences. The second did not require psychological uniformity as a consequence of a culture's socialization practices, but concentrated instead on uncovering their most common (modal) outcomes. The third, national character studies, applied the assumptions of the first and the second to larger, national culture units in the search for essential characteristics of a country's general population.

9. George's reformulation of Leites' work led to a rich and continuing literature in international politics, bargaining and conflict theory (Mandell, 1986). Not the least of the contributions growing out of Leites's revised culture-as-belief-system approach to culture and crosscultural political analysis was the literature on misperception and conflict (Jervis, 1976). Avoidable wars, according to White (1970), could be traced to differences of perception and understanding rooted in distinctive cultural frames and historical experiences.

10. First, compare in this respect the work of Shweder (1990) and Cole (1996). Shweder calls for a cultural psychology whose core focus is on cognition and

whose methods are rooted in the interpretative branches of the social sciences and humanities. Cole does the same, but frames his methods in line with more traditional views of 'science'.

Then compare these two 'new' psychological anthropologists with Hsu (1972, 10), who introduced the term, psychological anthropology – not without objection from other 'culture and personality' theorists (cf., Spiro, 1972, 578). Hsu defined the term as including a focus on: (a) the conscious and unconscious ideas shared by a majority of individuals within a culture, and (b) the conscious or unconscious psychic materials governing the action patterns of many individuals.

11. The research is buttressed by the development of a journal devoted specifically to its interests, *The Journal of Cross-Cultural Pschology*, as well as annual yearbooks (Triandis and Brislin, 1980).

12. Such societies were not necessarily harmonious or peaceful. Intertribal warfare was frequent and detailed social rankings coupled with the dominant power of chiefs limited mobility and opportunity for many group members.

13. Hermans and Kempen (1998) argue that 'modern', 'hybrid' cultures make the assumption of cultural coherence problematic. Yet, it remains to be seen whether hybrid cultures that go against the basic cultural traditions of a community will become integrated, as opposed to a more surface level of accommodation. Or, in other words, just because Muslims in Iraq wear levis and listen to rock, should we assume that they share the major cultural values of the countries from which these items are imported?

References

Almond, G. and Verba, C. (1963) *The Civic Culture*, Princeton, N. J.: Princeton University Press.

Altemeyer, B. (1981) *Right-wing Authoritarianism*, Winnipeg, Canada: University of Manitoba Press.

Altemeyer, B. (1988) *Enemies of Freedom: Understanding Right-wing Authoritarianism*, San Francisco: Jossey-Bass.

Barnouw, V. (1963) *Culture and Personality*, Homewood, Ill.: Dorsey Press.

Bell, D. (1954) *The Cultural Contradictions of Capitalism*, New York: Basic Books.

Benedict, R. (1934) *Patterns of Culture*, New York: Mentor.

Benedict, R. (1939) *The Chrysanthemum and the Sword*, Boston: Houghton Mifflin.

Boas, F. (1911, 1939) *The Mind of Primitive Man*, New York: Macmillan.

Bond, M. H. (ed.) (1988) *The Cross-cultural Challenge to Social Psychology*, Newbury Park, Calif.: Sage.

Bock, P. K. (1988) *Rethinking Psychological Anthropology*, Prospect Heights, Ill.: Waveland Press.

Cole, M. (1996) *Cultural Psychology*, Cambridge: Harvard University Press.

DuBois, C. (1944) *The People of Alor*, 2 vols, New York: Harper & Row.

Duckitt, J. (1993) *The Social Psychology of Prejudice*, New York: Praeger.

du Preez, J. (1983) *Africana Afrikaner: Master Symbols in South African School Textbooks*, Alberton, South Africa: Librarius.

Durie, M. (1988) *Te mana te Kawantanga: The Politics of Maori Self-determination*, New York: Oxford.

Eckstein, H. (1997) 'Social Science as Cultural Science, Rational Choice as Methaphysics', in R. J. Ellis and M. Thompson (eds), *Culture Matters: Essays in Honor of Aaron Wildavsky* (pp. 21–44), Boulder, Co.: Westview.

Fish, S. (1998) 'Boutique Multiculturalism', in A. M. Melzer *et al.* (eds), *Multiculturalism and American Democracy* (pp. 69–88), Lawrence: University of Kansas.

Fiske, A. P. (1991) *Structures of Social Life: The Four Elementary Forms of Human Relations*, New York: Free Press.

George, A. (1969) 'The "Operational Code": A Neglected Approach to the Study of Political Leaders and Decision Makers', *International Studies Quarterly, vol. 13*, 190–222.

Gudykunst, W. (1988) 'Culture and Intergroup Processes', in M. H. Bond (ed.), *The Cross-cultural Challenge to Social Psychology* (pp. 165–81), Newbury Park, Calif.: Sage.

Harding, D. G. (ed.) (1956) *Personal Character and Cultural Mileau*, 3rd edn, Syracuse: Syracuse University Press.

Hermans, H. J. M. and H. J. G. Kempen (1998) 'Moving Cultures: The Perilous Problems of Cultural Dichotomies in a Globalizing Society', *American Psychologist*, vol. 53 (10), 1111–20.

Hofstede, G. (1980) *Culture's Consequences: International Differences in Work-related Values*, Beverly Hills, CA: Sage.

Hsu, F. L. K. (ed.) (1974) *Psychological Anthropology*, 2nd edn, Cambridge: Schenkam.

Huntington, S. P. (1996) *The Clash of Civilization and the Remaking of World Order*, New York: Simon and Shuster.

Inkeles, A. and D. J. Levinson (1954) 'National Character: The Study of Modal Personality and Sociocultural Systems'. In G. Lindzey (ed.) *The Handbook of Social Psychology* (pp. 977–1020). Reading, Mass.: Addison-Wesley.

Inkeles, A. and D. J. Levinson (1969) 'National Character: The Study of Modal Personality and Sociocultural Systems'. In G. Lindzey and E. Arronson (eds.) *The Handbook of Social Psychology, vol. 4*, 2nd edn (pp. 418–506). Reading, Mass.: Addison-Wesley.

Inkeles, A. (1990–91) National character revisited. *The Tocqueville Review, 12*, 83–117.

Inglehart, R. (1990) *Cultural Shift in Advanced Industrial Society*. Princeton: Princeton University Press.

Inglehart, R. (1996) *Modernization and postmodernization: Cultural, Economic and Political Change in 43 Countries*. Princeton: Princeton University Press.

Jervis, R. (1976) *Perception and Misperception in International Relations*. Princeton, N. J.: Princeton University.

Kaplan, B. (ed.) (1961) *Studying Personality Cross-culturally*. Evanston, Ill.: Row, Peterson and Co.

Kardiner, A. with R. Linton (1939) *The Individual and His Society*. New York: Columbia University Press.

Kluckhohn, C. and H. A. Murray (eds.) (1953) *Personality in Nature, Society, and Culture, Second Edition*. New York: Knopf.

Kluckhohn, C. (1957) *Mirror for Man*. New York: Premier.

Landes, D. S. (1996) *The Wealth and Poverty of Nations: Why some are so rich, and others so poor*. New York: Norton.

Leites, N. (1948) 'Psychocultural hypotheses about political acts', *World Politics, 1*, 102–119.

Leites, N. (1951) *The Operational Code of the Politburo*. New York: McGraw-Hill.

Linton, R. (1930) *The Study of Man*. New York: Appleton-Century-Crofts.

Linton, R. (1945) *The Cultural Background of Personality*. New York: Appleton-Century-Crofts.

Lomax, A., & Berkowitz, N. (1972) 'The evolutionary taxonomy of cultures'. *Science, 177*, 228–239.

Mandell, R. (1986) 'Psychological approaches to international politics'. In M. Hermann (ed.) *Political Psychology*, (pp. 251–278). San Francisco: Jossey Bass.

Mann, L. (1988) Cultural influences on group processes. In M. H. Bond (Ed.), *The Cross-cultural Challenge to Social Psychology* (pp. 182–195). Newbury Park, Calif.: Sage.

Maslow, A. (1954) *Motivation and Personality*. New York: Harper and Row.

Mead, M. (1935) *Sex and Temperament in Three Primitive Societies*. New York: Apollo.

Mead, M. (1939) *From the South Seas*. New York: Morrow.

Norton, A. (1998) 'The Virtues of Multiculturalism,' in Arthur M. Melzer, *et al.* (Eds). *Multiculturalism and American Democracy* (pp. 130–138). Lawrence: University of Kansas.

Pangle, L. (1998) 'Multiculturalism and Civic Education,' in Arthur M. Melzer *et al.* (Eds). *Multiculturalism and American Democracy* (pp. 173–196). Lawrence: University of Kansas.

Peabody, D. (1985) *National Characteristics*. Cambridge: Cambridge University Press.

Ross, M. H. (1993) *The Culture of Conflict: Interpretations and Interests in Comparative Perspective*. New Haven, CT: Yale University Press.

Schlesinger, A. Jr. (1996) *The Disuniting of America: Reflections on a Multicultural Society*. New York: Norton.

Schwartz, S. (1992) 'The universal structure and content of values: Theoretical advances and empirical tests in 20 countries'. In M. Zanna (ed.), *Advances in Experimental Social Psychology, vol. 25* (pp. 1–65). New York: Academic Press.

Segall, M., W. L. Lonner, and J. W. Berry (1998) 'Cross-Cultural psychology as a scholarly discipline'. *American Psychologist*, 53 (10), 1101–1110.

Shweder, R. A. (1991) *Thinking Through Cultures*. Cambridge: Harvard University Press.

Smith, P., & Bond, M. H. (1993) *Social Psychology Across Cultures*. New York: Harvester Wheatsheaf.

Sowell, T. (1994) *Race and Culture*. New York: Basic Books.

Spiro, M. E. (1974) 'An Overview and Suggested Reorientation,' in F. L. K. Hsu (ed.) *Psychological Anthropology, Second Edition*. (pp. 573–607) Cambridge: Schenkman.

Sumner, W. G. (1904) *Folkways*. New York: Ginn.

Triandis, H. & Brislin, R. C. (eds) (1980) *Handbook of Cross-cultural Psychology* (vol. 5). Boston: Allyn and Bacon.

Triandis, H., Bontempo, R., & Villareal, M. (1988) 'Individualism and collectivism: Cross-cultural perspectives on self-ingroup relationships'. *Journal of Personality and Social Psychology*, 54, 323–338.

White, R. K. (1970) *Nobody Wanted War: Misperception in Vietnam and Other Wars*. New York: Doubleday.

Whiting, J. W. M. and I. L. Child (1953) *Child Training and Personality: A Cross-cultural Study*. New Haven: Yale University Press.

Wilson, J. (1996) *When Work Disappears*. New York: Knopf.

Yang, K. (1988) 'Will social modernization eventually eliminate cross-cultural psychological differences?' In M. Bond (ed.) *The Cross-cultural Challenge to Social Psychology*, (pp. 49–67). Newbury Park, California: Sage.

2

The Elusive Concept of Culture and the Vivid Reality of Personality

Lucian W. Pye

The domain of political psychology is broad and variegated, for it encompasses a boundless variety of topics and methodologies, as the authors of this book manifestly demonstrate. Whereas other academic disciplines seem ever intent upon narrowing their focuses in order to concentrate energies on select minutiae, political psychology has constantly opened its arms to welcome new issues, insights and approaches. This is understandable, given the subject matter of the field and the numerous parent disciplines of its practitioners. Political life, defined in a variety of ways, can be thought of as always taking in some aspect or another of basic human behavior. Thus just about every field in the humanities and social sciences can legitimately hold that it has a contribution to make to the understanding of the workings of the human factor in politics.

Indeed, politics has no foundations other than human nature. Thus, to understand politics there is no escaping the need for an understanding of psychology. The discipline of political science can be seen as standing at a junction point of psychology and sociology in that all political theories rest upon assumptions about both the nature of the individual and the dynamics of the collectivity, the leader and the group, the citizen and the state. From the time of Aristotle all classical political theorists have utilized the most advanced psychology available to them. It is only in modern times, as the field of psychology has grown scientifically sophisticated, that questions have been raised about how far political scientists can legitimately go in utilizing psychological knowledge. Since no political scientist can avoid employing assumptions about the human personality, the only basis for criticizing some political scientists for having engaged in 'psychologizing' is that they must have overstepped an undefined boundary and embraced 'too much advanced psychology' and thereby caused anxieties among the critics who feel threatened by such knowledge.

Yet, there is a legitimate problem of people venturing too far afield into other disciplines and thereby engaging in superficial and perhaps quite wrong practices. The danger is not just that of people in political science

18

and other disciplines dipping into psychology and using some of its jargon without adequate grounding in the subject. There is also the problem of psychologists and psychiatrists becoming 'politicized' beyond their competence in matters of public affairs. The solution to this problem is that of normal science: Specialists will criticize and expose what is flawed and gradually in the process the good will be separated from the bad. Fortunately in political psychology the very breadth of the field means that there is not the danger of cultism whereby a small group of like-mined practitioners become a mutual admiration society and thus allow the bad to stand uncriticized. Indeed, the wide ranging character of political psychology guarantees that there are always a large number of knowledgeable critics who can insure that what has been produced has been respectfully criticized from a number of different perspectives. Fortunately normal science is the inverse of Gresham's law, in that 'good' science will eventually drive out 'bad' science.

It is possible to reduce somewhat the expansive and diversified character of political psychology by noting that most studies concentrate either on individual psychology, such as the behavior of particular leaders and that of individual citizens as voter and participant, or on collective behavior at either the group or national level. The psychological studies of individuals goes beyond just biographical studies of particular leaders and surveys of the opinions and attitudes of citizens to include more theoretical attempts to relate personality characteristics to ideological orientations, such as with the theory of the authoritarian personality. The psychology of collective behavior involves matters ranging from ethnic and other forms of group identities to crosscultural communications and questions about the causes of wars and the prospects for peace.

The true heart of psychology as a discipline has been the analysis of the individual, and therefore there has long been a somewhat troublesome problem of how to go from the richness of the knowledge we have about the individual to the 'psychology' of a collectivity that is an aggregation of individuals. This is the classic micro–macro problem that has long bedeviled political psychology. A collectivity's behavior is obviously based in some way of the character of the individuals who make it up, but it is equally obvious that a mere tabulation of the characteristics of the involved individuals is not enough to explain the behavior of the collectivity. As Fathali Moghaddam and David Crystal demonstrate in their chapter in this book, cultural changes at the macro and micro levels follow quite different rhythms. Macro political and economic changes can be fairly rapid, as happens with the establishment of a new political regime, while there is greater resistance to change at the level of the individual personality, and therefore everyday social practices tend to persist.

The micro–macro problem is particularly troublesome because of an odd contradiction: the individual personality is more complex than any national political system, yet paradoxically, we are on surer ground in our analysis of the individual. Karl Deutsch in the *Nerves of Government* (1963) observed that if we think of the flow of communications in a government as analogous to the human nervous system, it turns out that the human system is more complex because it has far more nerve synapses than the communications connections in the entire United States government.

The advanced state of knowledge in psychology also means that we have techniques for exploring in some detail relationships between political attitudes and sentiments, and for identifying a host of conscious and unconscious fantasies, needs and drives which determine people's understanding about the nature of power and politics. This leads, however, to another contradiction in the macro–micro problem, and this is that only a small proportion of the rich array of attitudes and feelings that people have about politics are ever brought into play in their actual political behavior. This means that the manifest operations of a political system involve only a small fraction of all the political attitudes and fantasies that its individual participants have. What is tricky is sorting out which attitudes and feelings are significant for explaining the operations of the system as a whole. We have literally thousands of surveys of public opinion in America, but it remains a mystery as to which ones can really inform us about where American politics is going.

Fortunately we are able to reduce somewhat the micro–macro problem by using the concept of culture, and by relating it to theories of personality. Therefore in appraising the state of political psychology it may be well to begin by examining the concept of culture as a useful entering wedge for exploiting the pay-offs of psychology for understanding collective behavior at both the group and the national levels.

The elusive but indispensable concept of culture

The concept of culture is probably unique in the social sciences in both its reach across discipline lines and in its cyclical rise and fall in popularity. Regardless of the discipline, the concept has been hard to pin down with any degree of intellectual rigor, yet it is also indispensable for serious thinking about the workings of human society and the behavior of people. Indeed, all of the social sciences in the last analysis are based on the fundamental fact that human society is only possible because of culture. Social behavior is essentially patterned and meaningful interactions of human beings who share the symbolic and subjective elements of what constitutes cultures. As the sociologist and historian Liah Greenfeld has written,

> Social reality is essentially cultural; it is necessarily a symbolic reality, created by the subjective meanings and perceptions of social actors. Every social order (that is, the overall *structure* of a society) represents a materialization, or objectivization, of its image, shared by those who participate in it. (Greenfeld: 1992, 18)

Indeed, Richard Wilson in his chapter examines very systematically the deeper subjective bases of political cultures by demonstrating that they all rest upon a particular set of moral norms. Starting with the American political culture, he notes that cultures can differ according to whether they stress the ideal of autonomy and self achievement or whether they uphold an ethic of care and empathetic concern for others. He then argues that commitment to autonomy tends to produce an individualistic political culture while an ethic of care is associated with an equalitarian political culture. Cultures moreover follow a law of change based on shifts in the moral basis of the norms and the implicit regulations and standards which provide order and structure to the society.

Historically the explication of the concept of culture has had different moments of popularity in the different disciplines, and in a strange way its decline in favor in one discipline seems only to open the way to a welcomed reception in another. Thus, the swings in its popularity have followed an odd dynamic. At times its heralded utility in one discipline has spread its popularity to adjacent fields, but at other times other fashions have seemed to rule the day, and it has been left to isolated disciplines to preserve the flame until the arrival of another phases of general acceptance.

The concept is also elusive because it straddles the line between objective, materialistic phenomena and the realm of subjective consciousness. Cultures have their material, concrete aspects, but they are also lodged in the mind, part of both the conscious and the unconscious domains of the human psyche. Thus, a culture can be identified in terms of objective artifacts, symbols, language and observable behavioral patterns, but the real potency of culture lies in its operations in the subjective realm where the powers of awareness and of the imagination seem to give it almost unlimited sway. The human mind easily assumes that all manner of actions and behavior can be attributed to the workings of culture, which in turn may have no other basis for existence except for the actions and behavior it purports to explain. This is a form of circularity of reasoning which is not easily dismissed because the imagination is so rich in the potency of awareness and the magic of consciousness.

Yet, fortunately, we have techniques for measuring deeper psychological and cultural differences, and thus we can separate to some degree cause and effect. For example, George De Vos in his chapter, and in forty years of research, has demonstrated that Thematic Apperception Tests (TATs) can reveal the deeper motivational drives and the feelings of self-esteem which are decisive in determining the effectiveness of people in different cultures. He reports on prior work which showed that the early socialization experiences of Japanese meant that even when they were sociologically disadvantaged, as when they were forced in America to live in urban poverty settings and were discriminated against because of the color of their skin, they were still able to advance themselves and become high achievers. He now reports that the same tests reveal differences which help explain the relative successes of southern Brazilians with European and Japanese cultural heritage, and northern Brazilians who have had different and less supportive socialization experiences and thus operate out of a heritage of exploitation and a culture of dependency. The tests help explain southern dynamism and economic growth and northern stagnation and dependency.

The richness and the complexity of the subjective dimension of culture is further heightened because it has both cognitive and affective aspects. Culture can be thought of as being the 'mental map' which provides the knowledge for guiding political behavior. But culture also has strong affective claims which explains why the 'clash of cultures' can be so intense.[1] Since a people's basic sense of identity is usually strongly rooted in their feelings of cultural distinctiveness, crosscultural interactions can be fraught with tension-filled misunderstandings. People are easily offended by the mere suggestion of cultural differences, but at the same time people need to feel that their culture is indeed distinctive and different, and therefore they can be offended if it is suggested that they are not different.[2]

The subjective character of culture also insures that the concept is loaded with meaning and interpretation, and therefore it also has a significant moral or evaluative dimension. Statements about cultures inescapable seem to carry either explicit or implicit judgments about what is good and bad in different patterns of behavior. As Marc Howard Ross demonstrates in his chapter, culture provides a powerful tool for analyzing ethnic conflicts and for suggesting policy approaches for solving them. Yet, those who strive to be objective and value-neutral in their analysis of cultures often find themselves charged with having 'hidden agendas' or of unconsciously upholding the superiority of one cultural perspective over that of another. This is a particularly troublesome problem for American social scientists who have to operate in one of the few cultures which treats ethnocentrism as a bad thing and which insists that one should not make judgments about the ways of other people. Indeed, no other known society could have produced a political-correctness movement to match the virulence of today's demands for conformity on some American campuses.

The subjective dimension of culture is particularly significant when it comes to political culture because politics always consists of a combination of values and power, both of which involve the imagination. There is always the question of how deeply embedded are the elements of a political culture in the subjective realm. Can we really 'map' a political culture by sample surveys based on questions about values and opinions, or is it necessary to dig deeper and look for patterns at the unconscious or subconscious levels? As Ofer Feldman points out in his chapter, there have been two major approaches to the study of Japanese political culture: the *nihonjinron* tradition of seeking to identify the key characteristics of Japanese culture and identity, and the sample survey approach which seeks to compare the attitudes of Japanese with those of Westerners according to the same sets of questions. Although there is a tradition of antagonism between the practitioners of the two approaches, in theory the two should interact to enrich each other, in that the speculative characterizations should suggest hypotheses for survey testing in both Japan and the West, and the findings of the surveys should provide strong foundations for formulating generalized views about Japanese character. Ultimately the accumulative results of large numbers of sample surveys will only have scientific value if they can provide us with a deeper understanding of the general characteristics of political cultures. Differences in survey answers are of only passing interest if they do not illuminate the more profound differences in the basic characteristics of the particular political cultures.

The problem of the elusive nature of political culture is, however, more complicated because at the heart of politics there is the matter of power, and the related concept of authority, two subjects which have an inordinate ability to stimulate the human imagination. Out of the process of childhood socialization people develop enduring and complex fantasies about the almost magical workings of power. Authority figures are imbued with a degree of omnipotence that defies cold reason, but which makes possible exaggerated notions of the degree to which governments can be either benevolent or malevolent institutions. Since the play of politics almost invariably favors some people and hurts others, it therefore easily stimulates suspicion and distrust, but it can also arouse exaggerated hopes and dreams. For every paranoid about government officials as imagined enemies there is the childish dreamer who believes that government can solve all problems.

Similarly the mystique of leadership stems from an idealization of the exceptional powers people want to attribute to authority. The actual differences among individual humans in strength and intellectual cunning is so marginal that the heightened power of national leaders exists only because of shared fantasies about the wonders of power in the minds of the public. Moreover, nobody can ever observe empirically the full workings of the political process because it consists of the subjective interactions of countless acts of speculation, judgment, calculation, and different perceptions of reality. Events can be reported but the chain of causality can only be imagined. Wildly different notions of cause and effect can result in the same manifest event taking on totally different significance for people of different sub-cultures. Ultimately there is, of course, coercive power, especially that of the state, but even the threat of such force makes up only a small element of the concept of power which is the life-blood of politics.

Since political power rests largely upon expectations, communications, and shared sentiments and values, politics is essentially a cultural phenomenon. Indeed, politics would be impossible without culture, and cultures, of course, differ according to time and place. Indeed there are few human skills that are as place specific as that of the politician. The qualities which insure election in one country would guarantee certain defeat in another. Hence the need for all students of politics to be sensitive to cultural differences.

Anthropology leads the way – both forwards and back

It is thus not surprising that historians from Heroditus to Gibbons, philosophers from Plato to Montesquieu and Hobbs have all had to employ notions about the human community and the variations in people's practices in different societies. This was true not just in Western intellectual history but with thinkers in all traditions, such as with Confucius in China, Kautilya in India, and ibn-Khaldun for Islam, who all made insightful comments about the customs and practices of different peoples. However, the modern concept of culture was unquestionably the child of anthropology, especially the product of those pioneers who sought to utilize Freudian depth psychology to create the sub-field of 'personality and culture'. The band included Franz Boas, Edward Sapir, Margaret Mead, Ruth Benedict, Clyde Kluckholm, Robert Redfield, Alexander Leighton and too many others to be named, but none of whom should be forgotten. The concept of culture was then quickly picked up in political science with the popularization of theories about 'political culture' by Gabriel Almond, Harold Lasswell and Nathan Leites among others. Historians, such as Peter Gay in his psychologically oriented study of bourgeois Europe, utilized the concept of culture as a more sophisticated way of analyzing the 'spirit of the times'. As social historians relied upon the concept, it was enthusiastically adopted by some social critics, such as Christopher Leach with his theory about Americans' 'narcissistic' culture. For a time it might have seemed that culture was about to become the sovereign concept of the social sciences, with only economics holding out as its practitioners insisted that they could study utility maximization without asking where or how preferences were developed.

Then, however, there was a general retreat as rigorous theorists claimed that the popularization of the concept of culture had made it far too elastic a notion to provide valid explanations about human behavior. Culture could be used to explain everything, and hence it explained nothing. Moreover, anthropologists in particular began to feel that culture was being used as a screen of respectability which allowed intellectuals to engage in the shameful practice of stereotyping other peoples. Consequently, in anthropology there was a dramatic retreat from seeking generalized theories and a shift to practicing 'thick description', that is, detailed ethnographic studies devoid of any explicit theoretical categories or interpretations.

This was followed in political science by the rise of rational choice theory, which for a time thought it could proceed as economics had without asking about the sources of preferences. Concurrently in psychology,

Freud was out and cognitive theories were in. Historians also joined the retreat as the popularity of psychohistory took a sharp decline. Seemingly the cultural approach had overreached itself, tried to do too much, too loosely, and therefore questions were being raised as to whether the practice of cultural characterizations was not little more than a form of crude labeling, carried out by intellectuals who pretend to be above prejudice, but who no doubt had their private biases.[3]

Then, however, there was a most startling change in fashions, coming from the most unlikely of sources, the Humanities. This was the movement involving in particular scholars of English literature who had grasped onto the thinking of French theorists, who in turn had surprisingly late in the game discovered Freud. Out of the techniques of deconstruction they generated 'critical theory' which needed the concept of culture both as a 'bad' hegemonic force and as the hopefully new forces of feminism, multiculturalism and political correctness. Evoking the names of Foucault, Derrida, Lacan, Althusser and Gramsci was seen as enough to do the trick of removing the concept of culture from any association with bourgeois propriety.

The new wave of anthropological research is thus able to once again tap into the powers of depth psychology, but generally with a more specific and concentrated focus than the 'personality and culture' school of anthropologists originally did in trying to study whole cultures. Thus, Allen Johnson in his chapter examines the psychology of dependency between landlords and sharecroppers in Northeast Brazil by employing the key concepts of splitting and idealization from Kleinian psychoanalysis. The result is a much richer understanding of patron–client relationships than was possible with older and more rationalistic theories.

Revival may or may not be progress

The cyclical history of the concept of culture does not mean that with each revival there was a return to the same understanding of the concept. The combination of the need to respond to the criticisms which led to the decline in culture theory and the peculiar circumstances which produced a restoration of its popularity in a particular disciple insures that the theory will have accumulated some additional intellectual baggage. Thus, on some occasions and in some disciplines there can be genuine progress, but in other instances the revival may only bring back a qualified and weakened theory of culture.

The initial popularity of the concept of culture, for example, emerged in part because the anthropologists wrote with a clarity and vividness that made their formulations understandable to a large audience. Margaret Mead had an easy style and an instinct for what was on the minds of young Americans; Ruth Benedict was a poet as well as a scientist; Eric Erikson knew how to captivate his reader's imagination by speaking to common human experiences. In a sense these early writers made it all seem too easy and therefore the next generation of anthropologists felt that the pioneers had over-simplified reality and that extensive qualifications were necessary because the real world was much more complicated. Indeed so complicated that ordinary people could not fully understand what it was all about. Yet, when the challenge to the Freudian-oriented vision of culture was mounted by a call for detailed ethnographic reporting in the form of 'thick description', its main practitioner was the elegant stylist, Clifford Geertz, who however seemed to feel uneasy about the possibility that his readers might jump to conclusions and not appreciate that what he had to say was more complicated than he was able to explain. Thus, after describing in great detail the Balinese spirit of cock-fighting, Geertz insists that it would be too easy to suggest that it had any direct connections with the brutal massacre of Communists on the island of Bali in 1967; yet at the same time there was, he conceded, some relationship between the two, in a deep down, complex way which should not be confused with a straight-forward propositional statement of a relationship.

This fear that readers might take a simple-minded view of cultural differences and try to explain too much with cultural considerations led to two reinforcing trends in anthropology. The first was a shying away from explicit concepts and generalizations, particularly if they could be easily employed to label other peoples. The second was the adoption of an ever denser, more turgid, more murky essay style, which then was compounded many times over when many anthropologists responded to the opening provided by critical theorists and deconstructionist in the field of English. Anthropology had been badly shocked in the 1960s and 1970s with the thought that its theories of culture might be a form of neo-colonialism, involving the imposition of 'Western ideas' on other peoples. Somehow the idea took hold that clear thinking and rigorous logic was a uniquely Western value and that other peoples might not be able to either appreciate or practice it. Therefore, it was safest not to impose any logically rigorous theoretical concepts upon ethnographic data. The 'crisis of faith' became so bad that Richard Shweder (1988) suggested that the discipline was in need of something like a 'farm subsidy program for Western intellectuals: to avoid flooding the market with ideas, pay them not to think'.

The restoration of ideas and a new interest in theorizing came when anthropologists, such as Jean Comaroff (1985), utilizing the thoughts of Althusser, Foucault and the deconstructionists, noted that culture was not the preserve of only the strong and hegemonic but it was also, to use the phrase of James Scott, a 'weapon of the weak', and thus one could again write about non-Western, common people's cultures – but only if the prose was appropriately dense and convoluted so as to signal that no simple-minded putting down of others was taking place. It is not at all clear, however, that the new efforts have been any less ethnocentric than the earlier anthropologists were.[4] Geertz himself helped to pull the discipline back from the extreme of intellectual nihilism by pressing for a point of view which held that, while theory building *a la* logical positivism was still out, some ideas might be useful. Thus, seeking a middle ground, he, more serious than joking, suggested that he was a 'post-post-modernist' (Geertz, 1995). Marshall Sahlins (1995) joined the restoration effort by challenging Gananath Obeyesekere (1992) argument that Western scholarship in anthropology was a form of Western hegemonic 'imperialism' by convincingly demonstrating that the Hawaiians did in fact believe that Captain Cook was a god. Sahlins showed that for sound scholarship empirical facts should be the ultimate test rather than ideological posturing. Facts may not speak for themselves and thus there is the need for the human imagination, but at the same time speculation and ideological debating positions cannot in themselves advance knowledge.

So in a sense the concept of culture has gone through the cyclical swings common in the social science which begin with the attempt to stretch to the limits of generalization a few observable facts and thereby to pronounce elegant theories. Soon there is a need to introduce qualifications as other facts create the need for adjustments in the theory. This is followed by a period of enthusiasm for just 'sticking with the facts' and engaging in 'thick description'. After a time however the accumulation of just facts loses its appeal, and there is a craving for the intellectual excitement of elegant theories. But the experience of the swings leaves scholars a bit more cautious and not quite as prepared to engaging in grand theory building. The appeal is then for 'middle range hypotheses'. This is the cycle that the theories of not just the cultural anthropologists have gone through but also the theories of Marx, Freud, Darwin, Keynes and those of all other great, creative thinkers.

The revival of political culture studies

In political science the revival of political culture came about in large measure as a consequence of two related historical developments: the collapse of Communism with an attendant rise in ethnic politics, and a significant world wide trend towards democracy. Schwartz and Bardi in their chapter demonstrate how the collapse of Communism in Eastern Europe has provided almost laboratory conditions for measuring why the various countries have different legacies from their common experiences with Communist rule. The more general erosion of authoritarianism, which was basic to the disintegration of Marxist regimes, and the 'third wave' of democracy, to use Huntington's (1991) phrase, brought political science back to concerns about modernization and the cultural basis of stable democracies. Significantly these were the very issues which were at the top of the agenda in political science when the discipline had its initial fascination with the concept of culture.

The essential character of democratic culture was the central problem that Gabriel Almond and Sidney Verba addressed in *The Civic Culture*. Arguably few empirical studies have had as great an impact on political science as this effort to find the cultural basis for stable democracies through sample survey analyses of values in five countries. That work generated over several decades innumerable studies which refined our understanding of the cultural bases of democracies. Most recently Kornberg and Clark (1992), relying on survey methods, refined the *Civic Culture* theory of democracy through a sophisticated analysis of Canadian attitudes about their governments.

The argument advanced in *The Civic Culture* that cultural factors are critical for stable democracy received a substantial boost with the appearance of Robert Putnam's, destined to be a classic study, *Making Democracy Work: Civic Traditions in Modern Italy*. Putnam demonstrated that the elements of trust and community, which were basic to Almond and Verba's concept of a civic culture, provide the best basis for explaining the relative successes and failures of democracy in different parts of Italy. Putnam shows that the cultural roots for successful democracy in the Italian regional governments can be traced as far back as the twelfth century.[5]

The enduring influence of *The Civic Culture* is particularly impressive because there has been such dramatic changes in the American political environment from the time it was written. The work reflects the political mood of America in the 1950s and academic thinking prior to the campus turmoil of the 1960s and 70s. At that time orderly participation and constructive civic values were more the norm. *The Civic Culture* thus provides a baseline for charting recent changes in values and attitudes. Ronald Inglehart (1990), for example, has used surveys to show that in the advanced industrial countries there has been a significant shift in values from essentially materialistic concerns to what he calls 'postmaterialist' values, such as concerns about ecology, and a wide range of social issues, such as abortion and gender considerations. These changes in values and attitudes has heightened concerns about an apparent decline in the American civil culture. Concerns about the proper balance in state–society relations for a healthy democracy has opened the way to debates about the state of Western culture and especially about the possibility that American society has become too individualistic and therefore lacking in adequate communitarian values. Robert Putnam has dramatized this issue with his 'Bowling Alone' article which pointed to a general decline in America for joining voluntary associations and group participation activities which presumable are essential for a healthy democracy. Anxiety about the social bonds in modern and postmodern societies has brought about increased interest in political culture among social critics, such as Lasch (1994), Elshtain (1995) and numerous others.[6]

The problem of keeping up with the times suggests the need to go beyond the 1950s and 60s issues about participation and civic association and address new sets of problems and issues which clearly have psychological roots. With politicians taking sharper adversarial positions on social issues and widespread signs of a fraying social fabric, there would seem, for example, to be an urgent need for scientific studies of political alienation. In the wake of the Oklahoma bombing, Kenneth Stern (1996) has studied the militia movement and the politics of hate, but his work is almost totally devoid of psychological insights. The journalist Fox Buttefield (1995) has written a sensitive analysis of a family tradition of murder that seeks to understand the place of violence in a particular American subculture. In doing so he has opened up a field that could benefit greatly from further psychologically oriented research. Indeed, the psychologists Richard Nisbett and Dov Cohen in *Culture of Honor* have done just this by showing that the higher homicide rates among white Southerners can be traced to the historic roots of Scottish and Irish immigrants with their traditions of upholding honor through violence, while the Puritans and Quakers who settled the North came from a more peaceful farming culture. Again like with Putnam and Fischer they are able to trace remarkable continuity in key cultural elements from generation to generation.

There are indeed many new fields waiting to be conquered in the study of political culture. We need to get beyond debates about the relative advantages of different approaches and to seek out ways in which the cultural dimensions can be incorporated into even theories which are frequently assumed to be antithetical to cultural analysis. For example, Aaron Wildawsky (1987) has shown that rational choice theory, which traditionally dismissed any cultural considerations, can in fact be greatly enriched by adding a cultural dimension in order to explain the sources and the nuances of the preferences of the actors. (See also, Ellis and Thompson, 1997.) Fiske and Tetlock in their chapter go even further and demonstrate that culturally and psychologically there are sever restraints on rational choice because of deeply held taboos about thinking in terms of tradeoffs when it comes to many critical values. Possibly rational choice theory in political science will follow the example of what has happened to rationality in economics after the introduction of 'rational expectation' considerations. That is, instead of treating rational choice as being just static decisions involving only trade-offs and preferences, the approach needs to be given a dynamic dimension by introducing considerations about how an actor's behavior is shaped by expectations of about how others will react in the strategic or game-playing situations which are so common to politics. 'I think that he thinks, that I think that he is going to do such an such, and so I will adjust my actions according to my expectations about his likely behavior.' By making the actor's behavior responsive to not just his or her internalized set of preferences, the rational expectations approach expands the analysis to include judgments about how others with behave, and such judgments always reflect cultural predispositions.

In short, the future of political culture studies is indeed bright, especially if we continue to welcome diversity in approaches and content, and if we avoid assertions of orthodoxy. Culture will inescapably have an enduring place in the social sciences because it is absolutely basic to the human condition. The challenge is to avoid the fads of paradigm change, and to focus on the need to address what are the challenging problems of the times. The popularity of political culture should not go up and down, but rather we should aggressively apply the approach to whatever are the new and urgent problems of society.

Notes

1. Since 'civilizations' are in a sense cultures writ large, it is understandable that Samuel Huntington's notion of a 'clash of civilizations' should have stimulated such heated debate. Indeed, precisely because such 'clashes' involve sentiments of basic personal identity, which in turn evoke questions of superiority and inferiority, they tend to be more emotionally intense than differences over conventional political and economic matters.
2. Melville Herskovits in *The Myth of the Negro Past* (1941) and other writings revealed that much of American black culture, including everything from motor behavior, codes of conduct, social institutions, family organization, language expression, to religious practices and art forms can be traced back to West Africa. At the time his report appeared, Herskovits was harshly attacked by Negro intellectuals, led by the sociologist Franklin Frazier, who declared that he had insulted their identities by associating them with Africa. They felt that their culture could and should be explained entirely in terms of their American experiences from slavery on. Since then there has of course been a total reversal in pride and identity as the term 'Negro' has been replaced with 'black', and African-Americans now take pride in their African roots.
3. Alex Inkeles seemed to have put a dagger into the heart of comparative cultural studies when he declared that 'national character' studies need to adhere to much higher scientific standards – indeed standards which seemed so high as to make them out of the reach of normal scholarship (Inkeles and Levinson 1954). But then forty years later he himself demonstrated that he was not opposed to the idea that there are national differences and that his standards for researching there were not so unreasonably high (Inkeles 1996).
4. Indeed, the labored analyses of some of the critical theory anthropologists do not always support their author's intended evaluative, that is moral, conclusions. For example, Jean Comaroff (1985) presents a detailed, and implicitly admiring, accounting of how the Tshidi of South Africa used features of their customs as 'proletarian' defenses against the 'bourgeois' values and practices of 'modernization', which she implicitly casts in a negative light. Yet, without any changes in the substance of the analysis, it is possible to see those behaviors she seems to admire as explaining the 'current condition of Africa', which stands in such sharp contrast to the current condition of dynamic East Asian where the people have been able, with great success, to achieve 'modernization' while holding to features of their ancient cultures, possibly even more successfully than the Africans have been able to do. That is, what she sees as cleverness in opposing 'modernization' may in fact be an explanation for African poverty.

5. In another impressive demonstration of the durability of cultural influences, the historian David Hackett Fischer (1989), using 26 quantitative and qualitative cultural indicators, has traced how the colonists from four culturally different regions of Britain settled in different locations in America, leaving folkway practices that still endure. He moreover argues that the overlapping of cultural similarities and differences has given the United States both stable democracy and political pluralism. The transplantation of folkways involved the Puritans of East Anglia going to Massachussets, Royalists elite and indentured servants to Virginia, people from the North Midlands and Wales to the Deleware Valley, and Scotch Irish to Appalachia. Subsequent immigrants from elsewhere have tended to acculturate to these regional variations of the four British cultures.
6. This debate has been picked up by some Asians, especially spokesmen for the government of Singapore, who argue that 'Asian values' of a communitarian nature are superior to Westen individualism. In their view Americans in particular have run amoke extolling individualism to the point that the American social order is on the verge of collapse. The argument is used mainly as a counter to American pressures for more respect for human rights and justice for the individual.

References

Almond, G. and Verba, S. (1963) *The Civic Culture*, Princeton: Princeton University Press.

Brint, S. (1995) *In an Age of Experts: The Changing Role of Professionals in Politics and Public Life*, Princeton: Princeton University Press.

Butterfield, F. (1995) *All God's Children: The Bosket Family and the American Tradition of Violence*, New York: Alfred A. Knopf.

Comaroff, J. (1985) *Body of Power Spirit of Resistance: The Culture and History of a South African People*, Chicago: University of Chicago Press.

Deutsch, K. W. (1963) *The Nerves of Government*, New York, The Free Press of Glencoe.

Ellis, R. J. and M. Thompson (eds) (1997) *Culture Matters: Essays in Honor of Aaron Wildavsky*, Boulder, Col.: Westview Press.

Elshtain, J. B. (1995) *Democracy on Trial*, New York: Basic Books.

Fischer, D. H. (1989) *Albion's Seed: Four British Folkways in America*, New York: Oxford University Press.

Greenfeld, L. (1992) *Nationalism: Five Roads to Modernity*, Cambridge: Harvard University Press.

Hunt, L. (1984) *Politics, Culture, and Class in the French Revolution*, Berkeley: University of California Press.

Huntington, S. P. (1991) *The Third Wave*, Norman, Okla.: The Oklahoma University Press.

Inglehart, R. (1988) The Renaissance of Political Culture, *The American Political Science Review*, vol. 4, pp. 1203–30.

Inglehart, R. (1990) *Cultural Shift in Advanced Industrial Society*, Princeton: Princeton University Press.

Inkeles, A. and D. J. Levenson, (1954) 'National Character: A Study of Model Personality and Sociocultural Systems', in G. Lindzey (ed.), *Handbook of Social Psychology*, Cambridge: Addison-Wesley.

Inkeles, A. (1996) *National Character: A Psycho-Social Perspective*, New Brunswick, N.J.: Transaction Publisher.

Kornberg, A. and H. Clark (1992) *Citizens and Community: Political Support in a Representative Democracy*, New York: Cambridge University Press.

Lasch, C. (1994) *The Revolt of the Elites and the Betrayal of Democracy*, New York: W. W. Norton.

Nisbett, R. and D. Cohen (1996) *Culture of Honor*, Boulder, Col.: Westview.

Obeyesekere, G. (1992) *The Apotheosis of Captain Cook: European Mythmaking in the Pacific*, Princeton: Princeton University Press.

Putnam, R. D. (1993) *Making Democracy Work: Civic Traditions in Modern Italy*, Princeton: Princeton University Press.

Sahlins, M. (1995) *How 'Natives' Think About Captain Cook*, Chicago: University of Chicago Press.

Shweder, R. A. (1988) 'The How of the Word', *New York Times Book Review*, 28 February.

Smith-Rosenberg, C. (1985) *Disorderly Conduct*, Oxford: Oxford University Press.

Stern, K. S. (1996) *A Force Upon the Plain: The America Militia Movement and the Politics of Hate*, New York: Simon & Schuster.

Thompson, E. P. (1978) Eighteenth-Century English Society: Class Struggle Without Class? *Social History*, vol. 3, no, 2.

Wildavisky, A. (1987) 'Choosing Preferences by Constructing Institutions: A Cultural Theory of Preference Formation', *American Political Science Review*, vol. 81, pp. 3–21.

Wilson, R. W. (1992) *Compliance Ideologies: Rethinking Political Cultures*, New York: Cambridge University Press.

3
The Relevance of Culture for the Study of Political Psychology

Marc Howard Ross[1]

Introduction

There is a powerful tension between the context-specific analyses which figure prominently in anthropology – and other social sciences – in recent years, and the emphasis on universal human dynamics which characterizes crosscultural psychology. These differences are reflected in each approach's principal goals, concepts, theories and methods. However, there are good reasons to think that a synthesis of elements of both the particularisms of contextual analysis and the generalizations of crosscultural psychology offers richer explanations than either might provide alone.

Cultural analysis of politics takes seriously the post-modern critique of behavioral political analyses and seeks to offer contextually rich inter-subjective accounts of politics which emphasize how political actors under-stand social and political action (Merelman, 1991). In cultural analyses, for example, interests are contextually and intersubjectively defined and the strategies used to pursue them are understood to be context dependent. Central to cultural analysis is the concept of interpretation. The interpreta-tions of particular political significance are built from the accounts – stories if one prefers – of groups and individuals striving to make sense of their social and political worlds and I use the term to refer both to the shared intersubjective meanings of actors[2] and also to the explicit efforts of social science observers to understand these meanings and to present them to others (Taylor, 1985). Actors' shared interpretations – worldviews – are important in any cultural analysis as they offer an important methodological tool, along with an examination of rituals and symbols, for examining both systems of meaning and the structure and intensity of political identity.

Culture and politics: key concepts and questions

Culture, a central concept in anthropology, has been defined in a variety of ways over time. A widely cited definition is Geertz's which views culture as 'an historically transmitted pattern of meaning embodied in symbols, a system of inherited conceptions expressed in symbolic forms by means of which men communicate, perpetuate, and develop their knowledge about and attitudes towards life' (1973b, 89).[3] This view emphasizes culture as public, shared meanings; behaviors, institutions and social structure are understood not as culture itself but as culturally constituted phenomena (Spiro, 1984). Culture is usefully thought of as a worldview which explains why and how individuals and groups behave as they do and includes both cognitive and affective beliefs about social reality and assumptions about when, where and how people in one's culture and those in other cultures are likely to act in particular ways.[4] For purposes of political analysis, to this conception of culture as a shared meaning system needs to be added the idea of a widely shared collective consciousness among people who have a common (and almost invariably named) identity which marks distinctions between the group and outsiders. Culture, in short, marks 'a distinctive way of life' characterized in the subjective we-feelings of cultural group members (and outsiders) that the way of life is unique.[5] While culture can be examined through the beliefs about the distinctiveness of a lifestyle and worldview which members of a group hold, it is expressed though specific behaviors (customs and rituals) – both sacred and profane – which mark the daily, yearly and life-cycle rhythms of its members and reveal how people view past, present and future events and understand choices they face. Cultural metaphors have both cognitive meaning which describes group experience and high affective salience which emphasizes the unique intragroup bonds – almost like a secret code – which sets one group's experience apart from others.

   Placing the concept of culture at the center of analysis encourages us to ask certain questions about political life and not others. For example, an interest in distinctive ways of life and worldviews leads to questions about how differences in worldviews might explain such universal phenomena as reactions to leaders, proposed collective actions, or external threats. At the same time, a concern with culture and cultural difference discourages inquiry into rational self-interest in political choice-making to the extent that such questions presume that interests and their maximization are more or less invariant across cultures and hardly need a theory of cultural variation to explain what is viewed as constant (Wildavsky, 1987). The five questions about culture and politics which I now present suggest how cultural analysis enhances our understanding of politics, but they are hardly the only questions we could raise about their interconnection (Ross, 1997).

1   Political prioritization: culture frames the context in which politics occurs

Culture orders political priorities (Latin, 1986; 11) meaning it defines the symbolic and material objects people consider valuable and worth fighting over, the contexts in which such disputes occur, and the rules (both formal and informal) by which politics takes place and who participates in it. For example, anthropologist Napoleon Chagnon (1967) invokes the cultural importance of the value of fierceness (*waiteri* complex) to explain the prevalence of high warfare among Yanomamo communities; political sociologist Edward Banfield (1958) explains the absence of political participation and civic society in southern Italy in terms of a cultural pattern he calls amoral familism; and political scientists Gabriel Almond and Sidney Verba (1963) explain differences in political attitudes and patterns of participation between the USA, Great Britain, Germany and Italy in terms of differences between participant, subject and parochial political cultures. A useful way to understand the cultural framing of politics is to consider how culture influences ideas about, and the organization of, community, authority and conflict (Ross, 1988).

Community

Political communities are defined by two elements. One is a sense of common identity, supported by what Deutsch (1957 has called a sense of 'linked fate', the idea that the welfare of community members is interdependent. Furthermore, Geertz (1973b) suggests that community members share 'schematic images of the social order' which need to be understood as responses to cultural as well as social and psychological strain. Most simply this identity is expressed through a common name, but it also must be added that patterns of action linking different communities for purposes, such as military action, ritual activity or decision making, produce other groupings which may be short-lived and are not always clearly named. The other key element in community is the existence of institutions and practices which, as Deutsch says, more or less insure the peaceful resolution of differences between members (1957).

While communities are distinct entities, they are also nested so that people belong to more than one community and develop multiple loyalties. Some loyalties reinforce each other, while others are cross-cutting meaning that different attachments pull people in more than one direction. Both anthropological and political theory has long emphasized the importance of cross-cutting ties – linkages of kinship, trade, ritual organization, or just friendship that can unite people in different communities in the same society. When ties are cross-cutting, we expect higher levels of collective action to be undertaken, and for disputes to be managed peacefully within the society, along with a greater ability to resist the pressures of outsiders.

Authority

Authority consists of regularized procedures for distributing tangible and symbolic goods which members of a community consider more or less legitimate – meaning that they consider the procedures in a community fair. Authority is about publicly sanctioned actions, involving compliance with allocation and other decisions, based on the use of force to back decisions taken in the name of the community. Power, in contrast, results in compliance based on coercion or force alone, while influence or persuasion produces compliance among relative equals based on arguments or other social pressures, but not physical force or right.

The establishment of legitimate authority is a historical process for a community (Arendt, 1958), and a psychocultural one for individuals which involves the development of an emotional attachment to particular procedures and styles. Affective aspects of political authority, associated with deep emotional needs, can be understood as collective identification with individuals occupying crucial authority positions in a society (Freud, 1922; Jones, 1936), and the sense of a linked fate among individuals such that they are willing to tolerate short-run hardship. Identifications with authority develop and are maintained through ritual experiences (including religious action) (Edelman, 1964; Kertzer, 1988; Shils and Young, 1953; Turner, 1957, 1968). Thus, political authority, both cognitively and affectively, connects people's everyday experience and anxiety to those of the collectivity, while the exercise of authority often results in attachment reassurance and order, but can also be mobilized for change or revolution.

Conflict

Conflict occurs in virtually all communities but there are important cross-cultural differences in its levels and forms. A basic distinction is between conflicts which take place within preexisting rules that members of a community accept, and conflicts about the rules themselves. The former reinforce existing authority patterns, while the latter seek to revise them. The importance of psychocultural dynamics can be seen in the analysis of conflict at the micro-level. Because similar events continue to produce different understandings and reactions, it is important to consider the interpretation of events as crucial to the conflict process. Why is it that taking an object from another person in a small Atlantic fishing community is variously viewed as theft when it is done by a social outsider and borrowing when a social insider is involved (Yngevesson, 1978)? Both psychological and cultural processes are central here as groups and individuals develop understandings, sometimes but not often explicit, about social action, about others in their world, about intentions, about what is valued, and about the goals of action.

2 Identity definition: culture links individual and collective identities

Culture offers an account of political behavior through shared world views which make particular actions more or less likely. The crucial connection at work is that of identification which renders certain actions reasonable and removes alternatives which on other grounds might be equally plausible (Northrup, 1989). Both individual and collection action, this view suggests, is motivated, in part, by the sense of common fate people in a culture share involving two distinct elements: (1) the strong reinforcement between individual and collective identity which renders culturally sanctioned behavior rewarding; and (2) the sense that outsiders will treat oneself and other members of one's group in similar ways.

From a psychoanalytic developmental perspective, identification occurs when a person constructs bonds to an external object and these attachments alter one's subsequent actions. Psychocultural analyses are, not surprisingly, interested in how people in a culture share these objects and develop common reactions to them. Objects of identification can be frustrating resulting in destructive actions (A. Freud, 1937; S. Freud, 1922). However, Freud also described another, more positive form of identification which arises from loss of love (Freud, 1914; 1917). When an object of identification is benign, Schafer says a child derives a sense 'of mastery, competence, or independence ... [and] there is an atmosphere of precious intimacy surrounding these identification – a glow of well-being that is also seen in fond embraces' (1968, 154). Identification is associated with the development of a superego which monitors behaviors and feelings and is a normal aspect of psychological maturation.

Contemporary psychoanalytic writing emphasizes identification dynamics in the construction of internal images of the external world. Many of the objects of identification involve primitive primary sensations such as smell, taste, and sound which acquire intense affective meaning and only later acquire a cognitive component. People sharing cultural attachments have common experiences which facilitate the developmental task of incorporating group identity into one's own sense of self. Cultures, especially when they are under stress, emphasize what in-group members share, giving greater emotional weight to the common elements and reinforcing them with an ideology of linked fate. The process is probably best viewed as a kind of 'psychocultural regression to the mean' which overemphasizes what is common within culture variations are selectively ignored and negatively sanctioned, and differences with outsiders exaggerated.

The political relevance of identification dynamics lies in the psychocultural construction of groups which both seem natural to people and provide the basis for social and political action. It should be stressed that culture is only one basis for linking individual to social identity. It can be a particularly powerful one, however, in situations of threat and uncertainty because cultural attachments are connected to very primary feelings about identity. While much of our language (in Western thought generally and psychoanalysis in particular) emphasizes an inherent conflict between the group and the individual, this emphasis on identity draws attention to ways in which social attachments are an integral way of strengthening individual identity not at odds with it.

3   Boundary definition and maintenance: culture defines the boundaries and organizes actions within and between groups

Culture defines groups and patterns of association within and between them. Cultural definition of groups variously defined by kinship, age, gender or common interests entail clear expectations about how people are to act. Consider such basic questions as where a couple lives after marriage, who spends time together, to whom is one most attached emotionally, who controls scarce resources, how property is transferred between generations, and how work is organized. The world's cultures provide very different answers to each of these questions, but most important the evidence shows that how each culture answers these questions has significance for how people act and expect others to behave (Naroll, 1970; Levinson and Malone, 1981). Cultural norms regarding intergroup relations (here we can consider relations between groups in the same culture such as age or ritual groups or groups from different cultures) can be highly elaborate and sometimes ambiguous as well. Cultures differ in how and when they restrict (and how they enforce such restrictions on) such relations but few are silent on this question.

Of course people don't often think about the origin of group categories which for most are seen as natural, often biological in character, when in fact they are cultural and political constructions whose 'reasonableness' needs to be regularly reasserted and taught to succeeding generations (Anderson, 1991). Weber, for example, shows how the nineteenth century French state through the institutionalization of a national education system, a developing system of transportation and universal male military service created a sense of national identity out of a myriad of regional loyalties (1976). All cultures, of course, provide specific, but not always explicit, socialization regarding ingroup and outgroup distinctions. Cultural learning involves messages about groups' motives, expectations about their behavior, and how one is to act towards members of each outgroup.

The rigidity of social distinctions and the clarity of group boundaries vary crossculturally and change over time. This is clearly seen in the literature on 'situational ethnicity' which shows how distinctions among groups can depend upon what other groups are in a social environment and what the particular political stakes are in a conflict. In East Africa, for example, speakers of *Kiluhya* whose homeland is in western Kenya, gradually developed since 1900 a political and social identity as *Luhya* people through contact with other ethnic communities in Nairobi, Mombassa, Kampala and other urban centers during this century. Earlier, however, their identity was as Marigoli or Samia, and other more localized Baluhya regional subgroups.

4 Interpretive frameworks: culture provides a framework for interpreting the actions and motives of others

In crosscultural encounters people most often make sense of another group's behavior, that is attribute motives to them, by drawing on their own cultural worldview since this intracultural way of understanding behavior is successful most of the time. This is a complicated process which I won't discuss here for I only want to distinguish between two contrasting strategies for encounters with other cultures. One is to apply the rules of one's own culture because they are, after all, what is best known (and often all that is known), assuming that outsiders will respond as insiders do. The second is to search for different rules, assuming that outsiders share few motives with people in one's own culture hence they will respond in 'heathen' ways and are likely to take advantage of any weakness shown to them – for they will not follow what are viewed as 'civilized norms'. The first strategy is that of generalization, while the second is one of differentiation.

An important question is the extent to which any culture characteristically exhibits generalizing or differentiating behaviors, at least in certain domains, in encounters with outsiders. For example, my crosscultural research on internal and external conflict and violence, shows that in some cultures the level of conflict with insiders and outsiders is quite similar (generalizers) while in others they are highly differentiated. The differences between the two groups of societies are quite clear: differentiating societies are characterized by many ties which link diverse groups in the society and which clearly mark it off from outsiders, while generalizing societies are those without strong mechanisms of internal integration and probably a key reason why insiders and outsiders are treated somewhat the same is because whether one is an insider or outsider *vis-à-vis* a group is defined contextually and not in absolute terms (Ross, 1993a, chapter 7).

Actions, like words, are often highly ambiguous and making sense of them requires a shared cultural framework to assure that the meaning which is sent is similar to, if not identical with, that which is received. Clearly, this is most visible in culturally homogeneous settings, but we also can see it in multicultural settings (such as large cities) where people from quite different cultural groups develop shared understandings in domains (such as the marketplace) with frequent intergroup interactions. Few behaviors are so universal that they require little or no interpretation. The work on the crosscultural (and even cross-species) interpretability of specific facial gestures, while fascinating, is also testimony to how few domains of human action are coherent outside of a shared cultural framework (Ekman, Friesen and Ellsworth, 1972; Masters and Sullivan, 1989). However, because most political and social action is complex, a capacity to decode only facial, and other obvious physical, gestures doesn't get one very far in understanding political life. It also provides little assistance in placing action in a broader context which offers an account of what someone has done, or, why he did it.

To do this requires saying something about motives which are central mechanism in a cultural analysis linking individual action to the broader social setting in which it occurs (D'Andrade and Strauss, 1992). Motives are located in individuals but are widely shared and transmitted at the cultural level and explain 'how culture works' to produce particular behaviors. This contrasts with Geertz's focus on 'inspecting events' to make sense of actors' interpretations of them, and his rejection of the idea that we should examine mental structures (1973a, 10–12). D'Andrade's (1992) cultural analysis of motives develops the notion of schema (what I am calling worldview), 'a conceptual structure which makes possible the identification of objects and events' (1992, 28) and he argues that schemas are culturally acquired and produce 'motivational strivings'. He emphasizes the importance of understanding the context-dependent nature of schemas as interpretive devices, and the need to spell out how they are acquired. D'Andrade and Strauss agree that we need to see cultures as 'both the public actions, objects and symbols that make shared learning possible … and the private psychological states of knowledge and feeling without which these public things are meaningless and could not be recreated' (1992, 6).

In important ways, motives in cultural analysis are much like interests in rational choice theory. In statements such as 'They were motivated by fear of their ancestors and so they sacrificed half of their livestock', or 'The blips had an interest in weakening the military capability of their enemy', both motives and interests offer a 'reasonable' account of why individuals or groups behave in a certain way. Yet there are also significant differences in the use of motives and interests as explanatory mechanisms which are central to the difference between cultural and rational choice explanations. Most basically, while rational choice theory assumes that interests are more or less transparent (some would say given), universal and rooted in the structure of a situation, cultural analysis emphasizes that motives are located in individuals in particular cultural contexts and only knowable through empirical analysis of each particular cultural context.[6] As a result, while turning to interests suggests that more or less any human group would behave the same way in a certain situation, an emphasis on motives is far more interested in explaining variation in behavior. Wildavsky (1987) argues that rational choice theorists make a serious error in taking interests as given. In fact, he says there is systematic variation in interests which an empirically-based cultural analysis shows.[7]

In an analysis of intracultural behavior, the difference between motives and interests is not always very consequential for in fact when interests are shared they certainly operate like motives, offering a readily available account of why people behave as they do. Furthermore, in most cultures, public discourse is about interests, not the motives which underlie them. When we consider crosscultural encounters the difference between interests and motives is more significant. Consider the statement above that a group of people are motivated by fear of their ancestors and therefore slaughtered half their domestic animals. To people in another culture in which such fears are unknown, that is they are not motives for action, such behavior is not comprehensible. Trying to transform such an explanation into an interest statement ('They had an interest in not making the ancestors angry') still begs the question of why the group understands the world in terms of 'fear of the ancestor'. Only an analysis which seeks to explain why this motive is important in one culture but not another is adequate here.

Shared cultural frameworks are rarely the subject of self-conscious analysis for people deeply internalize cultural assumptions and rarely see them as problematic. It is only when people run into problems that such questions might be raised. Yet even here there is a widespread (if not universal) ethnocentric tendency to suggest that 'there is something wrong' with a person who fails to offer or misreads an obvious cultural signal, and to take such behavior as evidence that something is 'wrong' with that person or of the inferiority of the other group. For the most part, culturally shared world views are protected and people will go to great lengths to resist changes which challenge their core elements.

5   Organization and mobilization: culture provides political resources to groups and leaders

Culture offers significant resources which leaders and groups use in political organization and mobilization (Kertzer, 1988; Laitin, 1985).[8] Certainly this is seen in the 'culture wars' found in American politics (and elsewhere) over issues such as abortion, gun control, school prayer, and textbook censorship. Anthropologist Abner Cohen (1968; 1981; 1974) spells out the political uses of culture emphasizing the importance of cultural organization as a political tool in situations where 'normal politics' is not possible for one reason or another. In Cohen's analysis of Hausa traders in Ibadan (Nigeria) and Creoles in Freetown (Sierra Leone), the two are small minorities so that using electoral strategies to pursue their economic and political goals would have likely resulted in massive defeats. Instead the two groups organized around cultural activities – a religious revival focused on the Tijaniyyi brotherhood in the case of the Hausa, and Freemasonry for the Creoles. In each case these cultural responses to changing political situations, result in intense within-group interaction and social exchange which to maintain control over the long distance trade in the case of the Hausa and the Creole's domination of the state elite.

Frequently groups use cultural organizations (not always consciously as Cohen points out) to achieve goals which cannot be pursued directly. He identifies six political problems addressed by cultural organization which bolster group solidarity and effective mobilization (Cohen, 1969, 201–10):

1. Such organizations help define a group's *distinctiveness*, meaning its membership and sphere of operation within the context of the contemporaneous political setting, through myths of origin and claims to superiority;

descent and endogamy; moral exclusiveness; endo-culture; spatial proximity; and homogenization (201–4);

2. Cultural organizations meet the political needs of groups for intense
   internal *communications* among their constituent parts (205);
3. Cultural organizations offer mechanisms for *decision-making* involving
   some formulation of general problems confronting the group and taking
   decisions about them (206);
4. They provide *authority* for implementing decisions and for speaking,
   where appropriate, on behalf of the group (207);
5. Cultural organizations can provide a political *ideology* often rooted in
   the language of kinship and ritual which gives legitimacy to power and
   converts it into authority (208–10);
6. Finally, cultural organizations meets the need for *discipline, through cere-
   monials and rituals which connect the ideology to current problems of the
   community* (210–11).

In discussing religion, the quintessential cultural basis for political organization, Cohen points out that:

> Religion provides an ideal 'blueprint' for the development of an infor-
> mal political organization. It mobilizes many of the most powerful emo-
> tions which are associated with the basic problems of human existence
> and gives legitimacy and stability to political arrangements by represent-
> ing these as parts of the system of the universe. It makes it possible to
> mobilize the power of symbols and the power inherent in the ritual rela-
> tionship between various ritual positions within the organization of the
> cult. It makes possible to use the arrangements for financing and admin-
> istering places of worship and associated places for welfare, education,
> and social activities of various sorts, to use these in developing the organ-
> ization and administration of political functions. Religion also provides
> frequent and regular meetings in congregations, where in the course of
> ritual activities, a great deal of informal interaction takes place, informa-
> tion is communicated, and general problems are formulated and dis-
> cussed. The system of myths and symbols which religion provides is
> capable of being continuously interpreted and reinterpreted in order
> to accommodate it to changing economic, political and other social
> circumstances.

> (1969, 210)

While Cohen's analysis is about the coping strategies of small cultural
minorities, it is clearly relevant to understanding how leaders of large
ethnic groups (often, but not always, majorities) have come to, and held
onto, political power. African politics since the 1960s provides many examples of ethnic mobilization around cultural symbols and fears, and so do

European settings such as Northern Ireland, France (with a strong anti-immigrant, anti-foreigner party) and Germany (with its numerous outbreaks of anti-foreigner violence). It is, however, in Eastern Europe and the former Soviet Union where we perhaps have the most to learn about the political manipulation of cultural symbols and rituals and their sometimes disastrous consequences. Here we must ask why the appeals to Serbian, Armenian or Hungarian identity are all so powerful. Yet, as Campbell (1983) has suggested, any such answer which relies on mechanisms of individual benefit only make sense if we can also account for the strength of individual attachments to groups such as those defined in abstract cultural terms.

Notes

1. I received helpful comments and suggestions on an earlier draft of this manuscript from John Bendix, Katherine Conner, Barbara Frankel, Phil Kilbride, Stanley Renshon, Alan Zuckerman and especially the late Donald T. Campbell who has particularly encouraged my work in this area while always offering thoughtful and non-obvious suggestions about ideas to explore and arguments in need of development.
2. Taylor uses the term 'common reference world' (1972, 38) to refer to what members of a culture share.
3. D'Andrade (1984, 88) points out the radical shift from the view of culture as behavior which could be understood within a stimulus–response framework to culture as systems of meaning in a number of fields. For a more complete discussion of culture as meanings and symbols see the excellent discussions in Schweder and LeVine (1984).
4. I do not distinguish here between the notion of worldview and the idea of a social schema which many analysts use in a similar way. Elsewhere (and below) I analyze conflicting terms of worldviews found in psychocultural interpretations which offer culturally shared beliefs about what is worth fighting about, how conflicts are to be waged, and what opponents' motives are (Ross, 1993a and 1993b; 1995).
5. Although he didn't write much about culture *per se*, Karl Deutsch (1957), who discussed both a distinctive way of life and we-feelings in his early writing about nationalism, was writing about culture as I use the term. Phil Kilbride (personal communication) notes the connections between the definition of culture present here and Goodenough's (1970) idea of culture as 'standards for proper behavior', with its cognitive emphasis on 'what you have to know to behave properly in a given society'.
6. There have been efforts to identify a fixed number of human motives such as Murray's (1938) and McClelland's (1961) work on three particular motives – achievement, affiliation and power. It is important to recognize that in both of these cases – especially McClelland's – it was clear that the relative importance of any single motive varied crossculturally and across individuals as well.
7. Of course, it would be interesting if rational-choice theorists would consider interests, as culturally determined and begin to analyze them subjectively. Doing this would mean treating interests much like what I call motives and would locate them in individuals in specific cultural contexts, not just situations alone.

8. Laitin (1986) offers a fascinating examination of what he calls the two faces of culture: one most associated with Geertz which emphasizes culture as meaning, and the other he links to Abner Cohen and emphasizes culture as a resource for political entrepreneurs. His subtle analysis of the two perspectives emphasizes their differences while my purposes are more to emphasize the central role of culture in each.

References

Anderson, B. (1991) *Imagined Communities: Reflections on the Origin and Spread of Nationalism*, London and New York: Verso.

Arendt, H. (158) 'What is Authority?' in Karl Friedrich (ed.), *Nomos I: Authority*, Cambridge: Harvard University Press (pp. 91–141)

Banfield, E. C. (1958) *The Moral Basis of a Backward Society*, New York: Free Press

Campbell, D. T. (1983) 'Two Distinct Routes beyond Kin Selection to Ultrasociality: Implications for the Humanities and Social Sciences', in D. L. Bridgeman (ed.), *The Nature of Prosocial Development: Theories and Strategies*, New York: Academic Press (pp. 11–41).

Chagnon, N. (1967) 'Yanomamo Social Organization and Warfare', in M. Fried, M. Harris and R. Murphy (eds), *War: The Anthropology of Armed Conflict and Aggression*, Garden City, NY: Natural History Press (pp. 109–59).

Cohen, A. (1969) *Custom and Politics in Urban Africa*, Berkeley and Los Angeles: University of California Press.

—— (1974) *Two-dimensional Man: An Essay on the Anthropology of Power and Symbolism in Complex Society*, Berkeley and Los Angeles: University of California Press.

—— (1981) *The Politics of Elite Culture*, Berkeley and Los Angeles: University of California Press.

D'Andrade, R. G. (1984) 'Cultural Meaning Systems', in R. A. Schweder and R. A. LeVine (eds), *Culture Theory: Essays on Mind, Self and Emotion*, Cambridge: Cambridge University Press (pp. 88–119).

—— (1992) 'Schemas and Motivation', in R. G. D'Andrade (eds), *Human Motives and Cultural Models*, Cambridge: Cambridge University Press (pp. 23–44).

D'Andrade, R. G. and C. Strauss, (1992) *Human Motives and Cultural Models*, Cambridge: Cambridge University Press (pp. 23–44).

Deutsch, K. et al. (1957) *Political Community and the North Atlantic Area*, Princeton: Princeton University Press.

Edelman, M. (1964) *The Symbolic Uses of Politics*, Urbana: University of Illinois Press.

Ekman, P. W. V. Friesen and P. Ellsworth (1972) *Emotion in the Human Face*, Elmsford, NY: Pergamon Press.

Freud, S. (1922) *Group Psychology and the Analysis of the Ego*, New York: Norton.

Geertz, C. (1973a) 'Thick Description: Toward an Interpretive Theory of Culture', in Clifford Geertz, *The Interpretation of Cultures*, New York: Basic Books, Harper Torchbooks (pp. 8–30).

—— (1973b) 'Religion as a Cultural System', in Clifford Geertz, *The Interpretation of Cultures*, New York: Basic Books, Harper Torchbooks (pp. 87–125).

Goodenough, W. (1970) *Description and Comparison in Cultural Anthropology*, Chicago: Aldine Horowitz, D. L. (1985), *Ethnic Groups in Conflict*, Berkeley and Los Angeles: University of California Press.

Huntington, S. (1993) 'The Clash of Civilizations', *Foreign Affairs*, pp. 22–49.

Johnson, S. K. (1991) *The Japanese through American Eyes*, Stanford: Stanford University Press.

Jones, E. (1936) 'The Psychology of the Constitutional Monarchy', in E. Jones (ed), *Psycho-myth, Psycho-history: Essays in Applied Psychoanalysis*, New York: Hillstone (pp. 227–234).

Kertzer, D. I. (1988) *Ritual, Politics and Power*, New Haven and London: Yale University Press.

Laitin, D. D. (1986) *Hegemony and Culture: Politics and Religious Change Among the Yoruba*, Chicago: University of Chicago Press.

Levinson, D. and M. J. Malone (1981) *Toward Explain Human Culture: A Critical Review of the Findings of Worldwide Cross-Cultural Research*, New Haven: HRAF Press.

Masters R. D. and D. G. Sullivan (1989) 'Nonverbal Displays and Political Leadership in France and the United States', *Political Behavior*, 11, 121–53.

McClelland, D. C. (1961), *The Achieving Society*, Princeton: van Nostrand.

Merelman, R. M. (1991) *Partial Visions: Culture and Politics in Britain, Canada and The United States*, Madison: University of Wisconsin Press.

Murray, H. C. (1938) *Explorations in Personality*, New York: Oxford University Press.

Naroll, R. (1970) 'What Have We Learned from Cross-Cultural Surveys?' *American Anthropologist*, 72: 1227–1288.

Northrup, T. A. (1989) 'The Dynamic of Identity in Personal and Social Conflict', in L. Kriesberg, T. A. Northrup, and S. J. Thorson (eds), *Intractable Conflicts and Their Transformation*, Syracuse: Syracuse University Press (pp. 55–82).

Ross, M. H. (1988) 'Studying Politics Cross-Culturally: Key Concepts and Issues', *Behavior Science Research*, 22, 105–129.

—— (1993a) *The Culture of Conflict: Interpretations and Interests in Comparative Perspective*, New Haven and London: Yale University Press.

—— (1993b) *The Management of Conflict: Interpretations and Interests in Comparative Perspective*, New Haven and London: Yale University Press.

—— (1995) 'Psychocultural Interpretation Theory and Peacemaking in Ethnic Conflicts', *Political Psychology*, 16, 523–544.

—— (1997) 'Culture and Identity in Comparative Political Analysis', Mark I. Lichbach and Alan S. Zuckerman (eds), *Interests, Ideals and Institutions: Advancing Theory in Comparative Politics*, Cambridge and New York: Cambridge University Press (pp. 42–80).

Schweder, R. A. and R. A. LeVine (eds), (1984) *Culture Theory: Essays on Mind, Self, and Emotion*, Cambridge: Cambridge University Press.

Shils, E. and M. Young (1953) 'The Meaning of the Coronation', *Sociological Quarterly*, 1, 63–81.

Spiro, M. E. (1984) 'Some Reflections on Cultural Determinism and Relativism with Special Reference to Emotion and Reason', in R. A. Schweder and R. A. LeVine (eds), *Culture Theory: Essays on Mind, Self and Emotion*, Cambridge: Cambridge University Press (pp. 323–46).

—— (1987) 'Culture and Human Nature', in *Culture and Human Nature: Theoretical Papers of Melford E. Spiro*, Chicago: University of Chicago Press (pp. 3–31).

Tambiah, S. J. (1986) *Sri Lanka: Ethnic Fratricide and the Dismantling of Democracy*, Chicago: University of Chicago Press.

Taylor, C. (1985) 'Interpretation and the Sciences of Man', in *Philosophy and the Human Sciences*, Cambridge: Cambridge University Press, 2.

Turner, V. (1957) *Schism and Continuity in an African Society*, Manchester: Manchester University Press.

———— (1968) 'Mukanda: The Politics of a Non-Political Ritual', in Marc J. Swartz, (ed), *Local-level Politics*, Chicago: Aldine.

Weber, E. (1976) *Peasants into Frenchmen: The Modernization of Rural France, 1870–1914*, Stanford: Stanford University Press

Wildavsky, A. (1987) 'Choosing Preference by Constructing Institutions: A Cultural Theory of Preference Formation', *American Political Science Review*, 81, 3–21.

Yngevesson, B. B. (1978) 'The Atlantic Fishermen', in L. Nader and H. F. Todd. (eds), *The Disputing Process – Law in Ten Societies*, New York: Columbia University Press (pp. 59–85).

4

Taboo Trade-Offs: Constitutive Prerequisites for Political and Social Life

Alan Page Fiske and Philip E. Tetlock

To be eligible for participation in any relationship, group or institution, people must show that they abide by the constitutive rules for its fundamental forms of interaction. If someone invites you to dinner at their home and then seriously tries to make you pay for the meal, you are unlikely to continue to be friends. If a politician proposed setting up a state bureaucracy to maximize aggregate well-being by determining who would be required to marry whom, the politician would not be re-elected. How long would a Marine volunteer last in boot camp, or a novice in a monastery, if he tried to organize a vote about when to get up in the morning? People very rarely do such things, but if they do, others generally assume that they must be joking, or insane, or from another very different culture. Actions like these terminate relationships because we cannot sustain relationships with people unless they adhere to the cultural rules for constituting those relationships.

Behavior of this kind shows a lack of commitment to the fundamental nature of these relationships: a person who acts like this shows that they do not know or care what this kind of relationship *is*. We regard such a person as lacking basic moral and social sensibilities, and we do not want to have anything to do with them: how could you relate to such a person? We regard such actions and their perpetrators as bizarre, disgusting, horrifying or evil.

As these examples suggest, *many violations of the constitutive rules of any culture consist of misuse of relational principles that would be perfectly valid in another context*. In these examples, people are presenting a bill for payment, voting, or using cost–benefit analysis. These are ordinary actions, but entirely inappropriate to the relational context in which they are performed. What this shows is that *sociality is organized with implicit reference to domains; different modes of interaction are required in different domains*. To function in any given culture, people have to recognize the way domains are socially defined and organize their action with reference to the relational structures that are culturally appropriate in each respective domain. Violation of the distinctions between forms of relationship that operate in different domains is violation of the constitutive rules that define what is going on at any given time and place. Such violations evoke strong aversive responses because they disrupt the cultural presuppositions that permit predictably coherent, meaningfully coordinated interaction.

From this theory of sociality we can deduce several hypotheses:

1. Relational models – including principles of exchange – that people take for granted in one domains may be morally and politically unacceptable in another domain.
2. A person who attempts to use an inappropriate relational model is thenceforth suspect and considered morally dangerous, *in general*: they cannot be counted on to do what is required in *any* relationship, and we tend to ostracize them.
3. Cultures differ in their delineation of domains and in their paradigms for implementing relational models in these respective domains. People more or less understand that these cultural differences exist, and sometimes this mitigates the above attributions and evaluations. However, these differences commonly produce misunderstandings and friction, usually resulting in negative emotions and evaluations about people from contrasting cultures.
4. People learn these cultural paradigms for assigning models to domains primarily by observation and imitation, with little or no explanation. Consequently, people will generally be hard pressed to articulate *why* a model is appropriate or inappropriate in any given domain. To the extent that they can give reasons, they will offer analogies: they will explain that this case is similar to some standard prototype domain in which people use this relational model.
5. However, as cultures change, ambiguities arise which often bring these cultural paradigms into question. This may result in articulate debate that amounts to strong ideological controversy about which models are appropriate in novel or refigured domains.

Trade-offs

In contrast to the relational models framework sketched above, the standard micro-economic perspective assumes that all values can ultimately be reduced to a single utility metric. Economists stress that people live in a world of scarce resources. Rational decision-makers appreciate that they must make painful trade-offs, even if it requires attaching monetary values to things that we prefer to think of as priceless, such as children, body organs, endangered species, and basic rights and responsibilities of democratic citizenship. In this spirit, many behavioral theories of decision-making assume that there are compensatory relationships among values, and that trade-offs among values can be captured through mathematical formalisms such as indifference curves and trade-off functions (Keeney and Raiffa, 1976).

However, converging observations from political philosophy, social psychology and cultural anthropology suggest that people are extremely resistant to certain trade-offs. This resistance is rooted, in part, in the familiar problem of cognitive incommensurability. People reject certain trade-offs because the requisite mental operations (inter-dimensional comparisons) are just too difficult. It is hard to judge how much of value *x* one should sacrifice to achieve a given increment in value *y* if one has neither personal experience nor cultural standards to draw upon in making such judgments. But the resistance also runs deeper: there are *moral* limits to fungibility. People reject certain comparisons because they feel that merely considering the relevant trade-offs would undercut their self-images and social identities as moral beings. Here it is useful to invoke the less familiar concept of constitutive incommensurability – a notion that plays an important role in both modern moral philosophy (Raz, 1982) and in classic sociological theory (Durkheim, 1976). Two values are constitutively incommensurable whenever people believe that entering one value into a trade-off calculus with the other subverts or undermines that value. This means that our relationships with each other preclude certain explicit comparisons among values. To transgress this normative boundary (for example, to attach a monetary value to one's friendships or one's children or one's loyalty to one's country) is to disqualify oneself from certain social roles. People feel that making such an evaluation demonstrates that one is not a true friend, or parent, or citizen. In brief, to compare is to destroy. Raising even the possibility of certain trade-offs weakens, corrupts and degrades one's moral standing.

This chapter, which is a condensation, reframing and update of Fiske and Tetlock,1997, develops an explanatory framework for taboo trade-offs. By a taboo trade-off, we mean any explicit mental comparison or social transaction that violates deeply-held normative intuitions about the integrity, even sanctity, of certain relationships and of the moral-political values that derive from those relationships. We draw on two traditions – Fiske's relational theory and Tetlock's value pluralism model – to answer three categories of questions:

1. *When do people treat trade-offs as taboo?* Relational theory identifies four elementary forms for organizing, interpreting, coordinating, and evaluating social life. We suggest that people view trade-offs as impermissible and respond with varying degrees of indignation whenever the trade-offs require assessing the value of something governed by the socially meaningful relations and operations of one relational model in the terms of a disparate relational model. Trade-offs between distinct relational modes are more than simply bizarre, illegitimate and reprehensible: they destabilize the social order.

In each culture there is a myriad of distinctive prototypes and precedents that determine which mode of relationship governs which entities. Hence a trade-off between two entities that both belong to the same relational domain in one culture may be commonplace and unremarkable; in another culture where the same two entities properly belong to two disparate relational domains, such a trade-off may be taboo.

2. *How do observers respond to violations of taboo trade-offs?* Violations of taboo trade-offs are not just cognitively confusing; they trigger negative cognitive, emotional and behavioral reactions.

3. Decision-makers are nevertheless required by resource scarcity and their social roles to make trade-offs that cross relational boundaries. How do decision-makers avoid social censure? Here we draw on the value pluralism model to identify psychological and institutional *tactics that policy makers adopt in order to deflect blame.* These tactics include compartmentalizing social life by invoking distinctions among spheres of justice (for example, family versus work), obfuscating the trade-offs, and adopting decision-avoidance tactics such as buckpassing and procrastination.

Relational theory

Relational theory posits four elementary models that generate and give motivational and normative force to social relationships (Fiske 1991, 1992; for a further overview of relational models theory, a complete current bibliography, and links to researchers working in this area, go to http://www.sscnet.ucla.edu/anthro/faculty/fiske/RM_main.htm). Within any given cultural domain, governed by one of the four respective models, people can usually make trade-offs without great difficulty; between the domains of disparate models, comparisons are problematic and ambiguous. Let us begin by characterizing the four fundamental models:

1. *Communal sharing* (CS) divides the world into distinct equivalence classes, permitting differentiation or contrast, but no numerical comparison. For example, everyone in a community may share in certain benefits (national defense, police protection) or resources (national parks, clean air) without differentiation, while non-citizens may be excluded entirely.

2. *Authority ranking* (AR) constructs an ordinal ranking among persons or social goods, thus permitting lexical decision rules. For example, veterans or minorities may be given priority in access to government jobs, or United States federal law may have precedence over state and local laws.

3. *Equality matching* (EM) is a relational structure that defines socially meaningful intervals that can be added or subtracted to make valid choices. For example, the US decided to bomb a Libyan army barracks in tit-for-tat retaliation for the purported Libyan sponsorship of the bomb-

ing of a US marine barracks in Lebanon: 1–1 = 0, which 'evens the score'.

4. *Market pricing* (MP) is a social structure that makes ratios meaningful, so that it is possible to make decisions that combine quantities and values of diverse entities. Thus we can draw up a federal budget that explicitly weighs competing priorities against each other or select an investment portfolio designed to maximize risk-adjusted return. In these types of decisions, the criterion is some kind of ratio: for example, price/earnings comparisons, productivity, or expected benefits/costs.

Relational theory thus describes the basic structures and operations that are socially meaningful. It distinguishes four principal schemas for organizing, coordinating, evaluating and contesting all aspects of relationships, including group decision-making, ideology and moral judgments. Relational theory posits that these models are discrete structures: there are no intermediate forms, and people think about their social lives in terms of these four models (for a review, see Fiske and Haslam, 1996). As social values they are fundamental, and also incommensurable in the sense that there is no general, higher-level schema that mediates among them.

Relational theory also posits that these four models are open, abstract or indeterminate: they cannot be used to guide behavior or evaluation without the use of implementation rules that specify when they apply, to what and to whom, and how. Cultures provide most of the broad implementation rules, but these implementation rules change, and they are often ambiguous at the margins or in novel circumstances. Within a culture, there may be vigorous debate about some aspects of some implementation rules, while others seem unchallengeably natural. For example, in the United States most people take for granted the Communal Sharing precept that we have some obligation to be compassionate to our fellow beings and preserve them from harm, but there is agonizing debate over whether an owl or a two month-old fetus should count as a fellow being.

Implementation paradigms, prototypes and rules specify when and where to apply each model with respect to what aspects of which entities. For example, any of the models can be used to organize a group decision: according to the collective consensus of the whole body (Communal Sharing); according to the will of the leaders and the powers that they delegate (Authority Ranking); according to a fair election based on one-person, one-vote suffrage (Equality Matching); or according to cost–benefit analyses and the resultant equilibrium between supply and demand (Market Pricing). Furthermore, the use of the models may be nested or recursive. For example, each model can be used ideologically to justify the selection of any of the four models as a mechanism for making social decisions. But in the final analysis, there is nothing in each model that tells us when, where, and how it should be applied.

This brings us to the question of grounds for implementation rules. The four relational models respectively define four ultimate grounds for value – paradigms for moral judgment. But they do not provide foundations for making judgments about their own implementations. The moral precept of Authority Ranking is, 'Do as you are commanded by your superiors', or, 'Respect and defer to your betters'. But Authority Ranking is neutral with respect to criteria for determining rank; it does not answer the question of whether obedience, deference and respect should be accorded to people as a function of age and gender and race, as a function of achievement or office, or on any other basis.

Most dyadic interactions and groups are built out of a combination of the four basic models, implemented in diverse ways in each social dimension. All societies and institutions, and most complex and extended interactions, are comprised of relational components drawn from more than one model (often all four models). However, there is no meta-relational schema that encompasses the four elementary models (see Fiske, 1990, 1991). Various contingencies link specific implementations of the models, and innumerable schemas, roles and institutions consist of coordinated combinations of them. But there is no comprehensive, overarching meta-model that governs the conflicts among models. The four models together do not form a logically integrated, coherently regulated social system.

This means that there is no simple, determinate, conclusive resolution of choices among the four respective models. When they conflict, when it is necessary to compare and weigh alternatives, there is no ultimate criterion for making the necessary trade-offs.

How people select the relational model to use

A culture is a more or less shared system of models and meanings. People within a culture tend to have an implicit operating consensus about where and how to implement each of the relational models, which is what makes coherent social relations possible. But complete consensus is an ideal case; consensus is never complete because the implementation rules are not explicit, because they are always more or less in flux, and because there is always ambiguity about how to apply the rules to concrete cases. Consequently, it is common for there to be conflict or confusion about how to apply a model or about which model to apply in a given domain. We now consider three principles concerning how people deal with problematic implementations and the trade-offs that become apparent when people have to reflect on how to implement their relational models.

Political ideologies

Hypothesis 1:   Political ideologies can be modeled as preferences for particular relational models and/or preferences for particular implementation rules concerning how, when, and with regard to whom each of the models should apply in salient problematic domains. Ideologies may also include precepts about how to combine the models.

Cultures contain congeries of prototypes and precedents that guide people in constituting their ongoing social interactions. Considerable implicit consensus is necessary for meaningful, predictable, coordinated social relations; but the consensus tends to be shifting and cannot be fully determinate. Most implementations seem completely natural, but contentious issues sometimes arise. When people disagree on the collective implementation of relational models, the issues tend to be formulated in terms of linked sets of implementations espoused by competing political movements or parties. These linked sets of implementations are ideologies. Political debate tends to be framed in terms of these ideologically formulated alternatives, ignoring other logically possible trade-offs. Ideologies represent frameworks for resolving implementation debates, highlighting problematic trade-offs and specifying how to make these trade-offs.

To a first approximation, political ideologies represent predilections for particular models. Thus, fascism and feudalism would be roughly characterized as predilections to apply Authority Ranking very broadly (in different ways). Green Party adherents apply Communal Sharing beyond the range of old-fashioned socialism, encompassing many non-human beings. Applying Market Pricing to a broad array of domains represents a kind of libertarianism, while the use of Equality Matching as a generic political model produces a certain flavor of populist liberalism.

A more sophisticated analysis of ideologies takes into account predilections for implementing each model in certain domains. Thus Marxism in its original form described Communal Sharing as the inevitable culmination of history and as the ideal fulfillment of human potential. (In practice, though, communist political systems were rather extreme forms of Authority Ranking.) The Marxist implementation of Communal Sharing applied it to the relations among workers resulting from their shared relation to the means of production, and hence their common plight and common interests. Communal Sharing looks quite different when the emphasis is placed on the shared responsibilities of all humans for the habitat that we share with future generations, and with other species. Applied in one way, the slogan of Communal Sharing is 'Workers of the world, unite!' Applied in another way, the maxim is, 'Love your mother [Earth]'.

Still more subtle analyses take into account the distinctions among ideologies with respect to the manner in which they implement each model. Thus, within the scope of Equality Matching there is ample room for debating what constitutes equality: affirmative action to rectify previous deprivation, or equal opportunity henceforth?

Ideologies can mix models, but it is interesting to observe that most ideologies emphasize a single model. As a result, ideological activists may be more monistic than ordinary citizens – who rarely subscribe to a unitary point of view and display little cross-issue consistency in their policy preferences. It would be misleading, however, to imply that all political ideologies are equally monistic. Advocates of moderate left and centrist causes are more likely than extreme leftists or extreme conservatives to engage in explicit integratively complex weighing of values linked to different relational models and explicit integrative efforts are significantly more common in policy makers than in the opposition currently out of office (Tetlock, 1981, 1984).

Precedent and prototypes

Hypothesis 2:   When people face novel situations that raise the possibility of alternative implementation rules, debate will revolve around analogies to more familiar situations that people use as prototype implementations of the competing relational models.

The cultural implementation 'rules' are usually not abstract propositions; they are more like traditions in which each implementation is a prototype (or occasionally a counterpoint or even a negative contrast) for further implementations. These paradigms, prototypes or rules leave considerable ambiguity about which model(s) apply to concrete current cases and how to apply them.

Cognitive and normative pressures conducive to integrative metarelational thinking should be most intense when a problem primes two or more contradictory precedents that suggest the appropriateness of fundamentally different relational schemas. For instance, a political leader who values the traditional Authority Ranking prerogatives of national sovereignty and also values the efficiency of free trade (Market Pricing) may experience acute dissonance when confronted by trade pacts such as NAFTA and GATT that enhance the latter value at some cost to the former. Or a politician who believes that there is a shared humanitarian responsibility to alleviate intense suffering (CS) but respects the need to preserve traditional prerogatives of national sovereignty (AR) may be deeply divided over the wisdom of intervening in the internal affairs of nations where there are human-rights abuses, murder or starvation (cf. Tetlock's, 1986, value pluralism model).

Decision-making schema and accountability

Hypothesis 3a: Each of the four relational models can be used as a schema for making group decisions. Although it is possible to use any model to make a decision to implement any other model to organize a given social activity, decision-makers will tend to implement the model that corresponds to the relational structure in which they *make the decision*.

Thus a monarch will tend to decree Authority Ranking policies, a legislature will tend to ratify Equality Matching policies, and a Quaker meeting will tend to adopt Communal Sharing policies. A cost–benefit analysis of alternatives or a decision based on the supply and demand of the market will tend to result in selection of the Market Pricing alternative.

Hypothesis 3b: Decision-makers may be accountable under social and ideological systems based on any of the models. Although it is possible to use any model to legitimize the use of any other model, decision-makers will tend to make a substantive choice favoring the model that corresponds to the model under which they are *accountable*.

Hence the expectation of justifying a decision in terms of Market Pricing values will favor implementation of a Market Pricing choice. So, for example, a corporate board with active stockholders will be more likely to buy components on the open market, while the manager of a privately-held, single-owner company will be more likely to opt for the hierarchical mode of making components within the company. A religious order whose members regard themselves as accountable to an authoritarian God is more likely to establish a hierarchical church structure than a religious order with a theology focused on brotherhood and sisterhood. In short, the relational model(s) that constitute the most persuasive justifications will influence the range of positions that decision-makers regard as politically viable. In a sense, this hypothesis is a variant of the acceptability heuristic (see Tetlock, 1992).

Thinkable and unthinkable trade-offs

The previous section considered how ideology, tradition and political systems affect the implementation of relational models within a culture when these implementations become publicly problematic. This sets the stage for addressing the central question of what kinds of comparisons and transactions people take for granted and what kinds of explicit trade-offs people regard as unthinkable.

Trade-offs between relational modes

This raises the central issue of trade-offs among the four relational models. Although the distinctions are merely heuristic, we can classify such trade-offs according to whether the incommensurability primarily concerns entities (things and actions), values or the relationships themselves.

Hypothesis 4a: People will be anxious and have difficulty taking action when faced with decisions that require explicit choices among *values* or *entities* derived from distinct models.

The incommensurability of Communal Sharing and Market Pricing values illustrates this point. Both types of relationships are meaningful and important, but it is awkward and inappropriate to compare the two. How much should you spend on your daughter's wedding? It would be gauche to put a monetary value on your love for her. That is why we remove price tags from gifts: *I don't want to know the price you are bidding for our relationship* and you don't want your gift valued in terms of its market cost. Why is it that you can buy a birthday present to give to someone but you can't sell a present you receive? (This contrast provides a possible alternative interpretation of the well-replicated endowment effect in which people display a reluctance to trade goods recently bestowed upon them by the experimenter; Kahneman, Knetsch and Thaler, 1991.) Love and friendship are demeaned when they are monetized. There are many cognitive complexities in weighing two business opportunities against each other but at least there is a common currency: expected profit in conjunction with risk. In contrast, how does someone reach a decision when they have an opportunity to take a job with a big raise, if it means that they would have to live apart from their family? Further, consider what you would think of an employer who asked you, 'How much would I have to pay you to move away from your family to take this job?'

One recurring dilemma in American life concerns the irreconcilability of Equality Matching and Authority Ranking. We can't resolve the fact that everyone is equal, yet some are clearly superior in status, rank and authority. Consequently, we feel ambivalent about the trappings of office. Should students call you 'Mary' or 'Dr Smith'? Should the president of a university or a major corporation have a limousine and chauffeur – or would we admire her for riding her bicycle to work? These are the delicate dilemmas of democratic leadership, since the norms of equality and authority are strong and irreducibly disparate.

Another ideological quandary results from the juxtaposition of two kinds of 'fairness' or 'equality', or of 'equality' and individual 'freedom'. This impasse usually results from the discrepancy between the norms of Equality Matching and the norms of Market Pricing: Shall we distribute resources so that each person gets the same thing, or give people equal chances to earn rewards in proportion to their performance? Alternatively, shall we allocate resources in proportion to need – and if so, need in terms of current deprivation, or to the capacity to benefit from the resource? For example, should all students in a school have equal access to computers? Should we give priority to the slowest learners, who have the greatest deficiencies to make up in order to function effectively as adults? Should everyone in the department get an equal raise this year? Or the same *percentage* increase? Or raises proportional to their productivity?

Hypothesis 4b: People will be particularly torn when faced with incompatibilities among social *relationships* of different types. When people are forced to choose between relationships so that they must violate one or the other of two irreconcilable relational obligations, people will experience great difficulty, discomfort and ambivalence.

In an important sense, all of the trade-offs we have been discussing are choices among relationships, in the sense of models for meaningful, co-ordinated social action and evaluation. However, many of the most tragic choices occur when people have long-term commitments to close relationships that involve frequent interaction in many important domains. Needless to say, sometimes such relationships are incompatible with each other, and there is no good choice: Should you desert your wartime post, dishonoring and placing in jeopardy your military unit in order to go home to care for your dying child?

This raises an interesting question: Do people react differently when confronted by two irreconcilable Communal Sharing relationships than they do when confronted by a Communal Sharing relationship that cannot be reconciled with an Authority Ranking relationship? Is the agony of the choice different when deciding between relationships of the same basic type and relationships of different types? We suggest that, holding constant the motivational force and moral value of the two relationships, people are most confused, most anxious, and most strenuously attempt to avoid confronting the choice when they are faced with incompatibility between relationships of different basic types. This hypothesis is based on the supposition that when people have to compare two mutually exclusive Equality Matching relationships with each other, for example, or when they must select between two opposed Authority Ranking relationships, people can fairly readily assess the relative 'strength' or 'value' of the two qualitatively similar relationships. Even two Communal Sharing relationships are important in the same way, resonating with the same relational motivation; that may make it possible to make a 'gut' choice between them, albeit one that perhaps cannot be reflectively analyzed and adequately articulated. But it is difficult to weigh Communal Sharing against, say, Market Pricing: the disparate qualities of the motives make them impossible to compare directly or consistently. They do not meet the same needs or derive from the same motives, do not share a common affective tone, do not have corresponding moral foundations, and do not operate within a common metric.

Culture, ideology and contention

Some readers may also have wondered whether people actually keep their Communal Sharing, Authority Ranking, Equality Matching and Market Pricing relationships as neatly compartmentalized and distinct as the previous discussion suggests. In fact, people both compartmentalize and combine the four elementary models, in accord with practices that depend on their culture. The central point of this chapter is an account of the kinds of trade-offs that people find confusing, unpleasant and difficult to make explicitly. However, the observation that people avoid making these trade-offs explicitly does not imply that they do not make them implicitly. Furthermore, while the four relational models are disparate and discrete, people constantly link and combine them. For example, in many traditional social systems, primary groups based on kinship embody Communal Sharing relations, yet for other purposes, in other respects, the people in these groups are internally differentiated according to Authority Ranking (often by age and gender). People use all four of the models in their relational repertoire every day: at different times people interact with the same person according to, say, Communal Sharing or with reference to Authority Ranking; and they may use each of the four models simultaneously with regard to different dimensions of a social event.

One clear conclusion from this analysis is that it is fallacious to suppose, as some economists have, that because people allocate limited resources (make implicit choices with 'shadow prices'), they necessarily are maximizing utility across alternatives. People typically segregate relationships in a certain sense: they avoid making explicit trade-offs among relational modes. In practice, even money is often segregated into different types, linked to different relationships and uses, without being integrated into a common psychological currency (Zelizer, 1994). Although relationships are linked in various ways and are often highly interdependent, this interdependence does not take the form of rational or even quasi-rational utility comparisons.

People use complex combinations of the four respective models to generate dyadic relationships, groups, institutions, and practices. Yet each aspect of each activity may be governed by different models without people ever perceiving any trade-off. Within a relatively stable social system, it is a matter of common sense to use each of the models according to the prevailing cultural prototypes, paradigms and practices. In another culture, or at another time or place, common sense may presume different models, but it is only at the interfaces and contact points where transitions occur that people recognize that every act is necessarily a choice that implicates a trade-off among opportunity costs.

When such choices do become salient, people develop shared, reflective, more-or-less elaborated principles for resolving problematic issues. These ideologies formulate preferences in relation to theories and values about society. Ideologies are often rather monistic, based primarily on a single relational model, but they can be more pluralistic. However, even an ideology generated from a single relational model must specify *how* to implement that model in the contexts at issue. Advocates of two ideologies based on the same model may disagree on how to implement it – and the disagreement may be so heated that proponents fail to recognize or care that they are implementing the same underlying model.

People are typically unaware of most of the trade-offs they necessarily make everyday because the routine allocation of time and energy accords with cultural prototypes and paradigms that people take for granted. Cultures are meaningful, self-reproducing practices that organize the application of disparate relational models. When a culture is comparatively isolated and stable, people confront relatively few unthinkable trade-offs. When cultures mix and transform, people more frequently face confusing, anxiety-provoking, or taboo trade-offs.

Responses to taboo trade-offs

Up to this juncture, we have been concerned with identifying when people recognize their actions as trade-offs, and when they regard such trade-offs as permissible. We now shift attention to two interrelated issues:

1. Why are people so intensely indignant about taboo trade-offs? What are the conceptual components of moral outrage? And what factors moderate the intensity of this outrage?
2. How do decision-makers – compelled by resource scarcity and their institutional roles to make certain trade-offs – cope with the perilous social predicament of attempting taboo trade-offs? How do they avoid becoming victims of the righteous indignation of observers who learn that sacrosanct normative boundaries have been transgressed?

Observers' responses: moral outrage

Drawing on the traditional tripartite division of attitudes, we can analyze the moral outrage into cognitive, affective and behavioral components. The cognitive component consists of trait attributions to anyone who seems prepared to consider proposals that breach the boundaries of the four relational models: What kind of person would place a dollar value on human life or the right to vote? People perceive the relational models and their implementation rules as deeply normative; it is generally inconceivable that a reasonable person could encode the social world differently. Hence we should expect, following the attributional logic, that people would perceive violators of these normative conventions as at best mildly offensive and at worst bizarre, insane or evil.

The emotional response to taboo trade-offs follows directly from the cognitive appraisal of norm violators as threats to the social order. A breach of the boundaries among basic relational models is a threat to the social order because it throws into doubt the taken-for-granted assumptions that are constitutive of that order. Taboo trade-offs break down the distinctions between, say, authority and tit-for-tat equality, or between communal solidarity and the market. Hence they throw into doubt our fundamental assumptions about what each relationship *is*. The response should range from anxiety and confusion to primitive, punitive rage.

Finally, the behavioral component follows directly from the cognitive and emotional components. People should want to punish those who breach normative boundaries – punish them for purposes of both retribution and deterrence. Transgression threatens the relationship; punishment restores that relationship. To re-invoke Durkheim, only reassurance that the wrong-doer has been punished by the collective should be sufficient to restore the moral *status quo ante* and to reduce whatever cognitive and emotional unease was produced in individual observers by the original trade-off transgression. Indeed, punishments are forceful impositions of the relational models themselves, reestablishing their validity and hegemony. Thus, for example, corporal punishment reasserts the authoritative power of the punitive agent and the subordination of the criminal. When deviance disrupts the integrity of a communal group, ostracism – with or without subsequent rites of reintegration – reestablishes it. If someone violates Equality Matching (EM), then restitution or payment in-kind (an eye for an eye, a tooth for a tooth) restores the balance; in contrast, payment of a fine redresses a violation of Market Pricing (MP). In each case, a definition of social reality is effectively imposed on the transgressor: his subjugation in the one case, his dependence on the group, his equality, or his market obligations, respectively.

From this standpoint, moral outrage is not a dichotomous variable that is switched off or on as a function of whether a taboo trade-off has been observed. Outrage is a matter of degree and subject to a host of potential moderators. Specifically, we advance the following hypotheses:

1. *Relationship moderators.* Taboo trade-offs implicating Community Sharing (CS) relationships may evoke the greatest outrage because, it seems, CS relationships can tap the deepest, strongest and most tenacious motives and moral sentiments. The motives and moral commitments to Authority Ranking (AR) relationships may also be strong, such that violations of AR – sins against the gods or breaches of filial piety – tend to evoke intense outrage. EM relationships have intrinsic value to people, but for the most part people are less deeply involved in EM relationships than CS or AR relationships. People typically are much less committed to MP relationships – MP relationships in themselves do not feel sacred and meaningful to the same degree as EM relationships.

2. *Ideological moderators.* Certain ideological groups are more likely to view taboo trade-offs as outrageous than are other groups. Tetlock *et al.* (1996) found that libertarians (who have an expansive view of the appropriateness of MP implementation rules) are less offended by proposals to buy and sell votes and body organs than are conservative republicans, liberal democrats and radical socialists. By contrast, radical socialists (with a very restrictive view of the appropriateness of MP rules) are much more offended by routine market transactions – which radical socialists may

regard as inherently exploitive – than are liberal democrats, conservative republicans and libertarians.

3. *Contextual moderators.* It is possible to amplify or attenuate outrage via experimental manipulations of the degree to which the taboo trade-off threatens a core political value. For instance, Lerner, Newman and Tetlock (1995) hypothesized that liberals object to MP rules for body organs and baby adoptions in part because of their fear that the poor will be coerced into deals of desperation. Although the effects were modest, it was possible to reduce outrage when people were reassured that all participants to the exchange were reasonably well-off. Lerner *et al.* also found that another reason that people objected to extending MP rules into 'new' domains, such as body organs, was fear of setting precedents that would destabilize the social order as they knew it.

This work raises the possibility that some ideological groups in late twentieth century America view CS relationships as a moral bulwark against the encroachments of market capitalism, protecting otherwise vulnerable populations. The research also raises intriguing questions about how political values are linked to when, where, and why people draw boundaries between spheres of exchange. If allowing MP implementation rules to operate unchecked produces consequences that we judge abhorrent (for example child labor, organ and baby markets), then we resort to AR solutions of governmental regulation and/or CS solutions of pooling resources and rationing by queues. But, even within the MP model there may be ways of attenuating the 'nasty' side-effects of MP implementation rules while simultaneously accruing efficiency benefits (for example school vouchers that target poor children for especially large transfer payments).

Decision-makers' response: deflecting the wrath of observers

Observers often react fiercely to taboo trade-offs. So it should not be surprising if decision-makers, compelled by realities of resource scarcity to make such trade-offs, should feel that their social identities as moral and rational beings are in jeopardy. The revised value pluralism model (Tetlock *et al.*, 1996) identifies a set of individual and institutional coping strategies designed to defuse potential outrage, including concealment, obfuscation, decision-avoidance, and demagoguery.

Concealment and obfuscation

The safest defense is to conceal cross-domain trade-offs by rendering the decision process opaque. Secrecy is one key ingredient, and committees charged with sensitive trade-offs are typically unknown to the vast majority of the population. (Who is responsible for allocating scarce resources such as body organs and admission to professional schools? Who decides how much we should spend on making air travel or the workplace safer?)

Moreover, the actual criteria used to weigh conflicting values can rarely be inferred easily from the cryptic public statements issued by these committees and regulatory agencies.

Rhetorical obfuscation also promotes ignorance of taboo trade-offs. To obscure the actual trade-offs being made, decision-makers will often resort to smoke screens such as vague appeals to shared values: 'the Federal Reserve seeks to maximize long-term prosperity', 'OSHA would never put a price tag on life', or 'the admissions committee believes that diversity is excellence'. These obfuscations disguise the politically unpalatable fact that decision-makers are indeed prepared to trade off current jobs to contain future inflation, the loss of lives in work-place accidents to reduce regulatory burdens on business, and the imposition of higher college admissions standards on some racial groups to compensate for past and perhaps current discrimination. Our point is not, of course, that these decision-makers are doing something immoral. The political merits of each policy can be debated endlessly. Our point is that decision-makers do not like to acknowledge in private and especially in public that they are making taboo trade-offs. In many cases, to discuss the trade-off candidly is to commit political suicide.

Decision avoidance

In democratic societies, it is difficult to keep taboo trade-offs a secret for long. Invariably, some faction will conclude that it has been shortchanged and will call the formally anonymous decision-makers to account. Medical organ-transplant committees will stand accused of using inappropriate criteria (race or social class); the Federal Reserve Board will stand accused of insensitivity to the unemployed or to the danger of inflation; university admissions committees will find themselves in the docket for either reverse discrimination or institutional racism; regulatory agencies will be denounced as either tools of business interests or oppressive bureaucracies that squelch innovation.

Experimental results reveal that value conflict can be highly aversive when one is publicly accountable for a decision that requires imposing a loss on one group in order to confer a greater benefit on another. For example, Tetlock and Boettger (1994) found a surge of interest in buckpassing (referring the decision to others) and procrastination (delaying the decision) whenever subjects were publicly accountable for deciding whether to allow a currently banned drug that would save 300, 600 or 900 lives at the cost of either 100 or 300 lives. Subjects did not want to take responsibility for making a decision either resulting in side-effect casualties or denying society the benefit of a drug that would save hundreds of lives. Caught in a no-win political conflict, decision-makers 'ducked'.

Such dilemmas are not unusual; they are the essence of political struggles over resources and entitlements. Given the well-established tendency for losses to loom larger than gains in value trade-offs (by a ratio of 2:1 in prospect theory), it seems reasonable to hypothesize a strong motive among politicians to delay or redirect responsibility whenever decisions require imposing losses on well-defined constituencies. In this political calculus, the friends one gains will be more than offset by the enemies one makes. Therefore it should not be surprising that both legislators and regulatory agencies cope with trade-offs in general and taboo trade-offs in particular by passing the buck and procrastinating (cf. Wilson, 1989).

Demagoguery

Trade-offs, even of the legitimate within-domain sort, are politically problematic. Acknowledging that one is prepared to give up this amount of value *x* to acquire that amount of value *y* usually has the net effect of putting one on the public-relations defensive. The bitterness of the losers generally exceeds the gratitude of the winners (at least so long as the losers know who they are and suffer a sufficient loss to justify the effort of complaining).

Taboo trade-offs can be politically lethal. Acknowledging that one is prepared to cross boundaries between relational models implies a lack of respect for foundational values of the social order. Love, life and loyalty are generally held to be priceless. When decision-makers nonetheless put prices on them, their constituents are likely to accuse them of gross insensitivity to the prevailing qualitative distinctions among spheres of justice, and to decide that they cannot be trusted with public authority (cf. Walzer, 1983). Politicians who are caught affixing dollar values to entities governed by CS, AR or EM rules should expect brief careers.

But taboo trade-offs are unavoidable. Although we do not want to face the issue, most of us are not willing to spend everything we own to maximize the health, happiness and education of our children, and are even less disposed to do so for the children of others. There is also a limit to the dollars we will spend to enhance our own personal safety at the workplace or in cars or airplanes, and we will certainly spend less for the safety of others. In our choices, we implicitly reveal our qualified commitments to love, life and loyalty.

This analysis highlights a recurring opportunity in democracies for political opponents of the governing party. Unconstrained by the responsibilities of making the actual decisions that allocate scarce resources, they are free to find fault. The opposition can explicitly draw attention to the taboo trade-offs that political leaders must make. Leaders obviously do not want to be held accountable for taboo trade-offs that outrage substantial segments of the electorate. It is equally obvious that opposition politicians want to hold leaders accountable for these trade-offs, and to portray them as callous and cruel. Opposition politicians are disposed to caricature the governing as cads who trade blood for oil, lives for money, and basic democratic rights for administrative convenience. Not surprisingly, opposition rhetoric tends to be shrill, self-righteous and integratively simple (Tetlock, 1981). In short, the opposition 'gives them hell'. Indeed, the major reality constraint on opposition rhetoric derives from the opposition's own past conduct when they were in power. Opposition parties that have recently held power and hope to hold it again soon may well choose to forgo immediate political advantage and temper criticism of decision-making procedures that they either recently employed themselves or might want to employ in the foreseeable future. Demagoguery, however, looks like the rational response for those who do not expect to wield power but do want to wield influence – or for those who believe that the electorate has a short memory.

Implications

We seem to be impaled on the horns of a dilemma. Responsible governance entails tradeoffs that transgress fundamental normative boundaries – trade offs, for example, that involve monetizing societal concern for the elderly, infirm or young (how much should we spend on Social Security, Medicare or Head Start?). But political survival requires denying that any relational boundaries have been breached and insisting that all obligations have been honored. A portrait of the political process emerges that is congenial to 'elitists' who have long doubted the competence of ordinary people to execute the critical-appraisal functions of democratic citizenship. People, in this view, are best 'left in the dark' and governance left to the cognoscenti. In closing, therefore, it is worth stressing that, although we recognize that some readers may draw an elitist moral from our argument, elitism is far from an inevitable prescriptive entailment of the analysis we have presented. Elsewhere Fiske and Tetlock (1997) have shown that relational theory and the value-pluralism models can just as easily be reconciled with proposals to create and enhance various forms of deliberative democracy based on a kind of moral comity. All people appreciate the inherent good of all four relational models *in some – albeit different – domains* and all humans are committed to the moral validity of *some* implementations of all of the models. This makes it possible, in the right framework, for people to find common ground for discussion that may enable them to develop a consensus on some reasonable combination of implementations of the four models that may be acceptable to all.

References

Durkheim, E. (1976) *The Elementary Forms of the Religious Life*, 2nd edn, London: Allen & Unwin.

Fiske, A. P. (1990) 'Relativity within Moose ('Mossi') Culture: Four Incommensurable Models for Social Relationships'. *Ethos*, vol. 18, pp. 180–204.

Fiske, A. P. (1991) *Structures of Social Life: The Four Elementary Forms of Human Relations*, New York: Free Press (Macmillan).

Fiske, A. P. (1992) 'The Four Elementary Forms of Sociality: Framework For a Unified Theory of Social Relations', *Psychological Review*, vol. 99, pp. 689–723.

Fiske, A. P. and P. E. Tetlock (1997) 'Taboos Trade-offs: Reactions to Transactions that Transgress the Spheres of Justice', *Political Psychology*, vol. 18, pp. 255–97.

Fiske, A. P. and N. Haslam (1996) 'Social Cognition is Thinking about Relationships', *Current Directions in Psychological Science*, vol. 5, pp. 143–8.

Kahneman, D., J. L. Knetsch, and R. Thaler (1991) 'The Endowment Effect, Loss Aversion, and the Status Quo Bias', *Journal of Economic Perspectives*, vol. 5, pp. 193–206.

Keeney, R. and H. Raiffa (1976) *Decisions with Multiple Objectives: Preferences and Value Trade-offs*, New York: Wiley.

Lerner, J., D. Newman and P. E. Tetlock (1995) 'Taboo Trade-offs: The Psychology of the Unthinkable', paper presented at the annual meeting of the American Psychological Society, New York, July 1995.

Raz, J. (1986) *The Morality of Freedom*, New York: Oxford University Press.

Tetlock, P. E. (1981) 'Pre to Post-Election Shifts in Presidential Rhetoric: Impression Management or Cognitive Adjustment?' *Journal of Personality and Social Psychology*, vol. 41, pp. 207–12.

Tetlock, P. E. (1984) 'Cognitive Style and Political Belief Systems in the British House of Commons', *Journal of Personality and Social Psychology*, vol. 46, pp. 365–75.

Tetlock, P. E. (1986) 'A value Pluralism Model Of Ideological Reasoning', *Journal of Personality and Social Psychology*, vol. 50, pp. 819–27.

Tetlock, P. E. (1992) 'The Impact of Accountability on Judgment and Choice: Toward a Social Contingency Model', in M. Zanna (ed.), *Advances in Experimental Social Psychology*, vol. 25, San Diego, CA: Academic Press (pp. 331–76).

Tetlock, P. E. and R. Boettger (1994) 'Accountability Amplifies the Status Quo Effect When Change Creates Victims', *Journal of Behavioral Decision Making*, vol. 7, pp. 1–23.

Tetlock, P. E., R. Peterson and J. Lerner (1996) 'Revising the Value Pluralism Model: Incorporating Social Content and Context Postulates', in C. Seligman, J. Olson, and M. Zanna (eds), *Eighth Ontario Symposium on Personality and Social Psychology: Values*, Hillsdale, NJ: Erlbaum.

Walzer, M. (1983) *Spheres of Justice: A Defense of Pluralism and Equality*, New York: Basic Books.

Wilson, J. Q. (1989) *Bureaucracy*, Cambridge, Mass.: Harvard University Press.

Zelizer, V. A. (1994) *The Social Meaning of Money*. New York: Basic Books (Harper Collins).

5
Substance and Method in Cultural and Crosscultural Political Psychology

Stanley A. Renshon and John Duckitt; with contributions by Marc Howard Ross, Ofer Feldman, Fathali M. Moghaddam, George De Vos, Walter G. Stephan and Kwok Leung

The important relationship of substance to method was a key insight in the development of the social sciences. Focus on the many different techniques developed – surveys, experiments, focused interviews – shared two common purposes. Primarily, they were designed to make our analyses more systematic and reliable. However, they also had the effect, in time, of making us more self-consciously aware of the advantages and limitations of the ways in which we gather information in support of them. This being the case, it was natural to ask whether it was possible to try and revitalize a founding tradition for a new subfield in political psychology without saying anything about method. We thought the answer to that question had to be no if (a) there was anything distinctive about studying culture, as opposed to say political attitudes, values, and so on, (b) there was anything distinctive about studying politics in different cultural contexts, or (c) there were any particular limitations or opportunities for the researcher who examines culture politically which have implications for theory and/or methods.

On these grounds we thought that there might well be distinctive aspects involved in the study of cultural and crosscultural political psychology. Even so, we faced two further dilemmas. First, we had no wish to restate or echo the excellent crosscultural methods discussions already available (Berry, Segall and Kagitgitçibasi, 1997; Kaplan, 1961; Naroll and Cohen, 1970; Van de Vijver and Leung, 1997). Second, the contributors to this book represent a diverse group both in theoretical focus and methodological preferences. Given the book's purpose, this strategy had much to recommend it. However, uniform perspectives on the relationship of method to substance in cultural and crosscultural political psychology were an unlikely by-product of such a choice.

Our solution was to ask a group of our contributors a basic question: Is there anything distinctive about the cultural or crosscultural study of matters interesting and important to political psychology? More specifically, we asked them to address issues found in the following four question areas:

1. Is there anything distinctive about the level of analysis that one must use in studying the interplay between culture and politics? Are there any specific theoretical or methodological implications that flow from these distinctions?
2. Is there anything distinctive about the variables used in studying the interplay between culture and politics? Could one as easily and legitimately use, say, political attitudes as political values to study such a relationship? If not, how would you frame and understand the relationship between the kinds of variables that one should use in examining the interplay of culture and politics? What are the theoretical and or methodological implications of these distinctions?
3. In studying political phenomena/processes within or across cultures are there any particular methodological problem(s) that make certain established methods more or less appropriate or requiring some sort of modification? If so, how have you addressed this in your work?
4. Are there particular limitations and opportunities for the researcher who shares (or does not share) the culture he or she is examining politically which have implications for theory and/or methods?

The brief essays which follow use these questions as their starting point to provide a basis for increasing our understanding of the particular issues that arise between substance and method in cultural and crosscultural political psychology.

Commentary: if culture is so important, why haven't political scientists emphasized it more?
Marc Howard Ross

The promising nature of cultural analyses of political life raises the question of why relatively few political scientists show much interest in it. Certainly, this has helped to slow development of crosscultural political psychology. Perhaps some of this is because of problems which opponents of cultural analysis raise and are worth noting. Perhaps the most significant problems arise over methodological issues such as the difficulty in defining culture as a unit of analysis or the issue of within versus between cultural variation. Others are concerned with the vagueness of the concept of culture and the difficulty in distinguishing culture from related concepts such as social organization, political behavior and values. Some are worried that since culture suggests relatively fixed, unchanging patterns of behavior, it is not terribly useful in accounting for changes in behavior and beliefs, a key feature of most contemporary political systems. Finally, there is concern that cultural analyses are not sufficiently explicit concerning the mechanisms linking culture and political action. Each of these is worth some brief comments.

The unit of analysis problem

Most political scientists are worried when the entities they study cannot be defined in a precise manner. Voters, states, wars, and international organization can all be defined and subject to a wide range of analyses. However, political scientists are far more squeamish about units of analysis whose core is imprecise. What is a culture?, some ask, meaning 'How do I know one when I see one?' since it is not a unit of social or political organization.[1] Furthermore, the imprecision of everyday language use makes it very unclear what are a culture's key properties. As a result we can hear references to Western culture, French culture, Breton culture, rural Breton culture and so on. Where does the parsing stop? Conceptually my answer is that the appropriate level depends on what one wants to explain, but this is not always a very useable methodological guide to someone conducting empirical research.

Huntington offers a similar answer when he describes a range of what he calls cultural entities starting with villages and moving to regions, ethnic groups, nationalities, religious groups and civilizations. Each has distinct cultural features which distinguish it from similar units in other cultural entities. The key for him is that the civilization is 'the highest grouping of people and the broadest level of cultural identity people have short of that which distinguishes humans from other species' (1993, 24). Which level of cultural identity is the most salient at any moment, he, following Horowitz (1985) says, depends upon where someone is and what they are doing with whom. Cultural identity from this perspective is layered and situationally defined.[2] The same person could variously define herself as a Breton, as French, or as a European depending upon who she is interacting with and what she perceives at stake in a particular situation.

The unit of analysis problem is about what constitutes the core of a culture and also how to identify its edges (Barth, 1969). Where does one culture stop and another begin? Since cultures, unlike states or political parties, are not formal units of organization, treating them as independent units of political analysis can be troubling indeed. No matter that states aren't as independent as our political and methodological theory leads us to believe. (Nor are voters, but that's another matter.) For purposes of most analyses we emphasize the independence of these units. However, since cultures are not often formally organized entities we are reluctant to do the same with them.

Probably the best answer to these methodological problems is to begin with the recognition that cultural identity is layered and situationally defined. People hold multiple identities, some identities partially overlap, and the group boundaries can shift across issues. Despite the methodological problems this can present, we cannot ignore culture if we think it is important, and we should make decisions about units of analysis based on what we are trying to explain rather than on abstract criteria intended to identify a set of cultural units akin to a list of all UN member states. In addition, there are a number of other procedures we can use to define cultural units in particular pieces of research. For example, we can use operational criteria such as asking people how they identify themselves and others and use social consensus about particular cultural groups and their boundaries. The point is that a task for research is to identify relevant groupings in whatever situation is under study. The fact that people can have multiple identities or that identities can change over time does not invalidate such analysis, it just makes the research more complicated. Good longitudinal data on socially defined cultural identities might be of real importance, for example, in understanding the breakdown of Yugoslavia and its recent civil war.

The within-culture variance problem

It seems easy to say what members of formal groups have in common. But what exactly do people of a given culture share? I emphasize a distinctive way of life and a shared world view. Operationally, this can be ambiguous, for we know that people who consider themselves to be part of a culture often differ in terms of values, life-styles, political dispositions, religious belief and practice, and ideas about common interests. The key point which LeVine makes is that common understandings of the symbols and representations they communicate means there is not necessarily a problem with within-cultural variation in thought, feeling, and behavior (1984, 68). In addition, Strauss cautions that while there may be some variation in schemas across individuals in the same culture, even those with very similar schemas do not internalize exactly the same things, and that the ambiguity of metaphor produces variation in responses (Strauss, 1992, 10–11).[3]

Another answer is that what is more crucial than agreement on content is that people share a common identity, although this still leaves open the question of different degrees of identification and differences in the actions people are willing to undertake in the name of that identity. Shared identities mean that people see themselves as similar to some people and different from others and are open to potential mobilization on the basis of these differences. Emphasis on self-identification stresses, once again, that the relevant critical aspects of cultural similarity and difference are defined in particular political contexts. It also points to beliefs about what people believe they share which may be at odds with reality. It is probably the case that people's perceptions of cultural unity take the form of a regression to the mean in which widely accepted norms are seen as more shared than they in fact are. In this dynamic, in-group conformity pressures will both lead people to selectively perceive greater within group homogeneity on critical characteristics than actually exists and to generate greater actual homogeneity and group conformity in situations where perceived threats to the culture are great.

The 'culture is everything so is it anything?' problem

Some uses of the concept of culture, such as some of the early work on national character, defined culture so broadly as to include society, personality, values, and institutions. In fact, nothing was excluded.[4] The tendency to use a concept like culture very broadly was also encouraged by early writers who emphasized culture as a way of understanding the social integration of a society. This perspective, probably clearest in functional theory such as British social anthropology, would use culture to refer to both distinct elements of social organization and to the 'fit' between different parts of a cultural system and the integration of the whole. Some more recent cultural analyses suffer from the same problem as culture becomes a master, all-encompassing, yet often undefined, phenomenon. The problem here isn't the concept of culture but the way it is used. As noted above, current anthropological investigations focus on culture as meaning systems and distinct from social structure, and behavior. D'Andrade's makes this particularly clear in his description of culture

> as consisting of learned system of meaning, communicated by means of natural language and other symbol systems, having representational, directive, and affective function, and capable of creating cultural entities and particular senses of reality. Through these systems of meaning, groups of people adapt to their environment and structure interpersonal activities. (1984, 116)

I find Spiro's clear distinction between culture as a system of meaning, and what he calls 'culturally constituted elements', referring to social structure, behaviors, beliefs, rituals and so on, particularly helpful here. Distinguishing between culture and culturally constituted elements allows us to separate cultural meanings and identity on the one hand and structure, behaviors and individual beliefs on the other. Structure, from this perspective, is reflective of (and to some extent derived from) culture, but it is independently measurable and an important empirical question concerns the conditions under which the correspondence between culture and various culturally constituted elements is high and when it is not. We also can examine hypotheses about change and examine how culture, structure, and other phenomena do and do not shift in patterned ways. Lastly, the distinction makes it feasible to compare societies in which the correspondence between culture and social structure are high and those in which they are low to test hypotheses about the impact of consistency on such things as citizen satisfaction with government, political involvement, and political stability.

Culture and change

Cultures are commonly viewed as slow-changing entities. How, then, can the concept of culture help comparativists deal with issues of political change, especially relatively rapid developments such as the end of military rule in many Latin American states during the 1980s or the break-up of the Soviet empire?

Three points are worth making. First, cultural analyses are no better than any other partial theories, such as interest or institutional ones, available in comparative politics. There are some phenomena for which each is most powerful, and some aspects of change are not best explained in cultural terms. Second, interestingly, while it is not clear that cultural theories would have explained the fall of the Soviet empire very well (many other comparative political theories share this feature), a political cultural analysis is probably a good deal better at accounting for the ebb and flow of politics in the region since 1989 than many of its rivals. Particularly in unstructured, changing settings cultural interpretations and assumptions about the motivation of others can be especially important in accounting for political processes in which there are few or no institutionalized procedures to guide action. Third, few contemporary views see culture as a static, unchanging phenomenon marked by fixed beliefs and unalterable practices (Eckstein, 1988). Rather, emphasis on the interactive, constructed nature of culture suggests a capacity to modify beliefs and behaviors, and for important shifts in the salience of particular cultural understandings and their connections to other cultural elements (Goode and Schneider, 1994; Merelman, 1991).

Culture can play a significant role in change not because culture itself changes so quickly when changes – or demands for change – are articulated in cultural terms and when change oriented groups and their leaders develop culturally meaningful narratives to articulate their goals and to mobilize supporters. Defining culturally legitimate possible alternatives both builds support and can challenge a regime. Brysk argues that this is particular powerful when it involves reframing elements of identity in a way which mobilizes supporters, produces agenda change, and challenging the legitimacy and authority of existing policies and institutions (1995, 580–2).

The 'how does culture work' problem

When we ask 'how culture works' we are really concerned with two different questions: (1) how does the organization of any particular culture produce the specific effects attributed to it?, and (2) why are appeals to cultural identity so powerful that people are willing to take high risks in its name? The first is about the organization of culture and the second about its mobilizing power.

Any theory which gives culture a central explanatory role must specify how the effects attributed to culture come about (Bohannan, 1995). It's not good enough to simply say, 'They did it because they're Chinese'. While this statement implies that non-Chinese people (such as the Japanese or Americans) would have behaved differently, and adding a clause to this effect doesn't really enhance the explanation a great deal. Only when one says why Chinese are likely to behave differently from how Americans behave (in what is presumed to be an equivalent situation), do we begin to have an adequate explanation. Anthropology, one might say, consists of many such 'middle-range' theories which answer questions about the effects of culture on social action.

Any adequate explanation of how culture works has to pay some attention to how it is learned and reinforced (Strauss, 1992; D'Andrade, 1992). Learning from the first days of life, (Stern, 1985) provides clear messages about appropriate behavior and contains both affective and cognitive content. Just as important, learning and reinforcement involve practice during which a person (child or adult), masters certain behaviors and often infuses them with emotional significance. Beatrice Whiting (1980) describes the importance of the placement of individuals in particular contexts; for example girls take care of younger siblings more than boys, and boys are more likely to take care of animals in all the cultures for which she has data. In these contexts a person learns what she calls 'mundane' behaviors, those culturally sanctioned daily actions and values which serve them throughout life.

Social experiences within institutions such as schools, religious organizations, kin groups, and later in work and leisure settings all provide cultural messages about values and expectations which are selectively reinforced. It certainly is the case that the messages from different domains are not always fully consistent. Sometimes there is a difference in emphasis, at others an outright contradiction, for example peer groups and families don't necessarily give adolescents the same messages. However, what is most important from a cultural perspective are the beliefs, customs, rituals, behaviors, expectations and motives which are internalized by individuals and widely shared among people in a culture. Culture is about what is held in common and regularly reinforced; there is a reward for 'getting it right' and a cost – which most people are willing to pay at times – for not doing so. Finally, it should be noted that cultural learning is not necessarily very conscious at all for it occurs when individuals in institutional roles pass on culturally sanctioned beliefs and behaviors to others. Through these experiences culture prepares people to make sense of – to interpret – the world and act 'effectively' in it.

The power of culture – the ability to mobilize action in its name – requires explanation for it is not always the case that people can or will exhibit solidarity around cultural identity just because a leader (or anyone else) asserts that there is an external threat. Various theories of ethnocentrism and ethnic identity (LeVine and Campbell, 1973; Ross and Campbell, 1989) provide answers to this question. For example, realistic group conflict theory (LeVine and Campbell, 1973; Taylor and Moghaddam, 1987) emphasizes cost–benefit calculations; sociobiological theory (a variation on cost–benefit analysis) stresses the transmission of genes; social identity theory points to the link between social belongingness and self-esteem, and psychocultural identity theory (Ross, 1995) locates group loyalty in early attachments. Each of these, although in very different ways, shares three core, often implicit key propositions: the ability of cultural groups to meet many basic needs; the importance of social connectedness and links to others both living and dead, and the interdependence of individual and group identity.

Cultural mobilization builds on individual fears and perceived threats consistent with internalized world views and regularly reinforced through high ingroup interaction and emotional solidarity. Such worldviews are expressed in daily experiences as well as significant ceremonial and ritual events which effectively restate and renew support for a group's core values and the need for solidarity in the face of external foes (Kertzer, 1988). In potentially threatening situations, the ability of a group to organize collective action which can range from unified voting to political demonstrations and violent action is tied to the plausibility of a worldview's explanation of a situation. The resonance between the definition of a situation and group-based action is often not explicit as Cohen's (1969) analysis points out. Nonetheless it is effective when group members act in unified ways in the face of perceived threats.

Commentary: Models and methods in cultural and crosscultural political psychology
Ofer Feldman

Generalizing from the case of Japan, many more variables other than 'simple' political attitudes and values need to be examined to study the interplay between culture and politics. On the macro level, the case of Japan illustrates that historical events and experiences (close to 300 years of isolation from other countries, defeat in the Second World War and the suffering of poverty and humiliation, late coming democracy, and so on), geographical conditions (keeping it from direct contact with the continent and other cultures, with a small island country a size close to that of California and a density of population today of about 123 million people), socio-demographical variables (a relatively linguistic and culturally homogeneous society with only a small minority of foreigners), and social organization (nuclear family system in a vertically constructed society) impacted the relationship between culture and politics; and, in particular, they have shaped and affected such factors as national character, images toward the self and others, political xenophobia, and communication (verbal and non-verbal) processes.

In examining the interplay of culture and politics on the micro level, it is necessary to look at such variables as child experiences (including customs at home, the role of the mother), socialization and education in general, all which impact adult Japanese to the extent that they are often characterized as having a sense of self-uncertainty at the motivational base of their social and political behavior. This sense of self-uncertainty has three main aspects. First is the combination of weak self-assertion, lack of self-confidence and a sense of inferiority in interpersonal relationships, expressed by such passive traits as faintheartedness, shyness, reserve, and resignation. Another side of this sense of self-uncertainty, however, is linked to a tendency to be concerned about maintaining harmony in interpersonal relationships by being considerate and gentle. In an attempt to overcome this sense of self-uncertainty, a third aspect, consisting of more active tendencies such as studiousness, aspiration and zeal for work come into play. In this way Japanese try to conquer their uncertain sense of selfhood (Minami, 1982).

In short, in order to understand political behavior one has to explore rather a wide range of dimensions, beyond what 'traditional' political science (or psychology) may offer, including historical, sociological, anthropological and linguistically variables.

On crosscultural equivilance in political psychology

In my own research I attempted to examine political attitudes (for example dogmatism and xenophobia) across cultures. In order to make crosscultural comparisons, I tried to utilize in Japan the same questionnaires that were used in other countries, but often I found it extremely difficult to ensure identical meaning to the questions used. Some basic Western concepts such as identity, ideology, anomie, personality, charisma and communication do not exist in Japan. These words must be either pronounced as they are in the Japanese way (*aidentiti, ideorogi, anomi, pasonariti, karisuma* and *komyunikeishon*, respectively) or explained in a short sentence. Of course most Japanese know the meaning of such a concept as communication (personal or mass), but only highly-educated people are familiar with the meaning of such concepts as personality or anomie.

On the other hand, there are, of course, reverse examples of concepts that are commonly used in Japanese but that would be difficult to find equivalents for in Western languages. Among them are concepts such as *amae* (translated generally as 'dependency'), *nemawashi* ('trimming of a tree's roots prior to its being transplanted'), *ishin-denshin* ('traditional mental telepathy'), and *haragei* ('the art of the abdomen'). Even if the translation of concepts is possible from the technical perspective, one is still left with the problem of connotations and nuances which are different in Japan. One example to illustrate this is the concept of 'public' and 'private'. In Western societies, 'public' refers to things that are in the general domain of understanding, are relatively objective and assessable to observation. In Japanese, however, the word for 'public' stand for institutional, socially observable functions and processes that are part of a common-wealth of objects, experiences and ideas and cover the notions of 'public building' or 'public awareness'.

In Western societies, 'private' refers to functions, possessions, ideas or fantasies that 'belong' to the individual and are not readily accessible to other persons. In Japanese, however, the parallel term conveys the connotation of strong personal subjectivity, which when compared with the rich application of the word 'private' in American life, is relatively hypocognated in the Japanese language. The terms 'public' and 'private' also have moral connotations in Western personal interaction. Moreover, the ideas of private is more extensively substantiated in Western constitutional and civil law, protecting the ownership of material goods, property and original ideas to a degree that is not as prominent in Japan (Johnson, 1993, 220–2).

Likewise, whereas in individualist cultures 'individualism' and 'rationalism' can be regarded as positive traits or virtues, in a highly group-oriented society like Japan these are often viewed in a negative way because Japanese tradition and practice place far less emphasis on individual and rational behavior than do Western societies. Japanese thus tend to consider the individual as insignificant and value a team player more than a solo star. They see the rational person as egoist, often selfish, one who tries to use others to maximize personal rewards and profit. And by the same token, in individualistic cultures a political leader must be decisive, powerful and determinate. But in Japan, rather than preferring a strong, visible articulate leader, the Japanese concept of leadership values the virtues of the behind-the-scenes consensus builder. Any charismatic leader who can motivate the masses is rejected, collective aspects are emphasized and much importance is attached to group dynamism and decisions.

Consequently, when translating a questionnaire I want to use in Japan I always consult Japanese social psychologists and ask them to look at the nuances of the questions to ensure that the real meaning of the questions will be conveyed to the respondents. To test this translation, I then do a pilot study with students and discuss problems they have in answering questions.

There are also several other problems related to response pattern of the Japanese. Traditionally, perhaps as a surefire way to cause the other individual not to lose face, Japanese do not give clear-cut answers but rather ambiguous, neutral and middle-of-the-road responses. In public opinion surveys, when asked for their opinion, needs or agreement with a certain phenomenon, a large number of individuals tend to answer most often 'I don't know' or 'it depends'. Nishihira (1987, 160) indicated that compared with Western societies, the percentage of 'don't know' and 'no answer' responses in public opinion surveys in Japan are considerably higher. For example, in the 1980s, the percentages of those who answered 'don't know' and 'no answer' in research in the USA were 2.6 per cent, France 5.4 per cent, the UK 7.3 per cent, Germany 9.6 per cent and Japan 12.5 per cent. For this reason, when interviewed, many Japanese try to avoid using vocabulary that in any way seems to pass judgment or make a commitment to a position, often hedging their comments with such words as *tabun* (literally 'probably'), *osoraku* ('perhaps') or *hyottoshitara* ('possibly').

The implication from this is that when conducting studies in Japan one has to ignore 'middle-of-the-way' option ('neutral attitude', or 'don't know') in order to enforce a selection of a clear answer on the respondents.

On being part/apart of a culture

The fact that I was not born and raised in the particular society (Japan) in which I work, enables me to examine political (and social) behavior and attitudes from another perspective, perhaps to be more neutral than the 'natives'. I can easily identify those things related to language, religion, ideology and customs which are considered by the 'natives' as 'common practice', and are taken at face value, but which are not so 'common' for me. To the extent that I do not seek the 'exceptional' and 'unique' and that I do not feel 'attached' to, or cultural identity with, this particular society, I can look at behavior patterns and developing events in the society from a distance, without getting psychologically involved. By looking on events from this angle I can explain behavior and attitudes by considering a wider circle of variables which perhaps are not seen and are not assumed at first place to directly affect a particular activity that takes place.

As a matter of fact, from living more than 16 years in this society and by knowing the language and the customs of the people, I have an interchangeable inside–outside perspective to evaluate and interpret individuals' behavior as well as trends in society in general. In many cases, I try to look at things from the inside and interpret them from the viewpoint of the natives, and at the same time I can provide the outside view as an explanation, putting it in a broader crosscultural context.

When examining political behavior and attitudes in Japan, there are various (advantageous) opportunities for foreign researchers in this country. In conducting field research and gathering data, for example, I found it very easy to meet with and interview a variety of people – social scientists, educators, journalists, government bureaucrats, politicians and political leaders. These individuals and others are willing to meet and host foreigners and answer as many questions as they are asked. Sometimes, as I experienced it, many of these people even answer more than they were asked, showing their willingness to give information, to explain in detail and to add their own views on issues in politics and society. The same people, particularly Diet members and government bureaucrats, seem reluctant to meet with Japanese scholars and cooperate with them. This is perhaps because they fear that their remarks about the political world, their colleagues, their orientations, and beliefs may be published and used against them. They also fear that reactions to certain ideas or views they espouse or personal data they reveal may be detrimental to their careers, hurting their status within their political party or the broader political world. Presumably, these Diet members and government officials feel no such threat from foreigner researchers. Many of those whom I have met and talked with felt that there is a need on their side to explain Japanese attitudes and behavior to the world, thus they welcome foreign researchers who want to study these issues.

Also, in collecting data through questionnaires from the general public as well as from students I get much support and assistance, probably because Japanese, in particular, would like to convey a good impression and image to the foreign researcher. Therefore, respondents often tend to answer in length and to detail their thoughts and opinions. Of course, some disadvantages limit the foreign researcher in Japan which may affect his or her work and potential theory. Inability to interpret correctly processes of communication and politics, to mention only two notable phenomena, may affect the way a researcher views attitudes in Japan.

Communication includes not only verbal but also nonverbal messages, which requires one to know the meaning and the significance of facial expressions, a smile, an eye contact, and gestures that people use in Japan. Communication in Japan also has certain distinguishing characteristics. In particular, the talk of Japanese politicians and government officials is often characterized by two distinctive features: *honne* (meaning the honest feeling, the obverse, the actual, or the genuine intent); and *tatemae* ('surface pretense', the formal, or the presented truth of a given issue). The two concepts of *honne* and *tatemae* reflect different attitudes of a person conversing on a given issue. When the speaker tends to disclose the real meaning of an issue, to reveal all and to openly disclose true feelings – regardless of the reception those feelings receive – it is *honne*.

In contrast, when everything said is carefully expressed in order to restrict the conversation to official positions, or is spoken of in generalities, avoiding direct opinion and display of any personal feelings through euphemisms, ambiguous generalities or lack of clear expression, it is *tatemae*. *Tatemae* is the most commonly used form of public speaking in Japan, because it is not socially acceptable to express personal feelings or opinions in a public forum, nor is it appropriate to interject personal opinions in what is regarded as public affairs. The distinction between public obligation and private matters must always be made clear (Yoneyama, 1971).

The foreign researcher, thus, who may find it difficult to distinguish between the two concepts, may interpret an official statement or a given answer to a question by officials as the real intent, whereas they might be different. An ability to distinguish between these two concepts, which are used so often in Japanese politics and management, might be a crucial factor for the student of Japanese political attitudes and behavior. Additionally, in observing political processes, much of Japanese politics is conducted in the *misshitsu seiji* ('political decisions made behind closed doors'), or *machiai seiji* ('behind -the-scene politics'). In order to avoid a direct and open clash of ideas or wishes and to achieve a mutual understanding among all the members, to resolve differences of opinion and to maintain harmony, each individual's opinion is usually adjusted informally in a kind of ground-work before the formal meeting takes place. This all involves secret political consultations among the various partners in the political game. There, representatives of political parties and factions quietly present to each other their stances on specific issues, express support for – or objections to the views held by other members on these topics, and try to resolve conflicts of opinions by involving all the relevant parties in the decision making process.

Diet proceedings, for example, constitute the face of the political process. This is where speeches on social and political issues are made, and procedures concerning the routine work of both chambers of the Diet are usually decided on by a vote in the plenary session. In fact, though, such votes merely ratify decisions already reached in negotiations between leaders of political parties and their representatives before the session began. Such negotiations, conducted far from the public's eye, are the back side of the Japanese political process. In these capacities, leaders of political groups meet and discuss, for instance, how each party will be represented in leadership posts, the duration of an extraordinary or special Diet session, and where each party's Diet members will be seated. Some bills introduced in the Diet are also first negotiated by representatives of the various political parties and are jointly endorsed by all the political parties involved.

All these aspects of the Japanese political process may not be easy for the foreign researcher – sometimes indeed even for the Japanese researcher – to follow and comprehend the course of events. This can impact the way the researcher interprets political behavior in Japan.

Commentary: elites and culture in crosscultural political psychology
Fathali M. Moghaddam

Those who enjoy greater power in society have the capability of shaping behavior and ultimately even culture. The influence of elites on culture, however, is seldom apparent and therefore seldom acknowledged. Most often, this influence is camouflaged, hidden, and even explicitly denied. This poses a problem for research methodology in crosscultural political psychology. Our methods have to be designed to get behind 'the masks' presented by respondents. To give an example, when Billig (1978) studied members of the National Front, an extreme right-wing organization operating in England, he found that traditional 'unbiased' questionnaire techniques did little to get behind the masks. Billig found it necessary to use in-depth interviews and work his way around the masks, and to explicitly use ideology to interpret the behavior of National Front members. Just 'taking the respondent at his/er word' actually led to warped views of the world, a view that justified the behavior of fascists toward minorities. The researcher, then, needs to adopt a skeptical stance, and use methods that uncover and penetrate different layers of meaning.

Another useful illustrative example is from Chagnon's (1992) research among the Yanomamo people in South America, particularly because it highlights the importance of layers of meaning in culture. Chagnon spent the first five months of his stay in a Yanomamo village learning all the names of the villagers, so that he could map out kinship relationships. He learned scores of colorful names, such as 'eagle shit' and 'asshole'. It was not until much later that he discovered that the Yanomamo have a strict taboo against mentioning the names of prominent people as well as those of dead relatives and friends. Among these people, the way to show respect is to not mention a person's name in public (rather different from the West!). In order to deal with this troublesome white researcher who wanted to learn their names and insult them by calling out names in public, the Yanomamo villagers fabricated names for Chagnon. The way Chagnon managed to discover this and many other features of the Yanomamo behavior is by not being satisfied with the first set of responses, and by using methods that allowed him to dig into deeper layers of culture.

In summary, then, a cultural approach implies that research methods should help allow the researcher to take a skeptical approach, to dig through layers of meaning, and to unravel the normative system that guides behavior in different contexts. Often these normative systems have been powerfully shaped by elites to reflect and protect their interests, and this goes unacknowledged by all, being embedded in the implicit understandings and meanings characterizing the culture. A cultural and crosscultural perspective, then, requires at its most fundamental level that researchers use methods powerful and penetrative enough to unravel such hidden meanings and examine the role of elites and power inequalities in establishing and maintaining cultures.

Commentary: projective test methods in a comparative cultural and political context
George De Vos

Working intermittently now for approximately 50 years, principally with the Rorschach and Thematic Apperception Test, in the field of endeavor best called cultural psychology, has exposed me to considerable differences of opinion in respect to the feasibility and validity of the tasks undertaken. However, I am a firm proponent of the feasibility and efficacy of using psychological tests crossculturally. I have read and listened to many opinions to the contrary by established individuals both in anthropology and psychology. Such individuals for the most part, without personal experience, have made *a priori* judgments about feasibly or validity. We cannot comment here without lengthy argument on the varying degrees of cogency found in such arguments, or on the number of published misadventures and questionable conclusions helping critics make their case.

There are semantic problems that need special attention in translating from one language to another; suffice it to say that by using a scoring system such as ours we do not eliminate some problems with shade or nuances of meaning, but by focusing on well-defined categories and subcategories we do force consideration of the particular affective or instrumental meaning of a narrative which for the most part does not depend solely on individual words, but is a meaning that flows out of the whole continuity of the narrative as it is given by the subject.

There are numerous issues encountered in the gathering, recording and scoring of material, as well as in the exercise of judgment necessary in making the eventual interpretations. Any interpretation derived from emic material must first be carefully and objectively scored before any interpretation can be attempted, hence my emphasis on developing a scoring system for manifest content for the TAT or any other narrative material. Sustained training towards objectivity is necessary for those entering the field, and remains a persistent endeavor for any true scientist.

The question most frequently raised is how can one assume that card 1, a boy with a violin, or any of the other TAT cards, means the same everywhere? What we are comparing is not relative familiarity with a violin, or simply the relative number of stories of achievement that are usually evoked by this card. But, as we demonstrate in our chapter, given the scoring system we are advocating, we are considering the relative kind of self-orientation or various interpersonal concerns evoked among the subjects tested. We are interested in what comes to mind, alternative to or more salient to the individual than any possible achievement theme. We are not simply concerned with measuring relative sensitivity to achievement taken out of its total social context. We are not only interested in normative themes compared crossculturally, we are also interested in deviant or aberrant themes that show up in a particular group but are notably absent elsewhere.

Another question sometimes raised is whether it would not be better to adapt the pictures used to reflect differences in cultural atmosphere. In our initial study in Japan we created new cards and modified the features, clothing and room interiors of the Murray cards. In another study we used Japanese modifications of the Murray cards wherein the features, clothes and background interiors of the scenes were altered to appear more

Japanese on one part of our large-scale sample of 800 records. We experimented with card 1 by changing the features of the boy and taking away the violin and replacing it with a book. However, we subsequently determined by comparing these results with other parts of our sample using the original Murray cards that the Murray and Japanese modified cards produced no significant differences in our scoring of the content. Henceforth, we have used only the Murrey cards and some additional Japanese scenes not found in the Murray set itself.

Collaborative work as essential

Research with any device takes place in some specific social context. What is termed 'fieldwork' cannot be avoided by anyone practicing cultural psychology. Individual fieldwork is insurmountably difficult for various reasons, and eventually all fieldwork must become *collaborative* to avoid individual bias. I have almost never worked individually in the gathering of data. Crosscultural work is a form of collaborative fieldwork. One cannot simply gather material without some prior knowledge of the social and cultural environment of one's informants. Fieldwork takes time. It changes what you thought you knew before. One cannot rush in and out of any setting and assume comprehension. Fortunately today, every society is producing individuals with some training in the social sciences, but, one danger that sometimes appears, however, is that such individuals put aside their own social perceptions to take on too completely the point of view of the training they may have received from outside their society.

In working with Japanese psychologists and sociologists for many years I came to see the hegemony of American social science in Asia, but I also observed, happily, that critical re-evaluation is possible in some circumstances. Part of collaboration is seeing the same events from somewhat different perspectives and continually checking one's perspective with what others see. In actually hearing what is said, an insider picks up nuances that would escape an outsider.

Let me point out one incident I experienced working with Hiroshi Wagatsuma. In our interviews with the parents of delinquents in Tokyo, Wagatsuma picked up in several of the parents the inappropriately overpolite expressions used toward authorities, particularly the police. This was a form of Japanese irony in language which indicated disparagement, not obsequiousness. Once it was pointed out to me, I was forever sensitized to this usage. While in Nagoya we did a survey of opinions from various districts in the city including those inhabited by Burakumin, the ex-untouchables of Japan. I found myself to be more relaxed in visiting outcaste neighborhoods than were the majority members of our Japanese research team, and my relaxation had a salutary effect on them.

Many more illustrations could make the point that fieldwork involves the relative sensitivity of the interviewers if we are to gain sufficient

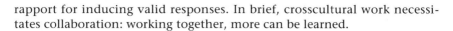

rapport for inducing valid responses. In brief, crosscultural work necessitates collaboration: working together, more can be learned.

The necessity of genuine rapport

Regardless of the setting, one must gain rapport to administer any form of testing. I have found no group that by and large, once rapport is established, could not enter the testing situation and understand the task presented, whether the telling of narratives to the TAT or creating perceived content for the Rorschach inkblots. The richness of imagination many distribute differently among groups, but among humans something can be evoked that indirectly reflects more about underlying attitudes or psychological functioning than the conscious material itself presents.

There are questionable studies reported in social science literature, however, that makes one wonder about the nature of the rapport achieved by particular examiners. Some groups are more suspicious than others. I have heard of notable failures to gain tests from Arab groups in the Mediterranean area, but I also worked with Horace Minor who had been acquainted long enough with the distrustful groups he came to test in Algeria to gain from them a willingness to be interviewed with the Rorschach tests as well as with direct expressions of opinion. In using a variety of tests in Japan in the 1950s, we found that certain of the administrators had great difficulty gaining valid results with particular tests such as eliciting drawings of human figures. Others, working in the same population had no such difficulty. Difficulty was not only in the task considered, but in the ability of particular administrators to overcome initial reluctance (in themselves as well as in their chosen subjects), and to gain sufficient relaxation for the test to be attempted.

Longitudinal potential

The TAT and other devices eliciting social narratives can be most helpful in documenting social change. They give a deeper, more immediate contextual view than can be documented by other devices such as social surveys. Indeed, in one of our earlier studies in the 1950s, previously reported, we were able to show that opinion surveys seemed to be in agreement with the acceptability of a free marriage. However, The TAT material suggested otherwise. Narratives about any free marriage tended to end in some form of failure or dramatic disaster. Attitudes about free as opposed to arranged marriage revealed in the TAT came closer to predicting the continuance of arranged marriages as the prevalent pattern of marriage for Japanese despite opinion surveys to the contrary.

The use of a device such as the TAT, or any psychological test, on samples *longitudinally* permits us by replication through time to gain some glimpse of changing attitudes that parallel other notable events occurring in society. Given lack of resources, such work is seldom attempted using the same population. It should be.

Commentary: using survey methodology in crosscultural political psychology
Walter G. Stephan and Kwok Leung

Crosscultural research into political processes is a daunting undertaking. It involves those methodological problems characteristic of most of the social sciences, as well as problems unique to cultural and crosscultural research on political psychology. One problem that is frequently underestimated is that political research is often highly sensitive. Participants in some countries may be reluctant to answer questions about political issues honestly, or refuse to answer them at all. For example, an Arab colleague told one of us that we could collaborate on any type of social research as long as it did not touch on politics or sex. In some countries the authorities may prohibit or 'discourage' research on political issues, and such governments may not gather or release information which might cast them in a negative light. The former Soviet Union was notorious for such policies.

Another characteristic problem of crosscultural political research is that the most appropriate participants are often the least accessible. For example, members of elites are much more difficult to access than the general population in most countries and almost impossible to access in some countries. The most relevant participant populations will usually be people who are eligible to be political actors, which in many countries means registered voters, and the social, economic, cultural, religious and political elites. However, members of the general public and sometimes even of elites often have differential eligibility to be political actors. This can mean that samples from different countries and cultures which are identical in socio-demographic terms may be politically non-comparable, and therefore produce quite different patterns of findings.

A particular difficulty in crosscultural political research is obtaining representative, random samples. While this is obviously desirable, it is often practically impossible. In such cases the best alternative strategy is to obtain equivalent samples in the different cultures, with the proviso that these samples must as noted above be not just socio-demographically but also politically equivalent. Having equivalent samples is particularly important if cultures are being directly compared using analysis of variance or similar inferential statistics, since socio-demographic equivalence of the samples increases the chances that observed differences in the results are due to culture alone (Leung, Lau and Lam, 1988).

A major issue in using questionnaires crossculturally is that of the equivalence of meanings across languages and cultural groups; and this problem looms larger the more sensitive the subject. For topics where evasions and euphemisms are common within a culture, the problems of creating crosscultural equivalence may become very difficult indeed. A second issue is that there may not be any widely accepted ways of measuring important crosscultural constructs; for example, the important and politically relevant cultural dimensions of tightness versus looseness (Triandis, 1994) and uncertainty avoidance (Hofstede,1980).

Faced with such difficulties, what are political psychology researchers to do? Several strategies seem useful. When studying theoretical processes involving cultures that differ along specified dimensions, it is important to use multiple cultures that are maximally different on those dimensions. Too often researchers have chosen two cultures that are thought to differ along a dimension such as individualism–collectivism, but have not measured the extent to which the cultures do actually differ along this dimension. A better research design would involve more than one culture representing each end of the continuum and ideally include multiple measures of individualism–collectivism. An entire range of techniques can and should be used to try to achieve equivalence of meanings across cultures, such as back translation, corrections for response bias, the use of multiple items and multiple measures, and related issues of instrument development and validation. It is often helpful to use focus groups to generate ways of phrasing sensitive issues in simple language to avoid biases. In short, researchers have to be sensitive about culture-specific issues to avoid the problem of imposed etics, that is the use of concepts and instruments that are not appropriate for a particular cultural group.

It is not impossible to do high quality crosscultural political psychology research, but it does require more persistence, ingenuity, subtlety, patience and resources than conducting similar research within cultures. However, the yield is definitely worth the effort, because without such efforts, we will never be able to develop anything resembling universal theories.

Notes

1. Renshon (personal communication) pointed out the parallels here with Greenstein's analysis of objections to the study of personality (1969, 33–62).
2. Another answer comes from Thompson, Ellis and Wildavsky (1990) who argue that culture is seen in distinct ways of life which they define in terms of Mary Douglas' grid-group analysis. Group refers to the extent to which an individual is incorporated into bounded units while grid refers to the degree to which a person's behaviors are circumscribed by externally imposed restrictions. Different individuals or states can, in their view, exhibit different degrees of each of the five combinations they identify over time, but viable social units, they argue are not characterized by the presence of only one culturally defined way of life. While I find much of their analysis of the interaction between values and social structure quite useful, it is less evident to me that making the way of life the unit of analysis provides a guideline that is easy for researchers to use.
3. Frankel (personal communication) suggests it is useful to think of culture as a reservoir from which each person dips a different portion, rather than as an invariant pattern.

4. Pye says that national character analyses tended to treat 'personality and culture as opposite sides of the same coin. Culture for them was the generalized personality of a people, in the sense that the modal personality of a people was their culture, and thus culture and personality were essentially identical factors shaping behavior' (1991, 494).

References

Barth, F. (ed) (1969) *Ethnic Groups and Boundaries: The Social Organization of Cultural Difference*, Boston: Little, Brown.

Berry, J., M. Segall and C. Kagitgitçibasi (eds) (1997) *Handbook of Cross-cultural Psychology*, Boston: Allyn & Bacon.

Billig, M. (1978) *Fascists: A Social Psychological View of the National Front*, London: Academic Press.

Bohannan, P. (1995) *How Culture Works*, New York: Free Press.

Brysk, A. (1995) '"Hearts and Minds": Bringing Symbolic Politics Back In', *Polity*, vol. 27, pp. 559–85.

Chagnon, N. A. (1992) *Yanomamo*, 4th edn, New York: Harcourt Brace Jovanovich.

D'Andrade, R. G. (1984) 'Cultural Meaning Systems', in R. A. Schweder and R. A. LeVine (eds), *Culture Theory: Essays on Mind, Self, and Emotion*, Cambridge: Cambridge University Press (pp. 88–119).

——— (1992) 'Schemas and Motivation', in R. G. D'Andrade *et al.* (eds), *Human Motives and Cultural Models*, Cambridge: Cambridge University Press (pp. 23–44).

Eckstein, H. F. (1988) 'A Culturalist Theory of Political Change', *American Political Science Review*, vol. 82, pp. 789–804.

Goode, J. and J. A. Schneider (1994) *Reshaping Ethnic and Racial Relations in Philadelphia: Immigrants in a Divided City*, Philadelphia: Temple University Press.

Greenstein, F. R. (1969) *Personality and Politics: Problems of Evidence, Inference, and Conceptualization*, Chicago: Markham.

Hofstede, G. (1980) *Culture's Consequences: International Differences in Work-related Values*, Beverly Hills, Cal.: Sage.

Horowitz, D. L. (1985) *Ethnic Groups in Conflict*, Berkeley and Los Angeles: University of California Press.

Huntington, S. (1993) 'The Clash of Civilizations', *Foreign Affairs*, pp. 22–49.

Johnson, F. A. (1993) *Dependency and Japanese Socialization: Psychoanalytic and Anthropological Investigations into Amae*, New York: New York University Press.

Kaplan, B. (ed.) (1961) *Studying Personality Cross-Culturally*, New York: Harper.

Leung, K., S. Lau and W. L. Lam (1998) 'Parenting Styles and Academic Achievement: A Cross-cultural Study', *Merrill-Palmer Quarterly*, vol. 44, pp. 157–72.

LeVine, R. A. (1984) 'Properties of Culture: An Ethnographic View', in R. A. Schweder and R. A. LeVine (eds), *Culture Theory: Essays on Mind, Self, and Emotion*, Cambridge: Cambridge University Press (pp. 67–87).

LeVine, R. A. and D. T. Campbell (1973) *Ethnocentrism: Theories of Conflict, Ethnic Attitudes, and Group Behavior*, New York: John Wiley.

Merelman, R. M. (1991) *Partial Visions: Culture and Politics in Britain, Canada, and the United States*, Madison: University of Wisconsin Press.

Minami, H. (1982) *Nihonteki jiga* [Japanese self], Tokyo: Iwanami Shoten.

Naroll, R. and R. Cohen (eds) (1970) *A Handbook of Method in Cultural Anthropology*, Garden City, NY: The Natural History Press.

Nishihira, S. (1987) *Yoron chosa ni yoru dojidaishi* [Contemporary history of public opinion polls], Tokyo: Brain Shuppan.

Pye, L. W. (1991) Political Culture Revisited', *Political Psychology*, vol. 12, pp. 487–508.

Ross, M. Howard and D. T. Campbell (1989) 'The Role of Ethnocentrism in Intergroup Conflict and Peacemaking: A Collaborative Integration of Theories', unpublished research proposal.

Stern, D. N. (1985) *The Interpersonal World of the Human Infant*, New York: Basic Books.

Strauss, C. (1992) 'Models and Motives', in R. G. D'Andrade *et al.* (eds), *Human Motives and Cultural Models*, Cambridge: Cambridge University Press (pp. 1–20).

Taylor, D. M. and F. M. Moghaddam (1987) *Theories of Intergroup Relations: International Social Psychological Perspectives*, New York: Praeger.

Thompson, M., R. Ellis and A. Wildavsky (1990) *Culture Theory*, Boulder: Westview Press.

Triandis, H. (1994) *Culture and Social Behaviour*, New York: McGraw-Hill.

Van de Vijver, F., and K. Leung (1997) *Methods and Data Analysis for Cross-cultural Research*, Beverly Hills, California: Sage.

Whiting, B. (1980) 'Culture and Social Behavior: A Model for the Development of Social Behavior', *Ethos*, vol. 8, pp. 95–116.

Yoneyama, T. (1971) *'Nihonteki shakai kankei ni okeru "kihongainen-gun"'* [Basic concepts in Japanese social relationship], *Kikan Jinruigaku*, vol. 2, pp. 56–76.

Part II

Culture, Psychology and Political Conflict

6
Culture, Personality and Prejudice

John Duckitt

The culture and personality approach emerged in the first half of the twentieth century as an ambitious attempt to understand the nexus between individual psychologies and their sociocultural contexts. While the approach produced some enormously influential work, such as Margaret Mead's classic studies of gender, by the 1960s the field of culture and personality had essentially come to an end. There were a number of reasons for this. Most fundamentally perhaps, as the first chapter in this volume suggests, the conceptual and methodological tools available at the time were far too primitive for such an ambitious task.

In this chapter I will argue that important conceptual and empirical advances have occurred in the latter half of this century that now make this enterprise feasible. Two developments have been particularly important, with both enabling critical conceptual linkages between individual and sociocultural context. First was the development within psychology of the concept of cognitive schema to describe how individuals represent knowledge in order to perceive, interpret and respond to the world, and its extension by psychological anthropologists (D'Andrade, 1992; Ross, 1993; Strauss, 1993) to that of cultural goal schema, or the cultural worldview, through which culturally derived interpretations of social reality generate shared motivational goals and responses.

The second important advance occurred in crosscultural psychology. It consisted of the elucidation and measurement of basic sociocultural value and attitude dimensions that differentiate cultures, and the demonstration that essentially similar dimensions differentiate individuals within cultures as well (Hofstede, 1980; Schwartz, 1996; Triandis, 1996). In this chapter I will show how these two developments enable linkages between cultural systems and their individual members, which cast new light on the sociocultural bases of social and collective behavior: in particular of conflict, prejudice and ethnocentrism.

The authoritarian personality

One of the culture and personality approach's most ambitious and flawed undertakings was the attempt to explain the emergence of Nazism in Europe after World War I, its virulent anti-semitism, and culmination in genocide and world war. Wilhelm Reich (1975) and Erich Fromm (1941) sketched in broad outline links between authoritarian societies, their family structure and socialization patterns, and an authoritarian personality structure. Their emphasis on the social and cultural dimension was embedded in a frank critique of capitalist culture and society.

In 1950 this approach was empirically developed and theoretically elaborated into the theory of the authoritarian personality (Adorno, Frenkel-Brunswick, Levinson and Sanford, 1950): an ambitious attempt to elucidate the psychological bases of ethnocentrism, generalized prejudice and fascism. These phenomena were seen as rooted in a particular complex of social attitudes, measured by the F-scale, and an underlying personality structure, which itself sprang from a particular family structure and kind of childhood socialization. However, the approach had already been narrowed. Influenced by the political, empirical and epistemological zeitgeist of America at the time, the theory now focused almost entirely on individual attitudes and personality, and their relation to family and socialization. The role of culture and society was, as Samelson (1993) has noted, 'passed over quickly in the introduction to disappear from sight afterward' (p. 36).

Initially the theory of the authoritarian personalty attracted enormous interest, but by the early 1960s it had collapsed completely under the weight of its numerous weaknesses. Particularly critical in this respect were the psychometric flaws of the F-scale, which largely derived from its lack of reliability and unidimensionality when acquiescent bias due to the all positive formulation of its items was controlled. As Altemeyer (1981) later showed, it appeared to be measuring several poorly related factors, and this was reflected in weak and inconsistent correlations with important validity criteria of authoritarianism.

Finally, in the early 1960s there was a marked shift in the prevailing zeitgeist: away from explanations of prejudice in terms of personalty towards explanations in terms of culture and society. The explanatory problem that now preoccupied social scientists was that of explaining prejudice in the American South and South Africa, where prejudice, as Pettigrew (1958) argued, seemed to be culturally and socially determined. Thus, a complete reversal had occurred from the 1950s when culture and society were ignored and prejudice explained in terms of personality, to the 1960s when personality based explanations were dismissed as inadequate. The original insight that both culture, society and personality could be dynamically interwoven and operate together to influence prejudice and ethnocentrism had been completely lost.

Altemeyer's authoritarian

In 1981 the theory of the authoritarian personality was revived by Bob Altemeyer. His research suggested that three of the original nine facets of authoritarianism described by Adorno *et al.* (1950), conventionalism, authoritarian aggression, and authoritarian submission, covaried strongly to form a unitary social attitude dimension, and developed his Right-wing Authoritarianism (RWA) scale to measure this dimension.

Subsequent research by Altemeyer (1981, 1988, 1998) and others (cf. Duckitt, 1994; Stone, Lederer and Christie, 1993) has shown that the RWA scale is a unidimensional and reliable psychometric measure of authoritarianism. It powerfully predicts a wide range of political, social, ideological and intergroup phenomena, as well as generalized prejudice to outgroups and minorities and chauvinistic ethnocentrism. Altemeyer's work has been massively important in reestablishing the idea of an authoritarian personality as a central explanatory construct in social and political psychology.

Altemeyer's approach did, however, have a cost: that of further narrowing the original construct (cf. also Samelson, 1993; Stone, Lederer and Christie, 1993). It completed the process of stripping away the social and cultural content of the original culture and personality view of authoritarianism. The view of authoritarianism as arising out of socially and culturally influenced socialization and family structure was completely discarded, and Altemeyer (1981, 1988) suggested that authoritarian attitudes were acquired through social learning in a purely individualistic manner, with the individual learning from significant others and from personal experiences.

Altemeyer's approach completed a narrowing of the original construct in a second way as well. Reich and Fromm had described an authoritarian personality or character type. Both the F-scale and the RWA scale consisted of items that did not refer to behavior or personality, but were statements of social attitude or belief (see also, for example, Feldman and Stenner, 1997; Goertzel, 1987; Stone, Lederer and Christie, 1993, 232). In both cases it was assumed that these relatively stable and enduring social attitudes and beliefs reflected a particular personality dimension, but this dimension was never directly measured, and merely inferred.

A second authoritarian

During the 1990s an important new perspective on group conflict and ethnocentrism, social dominance theory, was developed (Pratto, Sidanius, Stallworth and Malle, 1994; Sidanius and Pratto, 1993). Sidanius and Pratto suggested that societies minimize group conflict by promoting consensual ideologies that legitimize social and intergroup inequality and discrimination. Their theory centred on an individual difference dimension, Social Dominance Orientation (SDO), measured by their SDO scale, as a 'general attitudinal orientation toward intergroup relations, reflecting whether one generally prefers such relations to be equal, versus hierarchical' and the 'extent to which one desires that one's ingroup dominate and be superior to outgroups' (Pratto *et al.*, 1994, 742).

Research with the SDO scale has shown that it powerfully predicts essentially the same range of sociopolitical and collective phenomena that the RWA scale does. Both are particularly powerful predictors of generalized prejudice and ethnocentrism (Pratto *et al.*, 1994; Sidanius, Pratto and Bobo, 1994). Yet, the two scales appear largely independent of each other. Correlations between the two, while consistently positive, have generally been either non-significant or relatively weak (Altemeyer, 1998; McFarland, 1998; McFarland and Adelson, 1996; Pratto *et al.*, 1994). Second, the two scales show different patterns of correlation with other social and personal characteristics:

> Most notably, high SDOs are not particularly religious, but high RWAs usually are. Similarly, high scorers on the SDO scale do not claim to be benevolent, but high RWAs do. In contrast, social dominators have a wisp of hedonism about them, but authoritarians disavow such. The former do not need structure nor value conformity and traditions, but the latter do. Social dominators tend to be men; right-wing authoritarians do not. And quite strikingly, high SDOs do not see the world being nearly as dangerous as authoritarians do, nor do they appear to be nearly as self-righteous. (Altemeyer, 1998, 61)

And, third, a number of studies (Altemeyer, 1998; McFarland, 1998; McFarland and Adelson, 1996) have shown that the RWA and SDO scales predict generalized prejudice independently of each other, and together account for a very substantial proportion of the variance (for example, this ranged from 48 per cent to 58 per cent for Altemeyer's six studies). A large number of other measures of personality, social attitudes or values were included in these studies, but added only trivial amounts of explained variance.

Overall, these findings suggest that two relatively orthogonal social attitude dimensions independently predict a substantial proportion of the variance in generalized prejudice and ethnocentrism. Altemeyer (1998) has noted that the RWA and SDO scales both seem to relate to different sets of the original nine 'trait' clusters listed by Adorno *et al.* (1950) as descriptive of the authoritarian personality. He therefore suggested that underlying these two social attitude dimensions were two distinct kinds of authoritarian; the 'submissive' and the 'dominant'.

It should be noted that the empirical findings suggest that RWA and SDO are not perfectly orthogonal. While the typically positive correlations between them have been mostly nonsignificant and close to zero in student samples in North America, the correlations in older adult samples have been stronger, invariably significant, and weak to moderate in magnitude (cf. Altemeyer's, 1988, findings over six samples). Findings with New Zealand students have also shown a strong tendency for this correlation to increase with age (Duckitt and Wall, 1998). This suggests the possibility that these social attitudes may initially be acquired relatively independently during socialization, but later come to influence each other generating increasing consistency over time.

Sociopolitical attitudes and the two authoritarians

Typically the central factors or constructs that have emerged from many different empirical investigations of sociopolitical attitudes and value have shown strong similarities to the two 'authoritarian' dimensions. Thus, many investigations have reported that sociopolitical attitudes and values appear to be organized around two relatively orthogonal dimensions with one being an authoritarianism-social conservatism–openness/personal autonomy one and the other an egalitarianism/humanitarianism–economic conservatism/inequality one.

Eysenck (1954) found two orthogonal social attitude factors of radicalism–conservatism and toughness–tenderness, with the latter more appropriately re-labelled humane versus inhumane attitudes by Brown (1965). A number of investigations have found orthogonal dimensions of social conservatism and economic conservatism (with support for inequality the major component of the latter (for example, Hughes, 1975). Kerlinger's (1984) study of sociopolitical critical referents obtained orthogonal factors of conservatism (mainly Protestant ethic and traditionalism) and liberalism (mainly egalitarian and humanitarian). Tomkins (1964) similarly found orthogonal ideological belief dimensions of normativism and humanism. Katz and Hass (1988) found that socially conservative Protestant ethic beliefs were orthogonal to a humanitarianism-egalitarianism belief dimension. Forsyth (1980) studying ethical ideologies found two orthogonal dimensions of ethical ideology, relativism (endorsement of a relativistic as opposed to an absolutist moral code) and idealism (concern for the well-being of others and avoiding harm to them), with RWA and conservatism correlating very strongly with relativism but not at all with idealism (McHosky, 1996). Rokeach's (1973) classic investigation of values obtained two orthogonal terminal value dimensions, freedom and equality. Braithwaite (1994) found two independent sociopolitical value dimensions of national strength and order on the one hand, and international harmony and equality on the other hand. Ray (1985a) found that the ideological dimension of radical humanism was relatively uncorrelated with an F-scale measure of authoritarianism. Where available, correlations of these constructs with RWA and SDO have supported their conceptual similarity. For example, the correlation between RWA and various measures of social conservatism have been exceptionally high, suggesting that the two constructs are essentially isomorphic (Duckitt, 1993; McHosky, 1996; Ray, 1985b).

Other investigations, though also finding that sociopolitical attitudes were multidimensional with clear RWA-like and SDO-like factors represented, obtained on secondary analysis of the primary factors a single broadly bipolar left–right dimension (Wilson, 1970; Sidanius and Ekehammar, 1976). This seems to parallel those findings indicating that RWA and SDO may be significantly correlated with each other (for example, Altemeyer, 1998). Of the various measures and dimensions identified, RWA and SDO have been the most powerful and consistent predictors of politico-ideological and intergroup behavior, as McFarland (1998; McFarland and Adelson, 1996) and Altemeyer's (1998) recent findings have demonstrated. This may be because both are psychometrically highly reliable and unidimensional measures. It will also be suggested later that RWA and SDO, in relation to other measures of these dimensions, may be particularly direct social-attitude expressions of basic and universal motivational goals that powerfully influence social and collective behavior.

Cultural values and the two authoritarians

In the past two decades a number of important crosscultural investigations of cultural values have independently produced remarkably convergent findings with essentially similar basic value dimensions differentiating cultures and societies as entities, and individuals within societies (Fiske, Kitayama, Markus and Nisbett, 1998). The two most central cultural value dimensions that have emerged directly parallel the two 'authoritarian' social attitude dimensions.

The most methodologically sophisticated investigation has been that by Schwartz (1996) whose data from 54 countries and 44 000 participants indicated a circular ordering of value types around two basic dimensions: conservatism (conformity, security, tradition) versus openness (hedonism, self-direction, autonomy), and self-enhancement (hierarchy, power) versus self-transcendence (egalitarianism, social concern). These two pivotal dimensions were found to describe both individual differences within cultures or societies, and country differences – though the actual structuring of value types was simpler at the societal or global level (with seven value types for societies as opposed to ten for individuals). The correspondence between these two dimensions and the two 'authoritarian' social attitude dimensions has been empirically confirmed by Altemeyer's (1998) finding of generally powerful significant correlations between Schwartz's individual difference value types and RWA and SDO. The conservatism value types (traditionalism, conformity) correlated positively and the openness/ autonomy values (hedonism, self-direction) negatively with RWA, but were uncorrelated with SDO. The power-egalitarianism values correlated positively and negatively respectively with SDO, but not with RWA.

Similar dimensions have emerged from other investigations of cultural values. Hofstede's (1980) earlier investigation using only country level data identified four dimensions with close similarities to Schwartz's. The first two factors emerging in his research were individualism-collectivism (corresponding to Schwartz's conservatism versus openness) and power distance (the degree to which social inequality and hierarchy are accepted). Finally, Trompenaars and his coworkers (Trompenaars, 1993; Smith, Dugan and Trompenaars, 1996) used data from organizational employees from 43 countries. Their primary dimension opposed egalitarian commitment versus power and hierarchy, while their secondary dimension opposed a utilitarian orientation to others versus loyalty to one's ingroups.

These findings suggest two important conclusions. First, individual differences and differences between societies and cultures can be described and measured on essentially similar value/attitude dimensions. This seems to provide powerful empirically based conceptual tools for studying the linkages between cultures and individuals. Second, the two 'authoritarian' social value/attitude dimensions, shown to be pivotal in predicting collective and intergroup behavior in Western cultures, appear to have universal validity across cultures. Schwartz (1996) has argued that these values are universal because they directly express basic motivational goals that emerge out of universal requirements of human existence. Thus, the opposing goals of social control versus autonomy would be expressed in the authoritarian/conservatism value and attitude dimension, while the goals of power and dominance versus altruistic concern are expressed in the hierarchy/social dominance value and attitude.

The two dimensions as cultural goal-schemas

Schwartz's (1996) view that culturally general social value dimensions express universal motivational goals, may, however, be only a partial answer. Motivational explanations of psychological constructs or phenomena have been seriously criticized. Proponents of motives as explanatory constructs have been unable to satisfactorily specify a crossculturally valid set of universal motives, adequately identify them in behavior, and adequately account for situational variation in their expression (Mischel, 1968; Strauss, 1992). Psychological anthropologists, such as D'Andrade (1992), Strauss (1992) and Ross (1993), however, have provided a cultural analysis of motives that seems to largely resolve these problems.

According to D'Andrade (1992) motivational goals are not invariantly or universally present. They are activated or made salient for individuals by schema driven perceptions or interpretations of reality. As shared meaning systems, cultures provide their members with shared schemas about social reality that enable them to identify and interpret objects, events and situations. These interpretations of reality can instigate actions and act as goals. Highly generalized schema-based interpretations of reality, which

Ross (1993) terms cultural worldviews, will activate important motivational goals. D'Andrade refers to these together as 'cultural goal-schemas'. This analysis therefore suggests that certain motivational goals are culturally universal not because the motives themselves are invariant, but because they are triggered by certain interpretations of reality that reflect situations, experiences or events that are inevitable concomitants of human social existence.

The analysis suggests that the two opposing sets of motivational goals expressed in the two 'authoritarian' social attitude and value dimensions may be generated by the chronic accessibility of corresponding sociocultural schemas. In Ross's terminology, these schema-based beliefs about the nature of the social world are worldviews. There are clear indications from the empirical literature of what kinds of opposing schemas or worldviews seem to underlie the two 'authoritarian' dimensions. Thus, strong empirical relationships have been found between threat and authoritarianism for both societal and individual indicators (for example, Doty, Peterson and Winter, 1991; Sales, 1973; Sales and Friend, 1973). Most notably, Altemeyer (1988) has reported powerful positive correlations between his RWA scale and the perception of the social world as dangerous and threatening. A dangerous and threatening world therefore seems to be the schema or worldview that triggers the motivational goal of control expressed in the collectivist values of conformity, tradition and security, and in the authoritarian social attitudes of the RWA scale (for example, 'Obedience and respect for authority are the most important virtues children should learn'). A view of the world as safe, stable and secure on the other hand would activate the opposing nonauthoritarian motivational goal of autonomy expressed in the individualistic values of hedonism and stimulation (for example, the RWA item: 'Everyone should have their own lifestyle, religious beliefs, and sexual preferences, even if it makes them different from everyone else'). In D'Andrade's (1992) terminology these would be the opposing goal-schemas of threat–control and security–autonomy.

What kind of opposing worldviews would trigger the motivational goals of power-dominance versus altruistic social concern? A valuable clue comes from a Personal Power, Meanness and Dominance (PP-MAD) scale constructed by Altemeyer (1998), which correlated powerfully with SDO but not with RWA. The scale seems conceptually heterogeneous, since some items seem to tap personality and behavior, and others social attitudes and beliefs. A number of the social belief items, however, directly express a belief that the social world is a competitive jungle characterized by a ruthless and amoral Darwinian struggle for survival (for example, 'It's a dog eat dog world where you have to be ruthless at times'). Sidanius *et al.* (1994) in using a short alternative *ad hoc* version of the SDO scale also found that items expressing a ruthlessly competitive view of the world ('Winning is more important than how the game is played') scaled together with more typical SDO scale items expressing a belief in social inequality. Such a worldview permeated Hitler's speeches and writings. For example, in a speech at Kulmbach in 1928:

> The idea of struggle is as old as life itself, for life is only preserved because other living things perish through struggle...In this struggle, the stronger, the more able, win, while the less able, the weak, lose...It is not by the principles of humanity that man lives or is able to preserve himself above the animal world, but solely by the means of the most brutal struggle.
>
> (Cited in Bullock, 1962, 36)

This schema-based view of the world as a competitive jungle characterized by a ruthless, amoral struggle for resources and power in which might is right, power and winning are everything, and social relations are organized on the basis of dominance–submission, therefore unleashes the motivational goals of power and dominance. These goals are expressed in the values of power and hierarchy, and in the social attitudes expressed in high scores on the SDO scale: a belief in social inequality and a desire that one's group be superior and dominate others (Pratto *et al.*, 1994). The direct opposite would be a schema-based view of the world as one of cooperative harmony in which people care for, help and share with each other. This would trigger the altruistic motivational goals of helping and valuing others, and sharing with them as equals. Thus, this cultural goal schema of harmony-equality would be expressed in the social attitudes and values of egalitarianism and humanitarianism, reflected in low scores on the SDO scale.

The concept of cultural goal-schemas helps to explain why social attitudes can be generally stable over time, yet change quickly when social reality changes. Cultural socialization would make particular schemas highly accessible, generating stable interpretations of reality. But marked shifts in the nature of reality can activate different schemas, triggering new motivational goals that make different social attitudes and values salient. Altemeyer (1988), for example, found that when students were given scenarios in which a future Canadian society had experienced a long decline and was in economic and political crisis with massively escalating crime, unemployment, and terrorism, their RWA scores increased dramatically. This finding has a direct historical parallel with the catastrophic political and economic situation triggered by the great depression in 1930s Germany that catapulted the Nazis from political obscurity to state power in only a few years.

Cultural socialization of the two worldviews

How does cultural socialization make particular schemas highly accessible, and so generate stable worldviews? One possibility is that the content of worldviews are directly learned from others or from experience with the social world. Altemeyer (1981, 1988) has favoured this kind of social learning approach to the origins of RWA and reported a good deal of evidence for it. A second possibility, which could be simultaneously operative, is that certain culturally favoured socialization practices produce personality based dispositional tendencies in individuals to interpret and respond to the world in particular ways. This was the classical approach espoused by Adorno *et al.* (1950) whose evidence suggested that authoritarianism resulted from strict, punitive and harsh parental socialization.

Ross (1993) has recently reported powerful crosscultural evidence that suggests support for the second mechanism. He investigated the correlates of internal conflict and external warfare in 90 preindustrial societies. Internal and external conflict were highly associated with each other, and both were significantly and independently predicted by the degree to which two factorially distinct dimensions of socialization practices were characteristic of those societies: one dimension comprising strict, punitive versus permissive, indulgent socialization and the other affectionless versus affectionate (practices emphasising trust, generosity, affection, honesty and valuing children) socialization.

These two socialization dimensions seem to link directly to the two sets of cultural worldviews or goal-schemas identified. There is clear evidence indicating that strict, punitive socialization practices are favoured by persons with authoritarian social attitudes (Duckitt, 1994) suggesting that such practices are likely to be favoured in threat-control cultures. A link between strict, punitive socialization and personalities who are likely to adopt authoritarian social attitudes has been widely held (Adorno *et al.*, 1950; Milburn, Conrad, Sala and Carberry, 1995), though little attention has been given to identifying this kind of personality. However, a series of recent studies by Carolyn Wall and I, investigating the personality correlates of RWA and SDO found that the personality dimension of social conformity from Saucier's (1994) research consistently proved to be the most powerful predictor of RWA, but was unrelated to SDO (Duckitt and Wall, 1998).

Thus, the causal sequence that is suggested is that threat-control or collectivist cultures, characterized by authoritarian and conservative social values and attitudes, will favour strict, punitive socialization practices which tend to produce persons high on social conformity. This personality through a lowered tolerance of deviance and an attachment to conventional society will tend to be more likely to perceive threats to society, and see the world as dangerous and threatening. This personal worldview would also be directly transmitted and learned from the cultural worldview as well. Both personality and worldview give rise to the motivational goal of social control which is expressed in conservative values and authoritarian social attitudes.

The second socialization dimension, affectionless versus affectionate (practices emphasising trust, generosity, affection, honesty, valuing children and others: see Ross, 1993, 208) socialization, links clearly with the competitive-jungle versus cooperative-harmony worldview dimension. Competitive-dominance cultures seem likely to be relatively low in affectionate socialization practices. Such practices should tend to produce personalities who are interpersonally hard, tough, unfeeling, cynical, and low in trust, empathy, affection and generosity: that is tough as opposed to tendermindedness.

Both Goertzel (1987) and Eysenck (1954) have previously provided evidence that the personality dimension of tough versus tendermindedness was an important predictor of sociopolitical attitudes. The personality items contained in Altemeyer's PP-MAD scale, which correlated strongly with SDO but not with RWA, tend to express an extreme toughmindedness and rejection of tendermindedness and scaled together with items expressing a view of the world as a competitive jungle. A lack of empathy has been found to be related to both prejudice (McFarland, 1977) and the SDO scale (Pratto *et al.*, 1994). Finally, the research by Carolyn Wall and I investigating the personality bases of RWA and SDO found that personality trait ratings of tough versus tendermindedness derived from Goertzel (1987) and Saucier's (1994) measures were significantly correlated with SDO but not RWA in three different samples (Duckitt and Wall, 1998).

Thus, competitive-dominance culture through affectionless socialization will tend to produce toughminded personalities and a view of the world as a competitive jungle. These then evoke motivational goals of power and dominance which find expression in anti-egalitarian social values and attitudes. Overall, this suggests two distinct causal loops of psycho-cultural variables from culture to individual and back to culture that underlie and build in a generalized propensity to prejudice and ethnocentrism. In both these loops, which are depicted in Table 6.1, particular cultural dimensions use direct transmission and socialization to shape particular personalities and worldviews in individuals, these in turn make salient motivational goals that are then expressed in social values and attitudes. By their socially shared nature these values and attitudes then recreate the cultural pattern. These 'authoritarian' values and attitudes will then be the most direct, proximal causes of a generalized propensity to hold prejudiced and ethnocentric attitudes for both individuals and sociocultural groups.

A causal model of personality and prejudice

The theoretical framework summarized in Table 6.1 directly implies a more limited causal model of how individual differences in prejudice and ethnocentrism are determined. Shown in diagrammatic form. Each of the two personality dimensions, social conformity and toughmindedness, impact

Table 6.1 Two sets of psychocultural dimensions underlying prejudice and ethnocentrism, with causality running from left (culture) to right (individual differences) and then looping back (culture)

Culture	Socialization	Personality	Worldview	Motivational goal	Social attitudes
Collectivist vs Individualist	Punitive vs Indulgent	Conformity vs Autonomy	Threatening vs Safe/secure	Control vs Autonomy	Authoritarian vs Autonomy
Hierarchy/Power distance vs Equality/Social concern	Affectionless vs Affectionate	Toughminded vs Tenderminded	Competitive-jungle vs Cooperative-harmony	Power/dominance vs Altruism	Social dominance vs Egalitarian-humanism

on the two worldviews, beliefs in a dangerous and competitive-jungle world respectively, both of which then impact on the social attitudes of RWA and SDO, which in turn impact on prejudiced attitudes to outgroups and ethnocentric ingroup overvaluation. The model leaves open the possibility that there might also be direct paths from personality and worldview to in- and outgroup attitudes in addition to their primary effects mediated through social attitudes.

I conducted a partial test of this model using a sample of undergraduate students at Auckland University. The test is only partial because no measure of the competitive-jungle worldview was included so paths to and from it could not be tested. However, measures of all the other variables were available so that all other paths could be tested as well as the overall fit of the model to the data. The two personality variables were assessed using trait adjective rating scales: 16 items for social conformity (with pro-trait adjectives such as conforming, conventional, obedient; and contrait adjectives such as rebellious, unpredictable, unconventional) and 14 tough-mindedness items (with pro-trait adjectives such as hard, ruthless, toughminded; and contrait adjectives such as compassionate, caring, tenderminded). Worldview was assessed by Altemeyer's Dangerous World Scale. Twenty and 10-item shortened versions of the RWA and SDO scales were used (with items randomly sampled from the full scales, to give equal numbers of pro- and contrait items), as well as a set of scales to measure attitudes to four New Zealand ethnic groups: the majority Pakeha group (persons of European origin comprising approximately 80 per cent of the population) and the three main minorities, Maori, Pacific Islanders and Asians. The data analyzed were from the 183 Pakeha-European participants for whom there were fully completed questionnaires. Because attitudes to the three minority groups correlated strongly with each other, these scores were standardized and summed to give a single anti-minority attitudes score. The attitude to Pakeha scale then provided the measure of pro-ingroup attitudes.

All the measures had been used previously in a series of studies and had shown excellent reliabilities, as they did here (Duckitt and Wall, 1998). The data were analyzed using the powerful multivariate LISREL procedure to estimate path coefficients and the overall goodness of fit of the model to the data. The fit of the basic model shown in Figure 6.1, in which personality and worldview influence social attitudes which in turn then influence in- and outgroup attitudes, was compared with one in which personality and worldview had additional direct effects on in- and outgroup attitudes as well. The fit indices were acceptable for the first model with only mediating effects, but markedly better indicating very close fit for the second model which included direct impacts on group attitudes over and above the mediated effects (Model $Chi^2 = 1.61$, $df = 6$, $p = .95$; RMSEA = 0; GFI = 1.00). Figure 6.2 shows the standardized path coefficients obtained for this model, all of which were statistically significant.

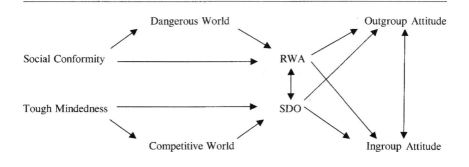

Figure 6.1.   A causal model of the impact of personality and worldview on the two authoritarian social attitude dimensions, RWA and SDO, and on prejudice and ethnocentrism.

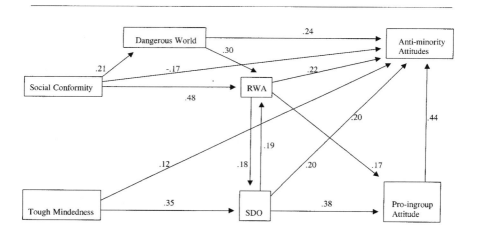

Figure 6.2.   Personality, social attitudes and prejudice: LISREL standardized maximum likelihood coefficients (all coefficients significant). Model chi^2 = 1.61, df = 6, p = .95. RMSEA = 0, GFI = 1.00.

Social conformity and toughmindedness impacted as expected on RWA and SDO respectively, and social conformity also influenced Dangerous World beliefs, which impacted significantly on RWA. Both RWA and SDO, which had weak reciprocal causal effects on each other, influenced pro-ingroup and anti-minority attitudes, with pro-ingroup attitudes also having a strong influence on anti-minority attitudes. A model with a reciprocal causal impact of anti-minority attitudes on ingroup attitudes was also tested but the path was nonsignificant, though the overall fit of the model was equivalently good. Thus the basic pattern of interrelationships that were expected theoretically was strongly supported. The weakest predicted effect was that of social conformity on dangerous world beliefs ($R^2 = .04$), which suggested that much of the variance in dangerous world beliefs might be derived from social learning of that worldview from significant others, education, the media and personal experiences.

In addition to the explicitly predicted relationships, the two personality variables and dangerous world beliefs also had direct causal impacts on anti-minority attitudes. This effect was quite weak in the case of tough-mindedness (though deleting the path markedly weakened the fit of the model) and moderate in magnitude for Dangerous World with both having the expected effect of increasing prejudice. The surprising finding was that social conformity had a weak direct though clearly significant *negative* effect on prejudice. This indicates two directly opposing effects on anti-minority prejudice for social conformity in this sample. First, social conformity had the expected effect of increasing prejudice indirectly through increasing RWA and Dangerous World (these mediated paths totalled to an overall indirect effect of .23). Second, it had the slightly weaker direct impact of reducing prejudice. The latter effect, though unexpected, is easily explicable in terms of the strong conventional norms of nonprejudice against ethnic minorities characterizing mainstream New Zealand society, and particularly amongst students. While there is a risk of overinterpretation here because this direct effect was not strong, this finding may have implications for the extensively studied finding of ambivalence in Euro-Americans attitudes towards African-Americans.

Overall, the model accounted for a substantial proportion of the variance in anti-minority prejudice ($R^2 = .58$) and in RWA ($R^2 = .44$). In the case of SDO, the proportion of variance accounted for was much lower ($R^2 = .22$), but this could well have been due to the absence of a measure of the competitive-jungle worldview. Data are currently being collected that includes such a measure and which will test the model in an entirely different population. These preliminary findings, therefore, suggest good support for the personality-prejudice model shown in Figures 6.1 and 6.2, and therefore also for the broader theoretical framework summarized in Table 6.1.

Cultures of prejudice

According to the model outlined in Table 6.1, particular cultural goal-schemas or worldviews are central to the interrelated patterns of psychocultural variables underlying prejudice and ethnocentrism, and quite probably a broader range of sociopolitical, collective and ideological phenomena as well. The research described in the previous section suggests that the framework is useful for explaining individual differences in prejudice and ethnocentrism. It should also be able to explain such differences between cultures and societies. Societies high on the threat-control or competitive-dominance goal-schemas or worldviews should be more prone to prejudice, ethnocentrism and conflict. Cultures high on both should be particularly so.

Unfortunately there is little directly relevant research, but what there is does seem broadly confirmatory. Meloen's world wide cross national study reported in this volume suggested that national levels of collectivism and power distance had powerful effects on authoritarian attitudes and authoritarian government in those societies, and on their involvement in violent conflicts. Ross's (1993) findings from 90 preindustrial societies, which have already been described, is also confirmatory, though Ross did not directly examine cultural values, attitudes, and worldviews, but inferred these very plausibly from dominant socialization practices. Bonta (1997) studying completely peaceful societies, in which aggression, violence and warfare are almost totally absent, found their primary distinguishing characteristic was a powerful normative emphasis on cooperation, with any kind of competitiveness being completely eschewed.

There is also ethnographic evidence indicating that cultures or subcultures particularly predisposed to ethnocentrism, conflict and violence are characterized by one or both the worldviews. One of the most prominent features of violent subcultures seems to be a view of the world as a competitive jungle and the associated goals of power, toughness and dominance. This tends to be the central feature of cultures of honor and respect, machismo and warrior cultures. It has been well documented in the American South by Nisbett and Cohen (1996), in the post-Vietnam paramilitary subcultures of America (Gibson, 1994), in fascist movements (Billig, 1978), and in violent underclass and gang subcultures (Toch, 1992). McNeil (1961, cited in Van der Dennen, 1987) describing his experiences in living with a group of 70 aggressive and anti-social boys noted how at first contact they immediately began a pattern of militant interpersonal and intergroup probing to establish an aggressive pecking order of dominance and submission. Toch (1992) and others (Staub, 1996), have also described such cultures of power, toughness and machismo, in which defence of ones honor and the establishment of dominance becomes a central value. In such cultures the social world is sharply divided into those who are strong and superior and those who are weak and inferior, and the dominant affect towards those classified as inferior is that of derogation and contempt, and the outcome, their dehumanization.

In many respects threat-control cultures may be quite different. Several powerful themes in authoritarian belief systems that contribute to the difference are fundamentalist religiosity, moral self-righteousness, and an intolerance of nonconformity and deviance (Altemeyer, 1988). These were salient characteristics of the White Afrikaner culture that gave rise to

Apartheid in South Africa. MacCrone (1937) has described how this culture was originally forged in the South African frontier situation. Once the Dutch colonists had spread from the original settlement at the Cape to the interior, the frontier situation and an enduring conflict with the more numerous indigenous black people and the more powerful force of British colonialism developed. The essential characteristics of the frontier situation were isolation, danger, war, and extreme insecurity. This created a society characterized by an intense group consciousness, an emphasis on group cohesion, conservatism, and conformity, and a pervasive ethnocentrism. In the atmosphere of omnipresent threat, intensely felt religious beliefs fused with racial distinctions, and the dichotomy between Christian and heathen, between good and evil, became the dichotomy between white and black. In threat-control cultures such as this, the distinction between ingroup and outgroup is between those who are seen as morally decent, normal and good and those who are bad, deviant and immoral. The affective dynamic is fear, and the outcome, moral exclusion.

In conclusion, therefore, prejudice, ethnocentrism, and violent conflict seem to be driven by two sets of conceptually distinct personal and cultural dynamics. These dynamics have their origins in particular worldviews that generate collective goals and come to be expressed in shared values and social attitudes. In terms of their underlying emotional dynamic, these are the cultures of fear and of contempt.

References

Adorno, T., E. Frenkel-Brunswick, D. Levinson, and N. Sanford (1950) *The Authoritarian Personality*, New York: Harper.

Altemeyer, B. (1998) 'The Other "Authoritarian Personality"', *Advances in Experimental Social Psychology*, vol. 30, pp. 47–92.

Altemeyer, B. (1981) *Right-wing Authoritarianism*, Winnipeg, Canada: University of Manitoba Press.

Altemeyer, B. (1988) *Enemies of Freedom: Understanding Right-Wing Authoritarianism*, Jossey-Bass.

Billig, M. (1978) *Fascists: A Social Psychological View of the National Front*, London: Academic.

Bonta, B. (1997) 'Cooperation and Competition in Peaceful Societies', *Psychological Bulletin*, vol. 121, pp. 299–320.

Braithwaite, V. (1994) 'Beyond Rokeach's Equality-Freedom Model: Two-Dimensional Values in a One-Dimensional World', *Journal of Social Issues*, vol. 50, pp. 67–94.

Brown, R. (1965) *Social Psychology*, New York: Free Press.

Bullock, A. (1962) *Hitler: a Study In Tyranny*, Harmondsworth, England: Pelican.

D'Andrade, R. (1992) 'Schemas and Motivation', in R. D'Andrade and C. Strauss (eds.), *Human Motives and Cultural Models*, Cambridge: Cambridge University Press (pp. 23–44).

Doty, R., B. Peterson and D. Winter (1991) 'Threat and Authoritarianism in the United States, 1978–1987', *Journal of Personality and Social Psychology*, vol. 61, pp. 629–40.

Duckitt, J. (1993) 'Right-wing Authoritarianism among White South African Students: Its Measurement and Correlates', *Journal of Social Psychology*, vol. 133, pp. 553–63.

Duckitt, J. (1994). *The Social Psychology of Prejudice*, New York: Praeger.

Duckitt, J. and Wall, C. (1998) *Personality and Prejudice*, Unpublished manuscript.

Eysenck, H. (1954) *The Psychology of Politics*, London: Routledge and Keagan Paul.

Feldman, S. and Stenner, K. (1997) 'Perceived Threat and Authoritarianism', *Political Psychology*, vol. 18, pp. 741–70.

Fiske, A., S. Kitayama, H. Markus and R. Nisbett, (1998) 'The Cultural Matrix of Social Psychology', in D. Gilbert, S. Fiske, and G. Lindzey (eds.), *The Handbook of Social Psychology* (4th edn, vol. 2, pp. 915–81) New York: McGraw-Hill.

Forsyth, D. (1980) 'A Taxonomy of Ethical Ideologies', *Journal of Personality and Social Psychology*, vol. 39, pp. 175–84.

Fromm, E. (1941) *Escape From Freedom*, New York: Rinehart.

Gibson, J. (1994) *Warrior Dreams: Paramilitary Culture in Post-Vietnam*, New York: Hill and Wang.

Goertzel, T. (1987) 'Authoritarianism of Personality and Political Attitudes', *Journal of Social Psychology*, vol. 127, pp. 7–18.

Hofstede, G. (1980) *Culture's Consequences*, Beverly Hills, CA: Sage.

Hughes, A. (1975) *Psychology and the Political Experience*, Cambridge: Cambridge University Press.

Katz, I. and Hass, R. (1988) 'Racial Ambivalence and American Value Conflict: Correlational and Priming Studies of Dual Cognitive Structures'. *Journal of Personality and Social Psychology*, vol. 55, pp. 893–905.

Kerlinger, F. (1984) *Liberalism and Conservatism: the Nature and Structure of Social Attitudes*, Hillsdale, NJ: Erlbaum.

MacCrone, I. (1937) *Race Attitudes in South Africa*, London: Oxford University Press.

McFarland, S. (1998) *Toward a Typology of Prejudiced Persons*, paper presented at the annual meeting of the International Society of Political Psychology, Montreal, Canada.

McFarland, S. and S. Adelson (1996) *An Omnibus Study of Personality, Values and Prejudice*, paper presented at the annual meeting of the International Society of Political Psychology, Vancouver, Canada.

McHosky, J. (1996) 'Authoritarianism and Ethical Ideology', *Journal of Social Psychology*, vol. 138, pp. 709–17.

Milburn, M., S. Conrad, F. Sala, and S. Carberry (1995) 'Childhood Punishment, Denial, and Political Attitudes', *Political Psychology*, vol. 16, pp. 447–78.

Mischel, W. (1968) *Personality and Assessment*. New York: Wiley.

Nisbett, R. and D. Cohen (1996) *Culture of Honor: the Psychology of Violence in the South*, Boulder, Colorado: Westview.

Pettigrew, T. (1958) 'Personality and Sociocultural Factors in Intergroup Attitudes: a Cross-National Comparison', *Journal of Conflict Resolution*, vol. 2, pp. 29–42.

Pratto, F., J. Sidanius, L. Stallworth and B. Malle (1994) 'Social Dominance Orientation: A Personality Variable Predicting Social and Political Attitudes', *Journal of Personality and Social Psychology*, vol. 67, pp. 741–63.

Ray, J. (1985a) 'Authoritarianism of the Left Revisited', *Personality and Individual Differences*, vol. 6, pp. 271–72.

Ray, J. (1985b) 'Defective Validity in the Altemeyer Authoritarianism Scale', *Journal of Social Psychology*, vol. 125, pp. 271–72.

Reich, W. (1975) *The Mass Psychology of Fascism*, Harmondsworth, England: Penguin.

Rokeach, M. (1973) *The Nature of Human Values*, New York: Free Press.

Ross, M. (1993) *The Culture of Conflict*. New Haven: Yale University Press.

Sales, S. (1973) 'Threat as a Factor in Authoritarianism', *Journal of Personality and Social Psychology*, vol. 28, pp. 44–57.

Sales, S. and K. Friend (1973) 'Success and Failure as Determinants of Level of Authoritarianism', *Behavioral Science*, vol. 18, pp. 163–72.

Samelson, F. (1993) 'The Authoritarian Character From Berlin to Berkeley and Beyond: the Odyssey of a Problem', in W. Stone, G. Lederer and R. Christie (eds.), *Strength and Weakness: The Authoritarian Personality Today*, New York: Springer (pp. 22–46).

Saucier, G. (1994) 'Separating Description and Evaluation in the Structure of Personality Attributes', *Journal of Personality and Social Psychology*, vol. 66, pp. 141–54.

Schwartz, S. (1996) 'Value Priorities and Behavior: Applying a Theory of Integrated Value Systems', in C. Seligman, J. Olson and M. Zanna (eds.), *The Psychology of Values: the Ontario Symposium*, vol. 8, pp. 1–24.

Sidanius, J. and Ekehammar, B. (1976) 'Cognitive Functioning and Socio-Political Ideology', *Scandinavian Journal of Psychology*, vol. 17, pp. 205–216.

Sidanius, J. and F. Pratto, (1993) 'The Dynamics of Social Dominance and the Inevitability of Oppression', in P. Sniderman and P. Tetlock (eds.), *Prejudice, Politics, and Race in America Today*, pp. 173–211. Stanford, CA: Stanford University Press.

Sidanius, J., F. Pratto, and L. Bobo (1994) 'Social Dominance Orientation and the Political Psychology of Gender: a Case of Invariance?' *Journal of Personality and Social Psychology*, vol. 67, pp. 998–1011.

Smith, P., S. Dugan and F. Trompenaars (1996) 'National Culture and Values of Organizational Employees: a Dimensional Analysis Across 43 Nations', *Journal of Cross-Cultural Psychology*, vol. 27, pp. 231–64.

Staub, E. (1996) 'Cultural-Societal Roots of Violence', *American Psychologist*, vol. 51, pp. 117–32.

Stone, W., G. Lederer, and R. Christie (1993) 'The Status of Authoritarianism', in W. Stone, G. Lederer, and R. Christie (eds.), *Strength and Weakness: the Authoritarian Personality Today*, New York: Springer (pp. 229–245).

Strauss, C. (1993) 'Models and Motives', in R. D'Andrade and C. Strauss (eds.), *Human Motives And Cultural Models* Cambridge: Cambridge University Press (pp. 1–20).

Toch, H. (1992) *Violent Men: an Inquiry into the Psychology of Violence*, Washington, D.C.: APA.

Tomkins, S. (1964) *The Polarity Scale*. New York: Springer.

Triandis, H. (1996) 'The Psychological Measurement of Cultural Syndromes', *American Psychologist*, vol. 51, pp. 407–15.

Trompenaars, F. (1993) *Riding the Waves of Culture*. London: Brealey.

Van der Dennen, J. (1987) 'Ethnocentrism and Ingroup-Outgroup Differentiation', in V. Reynolds, V. Falger and I. Vine (eds.), *The Sociobiology of Ethnocentrism*, London And Sydney: Croom Helm.

Wilson, G. (1970) 'Is There a General Factor in Social Attitudes? Evidence From a Factor Analysis of the Conservatism Scale', *British Journal of Social and Clinical Psychology*, vol. 9, pp. 101–07.

7
The Political Culture of State Authoritarianism

Jos D. Meloen[1]

In early May 1994, a small, but surprising item appeared in the world news: an 18-year-old American was arrested in Singapore for a minor offence and sentenced to six cane strokes. This shocked many Westerners, and President Clinton made three requests for leniency. Ultimately the Singapore government did not want to seem disrespectful to the American president, and the sentence was reduced to four strokes. In this prosperous Asian community corporal punishment is not uncommon with some 1000 convicted persons receiving cane strokes each year. In Western countries this is generally considered an infringement of human rights. A Singaporean official tried to explain: 'We in Asia consider the society as a whole more important than the individual. For us tough punishment is quite common, but not for you'.

This incident illustrates the ways in which political life and institutions can be influenced by the prevailing culture. What democracy is or should be, seems to depend on the culture one is part of, or, perhaps more appropriately, the political culture. The incident shows an important difference between Asian and Western democracies. In the West physical punishment has usually been long abandoned. In some countries subservience to the powerful and 'tough' measures are common, while in others egalitarianism and human rights are integral aspects of political life. Such variations can be viewed as basic to the concept of political culture. In this chapter I will explore the relationship of psychology, culture and politics to authoritarian state systems and authoritarian political cultures.

The concept of state authoritarianism

Psychologists have typically viewed the core issue in understanding authoritarianism in terms of authoritarian attitudes (or personalities) that lead

1 I would like to thank John Duckitt (University of Auckland, New Zealand) and Stanley Renshon (City University of New York) for their extensive, useful and professional comments that helped shape this manuscript.

populations to accept and sometimes even to support dictatorial and unde-mocratic rule. Political scientists on the other hand have analyzed the problem in terms of particular kinds of undemocratic government. Thus, most social scientists have defined the core of the problem of authoritar-ianism within their own discipline. As a result the study of authoritarian-ism has been defined in multiple, often unrelated, and fragmented ways. In this chapter the core of the problem of authoritarianism is redefined in terms of organized state policies and practices that violate human political and civil rights, that is, state authoritarianism. This follows the approach taken by several of the earliest investigators of the issue, such as Reich (1933), Brooks (1935) and Fromm (1941).

Authoritarian political culture

Studies of authoritarian regimes seem to agree on several key elements of authoritarianism (see for example Fromm 1941; Brooks, 1935; Brooker, 1995), that:

1. there is a set of rather extreme ideas, of an ideological (political, some-times religious) nature, that serve as absolute guidelines;
2. there is an organization devoted to these ideas; and
3. there are extreme actions advocated or undertaken for the propagation of these ideas.

Authoritarian ideas

Twentieth century authoritarian regimes and dictatorships have been con-sidered 'new' because of the primary role that ideology has often played in them (Brooker, 1995; Brooks, 1935). This was most clearly the case for fascism, nazism and communism, but also for fundamentalist and extreme nationalist ideologies. A set of 'coherent' political ideas or ideology pro-vided absolute guidelines for the party, state and people to proceed toward the 'glorious' goals of the regime. These related ideas were usually transmit-ted by a monolithic system of propaganda, so that everyone would believe the same absolute 'truths'. In this way these regimes could claim to repre-sent the people without being held accountable by a democratic electoral system.

Once formalized into 'Mein Kampfs' or 'little red books', the ideology turns into a political culture of psychological consequences. These conse-quences have been called *authoritarian conventionalism* in the case of support for right-wing authoritarian regimes (Adorno, Frenkel-Brunswik, Levinson and Sanford, 1950; Altemeyer, 1988), and core authoritarianism or dogma-tism in the case of both left and right-wing extremism (Rokeach, 1960). It represents a tendency to conform to the ideology or party line, and more broadly even, as Altemeyer (1988) has suggested, conformity to con-ventional religious and sexual beliefs and mores. The dominant ideology is portrayed as the epitome of conventional and traditional normality and is therefore intolerant of any competing or differing ideas.

Authoritarian organization

Authoritarian ideas need an organization to gain political power. Such ideas may remain dormant for long periods, nurtured and kept alive in small brotherhoods, secret societies and political fringe parties (Billig, 1978), and then rise to power under certain circumstances if, and only if, they acquire or develop an effective organization. Over time, authoritarian organizations have developed one prominent organizational principle: the authoritarian hierarchy, which in the case of fascism has been called the 'fuehrer principle' (leadership principle). Orders go from top to bottom without criticism from below.

In this way a political culture of blind obedience to the leader, party and state develops. Absolute loyalty and blind obedience are expected from the lower ranks in the organization. This hierarchical attitude becomes omnipresent, existing between the leader and the party, between the party and the state, and between the party and the citizens. It is this vertical and 'top-down' hierarchy of authority that seems fundamental to the concept of authoritarianism. It differs from democratic and even military hierarchy in its hostility towards any criticism from below, even when this would be in the interests of the organization. This hierarchical orientation has been called *authoritarian submission* (Adorno *et al.*, 1950; Altemeyer, 1988).

Authoritarian actions

There seems to be considerable agreement on what constitutes the most prominent feature of authoritarian regimes: the reign of terror. From the 'Republics of Fear' (Al-Khalil, 1989) to the Gulags and concentration camps of the totalitarian states of the twentieth century, terrorizing any possible enemy of the leader, party, or state, has been a central weapon to crush opposition and remain in power. The definition of 'the enemy' is often so vague that almost anyone could fear arrest, punishment, abuse, torture and even death.

A political culture of fear is probably the most characteristic feature of authoritarian regimes and dictatorships. It inevitably pervades the entire society and its institutions. The tendency to harshly punish any – presumed – violator has been called *authoritarian aggression* (Adorno *et al.*, 1950; Altemeyer, 1988). While the victims are usually the political opposition, they may often be nonpolitical, such as ethnic and national minorities. This is particularly the case when the dominant ideology involves racist or nationalist ideas, while for communist ideology certain social groups or classes are targeted and defined as 'enemies of the people'.

State authoritarianism

The main political and psychological components of state authoritarianism are therefore: (i) an authoritarian political ideology or belief system providing and reinforcing authoritarian conventional beliefs; (ii) an authoritarian organizational hierarchy conditioning people into authoritarian submission, and (iii) the use of terror in order to stay in power as an expression of authoritarian aggression. The emphasis here is on the state, as this is the main instrument through which authoritarian powers acquire 'legal' force.

State authoritarianism can therefore be formally defined as *the active organization of the state by an antidemocratic group (party, military faction, ideological extremists) characterized by three basic features: an authoritarian state ideology, an authoritarian hierarchy, and the use of force and terror by the state.* A political culture of authoritarianism is associated with state authoritarianism, and creates social and cultural conditions favorable for the establishment and maintenance of dictatorships. Possible constituents of this political culture, which are to be empirically investigated later in this chapter, are the formal political system, a traditional family pattern, a cultural pattern of hierarchical authority and power relations in society, and authoritarian attitudes among the people.

State authoritarianism is here viewed not simply as the absence of political and civil liberties (as is primarily the case for the Freedom House rating), but in terms of the actual organization and behavior of authoritarian regimes. While authoritarian systems are usually characterized by a lack of liberties and democracy, the denial of liberty and democracy serves a purpose: that of maintaining power. Thus, formal liberties may be tolerated and elections even held (though often predictably biased or rigged) as long as they do not threaten the regime's hold on political power. Therefore, it is not sufficient to study the legal and formal characteristics and behavior of these regimes. To do so would leave unrecognized many covert but well-organized acts (for example, 'final solutions', disappearances, secret death squads). For this reason the conception of state authoritarianism focuses on the actual behavior of states, and not just their formal and legal characteristics and institutions.

State authoritarianism in the world

A measure of state authoritarianism

In recent years, reliable data and country ratings have become available from international bodies, such as the United Nations, that make possible the development of a comprehensive measure of state authoritarianism that could be used for international comparisons. On the basis of the theoretical conceptualization presented here, a number of published empirical indicators were selected to provide an index of state authoritarianism (see also Meloen, 1996; Kidron and Segal, 1991).

Authoritarian beliefs

Three indicators represent authoritarian beliefs and morals, and the degree to which authoritarian norms, values, and attitudes are prescribed by the state, party or ruling class:

1. Imposing state beliefs or *ideology* is central to authoritarian rule. This was assessed by a four-point rating ranging from 'all beliefs being tolerated', to 'one belief being imposed, while repressing all the other ones'.
2. A repressive and intolerant official attitude to *homosexuality* is almost always present in authoritarian morality. A four-point indicator was used which ranged from 'lawful and tolerated' to 'unlawful and repressed'.
3. The legal status of *abortion* is also typically associated with authoritarianism. This indicator was rated as 'being legal on request' through 'being restricted', and 'most restricted' to 'only possible to save the life of the mother'.

Authoritarian submission

A further four indicators represent the suppression of criticism and opposition, and the imposition of authoritarian hierarchy and leadership.

4. The *suppression* by the state of deviation from official social norms is assessed by a five-point indicator ranging from 'affirmative action' through 'discouragement' to 'suppression'.
5. *Censorship* is the policy most widely used to curb anti-government criticism. A four-point indicator ranged from no censorship to rigid and arbitrary censorship practices.
6. Repression of the *opposition* is assessed in a combined three-point indicator of the existence of *prisoners of conscience* and *obstructing* human-rights bodies ('none', 'one violated', 'both violated').
7. The legal status of trade (labor) *unions* is assessed by a four-point indicator, ranging from 'legal' to 'illegal'.

Authoritarian aggression

And two indicators represent the more repressive aspects of state authoritarianism reflecting the extent to which the opposition is suppressed and persecuted and to which torture and killings occur.

8. The status and use of *capital punishment* is measured by a four-point indicator, ranging from 'abolished for all crimes' to 'retained and used for ordinary crimes'.

9. *State terror* or official infringement of human rights is measured by a three-point indicator ranging from 'no violations reported' to 'terror states, practicing disappearance, torture or assassination'.

And finally:

10. The number of *military per physician* represents the investment in the military over that in citizens' health and welfare, and was assessed as four quantified categories.

Summing these ten indicators thus provides an overall index of state authoritarianism. A reliability analysis of the overall index using these ten ratings for 95 countries for which data on all ten indicators were available produced an alpha coefficient of .83, indicating high internal consistency reliability (cf. also Meloen, 1996).

The validity of the state authoritarianism index

In order to assess the discriminant validity of the index, state authoritarianism scores were computed for each of 133 countries at the early 1990s and scaled from zero (low state authoritarianism) to 100 (high state authoritarianism). The number of countries that could be scored was increased to 133 by permitting either one or two missing indicators; a procedure justified by the high reliability of the overall index. To be regarded as valid, the state authoritarianism index should show high scores for known authoritarian dictatorships, and low scores for countries known to be free and democratic at the time. It should be noted that in the early 1990s many countries that were later democratized were still under dictatorial rule. As expected, the world map (see Figure 7.1) shows a belt of states with the highest state authoritarianism scores running from Africa (Sudan, Libya, Sudan, Ethiopia, Somalia, Angola) through the Middle East (Iran, Iraq, Saudi Arabia, Oman), to Southern Asia (Pakistan, Burma/Myanmar, Laos) and East Asia (China, North Korea). At the time, the Soviet Union and Yugoslavia were still intact and part of this belt. The highest scores were obtained for Iran (93), Laos, Burma (89), Ethiopia (86) and the Sudan (85), all of which were viewed as authoritarian states at the time.

The low state authoritarian countries are located primarily in North America, Western Europe and Australia, with some also in Asia (for example Japan), Africa (for example Botswana), and South America (for example Venezuela, Uruguay, Costa Rica). The lowest state authoritarianism scores were obtained in Scandinavia (Denmark, and Sweden 10, Norway 12), and for The Netherlands (0), Iceland (3), Canada (3) and New Zealand (12). The general picture therefore was overwhelmingly according to expectation.

The concurrent validity of the state authoritarianism index is strongly supported by its correlations with independent global ratings such as the

114

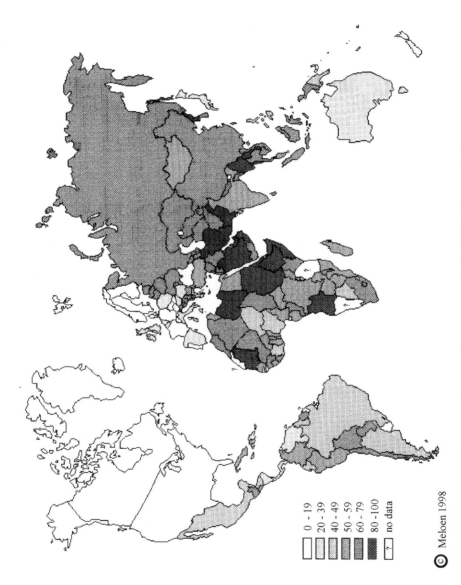

0 - 19
20 - 39
40 - 49
50 - 59
60 - 79
80 -100
no data

© Meloen 1998

Figure 7.1 State authoritarianism (early 1990s, 133 countries).

freedom rating by Freedom House (1993) (r = .82 for 76 countries), the UN human freedom index (UNDP, 1991) (r = .80 for 95 countries), and an inventory of gross human right violations by PIOOM (Gupta, Jongman and Schmid, 1993) (r = .79 for 84 countries). These correlations are all high, significant and in the expected direction. While these ratings are all measuring aspects of similar phenomena, the state authoritarianism index tends to be broader in scope than the others. For example the freedom rating tends to be based more on formal rights and liberties rather than on the actual behavior of authoritarian states.

Explaining state authoritarianism

Six causes of state authoritarianism

A number of causes of state authoritarianism have been proposed, involving political, cultural, psychological and developmental variables, and six main approaches can be identified:

- The first and most obvious approach views an *authoritarian government* as the main cause of state authoritarianism (Neumann, 1942; Perlmutter, 1981). This has often been considered self-evident, yet it clearly cannot be a complete explanation. Equally dictatorial or unrepresentative governments may differ, sometimes quite considerably, in how repressive, brutal, unpopular and behaviorally authoritarian their regimes are.
- The second approach focuses on *family traditions and practices* (Adorno *et al.*, 1950; Fromm, 1941; Horkheimer, Fromm and Marcuse, 1936; Schaffner, 1948; Todd, 1985). The rationale is that attitudes to authority are conditioned or learned in childhood, where the parents serve as a model for the authority relations in society.
- The third approach stresses the more indirect effect of an authoritarian, or basically *hierarchical culture*, which determines the degree to which relationships between individuals and in society in are organized hierarchically (Fromm, 1941; Hofstede, 1991).
- The fourth approach sees *authoritarian attitudes* (Adorno *et al.*, 1950; Altemeyer, 1988) as conditioning and reflecting a general mentality of the population, which influence the behavior and structure of the political and social institutions in the society.
- The fifth approach suggests that low levels of *education* may have effects on cognition and learning that result in authoritarian attitudes in societies (Goldstein and Blackman, 1978; Altemeyer, 1988).
- The sixth approach suggests a less direct, though potentially powerful influence: the *economic situation*. Economic instability or low levels of economic development may not only themselves dispose peoples and countries to become authoritarian, but they may create social problems that elicit authoritarian reactions from desperate peoples hoping for

'salvation' or grasping at political solutions, no matter how unrealistic, that might conceivably alleviate their situation.

An integrated multi-causal model

In order to explain state authoritarianism more adequately, the links between the different possible explanatory variables proposed and their causal trajectories need to be clarified in the form of an integrated multi-causal model. Such a model would show how the different cultural, psychological and political factors interrelate and combine to cause state authoritarianism, and could then be subject to empirical testing. It would therefore subsume the six approaches to the causes of state authoritarianism that have been described, and in addition, should specify some of the major effects of state authoritarianism.

The proposed model distinguishes between direct causes, such as type of government and authoritarian attitudes, less direct cultural causes, such as traditional family structure and hierarchical culture, and more distant socio-economic developmental causes, such as levels of educational and economic development.

Direct causes

Type of government.   One of the primary direct causes of state authoritarianism should be the existence of an authoritarian political system, which even if it initially does not have authoritarian policies and state practices should eventually develop them. In the model, *type of government* is therefore the main direct cause of state authoritarianism. Although it may seem obvious, a relationship between authoritarian types of government and state authoritarianism may not always be self-evident. For instance, there may be considerable variation in the degree to which equally undemocratic governments behave in dictatorial, militaristic, and aggressive ways.

For this reason, the type of government needs to be distinguished from state authoritarianism, and the relationship between them empirically investigated. In order to do this I used the classification of government types in terms of degree of democracy used by Freedom House (1993), and rank ordered them into four categories: no parliamentary democracy (one party state, monarchy, military government), parliamentary democracy dominated by the military, centralized democracy (strong presidential system) and decentralized democracy (strong parliament). The correlation of this ranking of governmental types with the state authoritarianism index was .71 ($p < .001$) for 92 countries.

Authoritarian attitudes.   A second direct cause of state authoritarianism may be the degree to which authoritarian attitudes are prevalent within the population, and such attitudes have been extensively studied in the social sciences since the 1930s. Many different approaches to explaining and predicting such attitudes have been developed, such as Fromm's research among workers in Weimar in 1929 (Fromm, 1984), the work of the Frankfurter Schule (Horkheimer *et al.*, 1936; Wiggershaus, 1994), and the approaches of Reich (1933), Adorno *et al.* (1950), Rokeach *et al.* (1960) and Altemeyer (1988).

Although the early work on authoritarian attitudes was primarily aimed at explaining the attractiveness of Fascism and Nazism, it later refocused, partly under American influence, to what was seen as its common core, the authoritarian character (Fromm, 1941; Maslow, 1943) or authoritarian personality (Adorno *et al.*, 1950). This latter concept has received most attention with the aim of discovering the psychological mechanisms that would make people vulnerable to authoritarian propaganda and lead them to submit to authoritarian ideologies and movements (Meloen, 1983, 1991, 1993).

Shils (1954) criticized Adorno *et al.*'s concept of the authoritarian personality, which was tied to right-wing extremism, by noting the lack of freedom and authoritarianism characteristic of communist regimes. Rokeach's (1960) concept of dogmatism or general authoritarianism was a response to this, but his measure of dogmatism seemed also to be primarily related to right wing authoritarianism, at least in western societies (Meloen, 1983; Stone, Lederer and Christie, 1993). Recently, evidence from the former USSR (McFarland, Ageyev and Abalakina, 1993; Popov, 1995) has helped resolve the 'mystery' of 'left-wing authoritarianism' by showing that supporters of the communist regime were clearly more authoritarian in their attitudes. Thus, authoritarian attitudes functioned to support the system in both right and left-wing centralized, antidemocratic states (cf. also Meloen, 1991, 1994).

In the absence of other data, an extensive review of cross-national empirical authoritarianism research by Meloen (1983, 1996; Meloen, Farnen and German, 1994) was used to provide national estimates of the level of authoritarian attitudes for 32 countries. The correlation of these national authoritarian attitude estimates with the state authoritarianism scores was .85 ($p < .001$) for 27 countries for which data on both variables was available.

Cultural causes

The cultural values and traditions of a country may be more distant and less direct causes of state authoritarianism. In particular, culture may shape family structures and the patterning of authority and power relations in societies, which may then mediate the impact of culture on politics (cf. Hofstede, 1991; Todd, 1985).

The traditional family structure. A relationship between family structures (traditions, attitudes, practices) and state authoritarianism has been suggested in research on authoritarianism since the 1930s (Horkheimer *et al.*, 1936; Schaffner, 1948). Adorno *et al.* (1950) believed that certain family structures and practices were causally related to authoritarian attitudes.

Research however, has not always found a relationship between the behavior of parents and the attitudes of their children (Hagendoorn, 1982).

One aspect that has received little attention is the idea that basic authority structures within the family might influence those outside the family. For example, the absolute rule of a monarch or leader might reflect the role of the father in the family. Thus, authoritarian states may be influenced by patriarchal or feudal family structures and practices. A global test of the relationship between state authoritarianism and family structures has not yet been done, but would be possible using the comprehensive anthropological classification of family structures proposed by Todd (1985).

Todd suggested a possible relationship between the structure of the family and the sociopolitical system, and that the totalitarianism of the communist world might be related to the structure of the family in those countries. These family structures could therefore constrain the development of democracy in these countries, even if the communist regimes fell; a suggestion that is not inconsistent with events in many of the countries that formed part of the Soviet Union. Todd's classification of family types was based on four basic features of families that seemed to be related to the degree of freedom and equality in the family.

1. the tendency for exogamous or endogamous relations, that is whether the marrying partner should be found outside the tribe, clan or group, or should be found inside;
2. the incest taboo, which is strict in certain cultures but less so in others where cousin marriage is permitted;
3. the degree of personal freedom permitted in spouse election; and
4. the degree of symmetry in inheritance, that is the degree to which the inheritance is divided equally or unequally between heirs.

These four family features were coded for 84 countries for which data was available. One of these features, symmetry in inheritance, showed little relation to the other three and was therefore disregarded. The other three were highly intercorrelated, suggesting that they comprised a single dimension ranging from exogenous families with strict incest taboo and full freedom to select one's partner at one pole to endogamous families where cousin marriage was permitted and where spouse selection was ruled by custom with little freedom of choice. This dimension was classified into traditional extended family type, mixed type, and modern nuclear type and this classification was found to correlate highly ($r = .74$, $p < .001$) with the state authoritarianism index for 50 countries.

Hierarchical culture.   Hofstede (1980, 1991) analyzed work value and attitudinal responses from 116000 IBM employees from 72 countries and found four basic cultural-value dimensions differentiating national cultures. Two of these, 'power distance' and 'individualism versus collectivism' are pertinent to the present research. The power distance dimension describes the degree to which inequalities in power and status, or hierarchy, are accepted or rejected in social life. In low power-distance societies egalitarian relations between people are seen as natural, while in high power-distance societies hierarchy is culturally accepted as the natural order of things.

A second dimension of cultural differentiation identified by Hofstede was that of individualism versus collectivism. In collectivist societies people are born into large 'extended families' and therefore are always embedded in a group. The group serves a protective function, and children learn to think in terms of 'we' rather than 'I'. Collective interests are more important than individual rights and privacy. Collectivist cultures are more commonly found among developing countries, and individualistic cultures more common in Western countries.

Empirical analysis showed that Hofstede's (1991) published country means for the power distance and collectivism dimensions were highly intercorrelated ($r = .67$, $p < .001$), indicating that practically both dimensions have much in common. Consequently, the two were combined to form a single index of *hierarchical culture* for 63 countries, ranging from collectivist, high power-distance, hierarchical societies to individualist, low power-distance, egalitarian societies. This hierarchical culture factor was scored from Hofstede's data and was found to correlate .68 ($p < .001$) with the state authoritarianism index for 57 countries.

Social and economic development as causes

The social and economic development of countries may be the most basic causal factor in the model. The focus here is on two indices: economic and educational development.

Economic development. Economic development can probably be considered the most basic cause, as it would determine a lack of means in almost every sense: material, social, medical. Economically poor countries experience a complex of associated problems that make escape from underdevelopment very difficult. Inglehart (1977) has suggested that the pursuit of the most basic human needs of nutrition, physical safety, health and a minimum of material possessions creates a culture of materialist objectives in social behavior, norms and values. Only after a satisfactory material level has been reached will a culture of post-materialism develop.

Economic conditions have also been viewed as the single most important cause of authoritarianism. Thus, the rise of European fascism has been linked to the economic collapse and unemployment of the great depression. However, this may be questioned since while one third of Germans voted for the nazis in 1932, Americans suffering even higher unemployment in the same year voted for a moderate liberal as president. It is possible therefore that there may not be a simple, direct relationship between the economic situation and political outcomes, but that, as Inglehart (1977) has suggested, economic factors may have effects mediated through their impact on culture.

Gross national product (GNP, corrected, per capita; UNDP, 1991; Freedom House, 1993) was used as an index of economic development. Its correlation with the state authoritarianism index for the 89 countries for which data was available was $-.60$ ($p < .001$), with state authoritarianism being higher in poorer countries.

Educational development.   Empirical studies since the 1950s have found educational level to be the strongest and most consistent social variable predicting authoritarianism (Meloen, 1983, 1993). The relationship has been discussed in terms of learning processes (Altemeyer, 1988), cognitive style (Goldstein and Blackman, 1978), cultural factors (Duckitt, 1992; Simpson, 1972), and nationalistic emphases in the content of education in authoritarian cultures (Meloen *et al.*, 1994).

Internationally, poverty implies a lack of educational infrastructure, such as schools, buildings, books, personnel and finance. However, education may also exert an influence distinct from economic development since nonmaterial consequences of education, such as literacy, knowledge and cognitive sophistication may reduce dependence on authorities and susceptibility to manipulation by them. Education may therefore counteract authoritarian tendencies.

The index of *educational attainment* provided by the United Nations (UNDP, 1991) was selected for this analysis, and its correlation with state authoritarianism was $-.71$ ($p < .001$) for 94 countries, indicating that higher educational attainment was associated with lower state authoritarianism.

Effects of state authoritarianism

Several effects of state authoritarianism can be hypothesized:

Gender gap.   One effect may be that authoritarian policies widen the gender gap; they tend to support male dominance and 'masculine' attitudes and activities. They would reinforce different social roles for men and women in the traditional sense, with men being prepared for military activities, and women to support the men, raise children and to stay out of social public life and politics. A composite four-point rating of the gender gap ranging from 'least equal' to 'most equal' opportunities for men and women (Population Crisis Committee, Kidron and Segal, 1991) was used, and found to be strongly correlated with the state authoritarianism index ($r = .78$, $p < .001$, for 84 countries).

Biased elections. A second effect of state authoritarianism may relate to the degree to which elections will be free or biased. Authoritarianism often leads to elections being abandoned completely or, if they are tolerated, to biased results. The index used was a five-point rating ranging from 'full', 'some' or 'slight participation in free elections' to 'virtually no participation with biased elections' and 'no elections held at all' (Kidron and Segal, 1991). The correlation with state authoritarianism was substantial and in the expected direction ($r = .65$, $p < .001$, for 91 countries).

Military conflict. A third effect of state authoritarianism may be military conflicts. Authoritarian rule may lead to territorial conflicts with neighboring states. In addition, negative attitudes to compromise and flexibility may aggravate existing minor conflicts. Sometimes external aggression may be used to distract attention from internal conflicts and problems. Generally democracies seem less prone to make war, and then typically in self-defense. The PIOOM four point rating of military conflict ('no military conflict', 'a serious dispute', 'low intensity conflict', 'a major armed conflict or war') was selected (Gupta *et al.*, 1993; Jongman, 1995). The correlation with the state authoritarianism index for 94 countries was .52 ($p < .001$).

The causal model

Economic development and educational level seem likely to be the most distal influences on state authoritarianism in the model. Education can be viewed partly as an effect of economic development as the economy provides its material conditions. Both economic and educational development seem likely to influence cultural values and the family system. In turn, hierarchical cultures seem likely to generate authoritarian social attitudes. The family system may also influence peoples values and attitudes, shape authority relations in society, and serve as a vehicle for the transference of authority between generations. Finally, the authoritarian social attitudes prevailing in a society and the degree to which the existing political system is authoritarian should be the most direct causal impacts on state authoritarianism. State authoritarianism in turn then may result in biased elections, a wide gender gap, and military conflict.

Testing the state authoritarianism model

LISREL analyses were used to test the causal model, which is shown in Figure 7.2. The availability of data for the variables ranged from a maximum of 174 countries (GNP), to 95 countries for the state authoritarianism index, 84 countries for Todd's family structures, 63 countries for Hofstede's cultural dimensions, and to 32 countries for which authoritarian attitude data was available. The data covered a wide variety of countries and cultures

122

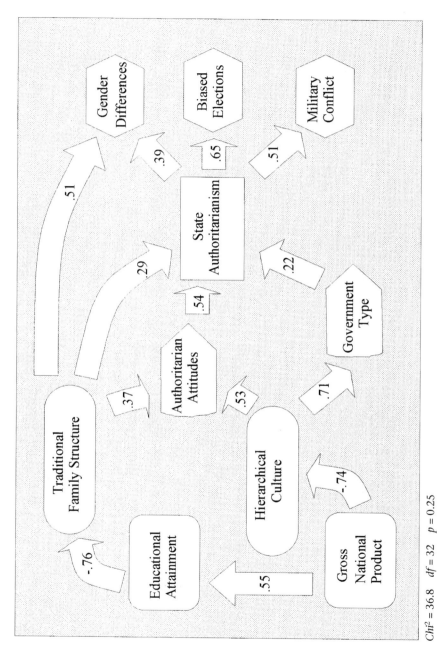

Chi² = 36.8   df = 32   p = 0.25

Figure 7.2   Model state authoritarianism.

on all continents. In order to use as much information and variance as possible, pairwise correlations were used for the LISREL analysis, which meant that on average data on 79 countries were being used. The LISREL analysis indicated that the model as a whole showed reasonably acceptable fit to the data (Full model: chi^2 = 36.8, df = 32, p = .25; ML method, no correlated errors allowed). Moreover, all the hypothesized relationships within the model were significant and reasonably powerful.

Economic development (corrected GNP) emerged as the most basic dimension, and proved to be a powerful influence on both educational attainment and hierarchical culture with a low GNP related to a more hierarchical culture. Higher levels of educational attainment in turn seem to result in the family structure being less traditional. The degree to which the family structure is traditional impacts on authoritarian attitudes in society as well as having a weaker direct impact on state authoritarianism itself. Authoritarian attitudes were also strongly influenced by the degree to which the culture is hierarchical, which also had a powerful effect on government type. Finally, the model also supported direct effects of both government type and authoritarian attitudes on state authoritarianism. The hypothesized effects of state authoritarianism were also supported, with higher levels of state authoritarianism leading to a wider gender gap, more biased elections, and more military conflicts. In addition a strong independent effect emerged for traditional family structure on gender differences.

Overall, therefore the model seems reasonably well supported by the data with most of the variance in state authoritarianism being accounted for within the model.

Conclusions

Before the conclusions are presented it is necessary to point out several limitations to this research that suggest that the findings need to be interpreted cautiously.

First, adequate data for the investigation of authoritarianism on a global scale are often not available; this is particularly so for cultural and attitudinal variables. In the case of authoritarian attitudes data was available for only 32 countries, though these did provide coverage of a variety of nations with respect to their political, religious, and cultural backgrounds and include most significant contemporary world powers. In addition, the availability of data may be distorted by the actual phenomenon being studied. Thus, when the number of authoritarian regimes decreases, the availability of more reliable social data may increase, since such regimes often censor or 'adjust' statistical data. However, this should only affect certain data (such as GNP, educational attainment), and not data derived from independent ratings.

A second limitation is that empirical techniques such as path analysis (LISREL) are only capable of assessing whether observed data are consistent with a theoretical model, and not of directly demonstrating causal relationships. More direct assessment of proposed causal chains require additional methodologies and data, which, however, tend to be rarely available.

A third limitation is that the data used here was obtained for only a limited period: the late 1980s and early 1990s. This period may be too specific for generalization to other historical periods. The reverse criticism would be that the data were not collected in the same year, but over a period of several years. However, this objection loses force to the extent that state authoritarianism is viewed as a relatively stable phenomenon. In addition, the basic indicators of economic development, educational attainment, and the cultural factors would also tend to be relatively stable over time. The period studied does have the advantage that most of the authoritarian regimes of the Cold War period were still intact then, and that many country ratings would simply not have been available before the 1990s.

State authoritarianism as the core problem

In this investigation state authoritarianism has been conceptualized as the core issue in the study of authoritarianism and dictatorship. It has been suggested that authoritarian regimes do show similarities in their basic ideas, structures and practices, despite the often substantial differences in their ideologies. Thus, they seem to involve a set of intolerant beliefs, a hierarchical political organization, and the use of violence and terror against opposition. This triad was considered the core of the concept of 'state authoritarianism'. The rationale for this is that the state is the main instrument through which dictators and authoritarian groups acquire and exercise power. In so doing they use the political structure, the military, the police, the bureaucracy and the legal system in order to secure absolute control over the population. The psychological equivalents of this core triad of key factors were termed authoritarian conventionalism, authoritarian submission, and authoritarian aggression, following Adorno *et al.* (1950) and Altemeyer's (1988) classic works on psychological authoritarianism.

A political culture of authoritarianism

The most important finding from this comparative and crossnational study would seem to lie in clarifying a powerful relationship between culture and politics. Authoritarian government is clearly not the sole cause of state authoritarianism: a political culture of authoritarianism seems at least as important an influence on the civil and human rights violations characterizing state authoritarianism. The most significant components of this political culture seem to be a traditional family structure and a culture characterized by hierarchical power relations and collectivism, which together generate, reinforce and maintain authoritarian attitudes in a society. Together these constitute a cultural climate conducive to authoritarian government and the policies and practices expressive of state authoritarianism. This authoritarian political culture itself is powerfully affected by the level of economic and social development of societies. The role of political culture in constraining democratic political change has often been commented on; with revolutions or other dramatic political changes all too often merely recreating the old authoritarian order in a new guise (Potter, Goldblatt, Kiloh and Lewis, 1997; Vanhanen 1997).

These findings also have implications for understanding previous research findings on authoritarian attitudes. Too often theory and research has examined authoritarian attitudes in isolation from the cultural context, and little or no empirical attention has been paid to the manner in which cultural variables might influence these attitudes. Although the role of the family has been stressed in relation to authoritarian attitudes, little progress has been made in actually unraveling this connection. Typically, research has simply correlated authoritarian attitudes with other social attitudes. The present model therefore has particular value in suggesting how these connections may operate and provides some empirical support.

The relevance of crosscultural studies of political psychology

A continuing problem in crosscultural research is that of whether the data and interpretations can be considered 'culture free' or not. The 'not culture free' argument maintains that an analysis originating in a western culture can only have significance for Western cultures, since other cultures would then be measured by Western standards, often to their disadvantage. While this argument does have merit in many respects, there is a problem. It is often used by apologists to justify authoritarian regimes and authoritarian practices in non-Western cultures. The counter argument is that human rights should be considered culture free and that the indicators used here do not involve value judgements, but are mere counts of incidents or denote the characteristics of existing laws and practices. Most fundamentally, however, crosscultural research by researchers from a variety of cultures is needed to reduce the risk that any particular analysis might involve ethnocentric biases.

The crosscultural and global approach of this analysis appears to have generated important insights that would not have emerged from traditional intra-national or intra-cultural research. Too often these have been analyzed independently of their cultural context, and only within one particular social science discipline. Research on authoritarianism has been multidisciplinary, crossnational, and crosscultural from its inception, and its relevance, methods and results in this respect may be considered a model for political psychology.

References

Adorno, T.W., E. Frenkel-Brunswik, D.J. Levinson and R.N. Sanford (1950) *The Authoritarian Personality*, New York: Harper & Row.

Al-Khalil, S. (1989) *Republic of Fear*, London: Hutchinson Radius.

Altemeyer, B. (1988) *Enemies of Freedom*, London: Jossey Bass.

Billig, M. (1978) *Fascists: A Social Psychological View of the National Front*, London: Academic Press.

Brooker, P. (1995) *Twentieth-Century Dictatorships: The Ideological One-Party States*, London: Macmillan.

Brooks, R.C. (1935) *Deliver us from Dictators*, Philadelphia: University of Pennsylvania Press.

Duckitt, J. (1992) 'Education and Authoritarianism among English- and Afrikaans-Speaking White South Africans', *Journal of Social Psychology*, vol. 132, pp. 701–8.

Freedom House Survey Team (1993) *Freedom in the World: The Annual Survey of Political Rights and Civil Liberties 1992–1993*, New York: Freedom House.

Fromm, E. (1941/1965) *Escape from Freedom*, New York: Avon Books.

Fromm, E. (1929/1984) *The Working Class in Weimar Germany: A Psychological and Sociological Study*, Leamington Spa: Berg Publications.

Goldstein, K. M. and S. Blackman (1978) *Cognitive Style*, New York: Wiley.

Gupta, D.K., A.J. Jongman and A.P. Schmid (1993) 'Creating a Composite Index for Assessing Country Performance in the Field of Human Rights: Proposal for a New Methodology', *Human Rights Quarterly*, vol. 15, pp. 131–62.

Hagendoorn, A. (1982) *Het Nazisme als ideologie* [Nazism as Ideology], Deventer: Van Loghum Slaterus.

Hofstede, G. (1980) *Culture's Consequences: International Differences in Work-Related Values*, Beverly Hills: Sage.

Hofstede, G. (1991) *Cultures and Organizations, Software of the Mind*, London: McGraw-Hill. Dutch Edition: (1991) *Allemaal andersdenkenden: Omgaan met cultuurverschillen*. Amsterdam: Contact.

Horkheimer, M., E. Fromm, & H. Marcuse (1936) *Studien über Autorität und Familie: Forschungsberichte aus dem Institut für Sozialforschung* [Studies on Authority and Family], Paris: Librairie Félix Alcan.

Inglehart, R. (1977) *The Silent Revolution*, Princeton: University Press.

Jongman, A.J. (1995) Contemporary Conflicts: A Global Survey of High- and Lower Intensity Conflicts and Serious Disputes. *PIOOM Newsletter and Progress Report*, 7, vol. 1, pp. 14–23.

Kidron, M., R. Segal (1991) *The New State of the World Atlas*, New York: Simon and Schuster.

Maslow, A.H. (1943) 'The Authoritarian Character Structure', *Journal of Social Psychology*, vol. 18, pp. 401–11.

McFarland, S., V. Ageyev and M. Abalakina (1993) 'The Authoritarian Personality in the U.S.A. and the Former U.S.S.R.: Comparative Studies. In W.F. Stone, G. Lederer and R. Christie (eds), *Strength and Weakness: The Authoritarian Personality Today* (pp. 199–229), New York: Springer.

Meloen, J.D. (1983) *De autoritaire reactie in tijden van welvaart en crisis.* [The Authoritarian Response in Times of Prosperity and Crisis], Amsterdam: University of Amsterdam, unpublished dissertation.

Meloen, J.D. (1991) 'The Fortieth Anniversary of "The Authoritarian Personality"', *Politics and the Individual*, vol. 1, pp. 119–27.

Meloen, J.D. (1993) 'The F Scale as a Predictor of Fascism: An Overview of 40 Years of Authoritarianism Research', in W. F. Stone, G. Lederer & R. Christie (eds.), *Strength and Weakness: The Authoritarian Personality Today* (pp. 47–69), New York: Springer.

Meloen, J.D. (1994) 'A Critical Analysis of Forty Years of Authoritarianism Research: Did theory testing suffer from Cold War Attitudes?', in R. Farnen (ed.), *Nationalism, Ethnicity, and Identity: Cross National and Comparative Perspectives* (pp. 127–165), London: Transaction.

Meloen, J.D. (1996) 'Authoritarianism, Democracy and Education: A Preliminary Empirical 70-Nation Global Indicators Study', in R.F. Farnen, H. Dekker, R. Meyenberg, and D.B. German (eds.), *Democracy, Socialization and Conflicting Loyalties in East and West: Cross-National and Comparative Perspectives* (pp. 20–38), London: Macmillan.

Meloen, J.D., R. Farnen and D. German (1994) 'Authoritarianism and Democracy', in G. Csepeli, D. German, L. Kéri, I. Stumpf (eds.), *From Subject to Citizen* (pp. 123–52), Budapest: Hungarian Center for Political Education.

Neumann, F. (1942/1966) *Behemoth: The Structure and Practice of National Socialism, 1933–1944*, New York: Harper and Row.

Perlmutter, A. (1981) *Modern Authoritarianism*, London: Yale University Press.

Popov, N. (1995) *The Russian People Speak: Democracy at the Crossroads*, Syracuse: University Press.

Potter, D., D. Goldblatt, M. Kiloh and P. Lewis (1997) *Democratization*, Cambridge: Polity Press.

Reich, W. (1933/1975) *The Mass Psychology of Fascism*, Middlesex: Penguin Books.

Rokeach, M. (1960) *The Open and Closed Mind*, New York: Basic Books.

Schaffner, B. (1948) *Father Land: A Study of Authoritarianism in the German Family*, New York: Columbia University Press.

Shils, E.A. (1954) 'Authoritarianism: "Left" and "Right"', in R. Christie, M. Jahoda (eds.), *Studies in the Scope and method of 'The Authoritarian Personality'*, Glencoe: The Free Press.

Simpson, M. (1972) 'Authoritarianism and Education: A Comparative Approach', *Sociometry*, vol. 35, pp. 223–34.

Stone, W.F., G. Lederer and R. Christie (1993) *Strength and Weakness: The Authoritarian Personality Today*, New York: Springer.

Todd, E. (1985) *The Explanation of Ideology: Family Structures and Social Systems*, New York: Basil Blackwell.

UNDP (1991), 'United Nations Development Programme', *Human Development Report 1991*, Oxford: University Press.

Vanhanen, T. (1997) *Prospects of Democracy*, London: Routledge.

Wiggershaus, R. (1994) *The Frankfurt School*, Cambridge: Polity Press.

8
Conflict and Injustice in Intercultural Relations: Insights from the Arab–Israeli and Sino-British Disputes[1]

Kwok Leung and Walter G. Stephan

Introduction

The remarkable technological achievements of this century stand in stark contrast to the plights and sufferings of millions of victims of the large-scale international conflicts that have occurred in the same period. After two world wars, the Korean war, the Vietnam war, the cold war, and numerous other regional wars, international conflicts are still rampant. The causes of such conflicts are obviously multi-fold, ranging from religious clashes and geopolitical conflicts of interest to cultural differences. In current analyses of international conflicts, the role of culture in triggering and fueling major international conflicts is relatively unexplored.

The present chapter attempts to analyze how culture shapes the development and resolution of international conflicts, and search for the cultural premises of the associated political actions. The value of this cultural approach is that it can reveal aspects of the cultural basis of political behavior, of which even the actors may not be aware, for most people are not aware of the extent to which culture shapes their thoughts, feelings, and behavior. This cultural perspective, we believe, will enrich our understanding of the meanings behind political events and actions in international conflicts.

Our specific focus will be on the role of perceived injustice in intercultural conflicts. Drawing upon Leung and Stephan (1998), we will argue that the particular perceptions of injustice that occur in intercultural conflicts are often directly related to dimensions of cultural differences. In this chapter we will focus primarily on two cultural dimensions: individual-

[1] The authors wish to thank Naji Abi-Hashem, Michael Bond, Peter Dorfman, John Duckitt,Hsin-Chi Kuan, Cookie Stephan, Joseph Schwarzwald and David Trafimow for their insightful comments on earlier versions of this manuscript.

ism–collectivism and power distance, although we acknowledge that other dimensions may also be important. Individualism–collectivism refers to the importance attached to the self vs the ingroup, whereas power distance refers to the extent to which power-related hierarchies are an accepted aspect of a society (Hofstede, 1980). In the discussion that follows, we will review the role of injustice perceptions in the creation of conflict between cultures that vary in individualism/collectivism and power distance. We will begin by discussing distributive justice and then examine procedural justice, retributive justice and reactions to injustice and their relationships to individualism–collectivism and power distance. We then apply this framework to two situations: the Israeli–Palestinian conflict and the Sino–British conflict over the return of Hong Kong to China.

Distributive justice

Distributive justice is achieved if all parties to a potential dispute regard their share of a resource as fair. To avoid a sense of distributive injustice, people must agree on the allocation rules to be used and the way these rules will be applied. Conflict can arise when cultural groups adhere to different allocation rules (for example, equity, equality, need). In individualistic cultures, equity is the preferred allocation rule (people's outcomes should reflect their inputs). In collectivistic cultures, the choice of allocation rules is affected by whether the recipient is an ingroup or an outgroup member (Leung, 1997; Leung and Bond, 1984). With ingroup recipients, collectivists tend to use the equality rule when their own input or contribution is high (each person receives an equal share of the resources, regardless of input), but the equity rule when their own input is low. With outgroup recipients, however, collectivists act like individualists and use the equity rule. Among collectivists, the preference for using the equity rule with outgroup members could lead to perceptions of injustice, if the other group adheres to a different rule (for example, equality).

Cultural groups with different levels of power-distance may react to allocation decisions in distinctive ways. In high-power distance cultures, people's acceptance or tolerance of unequal social prerogatives enhances their tolerance of 'unfair' treatment (Bond, Wan, Leung and Giacalone, 1985; Gudykunst and Ting-Toomey, 1988; James, 1993). That is, people in high power-distance cultures are more likely to accept an unequal distribution of resources than people from low power-distance cultures, although this acceptance may be much greater among low than high-status individuals in such cultures. In contrast, in lower power-distance societies, people's rejection of inequality makes them intolerant of any unequal treatment they receive. Consistent with this reasoning Gudykunst and Ting-Toomey (1988) found that there was a negative relationship between the power distance of a society and expressions of anger as a response to injustice.

Procedural justice

Procedural justice is concerned with the procedures and processes used in decision-making, and the fairness of their implementation. When people from two cultures prefer different conflict resolution styles, their attempts to resolve their conflicts could easily lead to perceptions of injustice. People from individualistic cultures favor styles of conflict resolution that are high on concern for the self, whereas collectivists are more likely to prefer styles that are high on concern for others (Gabrielidis, Stephan, Ybarra and Villareal, 1997; Morris *et al.*, 1998; Pearson and Stephan, 1998). In particular, people from cultures that prefer accommodative styles of conflict resolution (collectivistic cultures) are likely to feel unjustly treated by people from cultures that prefer competitive styles (individualistic cultures). People from competitively oriented cultures are less likely to regard such crosscultural negotiations as unjust because the outcomes are likely to favor them, given that the other side is accommodating to their wishes.

In high power-distance cultures, people who are high in status probably expect people who are low in status to withdraw from conflicts with them. In contrast, people in low power-distance cultures probably prefer collaboration to accommodation or withdrawal. Clashes in preferences for styles of conflict resolution between people from high vs low power-distance cultures may lead members of both cultures to perceive the outcomes of these negotiations as unfair to them.

Another important aspect of the procedures used during intercultural conflict is the manner in which members of the two cultural groups treat one another, sometimes referred to as interactional justice (Bies and Moag, 1986; Tyler and Bies, 1990). People who occupy the upper levels of the hierarchy in high power distance cultures are particularly likely to expect to be treated with respect and dignity during social interactions. Thus, 'disrespectful' interpersonal treatment will induce a sense of injustice in these people.

Retributive justice

In retributive justice, the focus is on perceptions of what constitutes fair punishments for harm-doers. Culture may affect how harm is perceived and defined, as well as what constitutes a fair punishment. Conflict between cultures can surface when cultural groups have to agree on a form of retribution to punish a harm-doer or when one culture punishes members of another for wrongdoing. When cultures differ in their views of what constitutes illegitimate behavior, the punishments meted out to offenders will almost inevitably be perceived as unjust by one cultural group. For instance, Americans would be unlikely to approve of a punishment such as cutting off a thief's hand, although traditional Muslim legal codes (*sharia*) call for just such a punishment.

One facet of individualism–collectivism that may affect perceptions of re-tributive justice is the distinction between ingroups and outgroups. It is poss-ible that collectivists are likely to engage in severe retributive actions against outgroup members, whereas toward ingroup members, they may be more lenient. In contrast, this difference should be less noticeable for individual-ists. In general, people from individualistic cultures are likely to see all justice principles (distributive, procedural and retributive) as universal, and use similar justice principles across group boundaries. In contrast, people from collectivistic cultures are likely to place greater weight on ingroup–outgroup boundaries, adopt a more contextual view of justice, and use different justice principles with different social groups (Leung and Morris, in press).

Reactions to perceived injustice

In most cultures people are motivated to seek redress for perceived injustice. In equity theory a distinction is made between behavioral and psychological responses to inequity (Walster, Walster and Berscheid, 1978). These two types of responses to inequity occur at the individual level. For intercultural rela-tions, it would seem that responses to injustice can occur at both the individ-ual and the group level, in much the same way that relative deprivation is thought to be either individual or fraternal (Vanneman and Pettigrew, 1972). Thus, it appears that there are four basic types of responses to injustice: indi-vidual-behavioral, individual-psychological, group-behavioral and group-psychological. Individual-behavioral responses include seeking redress through formal or informal conflict-resolution procedures, as well as through individual acts of sabotage, retaliation and revenge. Group-behavioral res-ponses include seeking formal redress as a group as well as rebellion, strikes and other forms of civil disobedience. Individual-psychological responses include changing one's evaluation of the ingroup or the outgroup, blinding oneself to the problem, and passive acceptance, as well as resentment and anger. Group-level psychological responses include collective attributions to fate, collective guilt, diffusion of responsibility, reconceptualizing the 'injus-tice' as legitimate, and shared feelings of anger or righteous indignation.

It is very likely that there are cultural differences in reactions to injustice. For instance, people in individualistic cultures may be disposed to individual-level interpretations and reactions to injustice, whereas people in collec-tivistic cultures may be more disposed to group reactions. People in high power-distance cultures may react differently to injustice depending on their rank in the hierarchy, and in general they may react differently than people from low power-distance cultures. In high power-distance cultures, people in high-status positions may be more likely to engage in behavioral responses. People low in the status hierarchy may be more prone to psychological responses, because their lack of power constrains them from responding behaviorally.

In the following sections, we apply our framework to analyze the role of culture in shaping conflict processes in two cases of international conflict.

The Arab–Israeli conflict

It is in the nature of conflict that the parties involved will perceive their causes as just. The Arab–Israeli conflict is no exception to this rule. The Israelis defend their behavior toward the Palestinians as self-defense against an enemy that has vowed to seek their extermination, and the Palestinians defend their behavior toward the Israelis as a case of fulfilling the right to self-determination (Bar-Tal, 1990; Bisharat, 1989; O'Brien, 1993). But beyond these broad justifications each side has cited a wide array of injustices that have played an important role in this conflict. Our task is to examine the extent to which these perceived injustices are influenced by the cultural dimensions of individualism–collectivism and power distance.

Although we do not regard collectivism–individualism or power distance as monolithic concepts which can be used to simply categorize cultures, we will try to locate Arab and Israeli culture on these two dimensions. Arab cultures appear to be more collectivistic than Israeli culture (Feghali, 1997). In support of this suggestion, Hofstede (1986) found that a group of Arab and Middle Eastern countries (Egypt, Iraq, Lebanon, Libya, Saudi Arabia and UAE) scored relatively low on his measure of individualism, whereas the Israelis score was somewhat high, but not as high as the USA or Western Europe.

Arab culture also seems to emphasize power distance to a greater extent than Israeli culture. Hofstede (1986) found that the Arab world in his sample scored very high on power distance, whereas the Israelis score was very low. The Arab World culture is more hierarchically structured, there are more rituals associated with respect and honor, dignity seems to be valued more, it appears to be more authoritarian, and inequalities are accepted more readily than in Israeli culture. Of course, there is great variability in both cultures with respect to these dimensions and the degree to which they are expressed in behavior depends on situational and social context factors (Barakat, 1993). There are also subgroups in both cultures who do not share the values of the majority. Nonetheless, we will attempt to show that the modal characteristics we have identified have had an impact on the types of injustices each group has reported experiencing in its relationships with the other.

Distributive injustice

Prior to the Oslo Accords (1993), which established a process for direct negotiations between the Israelis and the Palestinians, and autonomy for the Gaza and parts of the West Bank, the Palestinians maintained that the Israelis treated them unjustly by not distributing resources to them in accordance with their numbers in the population. The Israelis paid them low wages, annexed their lands, accorded them few legal rights, provided them with minimal social services, less water and electricity, and inferior roads and infrastructure (Hunter, 1991; Landau, 1997). After the Oslo Accords, the Israelis often excluded Palestinian products from Israel. The Palestinians have repeatedly asked to be treated equally. In a survey of 1140 Arabs and Jews living in Israel, 91 per cent of the Arabs said that the State of Israel should treat both groups equally, while only 16 per cent of the Jews felt this way (Smooha, 1987). It appears that the Israelis adhere to a conception of equity, one that is based on their perceptions of the what the Palestinians deserve. Thus, as suggested earlier, the Israelis (who appear to be relatively individualistic) rely on an equity rule when distributing resources. In addition, the Israelis appear to value their own productivity (their own outcomes) more than harmony or the well-being of the Arabs in their relationship with the Palestinians and these goals may also influence their reliance on an allocation rule (equity) that does not promote favorable relations between the two groups (cf. Leung, 1997).

The Palestinians clearly believe that they are being treated unjustly by the Israelis. Not only do they perceive their treatment as unequal, they also believe the way the Israelis treat them is inequitable (that is, they do not deserve to be treated so badly). Thus, the Israelis are violating both the distributive norm of equal treatment that prevails in collectivistic cultures, as well as the distributive norm of equity that people in collectivistic cultures expect to be used in relations between ingroup and outgroup members. The fact that the Palestinians are a low power group in this relationship may also feed this sense of injustice. That is, low power groups are likely to stress equality in relations with high power groups because it is in their interests to do so. Consistent with this argument, Azzi (1992) found that in both the USA and South Africa, members of minority groups were more likely to endorse the equality principle in allocating political power across groups than were members of majority groups.

Procedural injustice

When Palestinians and Israelis attempt to resolve conflicts they probably approach this situation with different styles and preferences. According to Griefat and Katriel (1989), Arabs approach interpersonal relations using an interpersonal style involving an array of politeness strategies emphasizing mutuality, cooperation, respect, concern, indirectness, subtlety, effusiveness, allusion and metaphor (see also, Feghali, 1997). In contrast, the Israelis often use an interpersonal approach relying on a style which involves direct, explicit, forceful, assertive, unembellished speech. These contrasting styles may lead to interactional injustice – feelings of injustice that can arise due to differences in communication styles (Bies and Moag, 1986; Tyler and Bies, 1990). The Palestinians may interpret the Israelis' lack of politeness as an indication the Israelis think they are superior to them. It also may be the case that the direct communication style of the Israelis is less persuasive to Palestinians than a more indirect style. As Suleiman notes, 'when non-Arabs speak, simply and unelaborately, they are not believed by Arabs' (p. 293).

On the other hand, Israelis often regard the indirect Arab communication style as deceptive and irrational. The differences in Arabs' and Israelis' communication styles may interfere with interactions between the two groups and may lead to dissatisfaction with the outcomes and process of negotiations. However, it should be noted that there are times when Arabs do communicate directly and use forceful language (Griefat and Katriel, 1989). This can be true when they are involved in conflict situations and when they are expressing deeply felt emotions. With respect to interacting with Jewish authorities, Griefat and Katriel quote one Arab young person as saying, 'In [relations with the Jewish] state one has to stand up for one's rights forcefully' (p. 130). Thus, when there is open conflict, the Palestinians and Israelis may adopt similar communication styles, but for more normal diplomatic and intercultural transactions, their contrasting styles may create difficulties.

Arabs also have a predilection for mediation and negotiation that is not shared by the Israelis. There is a long tradition in Arab societies of resolving disputes informally through the use of third parties (Witty, 1980). This may be one reason the talks leading to the Oslo Accords were successful, because they built on a conflict resolution procedure that was acceptable to the Palestinians. The discussions leading up to the Oslo accords were shepherded by a third party, they were informal, they took place in private, and they involved extensive interpersonal interaction. The Israelis entered into these negotiations very tentatively and were reluctant to commit high level government figures to the process until the very end.

Being treated with disrespect has been a central grievance of the Palestinians throughout the conflict. Issues of respect, dignity and honor are especially important in high power-distance cultures, particularly for individuals who hold positions of status and power. From the Palestinian perspective, the Israelis have constantly humiliated them and failed to treat them with the dignity and respect the Palestinians feel they deserve. Curfews have been imposed on them, they are subject to 'administrative detention', their press has been censored, their universities have been closed, and they have been tortured and abused by the Israeli security forces (O'Brien, 1993). The lack of respect that the Israelis have displayed toward the Palestinians has made the Palestinians very reluctant to negotiate with the Israelis. In contrast, in low power distance cultures, such as Israel, respect must be earned and issues of face, honor, and dignity appear to be less central to conflict resolution.

Retributive justice

The Israeli reaction to terrorism is an example where perceived retributive injustice occurs. Terrorist attacks on civilians are perceived as totally unjustified by the Israelis. Although there are many reasons that the Israelis resent the use of terrorism, including its cruelty and the fear and sense of hopelessness it engenders, for our purposes we wish to note that it is also resented because it is perceived as unjust and illegitimate. From the perspective of people in an individualistic culture such as Israel, it is not fair to punish people who are not responsible for acts of war or aggression. Thus, although the Israelis acknowledge that their security forces and the military are responsible for causing harm to the Palestinians, they maintain that terrorism is wrong because Israeli civilians are not responsible for this harm.

Reactions to injustice

Retributive justice focuses on perceptions of injustice. In this section we focus on reactions to injustice. It was suggested earlier that people in collectivistic cultures would be expected to respond to injustice at the group level. A good illustration of this notion is the intifada. The intifada was a group-behavioral reaction to perceived injustice, although there was a strong psychological element as well. The intifada did not involve armed resistance to the Israelis, but instead involved children and adolescents using less lethal forms of aggression (stones and sling shots – ironically the same weapon David, a Jewish child, used to defeat Goliath, a Philistine giant, in ancient times). The actions of the children were widely supported by the Palestinian community. The goal was not to defeat the Israelis through direct confrontation or conquest, but to reveal the moral weaknesses of the Israelis by provoking them to respond with greater aggression. The Palestinians were attempting to sway public opinion in Israel and the rest of the world by putting the brutality of the Israeli security forces on public display (Benvenisti, 1995; Bisharat, 1989).

Collectivism may also play a role in the choice of terrorism by some groups of Palestinians as a reaction to perceived injustice (for example, Hamas). Collectivistic cultures tend to make a greater distinction between ingroups and outgroups than do individualistic cultures and they may find it easier to treat outgroups in inhumane ways. The Palestinian terrorists seem to have made as great a distinction between the ingroup and the outgroup as it is possible to make. The terrorists view the Israelis as a dehumanized collectivity. Although the Islamic religion provides muslim Palestinians with a highly moral code of conduct (*sharia*) (Moten, 1996), the terrorists do not apply this code to the Israelis (see Opotow, 1990, for a discussion of moral exclusion). When an enemy is viewed as an entity that is subject to moral exclusion and all of its members are thought to be responsible for the repression of the ingroup, it may be considered justifiable to lash out at any of them, regardless of their direct individual involvement in the repression. As the well-known terrorist Abu Nidal said, 'Every Zionist is my enemy' (Nidal, 1986, 118). Terrorism is a group-behavioral response to perceived injustice that also has the psychological impact of striking fear into the hearts of the enemy.

The typical Israeli reaction to terrorism, particularly cross-border attacks, has been to counter-attack. There is a unique feature of Israeli history that is important in understanding the Israeli response to cross-border attacks. The holocaust imprinted a revulsion against being passive victims deeply in the minds of Jews. This experience predisposes the Israelis to respond actively to any aggression directed against them (Atran, 1990; Plaut, 1995). However, the low power distance and individualistic nature of Israeli culture appears to play a role in the specific nature of the counterattacks. The Israelis often justify the counter-attacks as responses to aggression directed against them. One reason for offering these justifications is that the Israelis do not wish to have their behavior seen as a dominant group overpowering a less able opponent. Even when they strike first, as they did in attacking the nuclear power plants that were being built in neighboring Iraq, they presented their attacks as defensive preemptive strikes. In line with their low power distance, the Israelis seemed to treat their enemies as equal in status, rather than as an inferior group which can be attacked at will.

A group-psychological reaction to injustice can be seen in the Israeli public's response to the intifada. During the intifada, the Israelis killed many Palestinians, but they did not do so without moral misgivings. One reason the intifada was successful was that many Israelis found the behavior of their own security forces morally repugnant. In doing so, they could hark back to the words of one of the founding fathers of Israel, David Ben Gurion, who said in 1924 that, 'Zionism does not have the moral right to harm even one Arab child, even if at that price it may realize all of its objectives' (cited in Benvenisti, 1995, 202). The Israeli emphasis on egalitarianism, which derives from their low power distance, may have contributed to this feeling of repugnance. That is, if all individuals are regarded as deserving equal rights, it is more difficult to dehumanize them and deprive them of those rights than if inequality is accepted as a natural part of the social order.

A group-behavioral response to perceived injustice by the Israelis that may reflect individualistic aspects of Israeli culture is the use of assassination. The Israeli security apparatus has sometimes used the assassination of individual leaders of terrorist groups as a technique of retaliation ('to bring them to justice'). It is interesting that this is not a technique that has been used with any frequency by the Palestinians against the Israelis (although it may be the case that Israeli security measures make assassination more difficult than terrorism). The Israelis may be more willing to use assassination than the Palestinians because they hold individuals responsible for acts of aggression against them, while the Palestinians seem more apt to hold all Israelis responsible for the injustices done to them. An example of the Israelis holding individuals responsible for their acts occurred after terrorists killed a number of Israeli athletes at the Olympic games in 1972. The Israelis spent years tracking down and killing the individuals responsible for this raid.

Sino–British conflict over the future of Hong Kong

The second case is concerned with the handover of Hong Kong from Britain to China in 1997. This is the first time in history that a highly developed capitalist city has been peacefully returned to a communist government. The Sino–British negotiations over the future of Hong Kong lasted over 15 years, and went on until just days before the handover. During this time, the relationship between the two nations changed from cooperative in the beginning to confrontational and verbally hostile at the end. The Chinese can be characterized as collectivistic and high in power distance, whereas the British are individualistic and low in power distance (Bond, 1996; Hofstede, 1980). As in the case of the Arab–Israeli conflict, some of the conflict between these two nations can be traced back to differences in these two cultural dimensions. However, because the nature of the conflict is different, the two cultural dimensions played out quite differently. These differences are manifested in the two cultures' views about treaties and contracts, definitions of democracy, and approaches to negotiation.

Historical background

Hong Kong was acquired by Britain as a colony after China lost the opium war, which was triggered by China's resistance to the importation of opium into China by Britain. Hong Kong Island was ceded to Britain in 1842 under the Treaty of Nanking. Subsequently, Kowloon and Stonecutters Island were ceded to Britain in 1860, and New Territories was leased to Britain for 99 years in 1898 (Wesley-Smith, 1980). In the late 1970s, investors and bankers began to express concern about their investments in New Territories because its lease would run out in 1997. Furthermore, the Chinese were calling into question the legitimacy of British rule in Hong Kong because it was based on unequal treaties.

Distributive justice

China and Britain had very different views of the status of Hong Kong before their formal negotiations in the early 1980s. China's position was that the agreements made between Britain and the Qing Government (China's last dynasty) concerning Hong Kong were unfair, and that they would not recognize these treaties signed by a previous government. As early as 1972, Huang Hua, China's permanent representative to the United Nations, requested the United Nations not to categorize Hong Kong and Macau (a Portuguese colony next to Hong Kong) as colonies (Cheng, 1984, chapter 2). In the language of distributive justice, China basically argued that distributive decisions made under threat were invalid, and that these unfair decisions, although accepted by the previous government, need not be accepted by the current government (Li, 1997). These arguments were used to put moral pressure on Britain. From the Chinese perspective, the moral course of action for

Britain to take would have been to right the wrongs that were committed in the last century by agreeing to terms that favor China.

In contrast, Britain regarded the treaties as basically valid and demanded that negotiations should be carried out in light of the treaties. Margaret Thatcher, Prime Minster of Britain at that time, repeatedly stated that the nineteenth-century treaties could be altered, but not abrogated. On one occasion, she added that if a country does not abide by an internationally binding treaty, it will not follow other treaties. Consistent with Western international law, Britain was trying to bring a trans-generational, decon-textualized distributive rule to the bargaining table. The basic argument was that a treaty is treaty. The circumstances under which it was signed and the legitimacy of the party who signed it should not be reinterpreted at a later time. This emphasis on the legality of the treaties suited Britain's purposes, but it is also consistent with the emphasis on contracts in indi-vidualistic cultures (see also below).

Given this discrepancy in views, the two sides did not agree on the legit-imacy of the treaties. This disagreement was never resolved, and the two sides simply ignored it and moved on to practical issues. To maintain a working relationship with Britain, China did not demand retribution from Britain for the opium war or the colonization of Hong Kong. Both sides obviously did not want to end up in a deadlock flooded by emotional, insulting rhetoric.

The sovereignty of Hong Kong

The initial British position was to return the sovereignty of Hong Kong Island to China in 1997, in exchange for retaining administrative control over Hong Kong for an extended period of time. The Chinese position was to reclaim both the sovereignty and the administration of Hong Kong from Britain. It is well-documented that collectivist societies are very concerned with face (an issue with direct links to interactional injustice), and China is no exception (Bond, 1996). Britain's suggestion was considered to be an affront to the face of the Chinese for two reasons: The British proposal implied that (1) China could not run Hong Kong effectively, and (2) that China endorsed the unequal treaties and colonialism. According to Li Hou, then Vice Director of the Office of Hong Kong and Macau Affairs Office, Deng Xiaoping, the informal leader of China at the time, made it very clear that China believed it would lose all legitimacy with its citizens and in the world if it agreed to the British proposal (Li, 1997). Given this background, it is not surprising that the initial negotiations were tense. Thatcher recalled the following exchange with Deng Xiaoping in 1982:

Deng: 'Look, I could walk in and take the whole lot this afternoon.'
Thatcher: 'Yes, there is nothing I could do to stop you. But the eyes of
             the world would now know what China is like. Everything

would leave Hong Kong. You'd have its prosperity and you would suddenly have lost the lot.' (Dimbleby, 1997, 55)

Although the bluntness of Deng's statement seems to clash with the emphasis on harmony that is characteristic of many collectivist cultures, the statement was directed at an outgroup and seems in accord with the idea that in collectivist cultures people often use confrontational techniques if the other side is an outgroup.

Britain eventually retracted its position because China made it clear that it would risk wrecking Hong Kong if an agreement could not be reached. As a practical matter, it would have been impossible for Hong Kong Island and Kowloon to survive under British administration, if New Territories, which constitutes the bulk of the land of Hong Kong, was returned to China when its lease was up.

Procedural justice

Representation of Hong Kong

The two sides also differed in their approaches to negotiation. China insisted on a bilateral negotiation between the two countries without the direct involvement of the people of Hong Kong, whose interests, they argued, would be represented by China. China would engage in consultation with leaders from different sectors on its own. This is obviously consistent with the benevolent authoritarianism that has been emphasized in Confucian traditions and reflects the high power distance of Chinese society (Pye, 1985). The Chinese stance also reflected their denial of the legitimacy of the Hong Kong Colonial government.

In contrast, coming from a liberal democratic tradition, Thatcher insisted that the people of Hong Kong should have a direct say in deciding their future, as might be expected from a culture that is individualistic and emphasizes the rights of individuals to determine their own destiny. The British felt that the Government of Hong Kong should represent the interests of the people of Hong Kong and seek advice from the Executive Council (whose members were appointed by the Governor to advise him on major policy decisions) with regard to issues about the transition. In 1983, Sir Edward Youde, then Governor of Hong Kong, stated in a press conference that he represented the people of Hong Kong in the negotiations. The Chinese side quickly pointed out that Youde only represented Britain and rejected any notion of a 'three-legged stool' negotiation situation, with Hong Kong as the third negotiating party (Li, 1997).

As was the case with the treaties, the problem of representation was never resolved and both sides eventually downplayed this disagreement and went on to other issues. A joint declaration was finally made by China and Britain in 1984, which spelled out the framework for the transition of Hong Kong's sovereignty from Britain to China in 1997. Hong Kong would become a special administrative region of China, with no change in political, legal, social and economic systems or the life style to which the people of Hong Kong had become accustomed. The details were to be contained in an annex, the Basic Law of the Hong Kong Special Administrative Region, to be formulated by China at a later stage.

Conflicts over the Basic Law

In 1989, university students gathered in Tiananmen Square in Beijing to protest against widespread corruption. This movement eventually developed into a campaign for democratic reforms, and soldiers and tanks were sent in to clear the Square of students. The military crackdown and the killings created an uproar of disapproval in the West and in Hong Kong. The Sino–British relationship dropped to a low point, and negotiations between China and Britain almost came to a halt. In 1992, Britain decided to replace the governor of Hong Kong, David Wilson, a diplomat and a sinologist, with Chris Patten, a well-connected politician, who was chairman of the Tory party during John Major's election campaign. The motivation, according to Douglas Hurd, then Foreign Secretary, was the need for the last governor to be 'in tune with the world of Westminster and the British media' (Dimbleby, 1997, 11). Many observers also pointed out that Britain was keen to switch from appeasement to a firmer stand toward China, as a consequence of the Tiananmen crackdown.

Patten was quick to introduce democratic changes to Hong Kong. The Basic Law required that in the first legislative council after the handover, 20 out of the 60 seats would be based on direct election. The remaining 40 seats were to be based on indirect elections, determined by a small, selected group of voters, so called 'elite' members of society. Given that the Joint Declaration and the Basic Law do not prescribe clearly how this selected group is formed, Patten noted that there was 'quite a lot of space, quite a lot of elbow room between the Joint Declaration and the Basic Law. What I propose to do is to find all those bits of elbow room for bedding down democracy or extending it' (Dimbleby, 1997, 115–16). Patten then introduced a reform that drastically increased the number and representativeness of the voters in this group, making the election close to a direct one. The thrust of the British reforms was an attempt to make the Basic Law more egalitarian and representative, which is in line with the democratic, individualistic cultural traditions of Britain.

Patten's democratic reform met with hostility from China (Li, 1997). When initial contacts failed to produce any change in Patten's plan, China bombarded him with vitriolic, hostile remarks and avoided official contact with him. Lu Ping, then Director of the Hong Kong and Macua Office, called him 'the criminal of all time'. Patten (1998) was unprepared for such personal attacks as he recalled that 'Lu's occasionally graceless tone and behaviour were surprising' (1998, 69). Nevertheless, Patten's responses to the Chinese Government and the Chinese officials were basically task-oriented and hardly personal. He openly proclaimed his willingness to negotiate with the Chinese. The two sides did not resolve their differences, and in the end, China set up a provisional legislative council that would replace the legislative council formed under Patten after the handover.

In individualist societies, such as Britain, contracts are taken seriously, and the content is considered to be binding. In collectivist societies, such as China, contracts often are taken as symbols of collaboration, and their contents are taken to signify common understandings, rather than prescriptions that are binding regardless of situational changes (see, for example, Lubman, 1988 for the case of China; Sullivan, Peterson, Kameda and Shimada, 1981 for Japan). Part of the conflict between Patten and China arose from the legalistic interpretation of the Basic Law and the Joint Declaration by Patten and the symbolic interpretation adopted by the Chinese. China made numerous remarks about how Patten violated the 'spirit' of the Basic Law. Patten (1998) recalled that

> Chinese officials ... would accuse me of having broken the Joint Declaration and the Basic Law. 'How have I done so?' I would respond. 'Show me where.' 'You know you have done so,' they would reply. 'You must have done so, or else we wouldn't have said it.' 'But where?' 'It is not for us to say; you must know that you have erred.' 'Give me a single instance,' I would argue. 'Well', they would usually claim somewhat lamely, 'you have at least broken the spirit of the Joint Declaration and the Basic Law'. 'What do you mean by the "spirit"? Do you just mean that you disagree with me? Why not then discuss what I have done? Put forward your own proposals.' 'We cannot put forward our own proposals until you return to the spirit of the texts.' (1998, 68–9)

Furthermore, Chinese officials also accused Pattern of breaking 'understandings' reached by the two countries in 1989 and 1990 (Dimbleby, 1997, 169). These 'understandings' were based on some exchanges between the foreign secretaries of the two countries, but were not clearly specified in the Basic Law. Again, Patten took a legalistic approach to this accusation, as he noted that three different teams of international lawyers concluded that his proposed reform was not a breach of these so-called understandings (Patten, 1998). Needless to say, the judgment of these international lawyers was based on Western international law.

Retributive justice

As noted earlier, Patten made many public declarations concerning his willingness to negotiate with the Chinese, but the Chinese refused to negotiate with him, arguing that lacking a common ground, further talks would be futile. This pattern of exchange is also consistent with how individualists and collectivists handle conflicts. Tse, Francis and Walls (1994) studied the ways in which executives from mainland China and Canada handled two types of conflict: task-related and person-related. When a conflict was caused by personal styles, Chinese executives were more likely to recommend discontinuation of negotiation, showed less satisfaction with the negotiation, and were less likely to be friendly than their Canadian counterparts. Leung (1997) also argued that Chinese are more likely to scrutinize whether someone can be trusted and accepted as an ingroup member. They are likely to avoid contact with people classified as outgroup members, and may even be hostile toward them. Given that Patten was seen by the Chinese as uncooperative, confrontational, and unreasonable, the vitrolic remarks directed at Patten should not be surprising.

The outcome of the dispute

The Sino–British conflict was mild in comparison with the Arab–Israeli conflict, although the stakes were nonetheless very high. Both sides were restrained and careful to avoid full-scale, open conflict. For China, it was important to maintain the prosperity of Hong Kong so as to reap the enormous financial benefits from its continued stability (Kuan, 1997). China also wanted to use Hong Kong to demonstrate to Taiwan that a peaceful reunification between two different social and political systems is possible (Weng, 1977). For Britain, it was important to protect British interests in Hong Kong after the handover and to maintain a cordial relationship with China so as to capitalize on its burgeoning market. The practical concerns of both sides created a long-term perspective that extended beyond the focal issues, contained the conflict, and moved the negotiations forward, despite fundamental differences.

Conclusions

We have presented a framework for understanding the role that culture plays in international conflicts, and two cases illustrating its usefulness. Like any methodological approach, case studies have both limitations and strengths. In a protracted conflict, such as the Israeli–Palestinian conflict or the negotiations over Hong Kong, it is probably possible to find evidence for a wide variety of hypotheses. Also, it is not easy to establish the validity of cultural explanations – that is one of the limitations of case studies. The strength of case studies, however, lies in their illustrative and heuristic value. Not only can they be used to illustrate a theory, they can also be used to generate hypotheses for systematic investigation. For instance, we discussed the possibility that the collectivistic nature of Palestinian culture may have made terrorism seem a less repugnant response to the conflict by some members of this group because collectivistic cultures emphasize the distinction between the ingroup and the outgroup. If the reasoning here is valid, then a crossnational study should show that collectivistic cultures are more likely than individualistic cultures to use terrorism as a response to perceived injustice. Similarly, it would be possible to test the idea that individualistic cultures may be more likely to use assassination as a tactic in intergroup conflict than collectivistic cultures. In the Sino–British conflict, we suggested that collectivists are likely to be confrontational and hostile toward an opponent who is judged to be untrustworthy and uncooperative. In contrast to the common characterization of collectivists as tolerant and harmonious, we may test the notion that they can be aggressive and unyielding, especially with outgroup members.

To sum up, we acknowledge that international conflict is produced and sustained by many factors, and cultural differences sometimes may not be the major cause. As shown in the Sino–British conflict, practical-mindedness on both sides kept the conflict under control, with no obvious damage to the long-term relationship between the two nations (Dimbleby, 1997, 533). However, some international conflicts are less restrained, and the Arab–Israeli conflict is a potent example of how tragic the consequences of such conflicts can be. Resolving international conflicts is like finding a safe pathway through a minefield. Culture is one of many mines that can be very destructive. It is our hope that this chapter highlights how cultural differences can trap nations in fruitless deadlocks and that knowledge of culture is crucial to avoiding these traps.

References

Atran, S. (1990) 'Stones against the Iron Fist, Terror within the Nation: Alternating Structures of Violence and Cultural Identity in the Israeli–Palestinian Conflict', *Politics and Society,* vol. 18, pp. 481–526.

Azzi, A. E. (1992) 'Procedural Justice and the Allocation of Power in Intergroup Relations: Studies in the United States and South Africa', *Personality and Social Psychology Bulletin,* vol. 18, pp. 736–47.

Barakat, H. (1993) *The Arab World,* Berkeley, Cal.: University of California Press.

Bar-Tal, D. (1990) 'Israeli–Palestinian Conflict: A Cognitive Analysis', *International Journal of Intercultural Relations,* vol. 14, pp. 7–29.

Bies, R. J. and Moag, J. S. (1986) 'Interactional Justice: Communication Criteria of Fairness', in R. J. Lewicki, B. H. Sheppard and M. H. Bazerman (eds.), *Research on Negotiation in Organizations,* Greenwich, Conn.: JAI Press (pp. 43–55).

Benvenisti, M. (1995) *Intimate Enemies: Jews and Arabs in a Shared Land,* Berkeley, Cal.: University of California Press.

Bisharat, C. (1989) 'Palestine and Humanitarian Law: Israeli Practice in the West Bank and Gaza', *Hastings International and Comparative Law Review,* vol. 12, pp. 325–71.

Bond, M. H. (1996) *Handbook of Chinese Psychology,* Hong Kong: Oxford University Press.

Bond, M. H., Wan, K. C., Leung, K. and Giacalone, R. (1985) 'How are Responses to Verbal Insults Related to Cultural Collectivism and Power Distance?' *Journal of Cross-Cultural Psychology,* vol. 16, pp. 111–27.

Cheng, J. Y. S. (1984) *Hong Kong: In Search of a Future*, Hong Kong: Oxford University Press.

Dimbleby, J. (1997) *The Last Governor*, London: Warner Books.

Feghali, E. (1997) 'Arab Cultural Communication Patterns', *International Journal of Intercultural Relations*, vol. 21, pp. 345–78.

Gabrielidis, C., Stephan, W. G., Ybarra, O., Pearson, V. M. S. and Villareal, L. (1997) 'Preferred Styles of Conflict Resolution: Mexico and the United States', *Journal of Cross-Cultural Psychology*, vol. 28, pp. 661–77.

Griefat, Y. and Katriel, T. (1989) 'Life Demands Musayara: Communication and Culture among Arabs in Israel', In S. Ting-Toomey and F. Korzenny (eds.), *Language, Communication and Culture*, (pp. 121–38) Newbury Park, Cal.: Sage.

Gudykunst, W. B. and Ting-Toomey, S. (1988) 'Culture and Affective Communication', *American Behavioral Scientist*, vol. 31, pp. 384–400.

Hofstede, G. (1980) *Culture's Consequences: International Differences in Work-related Values*, Beverly Hills, Cal.: Sage.

Hofstede, G. (1986) 'Cultural Dimensions of Management and Planning', *Asia Pacific Journal of Management*, January, pp. 81–98.

Hunter, F. R. (1991) *The Palestinian Uprising*, Berkeley: University of California Press.

James, K. (1993) 'The Social Context of Organizational Justice: Cultural, Intergroup and Structural Effects on Justice Behaviors and Perceptions', In R. Cropanzano (ed.), *Justice in the Workplace: Approaching Fairness in Human Resource Management*, (pp. 21–50) Hillsdale, N.J.: Erlbaum.

Kuan, H. C. (1997) 'Does Hong Kong have a future?' *Security Dialogue*, vol. 28, pp. 233–36.

Landau, S. F. (1997) 'Conflict Resolution in a Highly Stressful Society: The Case of Israel', In D. P. Fry and K. Bjorkqvist (eds.), *Cultural Variation in Conflict Resolution: Alternatives to Violence*, (pp. 123–36) Mahwah, N.J.: Erlbaum.

Leung, K. (1997) 'Negotiation and Reward Allocations Across Cultures', In P. C. Earley and M. Erez (eds.), *New Perspectives on International Industrial/Organizational Psychology*, (pp. 640–75) San Francisco: Jossey–Bass.

Leung, K. and Bond, M. H. (1984) 'The Impact of Cultural Collectivism on Reward Allocation', *Journal of Personality and Social Psychology*, vol. 47, pp. 793–804.

Leung, K. and Morris, M. W. (in press) 'Justice Through the Lens of Culture and Ethnicity', In J. Sanders and V. L. Hamilton (eds.), *Handbook of Law and Social Sciences: Justice*, New York: Plenum.

Leung, K. and Stephan, W. G. (1998) 'Perceptions of injustice in intercultural relations', *Applied and Preventive Psychology*, vol. 7, pp. 195–205

Li, H. (1997) *The Journey of the Return*, Hong Kong: Joint Publishing (H.K.) (In Chinese)

Lubman, S. B. (1988) 'Investment and Export Contracts in the People's Republic of China: Perspectives on Evolving Patterns', *Brigham Young University Law Review*, 1988(3), pp. 543–65.

Moten, A. R. (1996) *Political Science: An Islamic Perspective*, New York: St. Martin's Press.

Morris, M. W., Williams, K. Y., Leung, K., Bhatnagar, D., Li, J. F., Kondo, M., Luo, J. L. and Hu, J. C. (1998) 'Culture, Conflict Management Style and Underlying Values: Accounting for Cross-National Differences in Styles of Handling Conflicts among US, Chinese, Indian and Filipina Managers', *Journal of International Business Studies*. vol. 29, pp. 729–48.

Nidal, A. (1986) 'The Palestinian Goal Justifies Terrorism', In D. L. Bender and B. Leone (eds.), *Terrorism* (pp. 113–18) St. Paul, MN: Greenhaven Press.

O'Brien, W. V. (1993) *Law and Morality in Israel's War with the PLO*, New York: Routledge.

Otopow, S. (1990) 'Moral Exclusion and Injustice', *Journal of Social Issues*, vol. 46(1), pp. 1–20.

Patten, C. (1998) *East and West*, London: Macmillan.

Pearson, V. M. S. and Stephan, W. G. (1998) 'Preferences for Styles of Negotiation: A Comparison of Brazil and the USA', *International Journal of Intercultural Relations*, vol. 22, pp. 67–83.

Plaut, S. (1995) 'Continue the Peace Process? No, It's Heading for Disaster', *Middle East Quarterly*, vol. 2, pp. 23–28.

Pye, L. W. (1985) *Asian Power and Politics: The Cultural Dimensions of Authority*, Cambridge, Massachusetts: Belknap Press.

Smooha, S. (1987) 'Jewish and Arab Ethnocentrism in Israel', *Ethnic and Racial Studies*, vol. 10, pp. 1–26.

Suleiman, M. W. (1973) 'The Arabs and the West: Communication Gap', in M. Prosser (ed.), *Intercommunication Among Nations and People* (pp. 287–303) New York: Harper and Row.

Sullivan, J., Peterson, R. B., Kameda, N. and Shimada, J. (1981) 'The Relationship between Conflict Resolution Approaches and Trust: A Cross-Cultural Study', *Academy of Management Journal*, vol. 24, pp. 803–815.

Tse, D. K., Francis, J. and Walls, J. (1994) 'Cultural Differences in Conducting Intra- and Inter-cultural Negotiations: A Sino–Canadian Comparison', *Journal of International Business Studies*, vol. 25, pp. 537–55.

Tyler, T. R. and Bies, R. J. (1990) 'Beyond Formal Procedures: The Interpersonal Context of Procedural Justice', In J. S. Carroll (ed.), *Applied Social Psychology and Organizational Settings*, (pp. 77–98) Hillsdale, NJ: Lawrence Erlbaum Associates.

Vanneman, R and Pettigrew, T. F. (1972) 'Race and Relative Deprivation in the Urban United States', *Race*, vol. 13, pp. 461–86.

Walster, E., Walster, G. W. and Berscheid, E. (1978) *Equity Theory and Research*, Boston: Allyn and Bacon.

Weng, B. S. J. (1997) 'Mainland China, Taiwan and Hong Kong as International Actors', In G. A. Postiglione and J. T. H. Tang (eds.), *Hong Kong's Reunion with China: Global Dimensions*, Hong Kong: University of Hong Kong Press.

Wesley–Smith, P. (1980) *Unequal treaty, 1898–1997: China, Great Britain and Hong Kong's New Territories*, Hong Kong: Oxford University Press.

Witty, C. J. (1980) *Mediation and Society: Conflict Management in Lebanon*, New York: Academic Press.

9
Culture and Ethnic Conflict

Marc Howard Ross

What is the role of culture in the analysis of ethnic conflict? The power of cultural models of behavior and their value for the development of a comparative (and crosscultural) political psychology lies in their specification of cross-level links to explain collective behavior through individual-level learning mechanisms and the internalization of world views. The linkage between individual and group dynamics is seen in shared rituals and symbols of identity which emphasize a group's distinctiveness even where 'objectively defined' intragroup variation may be high. This linkage also draws our attention to the social reinforcement of shared worldviews and the distinctiveness of ways of life. These dynamics are especially relevant to considering the mobilization of group identity in ethnic conflict, a good account of which must explain why individuals behave as they do, how behaviors are learned, and why and how group loyalty matters. I try to emphasize these points below.

Ethnic conflict is an ideal question for comparative analysis. Few modern states are ethnically homogeneous, and as Gurr (1993) has shown, conflicts in which ethnicity is a central defining dimension are prevalent in all parts of the contemporary world. He counts 233 politically significant ethnic conflicts in the world from 1945 to 1989. Furthermore, as Huntington (1993) argues, conflicts rooted in cultural differences are likely to be even more common in the post-Cold War world. While ethnic conflict is widespread, it is not at all times equally virulent. Why some societies and certain groups handle ethnic conflicts more constructively than others, I suggest, is an important question for crosscultural political psychology.

Conflicts between ethnic groups are redefined in significant ways over time. A label, such as the Israeli–Palestinian conflict, may not shift although key goals of the parties and their interactions with each other may change in fundamental ways. Equally important for comparative analysis is that some intergroup situations are best characterized as cooperative when relations between the different groups are more or less peaceful and overt intergroup disputes are not a fact of daily life. Both conflict and cooperation need to be explained (Ross, 1993a; Worchel, Coutant-Sassic and Wong, 1993). Huntington, for example, writes about what he sees as the high potential for conflict between cultural groups, but at the same time we need to consider situations where cultural differences are great but where conflict is less than we might expect on the basis of these differences alone. In this regard, the present US– Japan relationship is interesting in that while there are clearly tensions and differences – some of which have been explained in cultural terms (Johnson, 1991) – the level of overt conflict is modest and overall one would have to describe the relationship for some time as more cooperative than hostile.

The question of why societies differ in their levels and forms of conflict is one which I have examined at length using a worldwide sample of 90 preindustrial societies (Ross, 1993). The data show strong relationships between conflict levels and psychocultural dispositions, orientations towards the self and others acquired early in life. In particular, violent conflict is much more likely in societies in which socialization lacks warmth and affection, is harsh, and where male gender identity conflict is high. These psychocultural practices, I argue, promote interpretations of the world as an uncertain place where potential enemies are ready to attack at any time. At the same time, while psychocultural interpretations predispose a group towards high or low conflict, its social and political structure is critical in determining who fights with whom. Cross-cutting social structures which link diverse groups in a society produce an interest in intra-group cooperation, and greater conflict with external enemies; whereas weak cross-cutting ties promote narrow group interests and greater intra-group conflict.

The relevance of these findings for ethnic conflict in the contemporary world is that they emphasize the key role of culture in interpreting potential and overt conflicts. Because so many social and political acts are inherently ambiguous, I emphasize the importance of psychocultural interpretations in the frameworks particular groups use to understand a conflict, and the need to address these powerful interpretations in any meaningful effort to manage the conflict constructively (Ross, 1995). Second, the results also make it clear that while we must take seriously the intense fears and threats parties feel, there is also a need to bridge the parties' often significant, and real, competing interests.[1] Addressing competing interests means doing something about inequalities while also building institutions which offer all sides significant benefits and a stake in future arrangements. One hypothesis is that when each side interprets the other's motives as very hostile, negotiation over interest differences and searches for mutually acceptable constitutional agreements are doomed to failure. For this reason, successful peacemaking in the most intransigent situations requires first taking seriously the parties' culturally-rooted interpretations and the fears and threats underlying them (Ross, 1995).

While the analysis of individual groups may show us a good deal about their propensity for intergroup conflict, studying dyads and regional clusters of societies can tell how conflict escalates between rivals. After all, it is not hard to find examples of a group which gets along fairly well with one neighbor and terribly with another. Because we know that conflict systems are highly interactive, comparative analysis of particular dyads – selected for theoretical reasons – can be especially valuable. Perhaps an obvious, but still interesting, comparison would be one which asked why the breakup of Czechoslovakia was so peaceful and that of Yugoslavia so violent. Huntington hypothesizes that conflict will be highest where cultural differences, particularly those defined by religion, are greatest. While that seems consistent with the outcomes here, are there other, perhaps more important factors at work as well?

Raymond Cohen's investigations into culture and negotiation offer a particularly useful starting point for dyadic analyses. In one study, Cohen (1990) examined Israeli–Egyptian negotiations, and in a second (Cohen, 1991) he looked at US negotiations with five different nations: China, Mexico, Egypt, India and Japan. In both studies, significant differences in cultural styles helped to explain why negotiations between each of the pairs of nations were often so drawn out and not successful. Cohen argues, for example, that intercultural communications such as diplomatic negotiations can be strongly influenced by disparate assumptions, the role of language and non-verbal gestures, and the nature and value of social relationships (1991). He is particularly interested in problems of communication in exchanges between members of what he calls individualistic and interdependent cultures. Different initial assumptions that people in different cultures make means that often the same words of gestures are interpreted quite differently if important cultural assumptions (worldviews) are not shared and each culture produces very different negotiation styles which is a source of tension when the two face each other (1991, 19–32). For example, he argues how Israeli's focus on the legal meaning of particular statements, and Egyptians stress the importance of context and metaphorical meaning produced a number of communications failures which have led to wars and missed peacemaking opportunities.

Psychocultural dynamics and ethnic conflict

Psychocultural dynamics are central in the development, escalation, and termination of ethnic conflict.

The cultural context of ethnic politics

Ethnic groups are cultural units whose distinctiveness is marked by contextually defined features such as language, food, clothing, religion, and a sense of identity and distinctiveness bolstered by an ideology of common descent which places emotional significance on real and fictive kin ties (Horowitz, 1985, chapter 2). The ethnic community, as Horowitz writes, is the family writ large; membership in the family separates insiders and outsiders. Some ethnic communities are formally organized as political units (such as states or autonomous regions in larger states) which make collective decisions and enforce ingroup rules on members. Often, however, in the contemporary world authority in ethnic communities is more informal but still can exert significant pressures over the behavior of group members, especially during periods of stress.

While the core of an ethnic group and consensus concerning who is part of the group is often high, a group's outer edges and the boundaries between one group and another are often fuzzy (Barth, 1969). In polities such as the former USSR which require citizens to carry internal passports identifying one's nationality, there are frequently multiple criteria for classifying a person allowing for movement across boundaries which follows systematic patterns (Karklins, 1986). Similarly, ethnic categories (and who is put in them) varies over time and context, reinforcing the importance of the subjective and changing character of ethnicity and possibilities for manipulating identity politically. In short, while cultural features distinguish one group from another, political dynamics are often central in deciding the relative importance of particular cultural features in any time and place. Political processes are crucial to shaping how and when cultural differences are emphasized. Culture, in this sense, does not cause conflict directly, but political groups and leaders use culture to mobilize followers in their pursuit of political goals.

Tightening the boundaries and defining action

Perceived threat frequently leads to calls for tightening the boundaries between a group and all outsiders (not just stated enemies). Groups become more careful to monitor how members interact with outgroups and there is sometimes an increase in sanctioning of interpersonal interactions with outgroups, exchanges across boundaries, and even expressions of positive feeling for members of other groups. The most extreme form – unfortunately not uncommon – involves ethnic purification in which groups seek to remove any traces of connectedness or interaction with the enemy. This often takes symbolic forms such as removing foreign words from the language or books from libraries and bookstores or rewriting history to emphasize a lack of connectedness between two groups which have shared the same territory for long periods of time (Tambiah, 1986). Finally, ethnic cleansing and genocide involve the removal and killing of any members of the outgroup (as well as in-group members about whom one has 'doubts'), as well as efforts to eradicate physical markers of its existence such as religious and other buildings and libraries housing culturally important manuscripts (Sells, 1996).

In escalating conflicts, groups frequently impose tests on their members requiring them to make public commitment to the group's cause, such as participation in group rituals which reaffirm the correctness of the group's position, such as taking an oath, wearing particular items of clothing, or giving up items of high value such as money or choice items of food. In such rituals, the group may focus particular emotional attention on individuals who in the past might have been critical of the group's position or even outsiders who support the group's cause as a way of emphasizing the righteousness of their cause.

Interpreting events

Ethnicity is not equally important everywhere as a marker of social position, as a determiner of political rights and privileges, or as a line of political cleavage. Where it is significant, however, ethnicity provides a culturally based framework to explain the motives and actions of others, particularly in situations where the actions themselves are highly ambiguous. Ethnic (cultural) frameworks offer worldviews which interpret inherently complicated and potentially puzzling actions to make sense of them and to guide appropriate responses. The frameworks (or schemas) of particular interest here are those marked by relatively high ingroup homogeneity because they are learned within the ethnic community and socially reinforced through the relatively homogenous ethnic networks in which many people spend much of their lives. Sharing and reinforcing interpretations increases as stress increases in conflict situations meaning that people have both less access to alternative interpretations and, more important, little social incentive to take seriously those they encounter.

At the core of psychocultural interpretations are the stories of the past and present which explain why an enemy behaves as it does and which justify a strong response from one's own group. Powerful metaphors help groups define the threats they face. Akenson (1992), for example, offers a masterful account of how many politically relevant Protestants in Northern Ireland, Afrikaners in South Africa, and Jews in Israel found great political meaning to the Old Testament idea of the sacred covenant from the story of Exodus. The metaphor of the sacred covenant explains their vulnerable and precarious situation in the world but also provides a course of action which tightens ingroups' resolve in the face of widespread external opposition. Such worldviews, he argues, are highly defended and difficult to change.

A similar powerful metaphor is found in what Volkan calls a *chosen trauma*, 'an event that causes a large group to feel helpless and victimized by another group' (1991, 13). In his writing, Volkan gives many examples of such events which clearly would include the Turkish slaughter of Armenians, the Nazi holocaust, the experience of slavery and segregation for African-Americans, and the Serbian defeat at Kosovo by the Turks in

1389 (Volkan, 1997). If a group feels too humiliated, angry or helpless to mourn the losses suffered in the trauma, he suggests that it then incorporates the emotional meaning of the traumatic event into its identity and passes on the emotional and symbolic meaning from generation to generation. The flip side is the *chosen glory* in which a group perceives triumph over the enemy; this is seen clearly in the Northern Irish Protestant celebration of the Battle of the Boyne in 1689 every 12 July (Cecil, 1993; Jarman, 1997). In escalating ethnic conflicts, the key metaphors, such as those in the chosen trauma or glory serve both as a rallying point and as a way to make sense of events which evoke deep fears and threats to existence (Horowitz, 1985; Kelman, 1978; 1987).

Cultural mobilization

Culture offers contextually defined resources for political organization and mobilization in ethnic conflicts as discussed above. Its ideology, for example, provides an explicit statement of what is often implicit in a group's worldview. While there is certainly great variability in the form and content of ideological statements, three politically critical themes which occur over and over in ethnic confrontation are:

- each side's feeling of relative *isolation* – 'People don't know what it is like to be a X', and 'We are alone in the world';
- expression of *vulnerability* – 'Unless we take extraordinary steps our existence is precarious; and
- a sense that the group constitutes the *chosen people* who will survive and triumph.[2]

The dynamics of increasing polarization involves mechanisms of selective emphasis on past events and selective perception of current ones, both of which are facilitated by the social and emotional separation between the group and others. In the creation of a politically acceptable past, the selective use of events is perhaps more important than outright distortions (Tambiah, 1986). It is not necessarily what groups get wrong that is as important as what they ignore. In fact, outside observers are often stuck at how little groups in conflict (even those living in the same small place such as Protestants and Catholics in Northern Ireland) know about each other, and how strikingly different are the accounts of the conflict each side provides – not so much because of outright disagreements but because each highlights such different events.

Selective perception is maintained when each cultural group, emphasizing its status as a vulnerable minority, is unable to empathize with the other side's past losses and present fears (Volkan, 1988; White, 1984). Ingroup accounts are selective but powerful for they resonate with what people have experienced and the way they have come to understand the past. Old wounds don't heal when (small) slights continue to keep them festering. The construction of powerful metaphors to symbolize a group's plight, the development of rituals of unity, and the destruction of social ties between groups all inhibit efforts to bridge differences and make further one-sided recounting of the conflict more likely.

Culture and ethnic peacemaking

If we take seriously the profoundly cultural nature of ethnic conflict, what are the prospects for peacemaking between two (or more) groups who have as basic a fear of and anger towards each other as the psychocultural dynamics described above suggest? Is it realistic to think that Protestants and Catholics in Northern Ireland or Tamils and Sinhalese in Sri Lanka can ever live together more cooperatively?

The first point to make is that there are many examples of situations where once extremely hostile ethnic groups have come to live side-by-side in more peaceful ways. The once hostile peoples of France and Germany have developed a new culture of European cooperation since the second world war which has not ended all differences between the former adversaries, but created a much less threatening, non-violent way of dealing with differences. Similarly, ethnic groups in Nigeria which fought a bitter civil war a generation ago have achieved significant reconciliation.[3] Such examples make it irresponsible and factually irrelevant to write off ethnic conflict as inevitable and unmanageable.

Emphasizing the cultural dimensions of ethnic conflict is at odds with the hypothesis that a first step to resolving serious group difference lies in finding the right formula (that is, constitution) to meet the core interests of each side. At best, such institutional arrangements might follow a much more complicated psychocultural process in which the groups come to believe that such arrangements are possible.[4] We have seen this at work in a number of recent examples of relatively partially successful ethnic conflict management, such as South Africa and the Middle East.

The theories of psychoanalysts like Volkan and cultural anthropologists like Geertz (1973a) agree that a natural starting point is making sense of the stories parties in a conflict tell. Taking seriously a group's worldview does not mean agreeing with it but rather trying to understand why a group has come to see the world as it does, the consequences of the view it holds, and what would have to happen for it to change its current understanding. There is no doubt that third-parties can be especially important in this process but the key here is getting the parties themselves to approach each other's accounts in ways that permit them to conceptualize future arrangements which are potentially more satisfactory than past ones. Volkan (1988, 1993) argues that in the most intense conflicts the inability to mourn past losses means that groups continue to fixate on the past. Cultural responses, such as building monuments, holding public rituals and other events which help groups acknowledge past suffering and mourn real losses are prerequisites to developing new relationships with old enemies.

Conclusion

An analysis of ethnic conflict requires that we account for the particular fears and threats competing groups perceive through a focus on the meaning of particular events and metaphors central to the conflict. Only through such detailed understanding might third-parties move not only towards understanding 'what a conflict is really about', but also towards being able to do something about it.

A complex problem such as the dynamics of ethnocentrism and ethnic conflict is likely to benefit from a better understanding of the psychological dynamics underlying cultural processes. After all, ethnic mobilization begins with perceptions of group differences rooted in shared cultural assumptions and is strengthened by dense within group social interaction. Cultural mechanisms provide selective reinforcement to group members for group-supportive behaviors and shared interpretations of the world which help account for the intensity of ethnic conflicts for participants which is, at the same time, generally puzzling outsiders.

The task of building a field of crosscultural political psychology, in this view, will rise or fall on the extent to which analysis can link the rich descriptions of contextually specific cultural understandings with the identification of psychologically general processes underlying culturally specific beliefs and behaviors. Psychocultural approaches to politics promise to broaden our comparative understanding of widespread (and probably universal) processes such as political participation, order and rebellion, authority and its legitimation, and conflict and its management.

Notes

1. Donald T. Campbell (personal communication) pointed out that ingroups can fear culturally very similar outgroups, and that in fact many arms races in history were between culturally very similar groups.
2. LeVine and Campbell (1972, 12) offer a more complete list of dimensions of ethnocentrism each of which can be, and often is, used to build a group's culturally grounded ideological rationales for hostility.
3. For a number of years now I have been asking groups for examples of more or less successful ethnic conflict management. My not very systematic list has produced several dozen cases, most of which I knew nothing about before they were presented to me. I would appreciate any examples readers might care to send.
4. Kelman's list of prerequisites (1978, 176–85) for an Israeli–Palestinian agreement is as useful a list of beliefs as I can imagine: (1) each side must acquire some insight into the perspectives of the other; (2) each side must be persuaded that there is someone to talk to on the other side and something to talk about; (3) each side must be able to distinguish between the dreams and the operational

programs of the other side; (4) each side must be persuaded that mutual conces-
sions will create a new situation, setting a process of change into motion; (5) each
side must be persuaded that structural changes, conducive to a stable peace, have
taken place or will take place in the leadership of the other side; and (6) each side
must sense a responsiveness to its human concerns and psychological needs on
the part of the adversary.

References

Akenson, D. H. (1992) *God's Peoples: Covenant and Land in South Africa, Israel and Ulster*, Ithaca, NY: Cornell University Press.

Barth, F. (ed.) (1969) *Ethnic Groups and Boundaries: The Social Organization of Cultural Difference*, Boston: Little Brown.

Cecil, R. (1993) 'The Marching Season in Northern Ireland: An Expression of Politico-Religious Identity', in S. Macdonald (ed.), *Inside European Identities: Ethnography in Western Europe*, Ann Arbor: Berg Publishers (pp. 146–66).

Cohen, R. (1990) *Culture and Conflict in Egyptian–Israeli Relations: A Dialogue of the Deaf*, Bloomington: Indiana University Press.

—— (1991) *Negotiating across Cultures: Communication Obstacles in International Diplomacy*, Washington, D.C.: USIP Press.

Geertz, C. (1973a) 'Thick Description: Toward an Interpretive Theory of Culture', in C. Geertz, *The Interpretation of Cultures*, New York: Basic Books, Harper Torchbooks (pp. 8–30).

Gurr, T. R. (1993) *Minorities at Risk: A Global View of Ethnopolitical Conflicts*, Washington, D.C.: United States Institute for Peace Press.

Horowitz, D. L. (1985) *Ethnic Groups in Conflict*, Berkeley and Los Angeles: University of California Press.

Huntington, S. (1993) 'The Clash of Civilizations', *Foreign Affairs*, pp. 22–49.

Jarman, N. (1997) *Material Conflicts: Prades and Visual Displays in Northern Ireland*, Oxford and New York: Berg.

Johnson, S. K. (1991) *The Japanese through American Eyes*, Stanford: Stanford University Press.

Karklins, R. (1986) *Ethnic Relations in the USSR: The Perspective from Below*, Boston: Allen & Unwin.

Kelman, H. C. (1978) 'Israelis and Palestinians: Psychological Prerequisites for Mutual Acceptance', *International Security*, vol. 3, pp. 162–86.

—— (1987) 'The Political Psychology of the Israeli–Palestinian Conflict: How can we Overcome the Barriers to a Negotiated Solution?' *Political Psychology*, vol. 8, pp. 347–63.

LeVine, R. A. and D. T. Campbell (1973) *Ethnocentrism: Theories of Conflict, Ethnic Attitudes, and Group Behavior*, New York: John Wiley.

Ross, M. H. (1993) *The Culture of Conflict: Interpretations and Interests in Comparative Perspective*, New Haven and London: Yale University Press.

—— (1995) 'Psychocultural Interpretation Theory and Peacemaking in Ethnic Conflicts', *Political Psychology*, vol. 16, pp. 523–44.

Sells, M. A. (1996) *The Bridge Betrayed: Religion and Genocide in Bosnia*, Berkeley and Los Angeles: University of California Press.

Spiro, M. E. (1984) 'Some Reflections on Cultural Determinism and Relativism with Special Reference to Emotion and Reason', in R. A. Schweder and R. A. LeVine (eds.), *Culture Theory: Essays on Mind, Self, and Emotion*, Cambridge: Cambridge University Press (pp. 323–46).

——— (1987) 'Culture and Human Nature', in *Culture and Human Nature: Theoretical Papers of Melford E. Spiro*, Chicago: University of Chicago Press (pp. 3–31).

Tambiah, S. J. (1986) *Sri Lanka: Ethnic Fratricide and the Dismantling of Democracy*, Chicago: University of Chicago Press.

Volkan, V. D. (1988) *The Need to have Enemies and Allies: From Clinical Practice to International Relationships*, New York: Jason Aronson.

——— (1991) 'On "chosen trauma"', *Mind and Human Interaction*, vol. 3, p. 13.

——— (1997) *Bloodlines: From Ethnic Pride to Ethnic Terrorism*, New York: Farrar, Straus & Giroux.

White, R. K. (1984) *Fearful Warriors: A Psychological Profile of U.S.–Soviet Relations*, New York: Free Press.

Worchel, S. D., Coutant-Sassic D., F. Wong (1993) 'Toward a More Balanced View of Conflict: There is a Positive Side', in S. Worchel and J. A. Simpson (eds.), *Conflict between People and Groups: Causes, Processes and Resolutions*, Chicago: Nelson Hall (pp. 76–89).

Part III

The Political Psychology of Change in Cultural Regions

10
The Political Unconscious: Stories and Politics in Two South American Cultures

Allen Johnson

Introduction

Central to political life in any society is the maintenance of a pattern of authority in spite of a certain inevitable tendency toward willful defiance (or uninhibited self-expression) on the part of at least some members of the group. In nonstratified societies – the bands and tribes of anthropological parlance – the management of aggression and anger-provoking behaviors like theft, infidelity and stinginess is among the most central political problems. In stratified societies – chiefdoms, feudal societies and states – the problem of aggression remains fundamental, but is often focused especially on the preservation of systems of inequality by managing the frustrations and resentments occasioned by poverty, repression and the general arrogance of power.

Intrinsically, maintenance of a system of authority in this sense is simultaneously cultural and psychological. Culturally, a set of (more or less) shared understandings describe the appropriate behaviors and values individuals are expected to conform to as good citizens. Rewards and punishments are also encoded culturally and are 'advertised' through explicit rules and implicit representations in dramas, stories and rituals. Psychologically, individuals face the need to control desire, insofar as impulsive gratification of anger, greed, lust and other culturally-constructed sins would arouse authority and bring punishment. Often enough, they will find ways privately to circumvent rules they endorse publicly, but they must still negotiate between sincerely-held citizenship values and the pressing but forbidden desires of the moment.

In this chapter I identify core emotion stories, or cultural emotion schemas, in the folk literatures of two contrasting societies: nonstratified native American forager-horticulturalists of the Peruvian Amazon (Matsigenka) and stratified peasant tenant farmers of northeastern Brazil (Boa Ventura). In each case the core emotion story represents a central political problem faced by audience members in everyday life: among the nonstratified Amazonians, the political problem is to maintain the coherence of the small kin group against the destructive conflicts arising from strong desires; among the stratified Brazilian tenant farmers, the political problem is to contain and, in a sense 'metabolize', the rage arising from humiliation by class superiors. Emotion stories are representations of these pervasive political-psychological issues and, therefore, open a window onto unconscious features of their political consciousness.

Political consciousness and the unconscious

If by political consciousness we mean the beliefs, values and attitudes that underlay people's political choices and actions, then a little reflection suggests that much of political consciousness is in fact unconscious, or at least inarticulate and inchoate. That is, although individuals when asked may describe their political beliefs and give reasons for their political choices, those descriptions and explanations frequently seem partial and inadequate – if not completely misleading – to outside observers. For example, political followers may describe their support for a leader or a cause in terms of ethnic or national pride, but may be unable to articulate the degree to which their own shared sense of humiliation and 'chosen trauma' (Volkan, 1997) can motivate cruel and violent political action (cf. Money-Kyrle, 1951).

Elements of political 'consciousness' may be unconscious in two senses. First, in terms of dynamic psychology, powerful political ideas and motivations may be denied or warded off because they would have to be acknowledged as wrong or shameful if made explicit. In racism and ethnic cleansing, for example, the need to describe the hated Other as filthy, immoral and subhuman is a defensive evasion of the self-criticism that would follow from cruelty toward fully human neighbors worthy of compassion. The Other simultaneously serves as a reservoir into which people can unconsciously project their own badness ('unintegrated "bad" fragments'; Volkan 1997, 104).

Second, political consciousness, like other information in the mind, is organized in schemas that may or may not be available to awareness. In the US, for example, men's political attitudes are partly organized by such schemas as 'American success values' and the male 'breadwinner model' (Strauss, 1992b). Although in interviews men can articulate some aspects of these schemas, others remain inchoate and their integration within larger and more personal systems of political beliefs appears to be completely unconscious (Strauss 1992b, 214), as is likely true of the majority of cognitive information processing (D'Andrade 1995, 144; Shore 1996, 52; Bucci, 1997).

Two cases

Since direct questioning can only take us so far in learning about an individual's political consciousness, we need ways to develop information about less readily articulated beliefs and values. Interviews themselves provide much indirect evidence of inarticulate political schemas; for example, the way sarcasm is used, or the juxtaposition of ideas from separate bounded schemas (Strauss, 1992b). Jokes, songs and poems also provide evidence for political ideas that cannot be more openly expressed (Scott, 1985; 1990). Here I explore the usefulness of folktales as one such line of evidence into unconscious constituents of political consciousness. First, I examine two cases as an inductive way into the subject; then I present the concept of cultural emotion schemas as a theoretical construct consistent with both kinds of unconscious and capable of accounting for a wide range of inchoate political consciousness.

I begin by examining the typical folktales of two contrasting societies. Although I have chosen them because I have extensive field experience in both and can explore with some confidence the deeper personal and cultural meanings of the stories, the contrast between them relates to an issue of broader significance, the different psychological demands made by life in nonstratified as contrasted with stratified societies. Elsewhere I have presented evidence showing that folktales from stratified societies reflect a much greater degree of 'repression' (resistance to open acknowledgment of forbidden desires) than those from nonstratified societies (Johnson and Price-Williams, 1996, 64–68). Here, I expand on that analysis by arguing that a specific difference between nonstratified and stratified societies is the far greater importance of humiliation (both conscious and unconscious) in the political-psychological dynamics of stratified societies.

Matsigenka: an egalitarian society

The Matsigenka are Arawakan-speaking native Americans of the Peruvian Amazon (Johnson and Johnson, 1988). Self-sufficient and virtually independent, they subsist from wild foods and horticulture, living in small scattered family groups that place the highest value on equality and non-interference. This intransigent autonomy – a source of continual complaint from missionaries and government officials who would like to unite them into villages and larger political units responsive to the state – often leads single families to break away from their extended-family hamlets and live in virtual isolation for years at a time. Yet the Matsigenka recognize full well that such isolation brings its own risks of exposure to nature and the possibility of human violence. Maintaining peace and harmony within the family and with other Matsigenkas in the vicinity thus becomes the central social – and, in effect, political – problem of their lives (Johnson 1997b).

The Matsigenka emotion story

The Matsigenka tell stories that nearly always have a similar emotional core (Johnson, 1997b). That there might be an emotional narrative, or emotion story, embedded in many folktales came to me by accident. Trying to learn

Table 10.1   Incidence of emotions and emotionally-charged outcomes in
29 Matsigenka folktales

Emotions/emotional outcomes	No. of occurrences	%
Desire (especially sex and meat)	81	28
Anger/frustration	51	18
Aggression	45	15
Admonition (includes warning, threat, suspicion)	27	9
Loss, sadness, remorse	21	7
Fear	19	7
Approval and gratification	19	7
Pain and suffering	16	5
Happiness/happy ending	12	4
Total	291	100%

more about Matsigenka emotions, I had gone over my collection of 29 folktales looking for emotion terms and emotional situations. It was as though
I had turned on a light that made only a few words and phrases in the folktales glow. This exercise produced two striking results. The first was that
Matsigenka folktales are overwhelmingly about strong emotions with negative outcomes (Table 10.1). By far the predominant emotions are desires,
especially for sex and meat. Most of the other emotions are negative in the
Matsigenka cultural context: anger, frustration, threat, loss, fear and suffering. Together, desire and negative emotions account for about 90 per cent
of the occurrences of emotions in the folktales. These numbers simply
confirm what is obvious to anyone familiar with these stories: most of
them are tragedies in which strong emotions cause trouble resulting in
violent death.

The second finding was remarkable: in virtually all the tales, emotions
appear in a sequence that constitutes the emotional essence of the tale, an
emotion story embedded in the larger tale. Furthermore, the emotion story,
with relatively few variations, takes a similar form in each tale (Figure 10.1).
A Matsigenka story usually begins immediately with a clash of desires. Either
two individuals want different incompatible things, or an individual wants
something inappropriate or forbidden. In either case, the result is frustration, followed by anger, followed shortly by aggression and violence.
Usually, by the end of a story, several individuals have died. The story may
end there or may further include expressions of loss, sorrow or regret, often
with a finger-pointing 'It's-all-your-fault' finale.

The pattern or structure in Figure 10.1 might be called a script (Schank
and Abelson, 1977), a schema (D'Andrade, 1995), or a cultural model
(Shore, 1996). As we will see, I prefer to call it a cultural emotion schema,
or more briefly, an emotion story. This cultural emotion schema helps
explain why Matsigenkas find listening to folktales an engaging pastime.

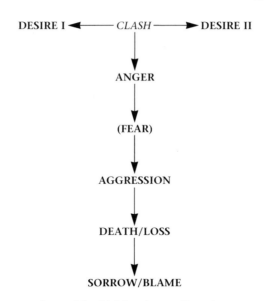

DESIRE I ◄────── *CLASH* ──────► DESIRE II

ANGER

(FEAR)

AGGRESSION

DEATH/LOSS

SORROW/BLAME

Figure 10.1   Common form of the Matsigenka emotion-story.

We may begin by establishing the cultural reality (validity) of the Matsigenka emotion story. *Narani, the Night Bird*, is an ordinary Matsigenka tale about a man who opposes his wife's wish to have children. The folktale, which I collected in the settlement of Shimaa in 1973, concerns a nocturnal bird known as *narani* (the Common Potoo, *Nyctibius griseus*) and the fate of a woman who encountered Narani in human form (*imatsigenkatanake*) and had sex with him.

Narani
(Roberto Yokari, Shimaa 1973)

There was a man who used to get drunk all the time and went off to drink by himself, leaving his wife home alone. He said he did not want his wife to have children because he wanted her to work only for him. One night, when the woman was alone, *Narani* appeared in human form and called to her. She was afraid he would kill her, but then she told him to come and give her a child. Narani entered and spent the night until her husband returned. Then Narani assumed his bird shape and flew out.

Her husband brought back a tinamou [*Tinamus guttatus*, a game bird]. When he asked her to open the door, she remained lying down. When he asked her to cook the tinamou she said she was too sick. When he offered her food, she said she was too sick to eat, she had a toothache. He asked, 'Why are you sick?' 'Because you do not know how to give me a child', she replied. He said, 'If I gave you a child, how would you work?' She said, 'I could work.' But the man knew from her illness that she had had intercourse with Narani and that his penis had broken her back.

That night, Narani came near the house (as a bird) and rested in a papaya tree. The man said, 'I will shoot him.' 'Do not kill your brother', the woman said. 'He is not my brother, he's a bird', the man said. His wife fell asleep and he shot Narani. When she woke up, she was cured. She got angry and tried to kill her husband, but could not. She said, 'Now, kill me.' He said, 'Wait until I finish eating.' Then he tied her to a tree and cut open her abdomen. Inside were thousands of tiny Narani babies. The largest was a few inches long and ready to be born.

Narani took her away with him [that is, her soul]. The man ran into the forest until he came to the house of his classificatory daughter. 'Where is my mother?' she asked. 'She is dead', he replied. 'Narani killed her. I want to sleep here.'

After some time, he returned to his former home. Narani was sitting up in the tree, very sad. The man cut some sugar cane and sucked it. The day was cloudy, no sun. On the way back to his daughter's house, he encountered his wife's spirit. She said, 'Why did you kill me before?' He said, 'Because Narani already killed you.' She said, 'Cut me open now', but the man fell unconscious because she was *ovegaga* (*kamagarini*, a very evil spirit). Later, he came to and went to his daughter's house. He was very sick. He slept on a sandy beach. He could not get up. 'Why can't you get up?' his daughter asked. He answered, 'Because I saw your mother earlier and she killed me.' In the morning, he was dead.

Narani begins with a strong emotional sequence: we learn that this selfish husband likes to drink manioc beer alone and does not want his wife to have a child because he wants her to 'work only for him'. Immediately, Narani appears in human guise and calls the woman to him – in the context of the story the audience clearly understands that he wishes to have sex with her. Her first reaction is fear, but this is followed immediately by a desire to have a child by him. This sets up a drama in which a man's wife gets pregnant by her lover, a love triangle of the most dangerous sort, in Matsigenka (and, I suspect, universal) terms.

This clash of will and desire between husband and wife unfolds in the next episode of the story, when the husband returns home with a game bird to find his wife ill: they argue over whether or not she could work and care for a baby at the same time. The anger implicit in the argument (including husband's implicit awareness of the infidelity) erupts shortly thereafter when the wife tries to kill her husband and ends up being killed by him. The rest of the story plays out the tragedy until the main characters are either bereft or dead.

The tale is cultural in the obvious sense that it is a well-known story that many individuals could tell and also in the sense that its many elements are familiar to Matsigenka audiences and have strong associations for them. For example, the episode in which the woman's belly is filled with narani chicks is culturally familiar, comparable to an episode in the tale *Kashiri* (Moon), where a woman who has intercourse with Moon has her belly cut open to reveal hundreds of baby snakes (Shepard, 1989). The woman's initial fear of Narani reflects the common belief that intercourse with spirits (who tend to have gigantic penises) is always fatal. The way the husband sickens and dies over a period of time is consistent with Matsigenka beliefs about how spirit-caused deaths occur.

Of particular interest is the theme of prohibiting a woman from having children so as not to lose her services. During my fieldwork in Shimaa in 1973, for example, two cases of infanticide occurred when young mothers were ordered to kill their newborn babies by an older woman who used the exact phrase, 'I want you to work only for me.' One was a girl's mother, the other a senior wife who told her junior co-wife that she was only a servant in the household. So even this odd-seeming conflict over a woman's reproductive rights at the outset of the story is meaningful to the Matsigenka – such self-centeredness in a husband is not good, but neither is it unfamiliar. Although infanticide has an effect of limiting population in this low-density society, we must see it and a man's reluctance to impregnate his wife, in psychological terms primarily as a selfish act by an individual who does not wish to be troubled by the needy presence of an infant.

The death of Pomokiri

That the whole story has an utter plausibility – a cultural taken-for-grantedness – to the audience, however, is best illustrated by an actual event that took place several months before the start of my field research with the Matsigenka in July 1972: the death of a young woman named Pomokiri during childbirth. Although the story came to me in several partial versions that I had to piece together, I report it here in its two main versions. The first represents a realistic version of what probably happened and is consistent with a tendency among the Matsigenka to explain many deaths in purely mechanistic or materialistic terms, without reference to spiritual agency:

The Death of Pomokiri, version I

Pomokiri was said to have had an affair with Ompira because her husband, Vasari, was old and did not want children. She became pregnant, but did not acknowledge the fact. Around her eighth month she became anxious that she was in labor but her baby was refusing to be born. After several weeks she asked a relative, who had knowledge of the drug *potogo*, a powerful herb [Spanish 'ojé'] that is supposed to induce labor and is often used as an abortificant, to prepare a potion. But, not being personally familiar with administration of the drug, he prepared an amount four times the usual dose. She drank the potion and soon had a seizure. As the narrator put it, 'her diaphragm tightened up so much she couldn't give birth and so she died'.

Over time, however, a more sinister (and exciting) version of Pomokiri's death emerged, one that has striking parallels to the folktale, *Narani*.

The Death of Pomokiri, version II

In the fall of 1971 Pomokiri and Vasari went on a collecting expedition up the Pogentimari and camped for the night along the river, making a caña brava shelter. Pomokiri left the house to defecate and encountered *Segamairini*, a demon who chased her into the woods. Later, she got back and told Vasari of her encounter. Some days or weeks later, she had a dream in which her father, who is dead, came to her and invited her to come live with him, saying "I have my son-in-law here' [*notineri*], but not meaning Vasari. After that, although she had not had intercourse for some time, she began to feel the presence of a mature baby inside her. She believed it was the demon's child. In December, although she was not feeling any serious birth complications, she complained to Maestro [the schoolteacher] and he examined her with a stethoscope [he was training as a sanitario]. He found her pregnant, probably with one child [there was some suspicion she might have twins] and apparently OK. In February, after Maestro had already left for teacher training in Yarina, she began 'labor', which continued painfully for the month of February. In order to help her Eriso prepared a brew of ojé ... She took the medicine and died.

Pomokiri was buried downstream on an island which has since been swept away by the changing currents of the river. Vasari burned the house down and his remaining family, along with several neighbors, fled upstream to escape Pomokiri's soul, which would be expected to return to the house to get her possessions [she was buried only in her cushma (gown) and beads]. The burning of the house makes it hard for the ghost to find its way and after a few days the danger is past. The real danger was not from her ghost, but from the spirit, *Segamairini*, who would have been in her company, being the one that 'spirited' her away, so to speak. *Segamairini* is a powerful and evil spirit, with an enlarged penis, capable of killing everyone in the vicinity of Vasari's' house. The neighbors, however, did not burn their houses and returned after four days.

The above account, from my journal, was mistaken about her ghost, however. According to Matsigenka belief, the dead wife did transform into a phallic demon capable of killing in order to take souls with her to relieve her loneliness in the next world.

In the second version, the story of Pomokiri's death takes on a 'true romance' stylishness in which its meaning comes very close to that of *Narani*. Indeed, it is likely that here the events surrounding Pomokiri's death have been recast to match the cultural schema that *Narani* represents (cf. D'Andrade 1995, 84). A wife, whose husband will not give her a child, sleeps with another man. She denies the adultery, but (probably feeling guilty) asserts she was attacked by the sexual demon, *Segamairini*, who has a large and lethal penis. When she experiences birth anxieties, she assumes the demon-child inside her is trying to kill her. After her death, she is buried downstream and her relatives and neighbors flee from her soul, which has now become a demon that would kill them in order to have companions in the next world.

We may say, therefore, that much of *Narani* is about what happens to a stingy husband and to the wife who is unfaithful to him. The audience is hearing a story that begins in the conflict of selfish desires between a husband and wife, proceeds to the danger of infidelity and ends in supernatural tragedy: the wife dies from her intercourse with Narani and the husband dies from contact with his wife's demonic soul (*ovegaga* in the Narani tale). The stories of Pomokiri's death and *Narani* converge on a common cultural meaning, a moral lesson about the consequences of selfishness and adultery. Had both husband and wife controlled their strong desires, the tragedy could have been averted.

A folktale like *Narani* engages its audience on many levels. It includes close-to-consciousness motifs like 'I want you to work only for me', desires close to biological nature ('you should give me a child'), social expectations ('you should be faithful to your husband') and cultural images, symbols and meanings (demons as dangerous phallic beings, a belly full of babies as wild fecundity). The listener, who is hearing on all these levels at once, is also being confronted with a moral lesson and is in a sense being invited to decide what to make of all this: Is the risk of extramarital sex really so great? Can I die from it? How am I to satisfy my desires in light of this information?

The emotion story represented in Figure 10.1 reoccurs in many different Matsigenka folktales and the same fear of strong emotional conflicts appears in other cultural contexts as well. The specific desires vary from story to story: theft, greed, lust, murder, cannibalism, jealousy. But the preoccupation with the destructive outcome of conflict resulting from such desires is a constant theme.

In an extended analysis of Matsigenka personality, social behavior and world view (Johnson 1999b), I argue that the control of emotions is their major preoccupation. Living as they do in small isolated groups with no overarching political system to resolve disputes, conflicts arising from strong desires are an ever-present danger. A response to this danger, deeply embedded in culture at all levels from child-rearing to social comportment to spiritual beliefs, is control over aggressive behavior and an emphasis on peace and cooperation in a local network of friends and relations. Strong emotions make the Matsigenka anxious. Although they tolerate great emotional expressiveness in small children, including a protracted temper-tantrum phase, the steady press of their socialization practices is toward calm, quiet, courteous behavior, within the household as well as between neighbors. Powerful emotional impulses break through this everyday self-control – especially during the beer-drinking festivities that accompany a full moon – threatening marriages, reviving old hostilities, fragmenting hamlets, even leading to homicides. The emotion story abstracted in Figure 10.1 is a cultural representation of this real danger that strikes at the heart of Matsigenka political life.

Boa Ventura: a stratified society

A single cultural emotion schema also has a major place in the folktales of nonliterate tenant farmers on a *fazenda* (plantation) in the backlands (*sertão*) of Ceará, northeastern Brazil (Johnson, 1971; 1997a; 1997c). The peasant householders of Fazenda Boa Ventura are landless and very poor: their access to farmland and housing, as well as to help and protection when disaster strikes, are dependent upon their relationship to a wealthy and powerful landlord. They seek and even welcome dependence on the patronage of such elites. As we shall see, their emotion story is quite different from that of the Matsigenka because the emotional conflicts in their case center on respect, humiliation and revenge.

A common emotion story in Northeast Brazil

In 1988 and 1989 my Brazilian colleague Carlos Caroso Soares and I recorded some 30 stories told by Zeca Paiva, a nonliterate tenant farmer of Boa Ventura. We tried to collect stories from a number of people, but none of the others wanted to tell us stories, saying that Zeca was the best storyteller in the region and that they themselves knew nothing. The disadvantage of this situation was that we could not get a sample of tales that might reflect variation within the community. The advantage was that we were getting what locals considered to be their best stories. Prof. Caroso Soares is native to the region, however and had heard these same tales in childhood from different storytellers on his grandfather's farm in Bahia and so could vouch for their wide distribution.

Zeca's stories tend to fall in two categories. One set of stories concerns a character, Camões, who is believed to have lived in a not too distant past when the land was ruled by a king. Camões liked to talk with the king, but there was always a tension between them because the king wanted to humble Camões, whereas actually Camões was more intelligent than the king and capable of coming out on top in any contest between them. The other set of stories concerns an ordinary man (*'Fulano de tal'*, roughly, 'a fella') who appears one day at a fazenda and is challenged by the *fazendeiro* (landlord) to undertake some difficult or impossible task. To the amazement and admiration of all, especially the fazendeiro, Fulano completes the task heroically.

Despite differences in the two types of stories, they have a similar underlying emotional structure. An elite person issues a challenge to a commoner, which contains an implicit possibility of failure and consequent humiliation. The challenge is generally either an intellectual puzzle (for example, 'Tell me the distance to the sun and the weight of the moon') or a physically dangerous undertaking (for example, 'Get rid of the jaguars that are killing my cattle'). In the Camões tales the king's challenge is usually meant to defeat Camões, leaving the king triumphant. In the Fulano tales, the challenge is simply a genuinely difficult and dangerous task that must be done. In either case, the implicit message is that the upper-class challenger does not believe the lower-class hero can complete the task. But the hero does successfully complete the task, leaving his upper-class challenger either amazed and grateful (Fulano-type), or defeated and humiliated (Camões-type), as in Figure 10.2.

Although rarely spelled-out in the stories, other evidence indicates that for the lower-class audience the meaning of the end of the story is that the elite man has been completely dominated by the commoner and left feeling envious and (in the king's case) frustrated. These stories are humorous tall tales and Zeca Paiva waits with barely concealed glee at the end of each

Figure 10.2   Common emotion story in rural Northeastern Brazil.

story for his audience to burst into laughter. The laughter celebrates the triumph of the commoner – through strength and cleverness – over the elite protagonist. Psychologically, the story reverses the humiliation and dependency experienced by tenant farmers in their relations with landlords and other elites; politically, it offers a channel for the expression of rage that has no access to more directly aggressive channels.

Two stories about Camões will illustrate the underlying emotion story.

A Tree Without Knots

Another time, the king called Camões, saying:
'I want you to cut me a cartload of wood, but I don't want a single piece with a knot, not a knot in the wood. You are to get me a cart of wood without a single knot.'
Now, all trees have knots. Wherever you have a branch there is a knot. We call it a knot [*no*]. You can cut it with an axe, but there is a knot, it stays. Then Camões said,
'King my lord, you want a cartload of wood without knots?'
'That's right.'
'And how am I to get wood without knots, without removing branches? If I remove the branches, there will be knots. If I don't remove branches, there will still be knots.'
Then the king went and said,
'Camões, you say you are the king of poets.
I want this cartload of wood without knots.'
So he went to the king's fields, where he had bananas growing, and cut all the banana trees down. He filled a cart and took it back to the king's palace. He said,
'Here my lord king, accept this cart of wood!'
'Camões, are those my banana trees you have cut down?'
'They are, because the only tree that does not have knots is the banana.'
Banana trees do not have knots – he took them all without mercy! And the king couldn't do or say anything to him.
Camões was tricky!

In this story, the king hopes to dominate Camões by posing an impossible task. But, from the standpoint of storyteller and audience, Camões is too clever for the king, and in the process renders him helpless and defeated. The storyteller is laughing with delight when he concludes, 'Camões was tricky!'

A King's Worth

The king had a meeting with Camões. He knew that Camões was king of the poets. He asked him to tell him the distance to the sun and the weight of the moon.

Then he went and said:
    'My lord king, it is very easy to answer this question, because the sun
    is only a day's journey away, since he rises at sunrise and sets at
    sunset. The moon when she waxes only weighs a fourth, when she
    wanes only weighs a half, because the moon has a quarter waxing and
    a quarter waning.'
Then the king said,
    'Camões you must also tell me my value, for I am the king and the
    king is worth much money!'
He replied,
    'You are only worth 29 cents.'
    'But why, Camões, is a king worth only 29 cents?'
    'Only because God was worth only 30 (don't they say that God was
    sold for 30 pieces of money?)'
The king said,
    'Very well, Camões, I won't punish you because you answered my
    questions as I asked you to.'

In *A King's Worth*, the king asks a question that would certainly puzzle a
nonliterate audience, the distance to the sun and the weight of the moon.
Camões answers in a way that the audience would consider clever. Then he
gets in a real dig at the king when the latter foolishly asks him his worth.
Camões gets away with an insulting answer by invoking the story of Jesus's
betrayal for 30 pieces of money: the king is only slightly less worthy than
Christ, but with a play on words Camões' real answer to the question,
'What am I worth?' is, 'Not much.'

Just as the core emotional content of the Matsigenka folktales concerns
the management of desire and aggression in a small, egalitarian community, the core emotional content of the stories of tenant farmers in northeastern Brazil concerns the management of humiliation and triumph in a
stratified society. Figure 10.2 represents a cultural emotion schema shared
by the popular folktales of rural northeastern Brazil. The emotional content
of the schema is a reversal of a common experience of humiliation suffered
by the rural poor in this highly class-stratified society.

Landlords and other wealthy people in the region (*os ricos*) are often
vastly wealthier than the rural poor (*os pobres*) who work for them and
depend upon them for basic resources like access to agricultural land and
housing, as well as emergency loans and health care (Johnson, 1997a). For
example, the landlord's house and furnishings in the state capital are worth
roughly 300 years of a tenant family's income. The poor are required to
show respect to elites, and elites are superficially courteous in their interactions with the poor. But elites are generally convinced that their great
wealth and power are reflections of their innate superiority, and in fact
show indifference to the plight of the poor through dismissive, disdainful
and arrogant behavior. The poor cannot afford to alienate the rich by

showing their anger and strong sense of injustice. But in their stories, heroic commoners dominate and at times humiliate elites.

This widespread phenomenon of reversing status inequalities through jokes, dramas and folktales is one among many 'weapons of the weak' (Scott, 1985). The powerless poor cannot afford to confront the rich directly, but they express their discontent, and their own disdain for the rich, in representations of elites as inept, ridiculous, dangerous and cruel. Psychologically, the reversal is satisfying and nourishes an implicit sense of practical and moral superiority in the lower-class audience. Politically, it serves as a container (and possibly as a pressure release valve) for inexpressible rage. It may also be said to constitute a kind of counter-consciousness to the dominant consciousness of political dependence and patronage (Johnson, 1997a), one that can be activated when the poor rise up against landlords, killing or humiliating them and their families, as happened in the aftermath of the Chinese revolution of 1949.

The psychodynamics of this reversal have been explored by Stoller (1985; 1987). Focusing on *humiliation* as a strong form of shame – deeply embedded in character, less available to awareness and more dangerous than shame because more likely to provoke retaliation – Stoller (1987, 305) graphically suggests the range of behaviors affected by it:

> ...We see [humiliation] at work unendingly in all of us: the suffering and maliciousness ('masochism' and 'sadism') in male–female relationships, highway accidents, warriorhood and impulses toward war, ambition and competitiveness, paranoidness, child–parent relationships, sibling rivalries...; in the construction of big cars, in table manners; in bowel habits...; in such complex uncertain gifts as art, science, humor, religious practice and theology, philosophy, politics, law. Even God is not exempt... When we observe the wreckage associated with humiliation, including the ease with which people die for and kill for self-respect, we can accept that humiliation is a fundamental element of behavior.

Humiliation is painful because it is an elemental destructive attack on the self: it conveys the attitude that the victim is intrinsically flawed or utterly worthless (Stoller, 1985,28–9). Stories about humiliation are popular among audiences that have experienced humiliation because they offer the opportunity to convert trauma into triumph. In such stories:

> The attackers of earlier times are defeated, undone, unable to persist in their attack. Now, each new episode of the trauma is constructed so that the victim is not defeated, though the experience is carried out using the same essentials that had earlier led to the disaster. Now the victim is the victor and the trauma a triumph...
>
> (Stoller, 1985, 32)

In such reversal, Stoller (1987, 306) writes of 'humiliation "cured" by retaliation.'

Discussion

The Matsigenka folktales rarely represent humiliation as a central motif. Where retaliation appears in the stories, it is for an outrage, like theft or murder. In fact, dominance and humiliation are not central features of Matsigenka political life because they are truly egalitarian at the household level, free to move away if any neighbor becomes overbearing. Although they use shame to try to keep others in line, it is of most value within the household and holds very little power between adults of different households.

On stratified Boa Ventura, however, householders cannot escape the class structure in which they are embedded. They must be most careful to show *respeito* ('respect,' see below) to their neighbors or violence may erupt, whereas they must be equally careful to swallow their pride when insulted by class superiors against whom retaliation is a practical impossibility. Control of aggression remains for them a central political problem just as it is for the Matsigenka, but in their case their stories focus on the aggression surrounding dominance, humiliation and retaliation.

I suspect this is a contrast that will be found in other stratified and non-stratified societies, but that must await further evidence. A valuable source of such evidence will appear in the form of cultural emotion schemas underlying significant proportions of the folk literatures of an array of communities.

Cultural emotion schemas

Emotion schemas originate in early childhood experiences and are continually reshaped throughout life. They take on particular cultural salience (they become *cultural* emotion schemas) insofar as they concern shared emotional conflicts in interpersonal and political life in a community. What are cultural emotion schemas and why are they so useful as means to represent unconscious features of political psychology?

As described by Bucci (1997), children learn early that family emotional life follows certain repetitive channels, such that given actions predictably call forth given emotional reactions from family members. Cognitively, these patterns begin to take the form of Representations of Interactions that have been Generalized (RIGs, *per* Stern 1985). RIGs are not memories of specific events but abstractions, schemas about what is likely to happen emotionally between child and caretaker in such common, repetitive activities as feeding, exploring, demanding, holding, hurting, defying. Even while still preverbal, children can abstract from patterns in their interpersonal interactions:

Somehow, the different invariants of self-experience are integrated: the self who acts, the self who feels, and the self who has unique perceptions about the self's own body and actions all get assembled. Similarly, the mother who plays, the one who soothes, and the ones that are perceived when the infant is happy or distressed all get disentangled and sorted. 'Islands of consistency' somehow form and coalesce. And it is the dynamic nature of episodic memory using RIGs as a basic memory unit that makes it happen.

(Stern, 1985, 98)

Bucci points out that these islands of consistency are in fact schemas, and are intrinsically emotional in nature:

'Emotion schemas' are defined as prototypic representations of the self in relation to others, built up through repetitions of episodes with shared affective states. The affective states consist of clusters of sensory, visceral, and motoric elements, which are largely subsymbolic... The prototypic episodes themselves, laid down in memory, constitute the structure of the emotion schemas. They are concrete events made abstract, metaphors of the contingencies of one's life, *incorporating what is likely to happen when one has a desire or need, what other people are likely to do, how one is likely to feel.*

(Bucci, 1997, 195–6; emphasis added)

Emotion schemas are linear, like scripts (Schank and Abelson, 1977): action (for example being compliant or defiant) is followed by reactions that have positive or negative charges (for example being hugged and kissed as opposed to being yelled at or struck). They are, in a sense, simple emotion stories that we tell ourselves, even though the 'telling' is initially nonverbal. For example, a teething infant is capable of implicitly knowing, 'If I bite this breast, my nursing will be interrupted, and I will be frustrated.' Since the child will also be frustrated by *not* biting, the abstraction constituting this RIG amounts to a simple story about a commonplace conflict situation in early childhood. In the inevitable debate over how much of an 'I' can be present in the infant, I favor the view that there is some rather than none, to the degree that from birth there is a sort of willfulness around which the first traces of a self begin gradually to cohere.

In psychoanalytic theory, common frustrating experiences in childhood are candidates for repression, particularly where the caretaker (working within a cultural meaning system) makes clear that only bad children behave in certain ways – in the present example, biting mother. And repressed ideas will out:

When these frustrations are general, and apply to every member of the community, then we can expect some manifestation of this pressure in folklore, religion and perhaps in other institutions.

(Kardiner, 1939, 445)

Therefore, a subset of an individual's emotion schemas, which are predictions about how others will react emotionally, will be so widely shared with other individuals throughout the community that they may become a focus of cultural attention.

In the present case, it is core political problems associated with the management of aggression and humiliation that come into focus in the folktales. The stories are representations of political problems that link directly to intrapsychic conflicts over control of aggression. Although these stories will be about many things in particular, and may be full of creative elaborations, the schema they have in common, though unconscious and embedded in the actual narrative, are shared and have unconscious meaning.

The political unconscious

Our usual way of talking about consciousness involves assumptions about the role of language in making mental contents conscious: quite simply, conscious contents of the mind can be articulated in speech (and other forms of symbolic expression). In psychoanalysis, the repressed contents of the mind represented by primary process only become conscious through the language-based transformations of secondary process (which modifies them to allow them to pass the repression barrier). The essence of psychoanalytic treatment, the 'talking cure,' amounts to finding ways of making the unconscious conscious, of moving ideas from the id to the ego, from the inarticulate preverbal or nonverbal realm to the realm of words (Herzog, 1991, 89).

In cognitive psychology and anthropology there has been less concern with whether schemas and related mental structures are conscious. It is taken for granted that many, perhaps most, of the patterned complexes of meanings – paradigms, taxonomies, schemas – identified by cognitive anthropologists are not conscious in the course of everyday life. But it is accepted that they may be articulated – may move into and out of awareness – situationally. This cognitive unconscious, not being dynamic – that is, not being created by the intent of some agency of the mind to ward off painful ideas – is viewed benevolently, as a convenient place where crucial thought processes may be most efficiently completed, free from the intrusions of conscious/rational thought. Sometimes subjects can collaborate with researchers to verify that the models discovered by the anthropologist have psychological reality, but often the models themselves remain covert, inarticulate, inchoate.

The emotion stories in the Matsigenka and Boa Ventura cases are unconscious in both senses. From a cognitive perspective, in talking about their folktales the Matsigenka do not address what the story means. They will discuss the facts of the tale ('Did Pomokiri have an affair?' 'Did the husband know Narani took human form and had intercourse with his wife?'). But all interpretive questions like, 'Why did the man finish eating before cutting his wife's abdomen?' or, 'Why do so many stories have the same sequence of emotions in them?' evoke only puzzled stares or awkward silences. Similarly, Zeca Paiva can recite the details of his stories, but cannot talk about them as tales of a type, even when asked. He believes Camões to have really existed, perhaps in his grandfather's time, and the events in the stories to have really happened. Although emotion schemas are real abstractions in the mind and constitute a form of knowing, neither Zeca nor the Matsigenka can talk about the shared emotion schemas in their stories, nor do they have any language or cultural mechanism for making such knowledge conscious.

Repression

For all practical purposes, Freud divided the world into conscious thought and the dynamic unconscious that is created through the act of repression. Freud's 'preconscious,' which we might be tempted to compare with the cognitive unconscious as I am using the term here, is for Freud not really distinct from the category 'conscious,' because preconscious contents of the mind can easily be made conscious by an effort at retrieval (Freud, 1900, 614–15; 1915,173). True, Freud acknowledged the existence of a *nonrepressed* portion of the unconscious (Herzog, 1991, 94), that he believed included symbols and dispositions from our 'achaic heritage' (Freud, 1939,98–9). This can be seen in his model of the mind (Figure 10.3), where the id is only partially separated from the ego by a repression barrier (in

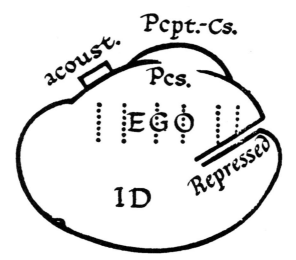

Source: From *The Ego and The Id* by Sigmund Freud (1923), translated by James Strachey. Translation copyright © 1960 by James Strachey, renewed 1988 by Alix Strachey. Reprinted by permission of W. W. Norton & Company, Inc.

Figure 10.3   The later Freudian unconscious

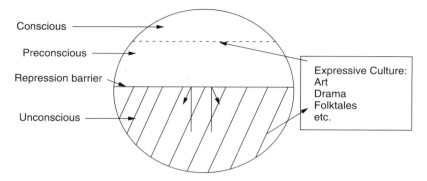

Figure 10.4   The 'Angler's Float': a psychoanalytic folk model of the unconscious.

Figure 10.3, 'Pcs.' is the preconscious, and 'Cs.' is consciousness). Indeed, Figure 10.3 leaves room for both the dynamic and the cognitive unconscious. But Freud's attention was clearly focused on the dynamic unconscious, and this focus has entered psychoanalytic anthropology as a kind of folk model (that I call the 'angler's float') in which the only meaningful unconscious is dynamic (Figure 10.4).

In addition to a cognitive unconscious, both Matsigenka and Boa Ventura emotion stories implicate a dynamic unconscious, the product of active repression, with all the theoretical complexities that entails (Johnson and Price-Williams, 1996, 77–89; Johnson, 1998). Repression is responsible for some of the inability of the Matsigenka to articulate the meanings of their stories. They will deny their own strong emotions (such as anger at a co-wife) and use defense mechanisms – particularly projection – to locate blame outside themselves, in order to protect themselves from anxiety deriving from self-blame and guilt (Johnson, 1997b). For example, Pomokiri tried to deny her extramarital affair by blaming her pregnancy on an encounter with a demon. Although other people seemed quite certain that she did have an affair with Ompira, she was not simply trying to throw them off the track: she herself clearly believed that she had been raped by a demon.

Matsigenka religion makes such a leap into fantasy easy, because demons are said to take the form of a lover when they seduce us – we think we have had a pleasant interlude, only to discover later when overcome by illness that our partner was really a demon. It is likely that Pomokiri felt unconscious guilt about her adultery and came to believe that there was a demon involved and that she was being punished. This would explain her terror about a pregnancy that the schoolteacher diagnosed as normal and healthy, a tragic anxiety that led her to intervene in her pregnancy with disastrous results.

Ample evidence implicates repression in the Boa Ventura case as well (Johnson, 1997a, 425–34). When Zeca Paiva concludes his stories with

'Camões was tricky!' he is both admiring the feisty commoner and distancing himself defensively, in effect saying, 'I would never do what that rascal did.' Making the king into a fool is part of a larger pattern of positive and negative idealization (splitting) that goes on constantly as tenants construct good vs bad landlords, and landlords construct good vs bad tenants. It is interesting, in light of the Stoller quote above, that tenants also see God as jealous and demanding of humility and respect (Johnson, 1997a, 427–8). And, at a deeply repressed level, they link dependence on a landlord with homosexual submission (Johnson, 1998).

On the comparison between Matsigenka and Boa Ventura

Two cases do not make a crosscultural generalization, but they can suggest new lines of comparative research (Johnson, 1999a). The cultural emotion schemas represented in typical folktales in Matsigenka and Boa Ventura differ fundamentally. The Matsigenka schema represents the danger of the clash of desires that produces violence and the breakdown of social order in small, isolated, highly interdependent family groups. The Boa Ventura schema represents the reversal of painful humiliation by elites. In both societies we could imagine that many kinds of emotional scenarios would be important to people, yet it appears that in each case a basic concern has outweighed others to dominate the storytelling field.

The Matsigenka schema actually allows most of their commonly experienced situations of emotional trouble to be represented: infidelity, hoarding meat, laziness, impulsive violence, and other dangers to group cohesion are all represented in specific tales. The Boa Ventura schema appears limited by comparison, in that the central conflict is usually between commoners and elites. This focus is certainly understandable, but what is a bit unexpected is that other sources of conflict, such as between family members or neighbors, are seldom explored in these stories.

This selective emphasis in the tenant farmer's folk literature suggests that in some sense humiliation by elites is their most salient emotional experience. The following points put this conclusion in context:

1. In both cases, the cultural emotion schemas represented in folktales are political in nature. The pain and anxiety of the emotion schemas concern central aspects of the respective political economies. It may be that the public forum in which the storytelling takes place tends to favor the representation of political conflicts, but surely even the most private of family dramas have a central place in most folk literatures (Johnson and Price-Williams, 1996). That other emotional concerns fail to find representation in the folktales does not mean they are not also important. They may be represented in other modalities (jokes, children's songs,and so on). Or, they may remain unrepresented, 'hypocognized' and, in effect, 'culturally invisible' (Levy, 1973, 324; Hollan, 1997, 8).

2. On Boa Ventura the experience of humiliation is not limited to the sphere of class relations. Although tenant families are loving and supportive of their children, who are charmingly open and friendly, there is an undercurrent of mean tricks, including humiliation of younger siblings by older ones, that reveals itself in small moments when children think no one is watching (Johnson, 1997a, 418–22). And, although my observations showed fathers to be respectful and often warm toward their sons, sons were almost too cautious and stereotypically respectful toward their fathers. Furthermore, the tenant farmers' view of God was of a jealous, punitive deity, intolerant of mortal pride and presumption (Johnson, 1997a, 427–8). It would seem likely, then, that the experience of humiliation in class relations is replicated to a degree in relations both within the family and with God. In a sense, God, landlord and father become collapsed into one cultural-emotional category: a father figure as a powerful store of good, but also of punishment, before whom one must be humble, respectful and fearful.

3. As Strauss (1992a, 11) writes, '...it is not enough to know *what* information people are exposed to; we also have to study *how* they internalize that information.' In the tenants' case, the idea of *respeito* (respect) is deeply internalized. God must be respected or he will send drought. Zeca tells us at one point, after saying that Camões did not respect the king, '...but the king must be well-respected.' And men go out of their way not to appear disrespectful toward their neighbors (Johnson, 1997a). Perhaps most dramatic for our purposes is the local practice, observed without exception, of respecting the flimsy gate that separates the landlord's low verandah from the ground outside his mansion on the fazenda. Tenants pause at the gate but do not come onto the verandah without an invitation from the landlord or his family. And when they do come, they leave all tools and implements – anything (even a walking stick) that could possibly construed as a weapon – on the ground outside the gate. This is a deeply internalized value that tenants would not think of violating. The disrespectful stories they delight in hearing, therefore, are in conflict with the strongly internalized value of respeito, and are to that degree unconscious.

Conclusion

Political life is about conflict. The more is at stake in a conflict, the more salient it becomes as a political issue. When a political issue becomes represented in typical stories that are popular throughout a political community, we may be certain that something important is at stake. Furthermore, it is a good bet that embedded in these stories is a core emotional conflict intrinsic to the political issue being represented.

People find it hard to talk about emotions. Part of the reason is repression: emotions get us into trouble and denying them becomes a way out of trouble. The other part of the reason is that, in our modular minds, emotions are processed and experienced far from the regions of the mind where experience is 'represented in a code that is composed of discrete lexical items, represented in discourse in the single-channel, sequential format of speech, and also registered in semantic memory in logical and hierarchical organization' (Bucci, 1997, 215). This is why the representation of emotion is the special province of the artist and the poet.

Folktales are one of the art forms where emotions can be communicated – perhaps this is why Zeca Paiva reminds us twice that Camões was 'king of the poets.' The folktale is experienced consciously – a member of the audience can describe the storytelling episode later, and summarize the story in many essentials. Yet the emotion story at its core is experienced unconsciously. That this core emotion story is about something basic, a dilemma of constant relevance in everyday life, means that folktales, and other stories, are avenues of access to emotional truths that people are usually not aware of and cannot find words to express directly.

* I am grateful to Daniel Fessler, Susan Phillips, David Sears, and Claudia Strauss for their comments on earlier drafts of this paper.

References

Bucci, W. (1997) *Psychoanalysis and Cognitive Science: A Multiple Code Theory*, New York: The Guilford Press.

D'Andrade, R. G. (1995) *The Development of Cognitive Anthropology*, New York: Cambridge University Press.

Freud, S. (1900) *The Interpretation of Dreams*, Standard Edition. Vols 4–5, London: Hogarth Press.

——— (1915) *The Unconscious*, Standard Edition, Vol.14, London: Hogarth Press.

——— (1923) *The Ego and the Id*, Standard Edition, Vol. 19, London: Hogarth Press.

——— (1939) *Moses and Monotheism*, Standard Edition, Vol. 23, London: Hogarth Press.

Herzog, P. S. (1991) *Conscious and Unconscious: Freud's Dynamic Distinction Reconsidered*, Madison, Conn.: International Universities Press.

Hollan, D. (1997) 'The Rediscovery of Dissociation Theory: Implications for Psychocultural Anthropology', paper presented in the panel, 'Universalism and Relativism in Psychoanalytic Anthropology' (Chair, Suzanne Kirschner). Bienniel Meeting of the Society for Psychological Anthropology, San Diego, Cal., 11 October 1997.

Johnson, A. (1971) *Sharecroppers of the Sertão: Economics and Dependence on a Brazilian Plantation*, Stanford: Stanford University Press.

——— (1997a) 'The Psychology of Dependence Between Landlord and Sharecropper in Northeastern Brazil', *Political Psychology*, vol. 18, pp. 411–38.

——— (1997b) "Inchoate Culture: Emotion Stories in Folk Literature', paper presented in the panel, "Universalism and Relativism in Psychoanalytic Anthropology" (Chair, Suzanne Kirschner). Bienniel Meeting of the Society for Psychological Anthropology, San Diego, CA., October 11, 1997.

—— (1997c) 'Modeling Unconscious Culture: Folktales' Emotions Stories as Inchoate Meaning', paper presented in the panel, "How Children and Ethnographers Learn a Culture" (Organizer Alan Fiske). Annual Meeting of the American Anthropological Association, Washington, DC, November 20, 1997.

—— (1998) 'Repression: A Reexamination of the Concept as Applied to Folktales' *Ethos*, vol. 26, pp. 295–313.

—— (1999a) 'Political Consciousness on Boa Ventura: 1967 and 1989 Compared', in, J. R. Bowen and R. Petersen (eds.) *Rethinking Comparisons*, New York: Cambridge University Press, pp.173–95.

—— (1999b), 'Matsigenka: In Nature and Culture', UCLA: Ms.

Johnson, A. and O. Johnson (1988) 'Time Allocation among the Matsigenka of Shimaa', *Cross Cultural Studies in Time Allocation*, Vol. 1, ed. A. Johnson, New Haven: Human Relations Area Files.

Johnson, A. and D. Price-Williams (1996) *Oedipus Ubiquitous: The Family Complex in World Folk Literature*, Stanford: Stanford University Press.

Kardiner, A. (1939) *The Individual and His Society*, New York: Columbia University Press.

Levy, R. I. (1973) *Tahitians: Mind and Experience in the Society Islands*. Chicago: University of Chicago Press.

Money-Kyrle, R. E. (1951) *Psychoanalysis and Politics: A Contribution to the Psychology of Politics and Morals*, London: Duckworth.

Schank, R. C. and R. P. Abelson (1977) *Scripts, Plans, Goals, and Understanding: An Enquiry into Human Knowledge Structures*, Hillsdale, NJ: Erlbaum.

Scott, J. C. (1985) *Weapons of the Weak: Everyday Forms of Peasant Resistance*, New Haven: Yale University Press.

—— (1990) *Domination and the Arts of Resistance*. New Haven: Yale University Press.

Shepard, G. (1989) 'The Moon Brings Manioc to Mankind', Berkeley, CA: Ms.

Shore, B. (1996) *Culture in Mind: Cognition, Culture and the Problem of Meaning*, New York: Oxford University Press.

Stern, D. (1985) *The Interpersonal World of the Infant: A View from Psychoanalysis and Developmental Psychology*, New York: Basic Books.

Stoller, R. (1985) *Observing the Erotic Imagination*. New Haven: Yale University Press.

—— (1987) 'Pornography: Daydreams to Cure Humiliation', in D. L. Nathanson, ed. *The Many Faces of Shame*, New York: The Guilford Press.

Strauss, C. (1992a) 'Models and Motives', in, R. G. D'Andrade and C. Strauss (eds.), *Human Motives and Cultural Models*, New York: Cambridge University Press.

—— (1992b) 'What Makes Tony Run? Schemas as Motives Reconsidered', in, R. G. D'Andrade and C. Strauss (eds.), *Human Motives and Cultural Models*, New York: Cambridge University Press.

Volkan, V. (1997) *Bloodlines: From Ethnic Pride to Ethnic Terrorism*, New York: Farrar, Straus, and Giroux.

11
Cultural Nationalism and Beyond: Crosscultural Political Psychology in Japan

Ofer Feldman[1]

Introduction

Japan's cultural heritage, historical experience and ethnic and linguistic homogeneity reinforced by geographical isolation offer a fascinating opportunity for cultural and crosscultural research into human political behavior and attitudes. With Japan celebrating 50 years since the end of the World War II, it has also experienced in the last few years social and political confusion and fluidity. Japan now faces issues it has rarely faced before, which will require new and perhaps far-reaching economic, political and administrative reforms. It does so, however, with a cultural psychology that is deeply embedded in its political and social practices.

In this chapter, I examine a range of studies which provide a broad picture of current trends in cultural and crosscultural political psychology in Japan. These studies examine areas such as political attitudes, voting behavior, political socialization, party identification, media use and effects, and political leadership, among others. Indeed, there are two contrasting approaches concerned with detailing Japanese social and political behavior within a crosscultural context. One claims that the only possible way to compare Japan to other cultures is by finding out how Japan is unique. This line of study emphasizes the idiosyncratic features of the Japanese environment, arguing that no social theory developed in the West can be applied to Japanese society because basic Japanese values and assumptions are different. While politics is not the focus of this line of research, most studies address issues related to social attitude and behavior, and thus indirectly affect researchers of politics in their analysis and explanation of political behavior.

The opposing approach is characterized by field research, and includes studies which collect quantitative data through various methods. This

---

[1] I am grateful to Andrew Barfield, John Duckitt, Rotem Kowner, and Stanley Renshon for their valuable suggestions and comments on earlier drafts of this article. This chapter draws on Feldman (1997).

second approach takes social theories developed in the West and tries to apply them to Japan to see whether they can explain Japanese behavior and attitudes. It tries to detect similarities and differences in social behavior between Japanese and Westerners in order to develop a broad theoretical perspective on human political attitudes in general. In spite of the traditional antagonism between adherents of these two approaches, the two in fact interact together and enrich one another to the extent that they both provide important tools in formulating generalizations about Japanese political culture, attitudes and behavior. Let us now look at both approaches in more detail.

Discussions on cultural nationalism

The so-called *nihonjinron* (literally, 'discussions of the Japanese' or 'theorizing on the Japanese'), *nihonbunkaron* ('discussions of Japanese culture'), *nihonshakairon* ('discussions of Japanese society'), *nihonkyosetsu* ('theorizing on Japaneseness'), or *nihonron* ('discussions on Japan'), form a genre of writings on Japanese society that focuses on the uniqueness of Japanese culture, society, and national character (Mouer and Sugimoto, 1986). These may be viewed as works of cultural nationalism concerned with the ostensible 'uniqueness' of Japan in any aspect, and which are contrary to both individual experience and the notion of internal sociohistorical diversity (Dale, 1986, ii). It is a discourse of 'thinking elites', who mobilize the ordinary sections of the population by transmitting them their ideas of national identity (Yoshino, 1992). Indeed, all this 'theorizing' actually is related to real cultural phenomenon.

Japanese, as Minami (1994) notes, seem to like discussing their national character, a term he defines as the traits apparent in the consciousness and behavioral tendencies shared by the majority of the population. In the case of the Japanese people, Minami reveals, this includes a special sensitivity to relations with others and a strong tendency to compare themselves with people from other countries. *Nihonjinron* exists ultimately in all aspects of life, including cultural values, ecology, landscape, and mentality. The proponents of *nihonjinron* are not confined to academia but also include journalists, critics, writers, and businessmen. They have published hundreds of books on the subject, a large number of which have undergone several printings and been translated into several foreign languages (for example, Ben-Dasan, 1972; Doi, 1986).

Nihonjinron tries to demonstrate that the Japanese are incomparably different; to perpetuate a view that Japanese culture and behavior are somehow exotic and removed from the experience of other societies; and to explain daily events in terms of culture or values considered peculiar to the Japanese (see for example, Araki, 1973; Hamaguchi, 1977; Kawai, 1984; Yoneyama, 1976). Japanese writers make claims for the peculiar status of their national culture, and characterize it as having a 'distinct character', being 'unparalleled' and 'difficult for foreigners to understand and perceive'. *Nihonjinron* assumes that culture itself precedes and determines existence. It depicts Japanese individuals as having no motives other than those implanted in them by their own culture. So culture trumps psychology.

Virtually anything can become subject matter for *nihonjinron*, so that *nihonjinron* may explain what, in cultural terms, is behind any particular subject. For example, *nihonjinron* has attempted to explain Japan's rapid economic growth and success in terms of what it views as the unique national character of Japan. Likewise, *nihonjinron* suggests that not only was Japan, as a 'late developer', able to adopt industrial technology and successfully industrialize, but it also solved many of the problems associated with the transition to becoming a post-industrial society, including crime and social integration (Dore, 1973; Vogel, 1979). Moreover, when the issue of trade imbalance between the USA and Japan emerged, on the one hand, the Americans perceived the issue largely in economic and political terms, and, on the other hand, Japan tended to explain the issue in cultural terms (Yoshino, 1992, 10). The implication is that the cultural argument is often directed at diverting attention from the real problems at issue. Differences of opinion and disagreement in the international arena may be regarded by Westerners, Americans for example, as more of incompatible 'interests', but for Japanese they are perceived as the failure of the foreign country or negotiator to understand all the variables of Japanese culture. Culture becomes an excuse for withdrawing from negotiations with partners, for not fulfilling agreements and contracts, and for maintaining systematic exploitations and legal abuses in the international community.

Nihonjinron writers present a series of contrasts in social structure and beliefs and give a set of contrasts in intellectual styles between Japan and the West. They see Japan as a homogeneous, monoracial, vertical society based on hierarchy, shame, duties, harmony and dependence. The West, on the other hand, is viewed as a heterogeneous, multiracial, horizontal society, based on egalitarianism, guilt, rights and independence (Dale, 1986, Chapter 4).

The linguistic and communicative mode of Japanese is characterized in the *nihonjinron* by nonlogic, taciturnity, ambivalence, situational ethic, emotionality, particularity and *haragei* ('the art of the abdomen'). This mode emphasizes silence as the art of communicating between individuals, and refers also to a common way of achieving a difficult consensus, without the use of direct assertions (Nishida, 1994). Tsujimura (1987), for example, argues that much of Japanese communication is based on

1. *ishin-denshin* ('traditional mental telepathy', 'heart to heart communication', or emphathtic understanding);
2. taciturnity;

3. *kuuki* ('air', 'mood' or 'atmosphere'); and
4. respect for reverberation (indirect communication).

Communication in the West, on the other hand, is viewed as being based on language that values rhetoric, logic, talkativeness, rationality, rigid principles, and universality. Tsujimura (1977) claims that the main reason for Japanese reticence is the homogeneity of the Japanese race. The Japanese often understand each other without any verbal communication because of their relatively homogeneous culture, and have developed abundant non-linguistic codes, he argues.

Typically, the writers of *nihonjinron* have used attention-catching key concepts to describe Japanese uniqueness, such as *enryo* ('social reserve'), *uchi* ('inside') and *soto* ('outside'), and *tatemae* ('formal truth') and *honne* ('the real intention') (Rosenberger, 1992; Bachnik and Quinn, 1994).

Dimensions of Japanese culture

Benedict (1946), for example, identifies the concept of 'shame' as the most significant dynamic in Japanese social relations. She describes Japan as a 'shame culture', in which individuals are controlled by social threats to personal honor and reputation, whereas the West operates by 'guilt culture', in which individuals are controlled by internal sanction against the violation of a moral standard.

Other observations on Japanese society are offered by Doi (1973), who identifies various psychological processes supporting a vertical social structure. Doi views *amae* (indulgent love) as a key concept for exploring the essence of the Japanese personality. He argues that *amae* is a unique Japanese concept used to describe relations between mothers and their children, as well as other social relations in Japan. *Amae* means the quality of love an infant feels for a doting and loving mother. It involves the desire to be passively loved, a sense of dependence, and an unwillingness to be separated from the mother and cast into the world of reality. It is Doi's contention that in Japanese society this attitude of dependence is prolonged into adulthood, thereby shaping the entire attitude of a Japanese person to other people. Dependence on another's benevolence is encouraged during socialization, so that a Japanese adult may continue to seek emotional dependence in social relations other than the family (Johnson, 1993).

This type of dependency is considered to occur typically as a quasi-parent–child relationship in companies and political factions, where a person in a subordinate social position assumes the role of a child towards his superior, who then plays the role of a parent. The child-role player can seek dependence upon the parent-role player for security and protection; the latter is expected to display his benevolence like a protective parent. The subordinate is then expected to reciprocate his debt through loyal service. In this type of relationship, the Japanese prefer to remain passive participants carried along in a comfortable emotional environment without having to do, or decide, anything by themselves.

The reciprocity of *amae* is regarded as the essence of social (and political) control. Mitchell (1976, Chapter 3) views *amae* as the source of authority; he claims that the idea of authority is entirely secondary in Japan to that of dependency. He suggests that in its operation in the family and society, *amae* results in mutual dependency. The reciprocity inherent in the parent-child relationship reflects a unique Japanese attitude toward authority. Submissiveness of the Japanese to authority is balanced, reciprocated by indulgence dependency. A submissive individual thus maintains basic trust in authority. Moreover, because he is willing to have matters taken care of by those in positions of leadership, he finds it easier and natural to follow the directives of others. This attitude is based on trusting that benevolent attention will be paid by the leader as soon as needs emerge. Consequently, by being responsive to their followers' dependency, and providing them with warmth and an emotional security blanket, leaders may retain their authority, obedience, and trustworthiness (Mitchell, 1976).

Further, Doi (1973) suggests the role of *amae* in the Japanese reliance on non-verbal communication. It expresses itself as an expectation that an interlocutor may understand another without that person having to verbalize his or her needs and feelings. Because of the emphasis on indirect and nonverbal communication in Japan, individuals need to know whether others understand them when they do not verbally express their feelings. This is in order to reduce uncertainty. The *amae* expectation requires an interlocutor to exercise *sasshi*, meaning conjecture, surmise guessing, or judgment about what someone or a sign means (Nishida, 1994; Miyanaga, 1991, 85–6). It implies that an individual can guess the real intention of others in spite of their surface disguise.

Likewise is the concept of *awase* ('to adopt oneself to the other person, particularly to the guest'). According to *awase*, an individual is not assumed to have control over his environment. It is clear in the *awase* behavior that an individual, in the process of adjusting to his interlocutor's needs and feelings, is expected or supposed to downplay assertiveness and help the interlocutor to keep a low profile of himself. Thus, for a Japanese to operate with *awase* principles means to give up direct control over one's interlocutor at least overtly and for the short time. Okabe (1983) notes that in individualistics cultures people use an *erabi* ('selective') worldview. With respect to verbal communication, they believe that the speakers consciously constructs their message for the purpose of persuading and producing attitude change. People in collectivistic cultures, such as Japan, in contrast, hold an *awase* worldview. With respect to verbal messages, they believe that the speakers should attempt to adjust themselves to the feelings of their listeners.

Harmony and leadership

Nakane (1972) identifies peculiarly Japanese forms of social organization and interactions by using the key concept of 'vertical society'. That is, the society is not one of horizontal stratification by class or caste, but of 'vertical stratification by institution or group of institutions' (Nakane, 1972, 87). The Japanese are described as a group-oriented (*shudanshugi*) people, preferring to act within the framework of a group. Groupism refers also to the individual identification with, and immersion in, the group. Identity is perceived invariably as a 'group orientation', and the term comes to imply the submergence of the individual within society. It denies thus the existence of an individual, uniquely personal identity. This group orientation fosters the strength of the company or organization, distinguishes one's own group from other groups, and makes the organizational unit the basis of Japanese society.

According to *nihonjinron*, each group is hierarchically organized based on the relationship between paternalistic superiors and their subordinates, as well as the relationships between members differentiated by their time of entry into the group. In these hierarchical relationships, often expressed in terms such as *oyabun–kobun* (boss–employee or master-follower) or *sempai–kohai* (senior–junior), the seniors are expected to protect the juniors, to give them benefits and help. In turn, the juniors demonstrate deference to their seniors, offer their service whenever the seniors require it, and show loyalty and commitment (Nakane, 1972, 42).

The system is thus an intense relationship of mutual obligation, and the dynamics of the group are primarily the vertical interactions between leaders and followers. Almost all group members occupy the place of leader in relation to some and followers in relation to others. Individuals' participation in the group is regulated by their established relationship to a given group member. Thus, the individual's identity with their group takes place first through a concrete personal relationship with a leader, who acts as the focal point for group loyalty.

In his theory of Japanese democracy, Ike (1978) applies to the political arena this characteristic of vertical society, namely the highly personalized relationships between superiors and inferiors. The individual at the bottom appeals to his patron (who is a client of a higher patron) and through him goes up the chain step by step. Individuals are thus related to the political system through personalized channels. Those who can use such personalized channels feel assured that they have access to the system. They are likely to have a sense of political competence and feel that they are part of the system and that it will respond to their needs and demands. In turn, they tend to support helpful politicians in each election.

Political leaders and followers thus exist in a relationship of mutual dependence. The lower ranks are dependent on the help and protection of the leader, while the leader is dependent on the support of his subordinates.

Assistance, protection, and generosity on the part of the leader generate support and loyalty on the part of the followers. On the one hand, a pyramidal political structure is more likely to be found in rural areas. In large cities, on the other, the average citizen has almost no opportunity to establish personalized relationships with political activists who can put him in contact with politicians. Such individuals are not able to relate to the political system in a personalized way. Hence they may not view the system as responsive to them, and may feel politically alienated, as well as have a low level of political efficacy.

Another implication of personalized politics is that candidates are often more important than issues or party labels. Some voters are willing to vote for candidates recommended by local influentials; others tend to prioritize the personal qualities of the candidates; that is, the candidates' characters are more likely to be evaluated than their position on policy matters. After each election, supporters let the successful candidates know what they want by submitting various requests. Their reward is to have their needs and interests represented. In other words, the voters supply votes in turn for the personal and constituency benefits that they trust their representatives will provide. As a result, issues that are important for the nation as a whole have rarely been at the center of the national elections in Japan. Moreover, voters tend often to judge their Diet representatives by their ability to obtain commitments from the central bureaucracy for roads, hospitals, railways, and schools rather than by their ability to initiate laws or to assume a role in national or international matters (Ike, 1978).

The 'group orientation' concept of Japanese society as described by *nihonjinron* also entails conformity and loyalty to group causes, and consensus and the lack of conflict among group members. Social control of individuals is possible through the conformity of individuals to the expectations of others in social interaction. Japanese groups are thus characterized by harmonious relationships among their members, and Japanese society is both conflict-avoiding and consensus-oriented. Harmony is viewed as one of the most important concepts that Japanese can strive to achieve in any social interaction. To prevent open clashes of opinions, the Japanese often prefer subtle ways to adjust conflicts and to achieve mutual understanding among all the members of the group (Rohlen, 1975; Clark, 1979).

The concepts of harmony and consensus-seeking behavior often appear as major characteristics in explaining the nature and dynamics of political leadership. Studies have suggested that in both traditional and modern practice, the Japanese approach to power and leadership differs from the concepts of leadership role found in the West (MacDougall, 1982). Political leaders in the West are expected to demonstrate their own personal style, determination and dominance in achieving political objects; leadership is thus usually associated with the demonstrated abilities, successful performance, and other personal attributes of the individual.

Culture and political decision-making

In Japan, emphasis is allocated to collective aspects, to group dynamism and consensus decisions. Leaders are like effective managers: they are expected to pay attention to the relations among all the members of the group they head; to be sensitive to the feelings of their subordinates; to cool emotional conflicts; and to elicit widespread support in attaining a common goal. It is consensus-building, not decision-making ability and authority, which is the mark of a good leader (Feldman and Kawakami, 1989).

Thus, Japanese leaders invest much energy in efforts to promote the collective interests, as well as to achieve cooperation between the disparate interests, of all the members of their group. When a decision must be made to resolve a conflict, leaders turn to the unique modes of *nemawashi* (literally, 'trimming of a tree's roots prior to its being transplanted'). This is the process of prior informal negotiation and persuasion among concerned parties before a proposed matter is presented to a formal meeting (Hashiguchi *et al.*, 1977). Through careful personal interaction, one can improve empathy and cooperation between all members of the group and obtain their complete support for a certain issue.

Another method which has been institutionalized in the bureaucratic policymaking procedure is *ringisei* ('a system of referential inquiry about a superior's intentions'). This is the procedure of circulating a memorandum along the hierarchy to the top of the organization to obtain approval of all concerned for a proposed idea. Along the way, members of the organization are required to approve the particular issue or proposal. The proposal may then be sent back to its initiator with modifications. But once the proposal reaches the desk of the top executive official, bearing the seals of approval from all intermediate levels of group members, its approval by the leader is virtually mandatory (Tsuji, 1968).

The operation of *nemawashi* and *ringisei* both illustrate the specific process of Japanese decisionmaking. Because both systems inform everyone concerned and give everyone an opportunity to contribute to the proposal, the expectation is created that all members will cooperate in its ultimate implementation once a decision is reached. In other words, the Japanese mode of decision-making is relatively slow in reaching decisions, but implementation can become steady and solid since the group's members support the decision during the course of consensus formation.

An important concept which appeared in the context of reaching a decision and acting upon is *kuuki* (mentioned above, literally 'air'). Yamamoto (1977) claims that the Japanese word *kuuki* has peculiar characteristics. Although *kuuki* usually means 'air' in a physical phenomenon, *kuuki* refers also to mental phenomenon of 'feeling', 'mood', 'atmosphere', or 'atmosphere requiring compliance', which exerts a pervasive pressure on Japanese and on their behavioral patterns. In English and also in other languages (perhaps with the exclusion of Hebrew, Greek and Latin) the word 'air' does not have this mental or emotional phenomenon in its meaning to the same extent.

Kuuki consists a characteristic feature of the Japanese in that it controls their behavior. Yamamoto (1977, 7–19) describes former government leaders and military generals who said after the Second World War that they could not stop the move towards the war or preventing many stupid suicidal military operations, because of *kuuki* at that time. Yamamoto claims that it was *kuuki* more than anything else that dragged Japan into the war. *Kuuki* in its emotional or mental meaning is as vague as its physical meaning. It broods shapelessly over the world, neither solid nor liquid but penetrating like a gas. *Kuuki* is the prevailing mood that has the power to render the final verdict and force a decision's acceptance. This is an intriguing phenomenon. It provides an indication that there is something capable of transcending and constraining all the arguments and assertions one may advance. This 'something' is a standard of sorts, one that can dictate one's response to major issues, everyday matters, and even accidents individuals find themselves caught up in.

Kuuki seems to be something that neither education, rational discussion, data, nor even scientific inquiry, can get its teeth into. Yamamoto claims that even though students or soldiers may be educated not to do certain things, despite all the admonitions, there may exist certain compulsions in *kuuki* whereby they find themselves doing the things they know they must not do against other people or their enemy. There is simply no clear way to identify any rational process by which a 'mood' leads people under its sway to a conclusion. Yamamoto calls this 'atmosphere' precisely because it is so elusive.

Ito (1990) notes that *kuuki* can be created in any social group: it can exist in family, local community, labor union, companies, meetings, and the whole nation. The concept of *kuuki* is especially important in a 'human relations society like Japan where good human relations, group harmony and consensus are specially and always emphasized' (Ito, 1990, 440). Ito further notes that if one focuses on society as a whole or a nation, because it is usually adopted as a standard unit of social change, *kuuki* may be considered to be determined by the degree of agreement among three major components: the government policies, the mass media, and public attitudes. In Japan, wherever these three components align, such as in the cases of the imperial system and the reversion of the Northern territories from Russia to Japan, the pressure of *kuuki* is extremely strong. Thus, criticizing the imperial system in public has become more than an explicit taboo; such an act may be perceived as a threat to the whole of society.

When the three components of policy, media, and public attitudes are divided into one versus two, the majority opinions and attitudes become *kuuki*. This then functions as a social pressure for compliance. It resembles the 'climate of opinion' in the 'spiral of silence' theory. Thus, the minority receives pressure for compliance through voting, demonstrations, protest and verbal attacks or criticism through various communication channels to the extent that they cannot help but concede to the majority. This is how a national consensus is gradually formed.

Ito (1996a) illustrate this claim by focusing on the question of media influence on governmental decisionmaking. He details the case of the United Nations Peace Cooperation Bill as was proposed by Prime Minister Toshiki Kaifu following the Gulf crisis in 1990 and the mountaining pressure on Japan for its contributions to the solution of the crisis. Prime Minister Kaifu announced in August 1990 his intention to propose a law to enable Japan to undertake prompt aid and peacekeeping activities outside Japan at times of international crisis. The purpose of this law was to assist the United Nations' peacekeeping activities. It was clear that this would not contradict the spirit of the Japanese Constitution. To the great disappointment of its supporters, the prime minister and other leaders decided to drop the bill. Ito suggests that some of the Japanese news media that opposed the bill influenced the prime minister's decision to drop it because they contributed to the creation and maintenance of a *kuuki* which went against the United Nations Peace Cooperation Bill. Likewise, Ito suggests (1996b) that some of the newspapers that opposed the consumption tax in 1989 influenced the Prime Minister' decision to amend the bill because they had contributed to the formation of the *kuuki* against the tax increase.

Criticism of *nihonjinron*

The *nihonjinron* approach to the study of Japanese culture started to be challenged from the early 1950s. Critiques (for example, Dale, 1986; Sugimoto and Mouer, 1989; Taketomo, 1986) highlight its weaknesses as a social theory on methodological, empirical and ideological grounds, illustrating that many phenomena such as the concept of *amae*, which have been supposed to be uniquely Japanese, can also be observed in other societies (Befu, 1989). Befu (1995) further indicates that certain *nihonjinron* writings are evidently the outcome of an identity quest. He places the current *nihonjinron* in historical perspective, in which the present is only one phase in the long swing that has characterized the Japanese identity. The relative strength of Japan *vis à vi*s a referent civilization, China in the past and the West since Meiji Restoration, has been instrumental in defining Japan in a positive or negative light. Since the 1970s, Japan's economical 'miracle' and social stability prompted the decline of postwar negative introspection and the reemergence of national self-confidence. It is in this milieu, Befu asserts, that *nihonjinron* has attempted to challenge Western perceived dominance by demonstrating the singular character of Japanese culture and social institutions (Befu, 1984).

Oguma (1995) details the myth of Japanese homogeneity, which, in his view, appeared after the Second World War. In contrast, in the prewar and wartime period, when Japan was in the process of colonizing its neighbors in the name of Asian unity, the theory of racial kinship between the Japanese and other Asian held sway in Japanese ideology. After the war, however, Japan's recognition of defeat, the radical reduction of its territory, and its desire to distance itself from the mounting Cold War tension in Asia, all helped install the theory of ethnic homogeneity as the new basis of national identity. Under the revised consciousness of self, Oguma claims, Japanese society was understood to have been, since antiquity, peaceful, homogeneous, and free from interracial conflict.

And whereas the *nihonjinron* explains Japan's economic success in terms of the unique national character of Japan, Crawcour (1980) has criticized the theory for neglecting the importance of such factors as the availability of advanced technology from abroad, high rates of investment, abundant supplies of labor, and a very favorable international environment. In particular, the revisionists express criticism against the heavy reliance on convenient examples of personal experiences in support of the 'group model', 'consensus model', or the images of harmony of Japanese society. In turn, the revisionists stress the importance of a 'conflict model' that emphasizes dissension between different groups.

Indeed, although the cultural model of harmony is more notable in Japan than in the West, research has pointed out the existence of conflict in Japanese society and politics (Apter and Sawa, 1984; McKean, 1981; Steinhoff, 1989). Following rapid economic growth during the 1960s, conflicts and disagreement intensified over the costs and benefits of industrialization, and over environmental and minority rights issues (such as those of close to three million *burakumin*, descendants of former outcasts). Rivalries between government and opposition parties also deepened. Further, the 1960s, 1970s and the 1980s saw consumer and student movements, antipollution and antiwar movements, and activities by various citizens' groups including mass protests, all reflecting severe generational cleavages as political alienation took place.

During that period, the opposition parties played a dominant role by sponsoring unconventional political activities and by encouraging their support groups to take part in them. The leadership of these parties, and of the interest groups and organizations these parties helped to form, adopted an ideological position on a specific issue in areas such as taxes or the American presence in Japan, before organizing campaigns that included demonstration of popular support for that position. Lower-level affiliates followed suit ideologically and provided the manpower for the demonstrations. Consequently, a large number of working class Japanese participated in union-sponsored protest rallies, and hundreds of strikes were reported every year. These elements of diversity and conflict in Japanese society illustrate that Japanese society is not the totally integrative and cohesive society that shares common values and disdains class-divided interests and values, as the *nihonjinron* tries to suggest. The existence of social conflict may be seen as a sign of dissent in common culture; it shows that individual members of Japanese society differentiate between their own interests and those of others.

However, it is noteworthy that social and political dispute actions often have a different meaning in Japan than in the USA and Europe. Political demonstrations, as well as the official response to them, are often ritualistic in nature (Mitchell, 1976, 125), and strikes are viewed as demonstrations of workers' will or readiness to fight. They are designed to attract the employers' attention. Because of this reason, strikes usually continue only a few hours and rarely continue more than a few days. Moreover, Japanese strikes are also different from Western ones in that a strike in Japan is rarely a walkout – it involves more often a 'walk in'. During strikes, union members usually stay in the working place and hold meetings or engage in various union activities (Hanami, 1984).

In his criticism of *nihonjinron*, Befu (1980a; 1980b) suggests that acceptance of this approach, with its emphasis on harmony and social identity as predominant factors influencing behavior, leads to *nihonjinron* proponents to overlook Japanese 'personhood' (for example, concepts such as *seishin*). Befu (1977) argues that there is a strong sense of 'personhood' in Japan, and behavior can be based on personal identity. Group orientation is more apparent than real, and behind the appearance of group solidarity, one will find individuals being loyal to the group because 'it pays to be loyal' (Befu, 1977, 87).

Crosscultural studies

In contrast to *nihonjinron*, the second approach concerned with detailing Japanese social behavior and attitudes seeks first to apply to Japan research methods theories and measures tested in empirical studies in the USA and European countries, and second to relate the Japanese case to a broad context of political behavior. It endeavors to elucidate aspects related to political attitudes in Japan by comparing them to those that exist in other societies, and by employing similar methodological procedures. For example, based on comparisons of thermometer evaluations of parties, leaders and groups in different countries, Richardson (1986) reveals that the emotional level of Japanese political culture is lower than that in most other industrialized countries. Japanese tend much more to emotional neutrality, feeling neither warm nor cold, or simply do not reveal their feelings toward political institutions, unlike citizens in other major democracies.

During recent years, an increasing number of books, periodical articles, conferences and panel discussions have been devoted to addressing from a comparative perspective issues related to Japanese social behavior and attitudes. The basic assumption of this extensive literature and debate is that the Japanese may have, like any other people, special cultural and sociological characteristics which distinguish them from other societies; yet, at the same time, the Japanese can be compared to other people, and such comparison is needed in order to deepen understanding and to develop a general theory of human behavior. Studies in this context focus in particular on several distinct areas of political behavior.

Similarities and differences

A number of studies have pointed to the similarities and differences in political attitudes in Western culture and Japan. Kabashima and Takenaka (1996), for example, note that in comparison to US voters, Japanese have a higher level of ideological consciousness. As many as 85 per cent of the Japanese voters locate themselves on a conservative–reformist scale, and more than 70 per cent of them distinguish each of the political parties on such an ideological scale. Kabashima and Takenaka detail changes in the Japanese belief system since the end of the Second World War.

In the 1960s, the liberal-conservative ideology of individuals was generally structured along with issues of national security and support for the prewar political system. In the 1970s, the ideology structure was further reinforced by dimensions of political participation and social equality. Although these dimensions remained apparent through the 1980s, public attitudes toward social and economic issues became more complex, and the attitude consistency somehow weakened. This may suggest a decline in ideological attitudes in Japan following the end of the Cold war.

In a thorough study of the various facets of political participation, Kabashima (1988, Chapter 5) notes that in comparison to other countries, involvement in politics in Japan is related to different factors. In many advanced industrial countries, participation is positively associated with socioeconomic status; that is, the higher the level of income and education, the greater the tendency to take active part in politics. Conversely, in Japan, income does not show a linear correlation with a willingness to take an active part in politics; in addition, education appears to be negatively related to voting participation. Kabashima explains this relationship by other causes of participation, such as cost-consciousness, strength of party identification, and feeling of identification with local neighborhood, which are all negatively associated with education. He concludes that if these social, geographical, and psychological factors are controlled, the effect of education becomes zero.

Hirano (1993) observes different outcomes when economic conditions worsen in the USA and Japan. In the case of the first, the American voter will refrain from supporting the incumbent government. In contrast, the Japanese voter tends traditionally to support the government in power in the hope that doing so will improve the economic situation. Focusing on the question of the relationship between the evaluation of the achievement of the government to voting behavior, Hirano found that in comparison to the USA, voter evaluation of the economic situation in Japan seldom affects voter evaluation of the performance of the government. While voters in the USA tend to perceive the course of economic direction as the responsibility of the government and the quality of daily life as the responsibility of the individual, the Japanese view the government as responsible for the quality of individual life, but at the same time feel that the economic situation is beyond governmental responsibility.

Analyzing the mechanism of voting decision-making at the election for the House of Councillors in Tokyo in 1989, Hirano (1991) reports that emotional reaction toward political issues and parties consists of positive and negative dimensions. Each of these two dimensions has an independent effect on party support. Yet, the influence of the positive emotion is relatively stronger. That is, those with positive feelings toward a particular party tended to support that party. Hirano notes that these results are consistent with results reported in the USA.

Several inquiries into the process and effects of political learning report that the level of party allegiance among Japanese children, from early in childhood through to adolescence, are similar to those prevailing in Western nations, such as the USA, the UK and France. The influence of the family on partisanship also seems similar in Japan to these countries. Like children in the UK, and more than their American counterparts, Japanese children have knowledge of their parents' partisanship; they also share their parents' party affiliation to a degree that approaches their Western peers. Japanese parents succeed in transmitting their partisanship to their children no less than Western parents do. Thus, the family plays a leading role in the child's early political socialization despite the large, rapid political, social and cultural changes that have been taking place in Japan, which include shifts in the political party system, occupational and geographic mobility, and value changes (Kawata, 1989; Massey, 1976).

In contrast to children in the USA, the UK, and France, Japanese children have no 'benevolent leader' image, but rather possess negative images of political leaders, particularly the prime minister. They view the prime minister as a distant, disagreeable figure, as one who lies, is wealthy, and does not do a very good job. The Japanese prime minister does not therefore appear to be either a dominant person or an object of trust and affection (Massey,1976; Okamura, 1968, 1974). Additionally, Japanese children tend to have a higher degree of political cynicism than their counterparts in other industrial advanced countries. Increase in age is associated with increasing cynicism. At the eighth grade, children are even more cynical than their parents about the concern and the responsiveness of the prime minister, the government, the Diet and political parties to people's desires (Massey, 1976). Increase in age is related also to a decrease in both political efficacy and feelings of being able to act effectively in politics (Massey, 1976, 133). University students, for example, tend to have an extremely low level of political competence (Kawata, 1985).

Low levels of efficacy are also major characteristics of Japanese adults' political attitudes. Nakamura (1975, 172–3), for example, reports that more than 65 per cent of the voters expressed cynicism regarding the extent to which their opinions are reflected in politics. In comparison to countries such as the USA, the UK and Germany, the proportion of Japanese who feel they are capable of influencing politics on both the national and local levels is low. In different from voters in these countries, however, relatively more Japanese feel that they are capable of influencing decision-makers through various groups rather than through personal contacts (Nakamura, 1975, 174–5). This is related perhaps to the fact that for many social relations in Japan, the basis is the group, and the Japanese tend to belong to some kind of organization more than, say, Americans do (Richardson and Flanagan, 1984, 231). Importantly, individuals' feelings of being able to have an impact on politics differ at the national and the local level. More people feel that they are politically competent in affecting decisionmaking processes at the local level more than at the national.

Last, crossculturally-related studies have examined aspects related to political leaders in Japan, including the prime minister (for example, Igarashi, 1989). This type of study received little attention, probably because Japanese prime ministers have, by standards of most other advanced industrial democracies, less real power either to establish new priorities for the nation or to enforce important measures. Usually, they do not have clear policy goals and/or agendas to advocate. Rather than being strong and assertive, the Japanese prime minister is remarkably weak and reactive (Hayao, 1993). As a result, prime ministers apply their energy to issues that happen to be salient at a certain moment, trying only to resolve them in some way. They do not take initiative for change and are not involved directly in the content of change. They try to coordinate broad policy programs or resolve major conflicts at crucial times, such as when the cabinet must reach a decision, or when the Diet is confronted by a vote on important legislation. Only a handful of studies have focused on the prime minister or other politicians in order to examine questions related to their motivation for political post, their role orientations, and other psychological aspects related to their attitudes.

One crosscultural study, which compared American and Italian politicians to Japanese, examines the belief system of Diet members. In particular, this study inquires how open or closed to change the belief systems of Japanese Diet members are and considered the significance of such findings for political behavior. The study reveals that as in Italy and the USA, dogmatic, authoritarian personalities as well as democratic, open-minded personalities function within the political system in Japan. In comparison to politicians from other countries, the proportion of Japanese Diet members who are dogmatic is neither as high as for Italian deputies nor as low as for American politicians (cf., DiRenzo, 1977). Thus, the Japanese case falls somewhere in between the Italian and the American cases – less dogmatic than the Italians but more dogmatic than their American counterparts. The study also found that Diet members are distinguished from nonpoliticians in terms of a dogmatic personality structure: Diet members are more closed-minded than nonpoliticians. Moreover, the personality structure of a Diet member is affected by previous political experience at the local level and by the desire to attain political position (Feldman, 1996).

Utilizing a theory and research method (the social-self symbol task) developed and applied in the USA to measure self-esteem, it was revealed that in comparison to the general public, newly elected Diet members tend to have a relatively lower level of self-esteem. Diet members with high and low self-esteem are distinguished from each other in terms of attitudes, motivation, work patterns, and their responsiveness to the electorate. A large number of Diet members who wanted to become politicians in child-hood tended to have lower self-esteem. The combination of a strong mother and low self-estimate led the child to want a future position in which he would be able to exercise power, such as in becoming a polit-ician. Such individuals are more likely to take an active part in public activ-ity even before they have reached the age of voting, such as serving in leading positions in student associations (Feldman, in press).

Conclusions

Today Japan faces daunting social challenges. The 1990s in particular have witnessed a growing number of events which shake Japanese society to the core. This in turn has put several pressing issues on the national agenda and led to renewed calls for urgent political, economic and administrative reform. These events include the Great Hanshin Earthquake; the scandal concerning hemophiliacs infected with HIV through the use of unheated blood products; the *Aum Shinrikyo* (Supreme Truth) cult, which attacked Tokyo's subways during the morning rush hour with sarin gas; the worsen-ing recession economy with increasing unemployment and job insecurity; accompanying political scandals of corporate and administrative corrup-tion; spiralling political malaise; a pervasive lack of business confidence; and the general public's growing cynical contempt for the government and its ability to manage.

The emergence of these new agendas and challenges are already radically affecting the way individuals behave and think politically in Japan; they are also impacting significantly the way foreigners and foreign countries view this country. Some traditions in Japanese society will clearly be helpful in meeting these new challenges; others will be found to be sorely deficient. In either case, the consequences will be profound, far-reaching and diffcult to bear.

References

Apter, D. E. and N. Sawa (1984) *Against the State: Politics and Social Protest in Japan*, Cambridge, Mass: Harvard University Press.

Araki, H. (1973) *Nihonjin no kodoyoshiki* [Patterns of behavior of the Japanese], Tokyo: Kodansha.

Bachnik, J. M. and C. J. Quinn (eds) (1994) *Situated Meaning: Inside and Outside in Japanese Self, Society and Language*. Princeton, N.J.: Princeton University Press.

Befu, H. (1977) 'Power in the Great White Tower', in R. D. Fogelson and R. N. Adams (eds.), *The Anthropology of Power*, New York: Academic Press (pp. 77–87).

Befu, H. (1980a) 'A Critique of The Group Model of Japanese Society', *Social Analysis*, vol. 5(6) pp. 29–43.

Befu, H. (1980b) 'The Group Model of Japanese Society and an Alternative', *Rice University Studies*, vol. 66, pp. 169–87.

Befu, H. (1984) 'Civilization and Culture: Japan in Search of Identity', in T. Umesao, H. Befu and J. Kreiner (eds.), *Japanese Civilization in the Modern World*, Senri Ethnological Studies, no. 16.

Befu, H. (1989) 'A Theory of Social Exchange as Applied to Japan', in Y. Sugimoto and R. Mouer (eds.), *Constructs for Understanding Japan*, London: Kegan Paul International (pp. 39–66).

Befu, H. (1995) 'Swings of Japan's Identity', in S. Clausen, R. Starrs, and A. Wedell-Wedellsborg (eds.), *Cultural Encounters: China, Japan, and the West*, Aarhus: Aarhus University Press (pp. 241–65).

Ben-Dasan, I. (1972) *The Japanese and the Jews* (trans. R.L. Gage). Tokyo: Weatherhill.

Benedict, R. (1946) *The Chrysanthemum and the Sword: Patterns of Japanese Culture*, Boston, Mass.: Houghton Mifflin.

Clark, R. (1979) *The Japanese Company*. New Haven: Yale University Press.

Crawcour, S. (1980) 'Alternative Models of Japanese Society: An Overview', *Social Analysis*, vol. 5(6), pp. 39–66.

Dale, P. (1986) *The Myth of Japanese Uniqueness*. London: Croom Helm.

DiRenzo, G.J. (1977) 'Politicians and Personality: a Cross-cultural Perspective', in M. G. Hermann (ed.), *A Psychological Examination of Political Leaders*, New York: The Free Press (pp. 147–73).

Doi, T. (1973) *The Anatomy of Dependence* (trans. J. Bester), Tokyo: Kodansha International.

Doi, T. (1986) *The Anatomy of Self* (trans. M.A. Harbison), Tokyo: Kodansha International.

Dore, R. (1973) *British Factory – Japanese Factory: the Origin of National Diversity in Industrial Relations*. Berkeley: University of California Press.

Feldman, O. (1996) 'The Political Personality of Japan: an Inquiry Into the Belief Systems of Diet Members', *Political Psychology*, vol. 17, pp. 657–82.

Feldman, O. (1997) 'Culture, Society, and the Individual: Cross-cultural Political Psychology in Japan', *Political Psychology*, vol. 18, pp. 327–53.

Feldman, O. (In press) *The Japanese Political Personality: Analyzing the Motivations and Culture of Fresh Diet Members*, London: Macmillan.

Feldman, O. and K. Kawakami (1989) 'Leaders and Leadership in Japanese Politics: Images during a Campaign Period', *Comparative Political Studies*, vol. 22, pp. 265–90.

Hamaguchi, E. (1977) *Nihonrashisa no saihakken* [Rediscovery of Japaneseness]. Tokyo: Nihon Keizai Shimbunsha.

Hanami, T. (1984) 'Conflict and Its Resolution in Industrial Relations and Labor Law', in E. S. Krauss, T. P. Rohlen and P. G. Steinhoff (eds.) *Conflict in Japan*, Honolulu: University of Hawaii Press (pp. 107–135).

Hashiguchi, O., T. Takeshita, K. Sugiura and T. Maruyama (1977) 'Taikenteki nemawashiron' [Empirical Study of 'nemawashi'], *Jichi-Kenshu*, vol. 203, pp. 2–17.

Hayao, K. (1993) *The Japanese Prime Minister and Public Policy*, Pittsburgh: University of Pittsburgh Press.

Hirano, H. (1991) 'Seijiteki soten to seito hyoka:89-nen sanin senkyo ni okeru tohyo ishi kettei no bunseki [Political Issues and Party Evaluation: Analysis of the Decision-making Process in the 1989 Upper House Election]. *Senkyo Kenkyu*, vol. 6, pp. 160–83.

Hirano, H. (1993) 'Nihon no tohyo kodo ni okeru gyoseki hyoka no yakuwari' [The Relationship Between Evaluation of the Government's Achievements and Japanese Voting Behavior], *Ribayasanu*, vol. 13, pp. 147–67.

Igarashi, J. (1989) 'Nakasone moto shusho ni okeru ridashippu no kenkyu' [A Study of the Leadership of Former Prime Minister Nakasone], *Ribayasan*, vol. 5, pp. 167–82.

Ike, N. (1978) *A Theory of Japanese Democracy*, Boulder, Col: Westview.

Ito, Y. (1990) 'Mass Communication Theories from a Japanese Perspective', *Media, Culture and Society*, vol. 12, 423–64.

Ito, Y. (1996a) 'Mass Media's Influence on Government Decision Making', in D. J. Paletz (ed.), *Political Communication in Action: States, Institutions, Movements, Audiences*, Cresskill, N.J.: Hampton (pp. 37–52).

Ito, Y. (1996b) 'Masses and Mass Media Influence on Government Decision Making', in D. J. Paletz (ed.), *Political Communication Research: Approaches, Studies and Assessments*, Norwood, N.J.: Ablex vol. 2 (pp. 63–89).

Johnson, F. A. (1993) *Dependancy and Japanese Socialization: Psychoanalytical and Anthropoligical Investigations into Amae*, New York: New York University Press.

Kabashima, I. (1988) 'Yukensha no hokaku to Nakasone seiji' [The Japanese Voter's Conservative–Progressive Idealogy and Nakasone's Politics], *Ribayasanu*, vol. 2: pp. 23–52.

Kabashima, I. and Y. Takenaka (1996) *Gendai nihonjin no ideorogi* [Ideology in Contemporary Japan]. Tokyo: Tokyo Daigaku Shuppankai.

Kawai, H. (1984) *Nihonjin to Aidentiti* [Japanese and Identity]. Tokyo: Sogensha.

Kawata, J. (1985) 'Konandaisei no seiji ishiki: showa 58-nen dai 37 kai shugiin senko wo tegakari to shite' [Political Consciousness of Konan University Students: a Case Study of the 37th General Elections for the House of Representatives in 1983], *Konan Daigaku Gakusei Hogaku*, vol. 14, pp. 1–45.

Kawata, J. (1989) *Hikaku seiji to seiji bunka* [Comparative Politics and Political Culture], Kyoto: Mineruba.

MacDougall, T. E. (ed.) (1982) 'Political Leadership in Japan', *Michigan Papers in Japanese Studies*, no. 1. Ann Arbor: Center for Japanese Studies, University of Michigan.

Massey, J. A. (1976) *Youth and Politics in Japan*, Tronto: Lexington Books.

McKean, M. M. (1981) *Environmental Protest and Citizen Politics in Japan*, Berkeley: University of California Press.

Minami, H. (1994) *Nihonjinron: Meiji kara konnichi made* [Nihonjinron: From the Meiji Period to the Present], Tokyo: Iwanami Shoten.

Mitchell, D. D. (1976) *Amaeru: The Expression of Reciprocal Dependency Needs in Japanese Politics and Law*, Boulder: Westview.

Miyanaga, K. (1991) *The Creative Edge: Individualism in Japan*, New Brunswick, N.J.: Transaction.

Mouer, R. and Y. Sugimoto (1986) *Images of Japanese Society: A Study in the Social Construction of Reality*. London: Kegan Paul International.

Nakamura, K. (1975) *Gendai nihon no seiji bunka* [Contemporary Japanese Political Culture], Kyoto: Mineruba.

Nakane, C. (1972) *Japanese Society*, Berkeley: University of California Press.

Nishida, T. (1994) *Iibunka to ningen kodo no bunseki* [Analysis of Cross-culture and Human Behavior], Tokyo: Taga.

Oguma, E. (1995) *Tanitsu minzoku shinwa no kigen: 'Nihonjin' no jigazo no keifu* [The Myth of Homogeneous society: The lineage of the Self-image of the Japanese], Tokyo: Shinyosha.

Okabe, R. (1983) 'Cultural Assumptions from Eastern and Western perspectives', in W. B. Gudykunst (ed.), *Intercultural Communication Theory*, Beverly Hills, CA: Sage (pp. 26–39).

Okamura, T. (1968) 'The Child's Changing Image of the Prime Minister', *The Developing Economies*, vol. 6, pp. 566–86.

Okamura, T. (1974) 'Seiji ishiki no kitei to shite no soridaijinzo: Gendai nihon ni okeru kodomo to seiji' [The Prime Minister's Image as the Foundation of Political Conciousness], in K. Taniuchi, B. Ari, Y. Ide, and M. Nishio (eds.), *Gendai Gyosei to Kanryosei (3)* [Contemporary Administration and Bureaucracy 3], Tokyo: Tokyo Daigaku Shuppankai (pp. 385–424).

Richardson, B. M. (1986) 'Japan's Habitual Voters: Partisanship on the Emotional Periphery', *Comparative Political Studies*, vol. 19, pp. 356–84.

Richardson, B. M. and S. C. (Flanagan 1984) *Politics in Japan*, Boston: Little, Brown.

Rohlen, T. P. (1975) 'The company work group', in E. Vogel (ed.), *Modern Japanese Organization and Decisionmaking*, Tokyo: Charles E. Tuttle (pp. 185–209).

Rosenberger, N. (ed.) (1992) *Japanese Sense of Self*. Cambridge: Cambridge University Press.

Steinhoff, P. G. (1989) 'Protest and Democracy', in T. Ishida and E. S. Krauss (eds.) *Democracy in Japan*, Pittsburgh: University of Pittsburgh Press (pp. 171–98).

Sugimoto, Y. and R. Mouer (eds) (1989) *Constructs for Understanding Japan*, London: Kegan Paul International.

Taketomo, Y. (1986) 'Amae as metalanguage: A Critique of Doi's Theory of *Amae*', *Journal of American Academy of Psycholanalysis*, vol. 14, 525–44.

Tsuji, K. (1968) 'Decision-making in the Japanese Government: A Study of Ringisei', in R. E. Ward (ed.), *Political Development in Modern Japan*, Princeton, N.J.: Princeton University Press (pp. 457–75).

Tsujimura, A. (1977) 'Nihonteki komyunikeshon no tokushitsu to shimbun no arikata' [Characteristics of Japanese Communication and the Function of the Press], *Senmon Shimbun*, vol. 1, pp. 7–24.

Tsujimura, A. (1987) 'Some Characteristics of the Japanese Way of Communication', in D. L. Kincaid (ed.), *Communication Theory: Eastern and Western Perspectives*, San Diego: Academic Press (pp. 115–26).

Vogel, E. (1979) *Japan as Number One: Lessons for America*, Cambridge: Harvard University Press.

Yamamoto, S. (1977) *'Kuuki' no kenkyu* [A Study of '*kuuki*'], Tokyo: Bungei Shunjusha.

Yoneyama, T. (1976) *Nihonjin no nakama ishiki* [Company Consciouness of Japanese], Tokyo: Kodansha Gendai Shinsho.

Yoshino, K. (1992) *Cultural Nationalism in Contemporary Japan: A Sociological Enquiry*, London: Routledge.

12
Change, Continuity and Culture: The Case of Power Relations in Iran and Japan

Fathali M. Moghaddam and David Crystal[1]

This chapter focuses on change and continuity in those aspects of cultures that influence the treatment of women, as well as authority relations more broadly. We bring a fundamental paradox to the surface: although cultures change, in some essential ways they remain the same. Very broadly, culture refers to everything that is influenced by humans and, more specifically, the normative system that prescribes correct behavior for people in different social roles and different social contexts (Moghaddam, 1998). Our thesis is that, in many cases, the impact of changes that occur at the macro level, such as changes in leadership, laws, and even political and economic systems, can be limited, opposed and even thwarted by stability at the micro level of common social practices. Such stability is sustained by what we term *social reductons*, elementary practices that implement norms and require the exercise of a related skill (Moghaddam and Harré, 1996).

Change poses a potential threat to majority groups, because it may be associated with alterations in power distribution. While issues of culture, power and inequalities are receiving some attention in traditional social (Gilbert, Fiske and Lindzey, 1998) and crosscultural (Berry, Poortinga and Pandey, 1997) psychology, there is need for a greater focus on cultural practices that perpetuate power inequalities. To illustrate our thesis that the influences of macro level changes are often limited by microlevel practices, we describe the situation of women and authority relations in Iran and Japan. These two ancient societies provide dramatic examples of cultural diversity and homogeneity, respectively, and in terms of history offer a sharp contrast to the younger North American cultures. We argue that similar relations between change at macro and micro levels exist in Iran and Japan, as well as the United States. We begin with a brief exposition of our theoretical framework.

---

[1]   We are grateful to John Duckitt, Stanley Renshon and anonymous reviewers for comments made on earlier drafts of this paper.

Theoretical approaches to culture and change

Change is an obvious feature of behavior and there have been some focused discussions on change in psychology (for examples, see Parkinson, Totterdell, Briner and Reynolds, 1996; Watzlawick, Weakland and Fisch, 1974). However, the cultural dimensions of change remain neglected. One reason is that the essential components of such change involve historical processes and an unfolding *collective* life (Moghaddam and Studer, 1997) that cannot be fitted into a one-hour laboratory study using psychology undergraduates as isolated participants (see Moghaddam, Taylor and Wright, 1993, 26–7).A number of social psychological theories of intergroup relations do address aspects of change, particularly theories concerned with social movements (see Taylor and Moghaddam, 1994, for a review), but they do not attend to processes associated with *continuity and stability*. In particular, they neglect the role of ordinary social practices in such processes. Other theories have attempted to tackle the issue of social change more broadly by focusing on national development (see for example, McClelland and Winter, 1969). However, the 'national development' models have typically derived from the reductionism that pervades mainstream psychology (Sampson, 1981), and which matches the American ethos of 'self-help' and 'personal responsibility'.

Social-reducton theory represents an attempt to address this gap by incorporating the idea of greater complexity in the ways in which cultural change occurs (Moghaddam and Harré, 1996). The theory focuses on the relationship between the speed of cultural change at the macro and the micro levels. In some cases changes (for example such as those in the domain of sexual practices) take place at the micro level of everyday social practices, but these are resisted at the macro level by authorities – through censorship, media manipulation, legal and education systems, religious rulings, and the like. An example would be changes reflected by the 'sexual liberation' and the 'gay rights movement' of the 1960s, and the reactions of religious and government authorities, who continue to support traditional lifestyles. However, there are also many instances in which macro level changes meet resistance at the micro level, where changes materialize at a far slower speed. For example, government legislation banning discrimination on the basis of race has been resisted at the level of everyday interactions at least in some communities.

Social-reducton theory proposes that the maximum speed that change can take place at the macro level, including the political and economic sectors, is faster than the maximum speed of change that is possible at the micro, social-psychological level. This means that while government policy, such as that on gender equality, can change fairly rapidly, the actual behavior of people in their everyday lives changes more slowly. Thus, instead of asking, 'why does change come about?' the point of departure for the theory is, 'Why do certain patterns of behavior persist?' Instead of asking 'why do revolutions occur?', the theory asks 'why do revolutionaries often fail to implement fundamental change even when they gain power?'

Social-reducton theory, then, addresses the age old question, 'why is it that in many cases, the more things change, the more they stay the same?' (Moghaddam and Harré, 1996). This theory is in line with some other research developments in interdisciplinary studies that focus on what Middlebrook (1995) has termed *the paradox of revolution*: the fact that popular mobilization and socioeconomic transformation often give rise to new forms of authoritarian rule. This tendency is captured in a *Washington Post* headline, 'Only the faces change' (Duke, 1998), which referred to developments in the Congo since the 'revolutionary' government of Laurent Kabila ended the 30-year dictatorship of Mobutu Sese Seko. Continuities of government style in the Congo include ethnic favoritism and discrimination against minorities.

In social-reducton theory, the concern to provide an explanation for continuity, rather than change, leads to a focus on the 'stabilizing' or 'anchoring' function of everyday social practices within the context of societal transformation. The theory assumes that psychological change is structured by *social-reducton systems*, 'interconnected networks of locally valid practices, implemented through implicit norms and related social skills that realize social relationships in particular domains' (Moghaddam and Harré, 1996). For example, 'authority relationships' are realized in a social reducton system that implements norms and skills relating to leader–follower, male–female, and various other types of high-status–low-status relations.

Change in pre and post-revolution Iran

Iranian government policy in the twentieth century has been consistent in trying to achieve a homogeneous national lifestyle, 'modern' before the revolution and 'Islamic' after the revolution. This consistency is reflected in (1) the treatment of women, and (2) authority relations more broadly.

Women in Iran

Our objective in this section is to show how both before and after the 1978 revolution women in Iran have in some respects served as pawns in a power struggle between competing groups of elite men. This trend may best be seen in government policy toward the veil, traditionally worn by women in Iran. The veil symbolizes different things to different groups. Some have argued that the veil 'frees' women by allowing them to escape being viewed as sex symbols, thus protecting their 'honor'. Others claim that the veil prevents women from achieving a modern, egalitarian gender role because it stigmatizes them and severely restricts their activities outside the home.

Although on the surface the situation of Iranian women has changed dramatically several times during the twentieth century, as symbolized by the banning and legalization of the veil by different regimes, at a deeper level gender relations have remained static. Both the 'modern Iranian woman' of the pre-1978 Pahlavi era (Abrahamian, 1982) and the 'Islamic female warriors' of the post-revolution era (Reeves, 1988) are creations of elite males.

The 'modern' Iranian state was launched soon after the first major oil find in the Middle East in North-Eastern Iran in 1908 (Graham, 1990). The collapse of the Qajar dynasty (1796–1921) created an opportunity for Reza Khan to seize power and establish his own Pahlavi dynasty (1926–78). Although during the latter part of Reza Shah's reign Iranian women were forcibly unveiled, as soon as the Shah lost power in 1941 many women went back to the veil, either voluntarily or because their fathers, husbands and other men forced them to do so. The abdication of Reza Shah in 1941 and the occupation of Iran by Allied forces coincided with a weakening of the central government. Reza Shah was replaced by his son, Mohammad Reza Shah (1941–79) who, for many years, was unable to dominate the larger national scene. During this time the veil once again became the normal covering for women in public places, although a minority of modernized women did appear in public without the veil. There also evolved a pro-democracy nationalist movement, led by Mossadeq who become prime minister in 1951, but it was thwarted by a coup supported by the United States, bringing the Shah back to full power after a brief exile in 1953.

From about the mid-1950s to the mid-1970s, the Shah used Iran's oil revenues to create a much more centralized and homogeneous Iranian state. Part of 'becoming modern' meant forcing women to abandon the veil. By the mid-1970s, it had become normative for women to be without the veil in the larger urban centers, such as Tehran, Mashad, Tabriz, Isfahan, Shiraz and Rasht. Indeed, during this era any female who wanted to take advantage of opportunities in higher education or to work in the modern sector of the economy was forced to abandon the veil and become 'be-hejab' (without the veil). It became customary to see traditionally dressed women take off the veil at the entrance to universities, government ministries and modern offices, and then return to the veil when they left such places to go back to their homes, because back in the family domain their fathers, husbands and brothers would often insist on them wearing the veil. Thus, at this period in Iran's history, women were forced by one group of men to take off the veil in official, government-controlled spaces, but forced by another group of men to put on the veil in informal spaces not directly controlled by the government.

A dramatic change came about after the 1978 revolution, eventually leading to women being forced to wear the veil in public ('ba-hejab' again!). This change started several years earlier, when some women went

back to the veil to indicate their opposition
became normative for women to be veiled durin
mass demonstrations of 1976–78 against the
become used to being unveiled now put on t
demonstrations, but they could, and most of th
once more to return home. But within a few years
political climate had changed dramatically, so that
choice – they had to adhere strictly to Islamic dress

On the surface, this new Islamic identity seems v ....om the
Shah's Iran (Simpson, 1988). However, both before a..u after the revolution
'correct' behavior for women has been established by an elite group of all-
powerful men. A pervasive social reducton system endorses the view of
women as objects of enjoyment for men. In her analysis of marriage in
Shi'i Iran, Haeri (1989) demonstrates continuity in the practice of temporary marriage, which is a contract, often verbal, between a married or
unmarried man and an unmarried woman. It is considered 'correct' behavior for men to be driven by sexual urges, but for women to be ambivalent
toward sex. Thus, a Shi'i Muslim man is legally allowed to contract simultaneously with as many temporary wives as he desires, in addition to the four
wives legally permitted to all Muslim men. A woman can only have one
husband of any kind at a time.

These marriage customs are based on everyday social practices guided by
rules about correct gender relations that span across centuries, and have
been only slightly altered by recent political events. The power of these
seemingly trivial everyday practices is that they operate at an implicit and
micro level. Temporary marriage is seldom publicly acknowledged, because
it is regarded as something shameful (despite its being legal), perhaps
because women often enter such contracts out of financial need. Thus,
temporary marriage is considered by some to be a form of prostitution. As
long as these everyday practices remain intact, large-scale political changes
may take place without influencing the status of women in Iran.

The same trend is evident in a number of other Eastern societies.
Mernissi's (1989) field research among Moroccan women reveals that while
the role of women has changed in the public, formal domain, change in
private life has been much slower. Many Moroccan women still have little
control over money, time, contraceptives, and other important matters
that shape their *daily* lives (the main title of Mernissi's book, *Doing Daily
Battle*, underscores the importance of the informal, everyday aspects of
social life). This disparity between the formal and the informal is pervasive
in many Arab societies (Sabbagh, 1996).

Authority relations

At a surface level, leadership changed after the revolution because the Shah
was replaced by a religious leadership: a 'grand ayatollah', or, if the clergy

ee on who this man should be, then a small group of ayatol-
sh, 1984). However, at a deeper level authority relations did not
because, in practice, there has been a continuation of the 'cult' of
ll-powerful leader (Abrahamian, 1993). Arjomand (1988) best captured
this theme with his phrase, 'The turban for the crown', implying that
the symbols of power had changed without a transformation in power
relations, and others have pointed to the deeper, more long-term cultural
basis for the contemporary political situation in Iran (Amirahmadi and
Manouchehr, 1988; Behnam, 1991). Many normative aspects of Iranian
culture can be traced at least to medieval times (Lambton, 1988), but we
believe norms governing authority relations have roots in pre-Islamic times
and that Iran represents a society where style of authority relations has persisted across major economic and political transformations. As Mackay
states in her analysis of Iranian culture, '...the authoritarian tradition of
father, king, and cleric have shaped a whole culture into a pattern of dominance and subservience' (1998, 93). Continuity in style of authority relations is evident in a number of other societies, as suggested by the cases of
Mao Zedong, Emperor Napoleon and other revolutionary leaders who came
to rule in the style of emperors they deposed.

In Iran only the surface elements of what have been termed 'political
culture' (Mashayekhi and Sami, 1992) have changed. Political personalities
at the very top are different, but the deeper structure of authority relations is
not. The Shah's 'Rastakheez' ('resurrection') party has been replaced by the
'Islamic Republic Party', but both before and after the revolution only one
'party line' has been tolerated. Members of the political opposition still face
oppression, persecution by the secret police, and even torture (Arjomand,
1988; Regal, 1993). One facet of this continuity is that although many political personalities changed, most of the 'new' personalities came from the
same extended families as the old. Again, this is not a new phenomenon.
Schama (1989, 516–17) has pointed out that the political leadership following the French Revolution was in large part a continuation of the cultural
climate of the *ancien regime*.

But the real key to cultural stability often lies in the details of how everyday social interactions are conducted. Consider, for instance, the example
of seating arrangements. If one enters a middle- or upper-class Iranian
home in the 1990s, on first impression it may appear that everything, particularly the furniture, is just like that in Western homes. However, a
careful examination of how Western furniture is used in most Iranian
homes reveals change that has only taken place at a surface level. Seating
arrangements continue to uphold traditional authority relations. Although
the chair with a high back and a seat supported by four upright legs has a
long history of association with Iranian kings, in everyday life Iranians followed the custom of sitting directly on carpeted or matted floors. *How* and
where a person sat was determined by their status. With respect to *how*,

Iranians would sit on their heels in the presence of a superior, cross-legged in the presence of an equal, and anyway they chose in the presence of inferiors. As regards *where*, those with highest status would sit in the center, furthest from the entrance door.

The essential function of seating arrangements has been to *maintain status hierarchies*, and this traditional function continues to be served by Western furniture,

> Although seating customs have been modified by the chair, the established protocol for receptions with eminent persons being seated in the center and lesser persons to the side has not been significantly changed except in extreme examples of Westernized homes and offices. Indeed, rather than Iranian protocol being changed by its occurrence, it is the modern chair which has been modified by Iranian use ... it has continuously been adapted to conform to traditional seating practices. (Peterson, 1981, 390)

*   *   *

We next turn to consider the experience of women in Japan. Japan is a classic case of a society that, on the surface, looks changed and Westernized, but in which the modern has actually been transformed to uphold traditional social relations. As with their Iranian counterparts, the situation of Japanese women demonstrates the interplay between change and constancy implicit in social reducton theory, and the influence of intransigent authority relations in maintaining the status quo.

The situation of women in Japan

From Japan's early history until the end of the eighth century, Japanese women frequently ruled the land as goddesses, queens and empresses (Ryusaku, de Bary and Keene, 1959). However, with the introduction of Buddhism from Korea in the middle of the sixth century, and the gradual absorption of Confucianist ideas from China, the spiritual landscape of Japan began to change. Under the patronage of Prince Shotoku (Regent from 593–622), Mahayana Buddhism especially began to flourish, with its sutras that spread discriminatory teachings about women. The establishment of a national system of administration in the seventh century resulted in women being excluded from posts in major religious institutions (Okano, 1995). These political changes, driven largely by the spread of Buddhist teachings, in addition to a civil war precipitated by the political scheming of Empress Shotoku (764–70) and her Buddhist priest lover, marked the beginning of a decline in Japanese women's social and political power (Robins-Mowry, 1983).

This decline became particularly precipitous during Japan's Tokugawa period(1600–1868), when the Japanese populace was inculcated with a combination of Buddhist and Confucianist ideas aimed at creating a tightly-controlled and rigidly hierarchical society. Both Buddhism and Confucianism, however, were strongly male-oriented, containing blatantly negative and deprecating views of women.

As a result, early in the Tokugawa period women lost their rights to own land or to file for divorce. Adultery by women was punishable by death. The Tokugawa shogunate promulgated the belief that women's chief value, in essence, lay in bearing children and perpetuating the family line; as help-mates, women were enjoined to be subservient, uncritical of and loyal to men. For Japanese women, the feudal era was the nadir of a slow but con-stant process of attenuation of power and influence that had begun a thou-sand years previously. For the next three hundred years, during which time Japan was virtually cut off from the outside world, images of women as sub-missive, docile, and powerless, and the thousands of daily interactions that instantiated these images, became ingrained in the minds and hearts of the Japanese people. These are the images and customs that form the core of the social reducton system with which Japanese women must contend in their efforts to win freedom and equality in contemporary Japan.

Change and constancy

The major obstacles to freedom and equality for contemporary Japanese women lie in three areas: education, employment and politics. In each of these areas, we find that a patina of change in women's status, usually deriving from political or legislative reforms, covers a resistant bedrock of constancy in male–female authority relations. Of the three areas, the domain of education has seen the most progress in women's participation.

Education

After the Second World War, a spate of reforms in Japan opened up access for women to all educational levels, including the university, from which women had previously been excluded. At the opening of the Meiji era (1868), about 40 per cent of boys and 10 per cent of girls attended some kind of elementary school (Robins-Mowry, 1985). Today, a little more than a century later, approximately 99 per cent of Japanese children of both sexes receive compulsory education which includes six years of elementary and three years of middle school. Similarly, 95 per cent of girls and 93 per cent of boys go on to attend senior high school (Beauchamp, 1989). Enrollment of women in higher education has also seen enormous gains: a sevenfold increase in the proportion of 18-year-olds entering universities and junior colleges since the end of the Second World War (compared with a threefold increase for men) (Kumagai, 1996).

Beneath these surface improvements in educational opportunities, which have been undeniably impressive, we find that sex differences still persist, especially in higher education. First, more Japanese men than women enroll in higher institutions. Second, a large percentage of women who pursue higher education enter junior colleges rather than four-year universities, the latter being the overwhelming choice for men. Women account for only 22 per cent of university student populations, yet represent almost 90 per cent of the students who attend junior colleges (Fujimura-Fanselow, 1995).

Several explanations may be posited for sex differences in attendance at Japanese institutions of higher learning. For one thing, cultural attitudes still reflect traditional images of Japanese women as primarily wives, mothers, and homemakers (Kameda, 1995). For another, given the high cost of private four-year universities and the above-mentioned cultural attitudes toward women's proper role, Japanese parents are more likely to invest in a son's than in a daughter's university education (Kameda, 1995). Lastly, the proportion of men and women attending colleges and universities are often related to employment options: societies where employment opportunities for women are most plentiful are those where sex ratio in education approaches closest to parity (see for example Fujimura-Fanselow, 1985). In Japan, employment opportunities for men and women are far from equal, as elaborated below.

Therefore, despite the considerable educational gains made by Japanese women, widespread gender disparities in academic attainment persist in Japan. In many ways, this disparity derives from the long-standing gender-based authority relations and from a cultural stereotype that still portrays a woman primarily as a man's helpmate, who needs education only to make her a more attractive marriage partner rather than to prepare her for a career outside the home (Kameda, 1995). Adding weight to the stereotype is the fact that opportunities for Japanese women to pursue careers outside the home are still very limited.

Employment

In April 1986, when Japan's Equal Employment Opportunity Law (EEOL) went into effect, many of the legal obstacles preventing Japanese women from reaching economic parity with men were removed. The EEOL prohibited employers from discriminating against women in terms of on-the-job training and supplementary education, dismissal, retirement, and fringe benefits. It also forbid the establishment of specific hiring requirements only for women, such as having to be unmarried, to be below a certain age, or to commute to work from one's parents' house. Furthermore, the law encouraged, but did not force, employers to give men and women equal consideration in hiring, assignments, and promotions.

Evidence suggests that the EEOL has had some positive impact on women's employment opportunities in Japan (see for example Cannings and Lazonick, 1994), but the general consensus among many scholars is that not very much has changed in the workplace for Japanese women (Fukuzawa, 1995; Kawashima, 1995). For one thing, the EEOL seems to have had little effect on people's attitudes regarding women and work. It is still generally expected that Japanese women will quit their jobs when they get married, pregnant, or reach a certain age (Maruta, 1991). A majority of companies (46 per cent) still seek to place women in jobs in which their 'feminine characteristics' can be best utilized, as opposed to those companies (23 per cent) that are willing to place women in all kinds of jobs (Women's Bureau, 1989). About 70 per cent of the heads of 942 large corporations still believe that the highest position attainable by a woman is a section chief, which is just one step above kakaricho, or section manager (Fukuzawa, 1995). Such attitudes place serious limitations on the opportunities for women to rise to executive levels in major organizations (Cannings and Lazonick, 1994).

Furthermore, since the passing of the EEOL, a two-track employment system for university graduates – a 'managerial employee track' and a 'clerical employee track' – has appeared in numerous Japanese companies. In theory, both employment tracks are equally opened to men and women, but in practice the clerical track has become the equivalent of the 'mommy track' (Ehrlich, 1989; Schwartz, 1989) in the United States – a track for educated women who want to pursue a career, but are limited in their professional commitment by family obligations to children and spouses (Cannings and Lazonick, 1994).

A blending of economic and sociopolitical forces (that is, the worldwide women's movement) may be seen as contributing to the passing of the EEOL in Japan in 1986. However, the implementation of a piece of political legislation such as the EEOL, while anticipating cultural changes and sometimes acting as a vehicle for change itself, by no means signals that society has arrived at a hoped-for destination. Thus, although Japanese women are legally equal to Japanese men in terms of rights and access to employment opportunities, in fact, everyday business practices and the social demands of daily family life in Japan conspire to prevent women from realizing the economic parity promised by political legislation.

Politics

The realm of politics is the most intractable of the three main areas in which Japanese women are seeking equality. It was only with the Revision of the Election Law of 1945 that Japanese women were given equal rights to vote and to run for elected office. Since then, women have not had much success in breaking into the world of Japanese politics. The one exception occurred in 1986 when Takako Doi, a female scholar of constitutional law, was chosen to be chairperson of the Social Democratic Party of Japan (SDPJ). The party at that time was said to be in crisis and in need of a 'sacrificial lamb' (Iwao, 1993). Doi's cool, straightforward, and powerful style, however, became very popular on the campaign trail, especially with women voters, resulting in unexpected success for the SDPJ in the 1989 elections. The elections that year saw a record number of women voted into the House of Councillors and elected as assembly members of the Tokyo city government. The 'Madonna Whirlwind', as that summer was known (do Rosario, 1993), was seen as Doi's triumph and briefly introduced the possibility that a woman might become a prime minister. That possibility, however, quickly faded when Doi's uncompromising opposition to the use of Japan's Self-Defense Forces in the Persian Gulf War lost both her and the SDPJ the support of many voters in the 1991 local elections (Iwao, 1993). The following year, Doi resigned as the SDPJ chairperson.

At present, women are only minimally represented in the Japanese Diet. Of the 511 seats in the lower house, 2.7 per cent are occupied by women. This places Japan 110th among 130 countries in a recent United Nations survey of women's participation in elected legislatures (do Rosario, 1993). In Japan's upper house, as well, women only hold 35 out of 252 seats. Some female politicians estimate that it will take another 10 to 15 years before women will be able to enter Japanese politics in any significant numbers (do Rosario, 1993).

In all, the difficulty experienced by Japanese women in attaining social and economic equality may be clearly understood in the context of social reducton theory. Although the Japanese government has attempted to legislate equal access to education, employment, and political power, images of traditionally female roles as child-bearers, homemakers, and wives create expectations that are often subtle and informal, yet powerful. Given the longevity of the social reducton system that governs male–female power relations in Japan, it is not surprising that the pace at which Japanese women are winning equality is considerably slower than that of their counterparts in younger cultures such as Canada and the United States. Nevertheless, the same longevity of oppressive cultural dynamics also makes the progress Japanese women have attained in a relatively short time all the more remarkable.

Authority relations

As with many aspects of modern Japan, contemporary Japanese authority relations may be traced back to the Tokugawa era. The rigid hierarchy characteristic of Tokugawa society was based on Confucian teachings that linked harmony in the state to harmony and order in the family. Consequently, the structure of the Tokugawa government resembled that of the traditional Japanese family or household, known as the *ie*. The Japanese *ie* consisted of a main house, headed by the father, and a number of subordinate branch houses in which lived the sons of the father and their families. Within each house, relations between members were hierarchically organized along lines based on age, sex and expectation of permanency in the house. Younger members were seen as indebted to older members for their upbringing. Males, especially the father and the eldest son, were given power over females. The two main principles governing life in the *ie* were that the good of the *ie* took precedence over the good of an individual, and that the continuation of the *ie* was the chief goal of all its members.

Similarly, the Tokugawa government was constructed as a kind of *ie*. The 'main house' comprised the Tokugawa family, headed by the Shogun, the 'father' of the State. Beneath the main house were hundreds of 'branch houses', fiefdoms controlled by territorial lords called *daimyo* who, in turn, ruled over thousands of *hatamoto* or retainers. Each daimyo family might be considered a subordinate *ie*, with hundreds or thousands of retainers and their families under its control. The nature of the Tokugawa power structure, then, was essentially that of a huge network of hierarchically connected households (Ooms, 1985).

After the Meiji Restoration in 1868, the government attempted to break up the *ie* system through a series of political reforms. These political measures, however, did little to change the basic structure of interpersonal authority relations. As in the case of pre- and post-1978-revolution Iran, the basic elements of Tokugawa political rule were transferred to the political system of post-Meiji Japan and given new names. The Shogun became the Emperor, the Daimyo became the Kenrei (Governor), and the local leader became the Jinushi (Landlord) (Maruta, 1991).

Although the *ie* system has weakened considerably since the end of the Second World War, these general rules at the macro-level persist to the present and reach down to influence the most routine, everyday aspects of life at the micro level. Perhaps the most conspicuous example of how the *ie* system has infiltrated into the daily life of contemporary Japan may be found in modern Japanese companies. Just as the head of the *ie*, the father, expected loyalty and self-sacrifice from his children, so a company superior expects loyalty and self-sacrifice from his subordinates. The primary loyalty of the Japanese 'sarariman' is to the company, the 'main house', while the worker's own family, the 'branch house', comes second. Just as loyalty to the *ie* was rewarded with paternalistic protection and support, so in exchange for the sarariman's loyalty and devotion to the company, the superior promises to take care of him and his family, even to the extent of arranging a marriage for him. Just as in the *ie*, authority relations in the company are arranged on the basis of age, permanency in the house (company seniority), and sex (males occupy most of the authority positions in Japanese companies).

Given that the essential structure of authority relations in Japan has remained relatively unchanged for the past 400 years, it is not surprising that Japanese women, systematically oppressed during the Tokugawa period, find it difficult to improve their status in contemporary society. Any political measures that do not address the basic nature of this power structure in Japanese society are unlikely to produce any real change on a day-to-day level.

Reflecting back on ourselves

The cases of Iran and Japan act as a mirror, reflecting back to illuminate the political, economic and legal status of women in the United States. The formal macro system has changed dramatically for American women over the last century, and they now have the legal right to compete as equals in all major domains. However, critics of the *status quo* have argued that despite recent gains by women in the formal domain, inequalities persist. Women who work outside the home are still expected to take more responsibility than husbands for family life (Gappa, St John-Parson and O'Barr, 1982). Women are still concentrated in lower-status occupations, and receive lower pay even when they are in the same occupations as men (Blau and Ferber, 1992; Matteo, 1993).

Additionally, women continue to be excluded from political power (Cook, Thomas and Wilcox, 1994). The so-called 'year of the women' US elections in 1992 brought the number of women in the Senate to a grand total of six, and even young students do not see women as equally viable political candidates for top political positions (Ogletree, Coffee and May 1992).

In both developed and developing societies, women have tended to reach positions of power through a 'widow's mandate' or by being closely related to male leaders. Indira Gandhi and Benazir Bhutto come to mind most readily. A woman has never achieved national leadership in the United States, and it was not until 1979 that a woman, Nancy L. Kassebaum, was elected to the US Senate without being preceded in office by her husband. Research on Ancient Egypt suggests that the 'family ties' route to political power was used by women 5000 years ago, and probably before (Capel and Markoe, 1996). Hatshepsut, the best documented female ruler of ancient Egypt, gained prominence through her lineage and was often represented as a man in sculpture and painting (Bryan, 1996, 32). Perhaps this was a way of making herself a more acceptable ruler, just as Margaret Thatcher presented herself as even tougher than the men in her cabinet (Thatcher, 1993).

In explaining this paradox between the formal and the informal, we once again point to the resilience and subtlety of social reducton systems guiding micro-level social practices. A similar idea is expressed by researchers concerned with aspects of the 'new sexism' (Benokraitis and Feagin, 1986). A study of the brightest women scientists, recipients of postdoctoral fellowships from the National Science Foundation and other prestigious sources, found subtle barriers working against them (Sonnert and Holton, 1995). For example, women would not receive the same quality of informal support and information, often provided through chats in corridors or by introductions to visiting scientists. In sum, much like their Iranian and Japanese counterparts, American women's advancement toward economic and political parity with men has to a considerable extent been stymied by subtle and unchanging everyday social practices.

Concluding comment

Received wisdom tells us that cultural change is either an economically determined 'top-down' process, with economic factors acting as causal agents, or a 'bottom-up' process with 'mental mechanisms' acting as causal agents. Our view is that psychological factors are important in cultural change, not because 'the causes are in our heads', but because the normative systems regulating everyday social practices can resist, and even help shape, macro political and economic changes. Such normative systems are socially constructed, collectively shared, and upheld by communities. They are part of the seemingly 'trivial' details of everyday life, and it is exactly because they are so intricately imbedded in cultural life that they are often both overlooked, and resilient to change.

References

Abrahamian, E. (1982) *Iran Between Two Revolutions*, Princeton, NJ: Princeton University Press.

Abrahamian, E. (1993) *Khomeinism*, Berkeley, CA: University of California Press.

Amirahmadi, H. and P. Manouchehr (eds.) (1988) *Post Revolution Iran*, Boulder, Col: Westview Press.

Arjomand, A. A. (1988) *The Turban for the Crown*, New York: Oxford University Press.

Bakhash, S. (1984) *The Reign of the Ayatollahs*, New York: Basic Books.

Beauchamp, E. (1989) 'Education', in T. Ishida and E. S. Krauss (eds.), *Democracy in Japan*, Pittsburgh, PA: University of Pittsburgh Press (pp. 225–51).

Benokraitis, N. V. and J. R. Feagin (1986) *Modern Sexism: Blatant, Subtle and Covert Discrimination*, Englewood Cliffs, NJ: Prentice-Hall.

Berry, J. W., Y. H. Poortinga and J. Pandey (eds) (1997) *Handbook of Cross-cultural Psychology* (3 vols). 2nd edn. Boston: Allyn and Bacon.

Blau, F. D. and M. A. Ferber (1992) *The Economics of Men, Women and Work*, Englewood Cliffs, NJ: Prentice Hall.

Bryan, B. M. (1996) 'In Women Good and Bad Fortune are on Earth: Status and Roles of Women in Egyptian Culture', in A. Capel and G. E. Markoe (eds.), *Mistress of the House, Mistress of Heaven: Women in Ancient Egypt*, New York: Hudson Hills Press (pp. 25–46).

Cannings, K. and W. Lazonick (1994) 'Equal Employment and the 'Managerial Woman', in Japan. *Industrial Relations*, vol. 33, pp. 44–69.

Capel, A. K. and G. E. Markoe (eds.) (1996) *Mistress of the House, Mistress of the Heaven: Women in Ancient Egypt*, New York: Hudson Hills Press.

Cook, E. A., S. Thomas and C. Wilcox (eds.) (1994) 'The Year of the Women: Myths and Realities', Boulder, Col.: Westview Press.

do Rosario, L. (1993) 'Last Stronghold', *Far Eastern Economic Review*, 156, 27. Dowa Kyoiku Shiryu (1985). No. 7, Tokyo: Mombusho.

Duke, L. (1998) 'Only the Faces Change', *The Washington Post*, 17 May, p. A22.

Ehrlich, E. (1989) 'The Mommy Track', *Business Week*, vol. 20, pp. 126–34.
Fujimura-Fanselow, K. (1995) 'College Women Today: Options and Dilemmas', in K. Fujimura-Fenselow and A. Kameda (eds.) *Japanese Women: New Feminist Perspectives on the Past, Present and Future*, New York: Feminist Press.
Fukuzawa, K. (1995) 'Women's hiring woes', *Japan Quarterly*, April–June.
Gappa, J., D. St John-Parson and J. O'Barr (1982) *The Dual Careers of Faculty and Family: Can Both Prosper?*, Paper presented at the American Association for Higher Education, Washington D.C.
Gilbert, D. T., S. T. Fiske and G. Lindzey (eds.) (1998) *The Handbook of Social Psychology* (2 vols). 4th edn. New York: McGraw-Hill.
Graham, R. (1979) *Iran: The Illusion of Power*, New York: St Martin's Press.
Haeri, S. (1989) *Law of Desire: Temporary marriage in Shi'i Iran*, Syracuse, NY: Syracuse University Press.
Iwao, S. (1993) *The Japanese Woman: Traditional Image and Changing Reality*, New York: The Free Press.
Kameda, A. (1995) 'Sexism and Gender Stereotyping in Schools'. in K. Fujimura-Fanselow and A. Kameka (eds.), *Japanese Women: New Feminist Perspectives on The Past, Present and Future*, New York: New Feminist Press (pp. 107–24).
Kawashima, Y. (1995) 'Female Workers: an Overview of Past and Current Trends', in K. Fujimura-Fanselow and A. Kameka (eds.), *Japanese Women: New Feminist Perspectives on the Past, Present and Future*, New York: New Feminist Press (pp. 107–24).
Kumagai, F. (1996) *Unmasking Japan Today: The Impact of Traditional Values on Modern Japanese Society*, Westport, CT: Praeger.
Lambton, A. K. S. (1988) *Continuity and Change in Medieval Persia*, Albany, NY: Bibliotheca Persica.
Mackay, S. (1998) *The Iranians: Persia, Islam and the Soul of the Nation*, New York: Plenum.
Maruta, T. (1991) '"Be Single or Quit": Equal Employment Opportunity Law of 1986 and Inflexible Social Attitudes Toward Female Employees in Japan', *Konan Journal of Social Sciences*, vol. 4, pp. 1–33.
Mashayekhi, M. and K. F. Sami (1992) *Iran: Political Culture in the Islamic Republic*, London: Routledge.
Matteo, S. (ed.) (1993) *American Women in the Nineties*, Boston: Northeastern University Press.
McClelland, D. C. and D. G. Winter (1969) *Motivating Economic Achievement*, New York: Free Press.
Mernissi, F. (1989) *Doing Daily Battle: Interviews with Morrocon Women* (tr. Mary Jo Lakeland). New Brunswick, NJ: Rutgers University Press.
Middlebrook, K. J. (1995) *The Paradox of Revolution: Labor, State and Authoritarianism in Mexico*, Baltimore, MD.: Johns Hopkins University Press.
Moghaddam, F. M. (1998) *Social Psychology: Exploring Universals Across Cultures*, New York: Freeman.
Moghaddam, F. M., D. M. Taylor and S. C. Wright (1993) *Social Psychology in Cross-cultural Perspective*, New York: Freeman.
Moghaddam, F. M. and R. Harré (1996) 'Psychological Limitations to Political Revolutions: an Application of Social Reducton Theory', in E. Hasselberg, L. Martienssen and F. Radtke (eds.) *Der Dialogbegriff am End des 20. Jahrhunderts*, (The Concept of Dialogue at the End of the Twentieth Century) Berlin: Hegel Institute (pp. 230–40).

Moghaddam, F. M. and C. Studer (1997) 'Cross-cultural Psychology: the Frustrated Gadfly's Promises, Potentialities and Failures', in D. Fox and I. Prilleltensky (eds.), *Critical Psychology*, New Park, CA: Sage (pp. 185–201).

Ogletree, S. M., M. C. Coffee and S. A. May (1992) 'Perceptions of Female/Male Presidential Candidates', *Psychology of Women Quarterly*, vol. 16, pp. 201–08.

Okano, H. (1995) 'Women's Image and Place in Japanese Buddhism', in K. Fujimura-Fanselow and A. Komeda (eds.), *Japanese Women: New Feminist Perspectives on the Past, Present and Future*, New York: The Feminist Press (pp. 15–28).

Ooms, H. (1985) *Tokugawa Ideology: Early Constructs 1570–1680*. Princeton, NJ: Princeton University Press.

Parkinson, B., P. Totterdell, R. B. Briner and S. Reynolds (1996) *Changing Moods: The Psychology of Mood and Mood Regulation*, London: Longman.

Peterson, S. R. (1981) 'Chairs and Change in Qajar Times', in M. E. Bonnie and N. R. Keddie (eds.), *Modern Iran: The Dialectics of Continuity and Change*, Albany, NY: State University of New York Press (pp. 383–90).

Reeves, M. (1989) *Female Warriors of Allah: Women and the Islamic Revolution*, New York: Dutton.

Robins-Mowry, D. (1983) *The Hidden Sun*, Boulder, CO: Westview Press.

Ryusaku, T., W. T. de Bary and D. Keene (1958) *Sources of Japanese Tradition*, New York: Columbia University Press.

Sabbagh, S. (ed.) (1996) *Arab Women: Between Defiance and Restraint*, New York: Olive Branch Press.

Sampson, E. E. (1981) 'Cognitive Psychology as Ideology', *American Psychologist*, vol. 36, pp. 730–43.

Schwartz, F. N. (1989) 'Management Women and the New Facts of Life', *Harvard Business Review*, vol. 89, pp. 65–76.

Simpson, J. (1988) *Inside Iran: Life Under Khomeini's Regime*, New York: St Martin's Press.

Sonnert, G. and G. Holton (1995). *Gender Differences in Science Careers: the Project Access Study*, New Brunswick, NJ: Rutgers University Press.

Taylor, D. M. and F. M. Moghaddam (1994) *Theories of Intergroup Relations: International Social Psychological Perspectives*. 2nd edn. New York: Praeger.

Thatcher, M. (1993) *The Downing Street Years*. New York: HarperCollins.

Wazlawick, P., J. H. Weakland and R. Fisch (1974) *Change: Principles of Problem Formation and Problem Resolution*, New York: W. W. Norton.

Women's Bureau (1989) *Joshi sayo kanri kihon chosa*, [Basic Statistical Survey on Employed Women in Management]. Tokyo: Ministry of Labor.

13
Value Adaptation to the Imposition and Collapse of Communist Regimes in East-Central Europe[1]

Shalom H. Schwartz, Anat Bardi and Gabriel Bianchi

Does the political system in a country influence the importance that its citizens ascribe to the broad range of basic human values? Surprisingly, there is little direct evidence that this is the case. We address this question through a comparative, crossnational study. For this purpose, we take advantage of the natural experiment in Central and Eastern Europe constituted by the imposition of communist regimes over 40 years and their subsequent collapse. We seek to identify if and how the experience of living under communist regimes affected the basic values of citizens in East and Central European countries. (For convenience we refer to this region collectively as East Europe).

No longitudinal data on basic human values are available for the period preceding communist rule. We therefore adopt the comparative, cross-national approach, applied to study the impacts of socioeconomic and technological development on individual values (see for example Inkeles and Smith, 1974), to study possible impacts of the communist political system. To examine possible value changes following the collapse of the communist regimes in Eastern Europe, we draw upon data we gathered in Hungary, Poland and Slovakia in 1989–91 as compared with 1996–97.

Previous crossnational research on countries with different political systems has offered interesting hints (for example Hofstede, 1980). It has not, however, studied a broad range of basic values and it has not sought to relate such values systematically to the different types of political systems (for a partial exception, see Broek and Moor, 1994). Basic values may be seen as the very heart of culture (Hofstede, 1980; Schwartz, 1994a; Schwartz, 1999; Smith and Schwartz, 1997). Culture is manifest in everyday practices, symbols and rituals that outside observers can see. But the meaning of these manifestations remains unclear until the observer comes to understand how the members of a group evaluate them. These evaluations are expressed in basic *values* – what people believe is good or bad, what they think should and should not be done, what they hold to be desirable or undesirable. Cultural values (for example freedom, prosperity, security) are the bases for the specific norms that tell people what behavior is appropriate in various situations.

There are two primary processes through which basic values may have been affected in Eastern Europe – direct indoctrination of people in communist ideology, and adaptation of people to the life circumstances created by communist rule. We first consider direct indoctrination.

For more than four decades, residents of Eastern Europe were subject to lifelong political education in communist ideology (see for example Roskin, 1991). But the inculcation of communist ideology was only partly successful, and it often produced reaction against the regime and its symbols (for example Barghoorn and Remington, 1986). Many have argued that, in Central Europe, communism remained an alien ideology imposed upon citizens but not accepted by them (for example Rupnik, 1988). We have recently described how failed indoctrination drained some of the core values propounded in communist ideology of their usual meanings (Bardi and Schwartz, 1996). If communism did not have the intended influences on value priorities in the domains to which communist education was directly addressed, perhaps it had even less influence on human values in other domains. The conclusion of the one study we have found that compared values of citizens in Eastern and in Western Europe supports this inference. Broek and Moor (1994, 226) reported that East Europeans did not differ as a group from their Western counterparts in most values related to politics, religion and primary relations at the beginning of the 1990s. Only in the domain of work values were consistent differences reported. East Europeans showed less appreciation for initiative, achievement and responsibility in work.

These findings and speculations challenge the success of direct ideological indoctrination in Eastern Europe. However, there are stronger grounds to postulate that life under communist regimes substantially impacted the values of citizens through the second process mentioned above, adaptation to life circumstances. Research on the acquisition of basic values and on change in the value priorities of individuals over the life-course has demonstrated that adaptation to life circumstances, is important for value formation (for example Inkeles and Smith, 1974; Kohn and Schooler, 1983; Rokeach, 1973). Adaptation does not require acceptance of an ideological message. Rather, it refers to adjusting effectively to the opportunities and constraints that structure one's life chances. It might even entail finding effective ways to resist undesirable ideologies. Studies of Eastern Europe describe communist regimes as systematically structuring the living conditions of their citizens in the worlds of work, family, education, leisure, and so on (for example Kohak, 1992; Nowak, 1988). Hence, on theoretical grounds, adaptation should have led to a characteristic set of value priorities.

Adaptation to life circumstances influences value priorities primarily through two mechanisms – acclimation and compensation. For most types of values, people acclimate their values to their circumstances. That is, they form value priorities that are compatible with the reinforcement contingencies that their life circumstances afford. They upgrade the importance of values they can readily attain, and downgrade the importance of those whose pursuit is blocked. For example, people in jobs that afford much freedom of choice increase the importance of self-direction values at the expense of conformity values (Kohn and Schooler, 1983). The constraints on independence in the occupational experiences of East as compared to West Europeans may account for the Broek and Moor (1994) finding that East European workers appreciate initiative, achievement, and personal responsibility less.

When the attainment of values concerned with material well-being and security is largely beyond personal control, a compensation mechanism operates. These values are based on what Maslow (1959) called 'deficit needs'. Deprivation increases the strength of such needs and, correspondingly, of the valued goals to which they point (Bilsky and Schwartz, 1994). For example, people who have endured economic hardship and social upheaval attribute more importance to the attainment of wealth and the preservation of social order (for example Inglehart, 1991; Schwartz, 1994a).

The idea that value formation and change is an adaptive process forms the basis for deriving hypotheses regarding the impact of life under communism on the basic human values of citizens in Eastern Europe. If adaptation to life under communism affects values in a coherent manner, there should be a shared profile of value priorities that distinguishes East European countries as a set from other countries. We will compare these countries with countries from Western Europe, the region closest to Eastern Europe in terms of historical and cultural developments (Schopflin, 1990).

Of course, Eastern Europe is not a monolithic entity (Glenny, 1990). Lines of demarcation significant for value priorities can also be drawn within this geopolitical region. This too is relevant for assessing the effects of adaptation to communist systems. One line of demarcation is religious. The East European countries we studied encompass Roman Catholic (Czechia, Slovakia, Hungary, Poland, Slovenia), Orthodox (Bulgaria, Georgia, Russia), and Protestant (Estonia) countries. The partition between Roman Catholic and Orthodox countries overlaps two other important lines of demarcation. The Roman Catholic countries form a Central European region whose socioeconomic development and agricultural adaptation to world markets place it midway between East and West (Gunst, 1989). Moreover, these Central European countries were characterized by greater resistance to the penetration of communism and stronger oppositional movements (see for example Carpenter, 1997; Lewis, 1997; Zubek, 1997).

The variation within Eastern Europe along religious, economic and political lines may also relate to differences among these countries in value priorities. Variation in resistance and opposition to communism suggests that communism may have structured everyday life conditions less pervasively in the Central European countries than in Bulgaria, Georgia and Russia. If so, the impact of communism on values may have been weaker in the former set of countries than in the latter. A comparison of these two sets of countries is therefore an additional way to assess the validity of hypotheses regarding the effects of adaptation to communism.

Differences in level of socioeconomic development might also account for value differences between the two sets of East European countries. Economic development might account for value differences between Eastern and Western Europe as well. In the discussion, below, we consider national economic levels as an alternative for explaining the differences in values that our hypotheses attribute to adaptation to communist regimes. Examination of the empirical data will reveal that national differences in economic level do not provide an adequate alternative explanation.

Basic values appropriate for national comparisons

Hypotheses about differences in basic human values require a comprehensive set of value types on which it is appropriate to compare countries. For this purpose, we drew upon a theory of culture-level values, developed for crosscultural studies, that we have recently validated empirically (Schwartz, 1994a, 1999; Schwartz and Ros, 1995). This theory derived seven types of values by considering the basic issues or problems that societies must confront in order to regulate human activity: Conservatism, Intellectual Autonomy, Affective Autonomy, Hierarchy, Egalitarianism, Harmony and Mastery. The theory views values (such as success, justice, freedom, social order) as the socially approved goals used to motivate action to cope with the basic societal problems and to express and justify the solutions that are chosen. Table 13.1 lists the definitions of the value types.

The single values that are used to index each type are written in parentheses. (See references above for more complete explanations.) We next describe life circumstances in Eastern Europe that are traceable to the imposition of communism and we derive from them a set of hypotheses regarding value priorities.

Value priorities in East-Central Europe: hypothesis derivation

Following unsuccessful struggles against communist regimes in several East European countries during the 1950s and 1960s, people began to adjust to their circumstances in a manner described by Kohak (1992) as analogous to the adaptation of long-term prisoners to jail: They developed a set of skills and attitudes that enabled them to live reasonably under the circumstances. We would add that they developed a set of value priorities that acclimated to life under these circumstances or that compensated for its

Table 13.1   Definitions of the value types and the single items used to index them

---

Conservatism: emphasis on the status quo, propriety and restraint of actions or inclinations that might disrupt the solidary group or the traditional order – clean, devout, family security, forgiving, honoring parents and elders, moderate, national security, obedient, politeness, protecting public image, reciprocation of favors, respect for tradition, self-discipline, social order, wisdom.

Intellectual autonomy: emphasis on promoting and protecting the independent ideas and rights of the individual to pursue his or her own intellectual directions – creativity, curious, broad-minded.

Affective autonomy: emphasis on promoting and protecting the individual's independent pursuit of affectively positive experience – enjoying life, exciting life, pleasure, varied life.

Hierarchy: emphasis on the legitimacy of hierarchical allocation of fixed roles and of resources – authority, humble[2], influential, social power, wealth.

Egalitarianism: emphasis on transcendence of selfish interests in favor of voluntary commitment to promote the welfare of others – equality, freedom, helpful, honest, loyal, responsible, social justice, world of peace.

Harmony: emphasis on fitting harmoniously into the environment – protecting the environment, unity with nature, world of beauty.

Mastery: emphasis on getting ahead through active self-assertion, through changing and mastering the natural and social environment – ambitious, capable, choosing own goals, daring, independent, successful.

---

deprivations. In what follows we explicate how aspects of the experience of life under communism were likely to lead citizens in Eastern Europe to attribute greater importance to conservatism and hierarchy values. We also explicate how adaptation to these experiences was likely to reduce the importance citizens attributed to intellectual and affective autonomy, egalitarianism and mastery values. We derive no hypothesis for harmony values because adaptation required no particular acclimation of these values.

The communist regimes of Eastern Europe, like other totalitarian regimes, demanded that citizens conform to their superiors in all realms of life. Punishment for failure to conform was frequent and the fact that the rules and expectations were often obscure or unstable made life more difficult. Performing acts or expressing opinions that were not explicitly approved was therefore dangerous. In response, people learned to adopt a 'low profile'. They avoided taking any initiatives or risks, refrained from offering suggestions or criticisms, and related minimally to their superiors (Kohak, 1992; Marody, 1988; Nowak, 1988).

These adjustments to life under communism have clear value implications. Close supervision, strict rules and the suppression of initiative, risk and innovation all undermine autonomy values (Kohn and Schooler,

1983). This applies most obviously to intellectual autonomy values like curiosity and creativity, whose expression was not only frustrated but often negatively sanctioned. It also applies to affective autonomy values like exciting life, pleasure and enjoying life. The independent pursuit of affectively positive experiences was suppressed by the regime as a threat to reliable conformity and to conventional norms. Unable to pursue autonomy values successfully, people would be likely to adapt by downgrading their importance, according to the acclimation mechanism.

Mastery values were likely to suffer a similar fate. Such values as ambition and daring emphasize active self-assertion and attempts to change the status quo. Their pursuit is inappropriate and even dangerous in settings where conformity to role obligations is the paramount concern. We would therefore expect people to downgrade or even abandon mastery values as a way to acclimate to such settings.

In contrast, we hypothesize that people came to attribute greater importance to the values that could promote adjustment to this constraining and dangerous environment – conservatism and hierarchy values. By definition, conservatism values emphasize propriety and restraint of actions and inclinations that might disrupt the prevailing order. By pursuing such values (for example moderation, self-discipline, social order), people could avoid conflict with their superiors and insure more predictability in their lives. By attributing high priority to these values, people could justify the 'low profile' that they adopted. In addition, compensation for the sense of insecurity fostered by dangerous and unpredictable life circumstances might increase the importance of the security aspect of conservatism values.

When their environment is organized in an authoritarian manner, people can feel reasonably comfortable only if they come to view the hierarchical distribution of roles and resources as legitimate to some degree. Both those who exercised power over others and those who were constrained to acquiesce in meeting the rigid but unpredictable demands of the hierarchical system could more easily justify their actions and find meaning in their lives by upgrading the importance of such hierarchy values as authority, social power, and humility.

Close surveillance over words and deeds accompanied the demands for conformity under communist regimes (Kohak, 1992). Compliance was often enforced by informants such as fellow-workers and fellow-students. This, in turn, diminished the level of interpersonal trust (Marody, 1998; Nowak, 1988).

One likely outcome of reduced interpersonal trust is an undermining of egalitarianism values. These values call for voluntary commitment to the welfare of others, but if others cannot be trusted a commitment to their welfare is foolhardy at best and self-destructive at worst. Guiding one's life according to such egalitarianism values as equality, justice, and honesty makes little sense in settings where others are unlikely to reciprocate so there is a real risk of being exploited.

Increased endorsement of both conservatism and hierarchy values is another likely outcome of reduced interpersonal trust. Lack of interpersonal trust makes it better to avoid too much openness in relations with others and to rely upon established norms, roles, and expectations. The assurance that people will fulfill the mutual role obligations imposed by the hierarchical role structures in which they are embedded can provide certainty and security. Hence norms, rules, role obligations and hierarchical relations are more crucial for successful adjustment to life circumstances. We would therefore expect people to increase the importance they attribute to conservatism and hierarchy values, the values that support and legitimize the social structural arrangements that could provide some certainty. Within narrow solidary groups of close friends and family, interpersonal trust generally persisted. It was therefore especially critical not to disrupt these relationships. This too may have enhanced the importance of conservatism values – values principally concerned with smooth relations within the solidary group.

The paternalism of communist regimes in the social and economic realms fostered passivity, loss of ambition and loss of interest in the political process (Feher, 1982). People came to expect the state to provide them with jobs, basic accommodation, and an adequate standard of living (Lomax, 1997; Marody, 1988; Miszlevitz, 1997). This increased people's investment in the status quo. It was therefore likely to increase the importance of conservatism values that protect the status quo. It also lent some legitimacy to the 'beneficent' hierarchical order and, thereby, to the hierarchy values that justify this order. In contrast, by fostering passivity and lack of ambition, paternalism undermined mastery and intellectual autonomy values.

Another consequence of paternalism was to reduce citizens' sense of responsibility for their own actions (see for example Kohak, 1992). Abdication of personal responsibility is the opposite of the moral orientation expressed by egalitarianism values. Egalitarianism values call upon people to engage in the arduous negotiation of shared interests with others and to cooperate voluntarily in promoting the welfare of all segments of society. Hence egalitarianism values were likely to lose force under paternalism.

Finally, we note that the reinforcement system under communist regimes tended to foster mediocrity (Marody, 1988). Authorities typically failed to reward effort and excellence with increased material benefits or promotions. The criteria for rewards were often capricious and incomprehensible, which undermined people's motivations to strive, to innovate, and to develop their unique ideas and abilities. The likely consequence was a weakening of mastery and intellectual autonomy values that express these motivations.

In sum, our analysis of the life circumstances to which citizens adapted under communist regimes leads us to hypothesize a shared value profile in Eastern Europe characterized by

(a)   relatively great importance attributed to conservatism and hierarchy values; and
(b)   relatively low importance attributed to intellectual autonomy, affective autonomy, egalitarianism and mastery values.

This pattern should be revealed operationally in comparisons of East Europeans with West Europeans and, within Eastern Europe, in comparisons of samples from Eastern Europe with samples from Central Europe. Note that the hypotheses of increased importance for hierarchy and conservatism values and reduced importance for egalitarianism and autonomy values are opposite to what one would expect if the teachings of communist ideology influenced values directly. Next, we assess these hypotheses empirically. In the second part of this chapter we address the issue of value change after the communist regimes collapsed.

Methods

Samples

The ideal data for comparing countries is from representative national samples, but because there are no data on the broad range of human values of interest here from representative national samples in the relevant countries, we adopted another approach. For each country, we used data from samples that are matched on critical characteristics. In addition we replicated the study with two different types of samples, both from the majority ethnic group in their country. One set of samples consisted of urban school teachers who teach the full range of subjects in grades 3–12 of the most common type of school system in each country. The second set of samples consisted of college students majoring in the popular subjects in their own countries.

Of course, the value importance scores of teachers and students are not the same as those of representative national samples. What is crucial is that value importance scores for student and teacher samples *order* the countries in a manner similar to the order that would be found based on the differences for representative samples. The assumption of similar order is supported by an analysis of 12 nations for which we have values data for representative national samples or for samples roughly representative of the adults in major cities (see Schwartz and Bardi, 1997).

Teacher samples representing East and Central Europe were from Bulgaria, the Czech Republic, Estonia, Georgia, Hungary, Poland, Russia, Slovakia and Slovenia. Samples representing West Europe were from Denmark, Finland, France, West Germany, Greece, Italy, Netherlands, Portugal, Spain, Sweden and Switzerland. Student samples were from the same countries as teachers excluding Russia, Denmark and France, and adding Belgium and England. All samples included between 89 and 377 respondents (mean $N = 203$), and were gathered between 1988 and 1993. With the exception of the Polish teacher sample, all the East European samples were surveyed shortly after the fall of communism in 1989. However, our analysis of value formation as an adaptive process suggests that value priorities do not change quickly. In any event, if the passage of time weakened communist influences, it would have worked against the hypotheses.

Respondents in each sample completed the Schwartz (1992) value survey anonymously in their native language. They rated the importance of 56 single values 'as a guiding principle in MY life.' Responses ranged from 7 (of supreme importance) to 3 (important) to 0 (not important) to –1 (opposed to my values). For each of the seven value types, we computed an importance score by combining the ratings of the single values that index it. These values are listed in Table 13.1 above . These values fit the conceptual definition of the value type and have demonstrated empirical coherence in culture-level analyses (Schwartz, 1994a, 1994b; Schwartz and Ros, 1995). For each country sample, we computed an average country-level score across all the respondents in the sample, which we then centered on the international average to correct for response bias.

Socio-demographic questions followed the value survey. The follow-up study included additional questions about current social, economic and political conditions in the country and about perceived changes in these conditions over the preceding five years.

Results

Eastern vs Western Europe

Table 13.2 presents the relevant data for assessing value differences between Eastern and Western Europe. The first column of the table lists the mean importance attributed to each value type across the nine East European teacher samples. These importance ratings can be compared with the mean ratings attributed to the value types by the 11 West European teacher samples, found in column two. Similarly, one can compare the mean importance ratings of each value type by East and West European student samples – column three versus column four. What do these comparisons reveal?

The differences between Eastern and Western Europe were almost entirely as hypothesized. Conservatism and hierarchy values were significantly more important in Eastern Europe, whereas egalitarianism, intellectual autonomy and affective autonomy values were significantly less important. These differences replicated with the teacher and student samples. The differences were especially strong for conservatism and egalitarianism values, exceeding three standard deviations in both sets of samples.

Table 13.2   Mean ratings of values for sets of East-Central as compared to West European samples

Value type	Teacher samples		Student samples	
	9 East Europe	11 West Europe	8 East Europe	11 West Europe
Conservatism	4.15	3.51***	3.83	3.32***
	(0.14)[a]	(0.20)	(0.16)	(0.18)
Hierarchy	2.19	1.98*	2.23	2.01*
	(0.27)	(0.18)	(0.27)	(0.21)
Harmony	4.24	4.30	4.11	4.05
	(0.31)	(0.22)	(0.24)	(0.33)
Egalitarianism	4.74	5.35***	4.63	5.21***
	(0.20)	(0.14)	(0.19)	(0.16)
Intellectual autonomy	4.15	4.60*	4.23	4.61*
	(0.42)	(0.39)	(0.30)	(0.39)
Affective autonomy	3.13	3.76**	3.78	4.23**
	(0.25)	(0.42)	(0.24)	(0.30)
Mastery	3.84	3.98	4.22	4.27
	(0.14)	(0.23)	(0.15)	(0.27)

[a]Standard deviation across samples in parentheses.
***$p < 0.001$, **$p < 0.01$, *$p < 0.05$, 1-tail, comparisons between Eastern and Western Europe.

There was no difference between Eastern and Western Europe in the importance attributed to harmony values in either the teacher or the student sample set, nor had we predicted a difference. Mastery values were less important in Eastern than in Western Europe for the set of teacher samples, but the difference was only of borderline significance ($p < .07$). For the set of student samples, there was no difference between Eastern and Western Europe. Thus this hypothesis received only partial support.

Bulgaria, Georgia and Russia vs Central (Eastern) Europe

As noted, various East European countries differed in the extent to which communism succeeded in penetrating their social system or met with resistance from opposition groups. Among the countries we studied, penetration was presumably greater in Bulgaria, Georgia and Russia than in Czechia, Hungary, Poland, Slovakia and Slovenia. If so, the impact of the communist system on values should have been stronger in the first set of countries than in the second. We therefore compared the mean importance attributed to each of the types of values in these two sets of countries in order to shed further light on possible impacts of adaptation to communism. Formal statistical tests were not computed, given the small number of cases. We simply compared the mean importance ratings in the two sets of countries to assess whether the directions of difference conform to those we hypothesized.

Both conservatism and hierarchy values were more important on average in Bulgaria, Georgia and Russia than in Central Europe. This was the case in both the teacher and the student sample sets. This provides further support for the conclusion that adaptation to communism promotes these two types of values. Egalitarianism, intellectual autonomy and mastery values were more important on average in Central Europe than in Bulgaria, Georgia and Russia, in both sample sets. This provides further support for the conclusion that adaptation to communism undermines these three types of values. The evidence was inconsistent with regard to affective autonomy values. In sum, the comparisons within Eastern Europe were compatible with five of the six hypotheses and had conflicting outcomes for one.

Discussion

Influences of adaptation to communism

The literature discussing life under the communist regimes of Eastern Europe pointed to a set of value-relevant life circumstances to which citizens were constrained to adapt. We postulated that people would acclimate their value priorities to the reinforcement contingencies that these conditions created. We expected East Europeans to upgrade the importance of values that were readily attained or expressed (conservatism and hierarchy), and to downgrade the importance of values that were unattainable or whose expression or pursuit was likely to be self-defeating (intellectual autonomy, affective autonomy, mastery and egalitarianism). We also postulated that a compensation mechanism would lead East Europeans to attribute higher priority to conservatism values because they largely lacked certainty and security, the core goal of these values.

The analyses revealed a shared profile of value priorities that distinguished the East European countries as a set from West European countries. The findings for five value types (conservatism, hierarchy, egalitarianism, intellectual and affective autonomy) supported the explanation that this profile reflects people's adaptation to life in a communist social system. The hypothesized differences replicated in both the teacher and student samples. The findings for mastery values were in the direction compatible with this explanation, but the difference was significant only in the teacher samples.

The comparisons within Eastern Europe added further support to our view that adaptation to the communist social system influenced value priorities. Value differences between the countries that were penetrated more or less deeply by communism were in the predicted direction in 11 of 12 comparisons.

The two independent evaluations of the hypotheses – East/West comparisons and within-Eastern Europe comparisons – reveal that those hypotheses that received less than full support in one evaluation received full support in the other. The replication in the two types of comparison increases our confidence in interpreting the findings as reflecting adaptation to the communist social system. We next briefly consider possible alternative explanations for the observed pattern of value priorities.[2]

Alternative explanations

Economic level

Most East European countries have had a lower economic level than most West European countries for more than a hundred years. Hence, economic level might offer an alternative explanation for the observed East/West value differences. Theorizing about effects of socioeconomic level on values (Inglehart, 1991; Schwartz, 1993; Triandis, 1990) suggests predictions parallel those based on communism for five types of values. To evaluate the relative strength of the economic versus adaptation-to-communism explanations, we compared correlations of national value ratings with (1) gross national product per capita (GNP/c) in 1986 in the countries of Western and Eastern Europe, and with (2) the dichotomous variable of Western versus Eastern Europe – equivalent to noncommunist versus communist regimes.

Of course, the two predictors share considerable variance because communist countries were generally less-developed economically. Nevertheless, results of this comparison suggest that both factors contributed to value formation, though economic level may have been less important. Moreover, correlations between GNP/c and value importance across East and Central European countries exhibited no consistent pattern to support economic level as an alternative explanation.

Religion

Might the prevailing national religion explain the value differences between Eastern and Western Europe that we have attributed to adaptation to communism? It is necessary to compare countries with the same prevailing religion in order to disentangle effects of adaptation to communist rule and effects of religion. We therefore compared the five Roman Catholic countries from Eastern Europe with the six from Western Europe. For all six value types, the East/West differences in value importance were in the directions hypothesized on the basis of adaptation to communist social systems. Because holding religion constant had no effect on value priority differences, it is possible to dismiss prevailing national religion as an explanation for East/West differences in value priorities.

West not East

Our conclusions regarding values in Eastern Europe were based on comparisons with values in Western Europe. These comparisons therefore tell us about the contrast between East Europeans' adaptations to communist regimes and West Europeans' adaptations to democratic, advanced industrial social systems. However, comparing East and West European value profiles with those in other world regions makes clear that the differences reported here reflect characteristics of Eastern and not only of Western Europe. For example, East European samples attributed the most importance to conservatism values, samples from other regions of the world next most, and West European samples least importance. Distinctive characteristics of East European countries apparently contributed to these value differences.

Earlier History

Could the pattern of value differences observed here have pre-dated communism? Long before the advent of communist regimes, Eastern Europe was governed by more centralized and autocratic regimes than Western Europe, it was more agrarian and less developed economically and socially (see for example Rupnik, 1988). While earlier history may account for some East/West differences, we doubt that it provides an adequate explanation. The agrarianism and traditions of autocratic governance in Eastern Europe probably made it more vulnerable to the imposition of communism, but the degree of centralized authoritarian rule and the suppression of pluralism increased dramatically with the communist takeovers (Schopflin, 1990). Most important, history reveals a region of ethnic and religious heterogeneity, one with repeated and shifting conflicts and conquests among countries (for example Kittrie, 1988), whereas the value profile observed across the various East European countries studied here was relatively homogeneous.

In sum, the current study supports the view that adaptation to the life circumstances imposed by communist regimes had profound effects on the value priorities of East Europeans. This in no way contradicts the widely held opinion that communist ideology and indoctrination failed to convince most East Europeans. But, despite themselves, East Europeans were constrained to adapt to the communist social system in which they lived. The data examined here suggest that this adaptation deeply influenced their values.

Have value priorities changed in East-Central Europe following the collapse of communism?

Is it reasonable to expect value change in Eastern or Western Europe in response to the changes of the past ten years? Students of culture argue that culture change is a very slow process even in the face of major institutional transformations. For example, Moghaddam and Crystal (1997) trace the norms that govern authority relations (a central cultural feature we relate to egalitarianism, hierarchy, autonomy, and conservatism values) in Iran, China and Japan back many centuries, despite profound political and economic changes in these countries. Other analyses use cultural continuities over centuries to explain the roots of democracy in Italian regions (Putnam, 1993).

Although some change processes take centuries, it is possible that prevailing values may change even within a generation as people acclimate their values to changing life circumstances. Inglehart (1997) has demonstrated incremental shifts from materialist to postmaterialist values in many countries, with noticeable changes often found in 5–10 year segments of time. He attributes these changes largely to the adjustment by cohorts to the socioeconomic conditions in their preadult years. However, he also recognizes period effects due to sudden, extreme changes in life circumstances. Such extreme changes may have occurred in Eastern Europe. So it is not unreasonable to anticipate some accompanying change in values.

Since the collapse of communism in Eastern Europe during 1989, social, political and economic institutions have changed substantially (see for example Miszlevitz, 1997; Zubek, 1997). Our theoretical analysis of value formation as an adaptive process implies that institutional change generates value change when the actual life conditions to which people are exposed also undergo transformation. More is required than modifications of the political atmosphere and of prevailing ideological messages, however. Only changes in the opportunities and reward contingencies that people confront in daily life should induce shifts in value priorities. People will gradually acclimate their values to changed circumstances, upgrading the importance of values that become attainable and downgrading the importance of those whose pursuit is no longer adaptive. Moreover, if life becomes sufficiently secure and controllable, people no longer need to emphasize conservation values to compensate for their insecurity.

Below, we assess the nature of the change in relevant aspects of life in Eastern Europe since 1989. We rely both on the scholarly literature and on data we have gathered. If life circumstances in Eastern Europe have become more like those in Western Europe, the value differences between these two regions could be expected to shrink. Conservatism and hierarchy values should become less important in Eastern Europe and egalitarianism, intellectual and affective autonomy values more important. Of course, Western Europe has also undergone social change since 1989. It has endured prolonged periods of unemployment and economic strain and growing tensions between majority populations and ethnic and immigrant national minorities. Such conditions are conducive to weakening egalitarianism, harmony, and autonomy values and strengthening conservatism and hierarchy values.

Social developments in Eastern Europe have taken different paths in different countries (Vachudova and Snyder, 1997). Our 1996–97 data come from Hungary, Poland and Slovakia. Analysts describe Hungary and Poland as having changed more toward democracy, human rights and a liberal economy than Slovakia, though they consider the latter more democratic than such states as Bulgaria or Romania (Carpenter, 1997). Indeed, researchers hold that Hungary and Poland began to prepare for democratization during the 1980s (for example Lewis, 1997; Miszlevitz, 1997). We might therefore expect value change in Slovakia to differ from that in Hungary and Poland.

Vulnerability to social change may be greatest during adolescence (Brim, 1966), at which stage value priorities are less crystallized and less anchored in a large number of past experiences to which people have adapted over time (see for example Inglehart, 1991). Younger people may therefore adapt more quickly to the transformation of life circumstances. Our East European college student samples from 1996–97 were in their mid-teens when the communist regimes collapsed. They might therefore show greater change than the teacher samples. Adults, who discover that the goals they have come to cherish – their important value priorities – are no longer adaptive, are more likely to resist or to oppose social change rather than to acclimate their values.

Empirical evidence for change in life circumstances

What evidence is there that the life circumstances to which we attributed the distinctive East European value profile have changed since 1989? Recall that these circumstances included, most prominently: pervasive demands for conformity, close surveillance of word and deed, unpredictable application of rules and sanctioning of disobedience, an atmosphere of mistrust, suppression of initiative and freedom of choice and action, rewards often unrelated to effort and performance, and paternalism that encouraged passivity and abdication of personal moral responsibility.

Research on Eastern Europe suggests that, despite much apparent social and political change, many of these circumstances persist. The multiparty systems that have replaced the totalitarian regimes have not instituted true democracy or effective laws to protect human rights (for example Lewis, 1997; Lomax, 1997). The political elites remain corrupt, showing favoritism rather than rewarding merit, undermining trust, acting paternalistically, and exhibiting little concern for the basic problems that confront the average citizen (Lomax, 1997; Miszlevitz, 1997). In many countries the state is still deeply involved in overseeing the daily life of citizens, granting little room for initiative. Social order has broken down, ethnic strife has multiplied, and personal and economic uncertainty and insecurity have grown (Carpenter, 1997; Miszlevitz, 1997). Presumably, the situation is better in Hungary and Poland than in Slovakia, though it has improved in all three since 1993–94 (Vachudova and Snyder, 1997).

To examine value change after five–nine years, we used data from five East European and eight West European samples. Samples were drawn from the same schools and universities as the earlier samples in each country. East European data were gathered in 1996–97 in Hungary, Slovakia and Poland (students only) and West European data in 1995–97 in Belgium (students only), Denmark (teachers only), Netherlands, Spain (teachers only), Switzerland (students only), and West Germany. Sample size ranged from 119–682 (median $N = 186$).

These samples responded to questions about current conditions in their country and about change over the preceding five years. The responses provide subjective assessments of the life circumstances these samples have confronted. For an overall picture of the subjective situation in Eastern Europe, we averaged the scores for five samples: Hungarian and Slovak teachers and students, and Polish students. All but the Slovak student sample reported considerable deterioration of economic conditions over the preceding five years and a decline in their confidence in the economic system. Most respondents reported that they or the family breadwinner had been unemployed for at least a few months. Satisfaction with their current financial situation was well below the midpoint on a ten point scale, again except for the Slovak students. (West European samples were well above the midpoint, although some samples reported deteriorating economic conditions.) Thus, subjectively at least, economic insecurity posed a problem for all but one East European sample.

Regarding personal safety, the East European respondents reported that they feel unsafe (below the scale midpoint, whereas West European samples were well above the midpoint), that their level of personal safety had deteriorated, and that they had lost confidence in the legal and police systems over the past five years. They had also lost confidence in the political system, the educational system, and the health care system. In sum, the subjective reports suggested little change for the better in the life circumstances relevant to value formation. Confidence in the various institutions declined in the West European samples as well.

Empirical evidence for value change

Table 13.3 presents the data for assessing value change in Eastern and Western Europe. Data are available for the second time period only from a subset of countries. For each value type, we list the value ratings given by the parallel samples from these countries at time one (T1, 1989) and at time two (T2, 1996–97). The first question is whether this subset of countries yields the same conclusions regarding East/West value differences at T1 as did the full set of countries discussed in the first part of this chapter. Only if this is so can we assume that the theoretical arguments adduced to explain the effects of life under communist regimes apply to the subset of countries in which we have studied value change.

Comparing the T1 ratings in Tables 13.2 and 13.3 reveals that the East/West differences, both for the teacher and for the student samples, are virtually the same whether we use the whole set of countries (13.2) or only the subset of countries available at T2 (13.3). That is, the directions and approximate size of the differences in mean value ratings found to be significant with the whole set of countries (conservatism, hierarchy, egalit-

Table 13.3 Mean ratings of values for subsets of East-Central as compared to West European samples studied at both T1 and T2

Value type		Teacher samples		Student samples	
		East (Hungary, Slovakia)	West (Denmark, Netherlands, Spain, W. Germany)	East (Hungary, Poland, Slovakia)	West (Belgium, Netherlands, Switzerland, W. Germany)
Conservatism	T1	4.00	3.42***	3.72	3.10***
	T2	4.01	3.45***	3.82	3.12***
Hierarchy	T1	2.13	1.98*	2.05	1.86*
	T2	2.08	1.90*	2.14	1.96*
Harmony	T1	4.33	4.14*	4.15	4.10
	T2	4.07	4.07	3.97	3.88
Egalitarianism	T1	4.81	5.33***	4.63	5.20***
	T2	4.62	5.22***	4.64	5.15***
Affective autonomy	T1	2.93	3.75***	3.59	4.40***
	T2	3.04	3.94***	3.46	4.52***
Intellectual autonomy	T1	4.11	4.54**	4.29	4.74**
	T2	3.94	4.51**	4.12	4.65**
Mastery	T1	3.90	3.90	4.07	4.11
	T2	3.96	3.90	4.01	4.15*

Note: East/West mean differences are compared using the pooled standard deviation from time 1 for each value type, based on the 20 teacher samples for teachers and on the 19 student samples for students.
***Difference > 2 standard deviations
**Difference > 1 standard deviation
*Difference > 0.5 standard deviations
T1 = 1989, T2 = 1996–97

arianism, affective autonomy, and intellectual autonomy) were the same at T1 in the subset. As a way to convey the strength of these differences, the table shows their size in standard deviation units.

Comparing the T2 value ratings in Table 13.3 reveals that the earlier East/West differences persisted following the collapse of the communist regimes. The hypothesized differences confirmed at T1 all emerged at T2 in the same direction and with approximately the same size in both teacher and student samples. The strength of the differences in standard deviation units was also virtually unchanged. There is no evidence here that Eastern and Western Europe have converged toward a common set of cultural value priorities. Indeed, with regard to affective autonomy values, the gap has increased .7 standard deviation units.

As for value change within each part of Europe, it too has been limited. Comparing the T1 and T2 ratings of each value type, changes of at least half a standard deviation unit include harmony (down for all but the students from the East), egalitarianism (down for teachers in East and West), and conservatism (up only for students from the East). These changes were neither large nor widespread. However, all were in the direction one would expect if life conditions have become more conducive to focusing on the interests of the in-group rather than the full range of groups in society or on nature. The increased nationalism, ethnic strife, and concern for economic development described by analysts of the European scene in the past five–ten years are compatible with such value change.

Above, we inferred from several sources (for example Carpenter, 1997; Lewis, 1997; Miszlevitz, 1997) that value change in Slovakia might differ from that in Hungary and Poland. A separate examination of each East European sample provides no support for this inference. No single country differed consistently from the others in the magnitude or pattern of value change. In general, changes were small and unreliable. We also proposed that student samples might show larger value differences over time than teacher samples. Examination of Table 13.3 reveals no evidence to support this proposal. This finding does not contradict the assumption that adolescents' values are more vulnerable than adults' values to influences in their environment. Our subjective measures of change and the literature we cited suggest that, despite the collapse of the communist regimes, adolescents were exposed to value-relevant life circumstances quite similar to those adults had experienced under communism.

Conclusion

This research explicated likely effects of life under communist regimes on prevailing cultural values. As anticipated, samples drawn from Eastern Europe in the late 1980s and early 1990s attributed particularly great importance to conservatism and hierarchy values and low importance to egalitarianism, intellectual and affective autonomy values, when compared with West European samples. These same contrasts appeared when comparing East European countries in which communism had penetrated more versus less deeply. The interpretation of this pattern of findings as resulting from people's adaptations to the day-to-day reward contingencies and opportunities present under communist regimes accounts well for the findings. Alternative explanations based on economic, historical, and religious factors do not do as well. We therefore conclude that 40 years of pervasive communist rule sufficed to influence people's basic values.

Although much has been written about social, economic, and political change in Eastern Europe following the collapse of communism, our analyses uncovered no clear effects of this change on prevailing values. Two explanations for the failure to detect value change seem most plausible. First, as suggested by our respondents' reports and by analyses in the literature, the critical life circumstances to which people acclimate their values have not yet changed decisively. Second, the five or six year interval between our measurements at T1 and T2 is simply not long enough for value change to appear. Traces of the communist experience may continue to influence values over generations. Other influences on values should come to the fore in the next few decades, as life circumstances shift.

The East European value profile that we identified is ill-suited for the development of democracy. A commitment to egalitarianism and auto- nomy values is required to provide the moral basis of social responsibility needed to maintain a democratic system (Diamond, Linz and Lipset, 1990). Nor are the value bases for a free enterprise system well-established: autonomy and mastery values are not widely endorsed, suggesting reluc- tance to assume responsibility, to take risks, and to work hard to apply one's talents assertively. Instead, the emphasis on conservatism and hier- archy values implies a continuing desire for the government to take responsibility and to provide for basic needs. Not surprisingly, then, the former communist nations are experiencing serious difficulties introduc- ing and maintaining democratic institutions and a liberal economy (for example Lewis, 1997).

Socioeconomic and political developments in East Europe will probably continue to take different paths in different countries. Future studies of values in these countries can therefore test our theorizing about the rela- tions of specific aspects of life circumstances to the formation and modi- fication of particular types of values. One lesson of the current follow-up study is that even major political change may not affect people's basic values in the short run. In order to clarify the mutual causal influences of value priorities and social and political developments on one another, long-term longitudinal studies of basic values are needed. The current chapter provides a theoretically grounded set of values appropriate for such studies and a baseline for measuring change in the future.

Notes

1. This research was supported by grant no. 94-00063 from the United States–Israel Binational Science Foundation (BSF) to the first author, and facilitated by the Leon and Clara Sznajderman Chair Professorship in Psychology. Preparation of this chapter was partly supported by the Slovak Grant Agency for Science, grant no. 2/4160/97. We thank the following persons for gathering the data on which this article is based: Krassimira Baytchinska, Viera Rosova, Bartolo Campos and Isabel Menezes; Ake Daun, J.-P. Dupont, F. Gendre, Dario Spini and Thierry Devos; Johnny Fontaine, Adrian Furnham, James Georgas, Suzanne Grunert, Sipke Huismans, Maria Jarymowicz, Michael McCarrey and Vladimir Zahkarov; Leo Montada, Toomas Niit, George Nidharadze, Henri Paicheler and Genevieve Vinsonneau; Darja Piciga, Maria Ros and Hector Grad; Jan Srnec, Giancarlo Tanucci and Sonia Roccas; Antti Uutela, Markku Verkasalo and Zsuzsa Vajda.
2. For the theorizing underlying these alternatives and more detailed analyses that assess them, see Schwartz and Bardi (1997, 402–7).

3. Inclusion of the value 'humble'in the hierarchy value type points to the fact that legitimizing hierarchy entails accepting inferiority to some as well as superiority to others.

References

Bardi, A. and S. H. Schwartz (1996) 'Relations among Socio-political Values in Eastern Europe: Effects of the Communist Experience?', *Political Psychology, 17*, pp. 525–49.

Barghoorn, F. C. and T. F. Remington (1986) *Politics in the USSR* (3rd edn), Boston: Little Brown.

Bilsky, W., and S. H. Schwartz (1994) 'Values and Personality', *European Journal of Personality*, vol. 8, pp. 163–81.

Brim, O. G., Jr. (1966) 'Socialization through the Life-cycle', in O. Brim, Jr. and S. Wheeler (eds.), *Socialization after Childhood*, New York: Wiley (pp. 3–49).

Broek, A. van den and R. de Moor (1994) 'Eastern Europe after 1989', in P. Ester, L. Halman R. de Moor (eds.), *The Individualizing Society: Value Change in Europe and North America*, Tilburg: Tilburg University Press (pp. 197–228).

Carpenter, M. (1997) 'Slovakia and the Triumph of Nationalist Populism', *Communist and Post-Communist Studies*, vol. 30, pp. 205–20.

Diamond, L., J. Linz and S. M. Lipset (eds.) (1990) *Politics in Developing Countries, Comparing Experiences with Democracy*, Boulder, Col.: Lynne Rienner.

Glenny, M. (1990) *The Rebirth of History: Eastern Europe in the Age of Democracy*, Harmondsworth: Penguin.

Gunst, P. (1989) 'Agrarian Systems of Central and Eastern Europe', in D. Chirot (ed.), *The Origins of Backwardness in Eastern Europe: Economics and Politics from the Middle Ages until the Early Twentieth Century*, Berkeley: University of California Press (pp. 53–91).

Feher, F. (1982) 'Paternalism as a Mode of Legitimation in Soviet-type Societies', in T. H. Rigby and F. Feher (eds.), *Political Legitimation in Communist States*, London: Macmillan (pp. 64–81).

Hofstede, G. (1980) *Culture's consequences: International differences in work-related values*. Beverly Hills, CA: Sage.

Inglehart, R. (1991) *Cultural Change in Advanced Industrial Societies*. Princeton, NJ: Princeton University Press.

Inglehart, R. (1997) *Modernization and Postmodernization*. Princeton, NJ: Princeton University Press.

Inkeles, A. and Smith, D. H. (1974) *Becoming Modern*. Cambridge: Harvard University Press.

Kittrie, N. N. (1988) 'The Undoing of a Monolith: Responding to Diversities in the Eastern Bloc', in N. N. Kittrie and I. Volgyes (eds.), *The Uncertain Future: Gorbachev's Eastern Bloc*, New York: Paragon House (pp. 1–8).

Kohak, E. (1992) 'Ashes, Ashes ... Central Europe after Forty Years', *Daedalus, 121*, 197–216.

Kohn, M. L. and C. Schooler (1983) *Work and Personality*. Norwood, NJ: Ablex.

Lewis, P. G. (1997) 'Theories of Democratization and Patterns of Regime Change in Eastern Europe', *The Journal of Communist Studies and Transitional Politics, 13*, 4–26.

Lomax, B. (1997) 'The Strange Death of "Civil Society" in Post-Communist Hungary', *The Journal of Communist Studies and Transitional Politics, 13*, 41–63.

Maslow, A. H. (ed.) (1959) *New Knowledge in Human Values*. New York: Harper.

Marody, M. (1988) 'Antinomies of Collective Subconsciousness', *Social Research, 55*, 97–110.

Miszlevitz, F. (1997) 'Participation and Transition: Can the Civil Society Project Survive in Hungary?', *Journal of Communist Studies and Transitional Politics*, 13, 27–40.

Moghaddam, F. M. and Crystal, D. S. (1997) 'Revolutions, Samurai, and Reductions: The Paradoxes of Change and Continuity in Iran and Japan', *Political Psychology*, 18, 355–84.

Nowak, K. (1988) 'Covert Repressiveness and the Stability of a Political System: Poland at the End of the Seventies', *Social Research*, 55, 179–209.

Putnam, R. D. (1993) *Making Democracy Work: Civic Traditions in Modern Italy*, Princeton, NJ: Princeton University Press.

Rokeach, M. (1973) *The Nature of Human Values*, New York: Free Press.

Roskin, M. G. (1991) *The Rebirth of East Europe*, Englewood Cliffs, NJ: Prentice Hall.

Rupnik, J. (1988) *The other Europe*, London: Weidenfeld and Nicholson.

Schopflin, G. (1990) 'The Political Traditions of Eastern Europe', *Daedalus*, 119, 55–90.

Schwartz, S. H. (1992) 'Universals in the Content and Structure of Values: Theoretical Advances and Empirical Tests in 20 Countries', in M. P. Zanna (ed.), *Advances in Experimental Social Psychology*, New York: Academic Press, vol. 25, pp. 1–65.

Schwartz, S. H. (1993, July) *Toward Explanations of National Differences in Value Priorities*. Paper presented at the XXIV Congress of the Interamerican Society of Psychology, Santiago, Chile.

Schwartz, S. H. (1994a) 'Beyond Individualism-Collectivism: New Cultural Dimensions of Values', iIn U. Kim, H. C. Triandis, C. Kagitcibasi, S-C. Choi and G. Yoon (eds.), *Individualism and Collectivism: Theory, Method, and Application*, Newbury Park, CA: Sage, pp. 85–119.

Schwartz, S. H. (1994b) 'Are There Universal Aspects in the Structure and Contents of Human Values?', *Journal of Social Issues*, 50, 19–46.

Schwartz, S. H. (1999) 'A Theory of Cultural Values and some Implications for Work', *Applied Psychology: An International Review*, 48, 23–47.

Schwartz, S. H. and A. Bardi (1997) 'Influences of Adaptation to Communist Rule on Value Priorities in Eastern Europe', *Political Psychology*, 18, pp. 385–410.

Schwartz, S. H. and M. Ros (1995) 'Values in the West: A Theoretical and Empirical Challenge to the Individualism-Collectivism Cultural Dimension', *World Psychology*, 1, 99–122.

Smith, P. B. and Schwartz, S. H. (1997) 'Values', in J. W. Berry, M. H. Segall and C. Kagitcibasi (eds), *Handbook of Cross-Cultural Psychology, vol. 3*, 2nd edn Boston: Allyn & Bacon, pp. 77–118.

Triandis, H. C. (1990) 'Cross-Cultural Studies of Individualism and Collectivism', in J. Berman (ed.), *Nebraska Symposium on Motivation, 1989*, Lincoln, NE: University of Nebraska Press, pp. 41–133.

Vachudova, M. A. and T. Snyder (1997) 'Are Transitions Transitory? Two Types of Political Change in Eastern Europe since 1989', *East European Politics and Societies*, 11, 1–35.

Zubek, V. (1997) 'The End of Liberalism? Economic Liberalization and the Transformation of Post-Communist Poland', *Communist and Post-Communist Studies*, 30, 181–204.

Part IV
Political Psychology and the Dilemmas of Multiculturalism

14

Social Authority and Minority Status: Problems of Internalization and Alienation among Japanese and Koreans in Diverse Cultural Settings

George A. De Vos

Social responsibility and internalized constraint

Modern multiethnic states, moral authority and social identity

Hobbes was incorrect in generalizing that dominant force alone can keep human societies together. Systems based too directly or exclusively on force are inherently unstable, although at a great economic and social price they may persist for some time. But for the appearance and continuance of some relatively stable social forms, there has to be a proportion of individuals in a society who come to believe that the potentially coercive force of exercised authority is also moral and legitimate. A good proportion of individuals develop a sense of voluntary adhesion or loyalty to a state. In so doing they are expressing some form of 'social identity'.

A more or less internalized social identity may relate to a more special sense of *loyalty* to a particular social group governing voluntary behavioral conformity. Modern societies are segmented into various social divisions: complexities of ethnicity, minority status and social class adherence overlap with questions of ultimate loyalty of citizens to the state which involves voluntary submission to its social recognized directives and administrative system. Patterns of loyalty to more distant authority and more proximate reference group allegiances may come into conflict. One may maintain ultimate loyalty either to a primary family, to a peer group, to some face-to-face community, or to a larger political entity. Loyalty is related to acknowledgment of moral authority. Those who are simply coerced into obedience often lack such sense of loyalty.

In any psychocultural study, one must consider in its specific social context how concerns with moral behavior, duty or obligation appear in conscious thought. It is even more important to examine how, and in what specific context, any recognition of authority becomes related to an *internalization*[1] of social constraint or, conversely, experienced inwardly as alienation. It can also be expressed outwardly in patterns of anomic deviant behavior, including that of a political or criminal nature.

What is designated either as compliant or as deviant political or social behavior, however, is not all motivated psychodynamically on the same social-maturational level. The mistake of Marx and many other sociological theorists has been to assume that political conflict, even deviant behavior, is motivated prevailingly by rational adult motives. Forms of political dissidence, or the varieties of so-called anomic behavior are not all psychologically equivalent internally: the developmental vicissitudes governing human motivation and resultant behavior are far more complex. A subjective sense of alienation results from experiences occurring on different maturational levels.

The American experience of a multiethnic society

Political conflict in a segmented American society has, in recent years, been less concerned with past territorial or religious forms of ethnic tensions and more with social class differences and residues of racial-caste discrimination. Degrees of loyalty and social adaptation to the American state by immigrants have remained interwoven with various forms of ethnic and class persistence. These social differences are related to variations in social adaptation permitted or attempted by members of these various groups comprising our multiethnic society. In this respect Japanese and other Asians immigrants have much to teach us. I began by examining the adaptation of Japanese as an American minority with whom I had first contact in 1947. Later, my research efforts were further extended into Japan itself from 1953 on, and now more recently, in 1991, into Brazil where a large group of migrant Japanese have settled as Brazilian citizens.

In exploring the social adaptation, including political loyalty, of Japanese both as ethnic minorities as well as majority members of a nation-state over a 50-year period, I have been impressed most with how, in all social groups, patterns of adult social internalization are heavily influenced, first by a prior social cohesion experienced within the primary family, and then, later, by what is experienced as members of a pre-adolescent peer society. This general impression applies not only to Japanese, but to various other American groups, majority and minority alike.

Forms of ameliorative political or social acts, taken by various minority groups who find themselves in discriminatory situations differ significantly depending upon earlier family-cultural patterns as well as socially-derived later grade-school childhood experiences. Difficulties experienced in early family socialization can interfere with the maturation of mature forms of social loyalty and commitment or protest. In negative primary family circumstances social discontent is experienced and expressed more as personal alienation and problematic forms of internalization or guilt formation. The value of such a focus can be seen in the work of John Ogbu

(1978) who divides the differential educational and occupational adaptation of various racial-ethnic minorities in the United States between those whose histories have been those of voluntary migrants from Europe and Asia, and those who have been *involuntarily* incorporated into the American state; principally, American Natives overrun by an expanding frontier society, Africans coming in as captured slaves, and Mexican Americans who were incorporated into the American state by conquest.

Although these latter groups are now identified as minority 'Americans', their relatively poor adaptation to educational and occupational institutions, discriminatory practices aside, is now seen as less due to problems of biological disability and more to their unconscious as well as conscious resistance of youth to learning or 'internalizing' social and technical skills from teachers who represent an outer authority alien to now defensively-held ethnic minority identities. In effect, some minority group members are more loyal to each other than to an external, racially discriminating system seemingly being imposed upon them from above. However, in each of these involuntary minority groups we also find widespread evidence of a high incidence of dysfunctional early family experiences, many with only one parent in residence. These early socialization experiences contribute to patterns of personality maladjustment underlying their external maladaptive behavior (De Vos, 1983).

The more positive adaptive patterns of Asian minorities who have also faced discrimination have been seen as an anomaly by some social scientists. They have *not* exhibited the negative forms of maladaptation predicted for them by a number of sociological theorists. Chinese and Japanese in California, from the turn of the century on faced severe difficulties in finding any social acceptance. Yet, generally, their youthful American-born generations have conformed positively to external authority. They have been achieving high levels of performance within the public schools, and have *internalized* middle-class American adaptive practices educationally and vocationally. The forms of employment they were able to find were at one time far below the level of training with which they had prepared themselves. However, now they are in large proportions entering the American middle class occupational structure; domestically, they have continued to live in close, intact family units; and characteristically they did not become delinquent.[2] They did not become either personally or collectively alienated. The question is: Why?

Cultural continuity, internalization and achievement motivation

In the late 1940s, as they were being released from their internment camps, 17 000 Japanese in family units were moving into the cheap, run-down housing available to them within the high delinquency areas of the inner city of Chicago. The inhabitants of these areas were being thoroughly studied by sociologists and psychologists at the University of Chicago and at the state-run Institute of Juvenile Research.

Drawing on their previous studies of the negative effects of inner-city ghetto living of other groups, they predicted personal and family breakdown, and various other forms of social alienation for the Japanese being abruptly released from the government internment camps. However, when we began to study the incoming Japanese-Americans we found that they were not performing as negatively as would be expected of members of a minority facing strong, continuous discrimination and now living in areas of urban breakdown. They had been subject not only to the usual forms of racially directed prejudice, but also been wrenched from their homes on the American west coast by their government and put into special camps for several years. Yet they were not behaving according to negative predictions. How were we to explain why Japanese children and youth, unlike the other minorities residing in Chicago's zone of transition were doing so well in school, and those old enough were somehow now finding jobs and advancing in specialized occupations? They had overcome an initial reluctance to hire 'Japs'. Why? Because they were extremely competent workers. They were soon sought after rather than rejected.

Despite decades of massive discrimination their political and social allegiances remained quite politically conservative and were characterized by intense loyalty to the American society. The conduct of both the young and the old was not marked by much evident anger or resentment.

As a result of our work, which involved the use of psychological tests as well as interviews, Caudill, and I developed some psychocultural contentions about internalized achievement motivation (Caudill and De Vos, 1956) that contradicted any straight sociological or anthropological approaches to discrimination. Sociological theories that viewed deviancy solely in terms of the immediate situational social factors, such as those operative in American city ghettos, could not explain why different minority groups developed different patterns of adaptation or forms and frequency of alienation or internal maladjustment in response to discrimination and economic hardship. Anthropologists seemed prone to dismiss psychological universals and advocate a non-judgmental cultural relativism that ignored the fact that some forms of culturally persistent socialization are more problematical than others. We advanced the still controversial idea that cultural patterning was more determining of minority adaptive behavior than were immediate sociopolitical conditions of severe discrimination.

In 1953 I became acquainted with two socially despised Japanese minorities, the close to three million endogamous former outcastes or untouchables, called Burakumin, and the close to one million Koreans, the remnant of a much larger group of Koreans brought to Japan as unskilled labor during the Japanese military period starting in the 1930s. Most of these minorities lived in urban ghettoes in the larger Japanese cities (De Vos and Wagatsuma, 1966; Lee and De Vos, 1981).

The overall relatively low delinquency rates of Japan compared with other modern industrial states, especially the United States, was striking. More striking was who, selectively, became delinquent. As in America, delinquents came prevailingly from broken or dysfunctional homes and from specific minorities, but while there were many fewer dysfunctional family units in majority Japan, their minorities showed a high incidence of family disruption. Noteworthy in the Japanese minorities were the statistics on family breakdown and desertion and other social symptoms such as the very high rates of alcoholism and prostitution. Among the Japanese minorities, the rate of delinquency among the former outcaste Burakumin was close to five times that of majority, and the delinquency rate among Korean youth was seven times that of ordinary Japanese.

Also, needless to say, there was a very high incidence of negative early family experiences among the American minority youth. California statistics examined at the same time reported a delinquency rate among Mexican Americans of under five times that of majority Californians, and a rate among African Americans over five times that of the majority population.

In looking at the relative adaptation of minority children of different minorities in both the USA and Japan, it should be very evident that cultural, psychological and sociological factors *all* play a role in the behavior of minorities. However, both the unexpectedly better adaptation in the face of discrimination of the Japanese and Koreans as minorities in the USA, and the continuing problems manifest in some minorities, both in the USA and Japan, bear continual examination and explanation in a comparative context on all levels of analysis. Structural psychological problems can remain severe as they are passed on from one generation to the next by the inadequate or less adaptive parenting more common to some historically debased minorities. It follows, therefore, that psychological problems of a maladjustive nature are not simply or solely to be ameliorated by a diminution of outer social discrimination. There is a psychological lag (De Vos, 1973, 107–8) that persists generationally even after economic opportunities open and social acceptance is more receptive.

What has been remarkable about Japanese emigrants wherever they have settled in rather different social settings is the similarity of reported positive, adaptive socially-conforming patterns, whether in the United States and Canada in North America, or Brazil, Peru or Argentina in South America. In this report, I emphasize the cultural continuities that guide the adaptation of members of some ethnic traditions who have migrated to other societies. My more recent psychological material reflecting social attitudes, obtained from Brazil, again includes stories obtained by using the Thematic Apperception Test, which consists of a series of pictures to which the informant is requested to give an imaginative story. Dramatic differences are obtained when one juxtaposes material from Japanese Brazilians with narratives obtained from youthful Brazilians of Portuguese, Afro-Brazilian or Italian ethnic backgrounds.

However, in order to fully appreciate the social attitudes reflected in these data it is useful, first, to briefly discuss the Confucian heritage found evident not only in modern Japan itself but in several generations of Japanese Americans and Japanese Brazilians.

The state reinforces moral authority: duty and responsibility in the Confucian heritage

In considering moral or socially conforming behavior, duty or obligation one must consider it in its specific past social context as well as how it appears in present conscious thought. To illustrate the social-cultural context of internalized responsibility, we draw on some past writings on Japanese culture (De Vos 1960, 1972, 1973, 1992, 1993a, 1993b, 1993c, De Vos & Wagatsuma 1966, Slote & De Vos 1998).

The role of formal education in governmental indoctrination of a Confucianist morality

By the late Tokugawa shogunate period, in the nineteenth century up to 1868, when the emperor was restored to head the state, Confucianist education espousing obedient loyalty to government as a sacred principle was already well-established among the ruling samurai. The exercise of political leadership was ideally not simply a means of gratifying a need for power, but a fulfillment of a social duty. There were explicit quasi-religious moral teachings to this effect in the Confucianism that became part of everyone's primary training. In the Confucian tradition, politics was not to be the art of the possible, the choice of lesser evils, or the achievement of democratic compromise between conflicting interests. A good policy was a nurturing one which could *benefit* everyone. Confucian government policy, at least as espoused by neo-Confucianist scholars, was to be based on the political philosophy of a less complex hierarchical society in which political conflicts of interest should not exist between the ruled and the rulers. Enlightened government consisted in the kind of harmony produced by nurturant benevolence which would enable the existing rulers to enhance the general contentment for the benefit of all (Dore, 1965, 118).

Conversely, loyalty toward superiors was to be cultivated. This loyalty was not simple obedience to a controlling *authority*, but an active moral anticipation of what would benefit one's superior. A truly developed loyal person would seek out the ultimate benefit of the master rather than immediately gratifying any command. If need be, individuals might go against a superior's wishes when, in their deep judgment, obeying immediate commands would be detrimental to any ultimate loyalty and ultimate well-being.

Education intensified the diffusion of the samurai ethic, not only through the merchants and townsmen, but also throughout the rural population. This diffusion downward has had a profound effect on Japanese family life on into the contemporary period. The rigid four-class structure had been broken by the abolition of the samurai as a separate class. However, the universal education given to both boys and girls was directly based on samurai neo-Confucianist loyalty and responsibility, and further espoused an age-graded sense of purposeful endurance toward the realization of instrumental goals of achievement with a continuing emphasis on hierarchy within the family roles. In totally different social contexts we can illustrate from our Thematic Apperception Test, or TAT stories, reflections in present generations of Japanese, now living in the Americas, persisting attitudes about the primary family derived from their past internalized heritage.

The past generations of Japanese were very self-consciously aware of the inner tensions inherent in taking on Confucianism. It was viewed as supporting the intellectual-moral side of a continuing tension between instrumentally positive social obligation, or *giri* as opposed to more spontaneous, affiliative or nurturant emotional social feelings, *ninjo*. To attend to *giri* was to comply ritually with the anticipated and expected tensions inherent in one's social role. It was a more formal adherence to moral expectations as opposed to the spontaneity of love, passion and other sometimes socially disruptive human emotions.

Many Japanese intellectuals today wish to move toward a looser, less collective type of educational training realizing a more individualized sense of self. We have found in our research an attempted shift to a search for more expressive, subjectively experienced happiness, 'shiawase', as a desirable concept to guide educational policy. It is now a social goal to aim for a more spontaneous mode of existence. However, the Japanese also remain very cognizant of the potential chaos resulting from too great a shift toward Western individualism.

Family and group responsibility in Japan

The Japanese have developed strong social sensitivity in the context of honor or esteem (De Vos, 1992, chapter 2). On a conscious level, assuming authority requires a strong sense of personal responsibility, if something goes wrong, including the improper behavior of a subordinate or family member, it is the one in authority who must assume responsibility. One of the most useful findings derived from our use of the projective techniques in Japan was the indirect revelation in TAT materials of how patterns of guilt in Japanese related to a sense of responsibility to one's family. Such attitudes were found consistently depicted in the TAT stories obtained in 1954.

Guilt related to parental suffering: a traditional pattern of responsibility and control[3]

The relation of induced guilt to parental suffering is apparent in certain TAT narratives in which the death of the parent follows upon the bad conduct of a child. The two events seem to bear an implicit relationship, as expressed in the following summaries taken from research conducted in the agricultural village of Niiike in 1954.

> W, age 22 (Card J6GF)[4]   FA-love RC-pr-sex *DSC-disobey KD-death*
> PD-sad   A daughter marries against her father's opposition, but her husband dies and she becomes unhappy.
> M, age 23 (Card J18)[5]   HC-murder-FC-seduce-PA-crazed *RA-apology-DSA-forgive*   A mother strangles to death the woman who tempted her innocent son. The mother becomes insane and dies. The son begs forgiveness.

In such stories, a respondent first puts into words an unconscious wish of some kind, like following one's own desire. However, quickly such a thought is followed by an underlying sense that self-will is a transgression that injures a beloved parent, and one can be punished by fate bringing about the death of a beloved person. Such an unconscious association governs the sequence found in several stories, especially in records obtained from a traditional farm village where we sampled in the early 1950s.

One could also interpret such behavior related to cultural traditions of inducing behavior in others by threats of self-inflicted violence. It was not unknown for a mother to threaten to die as a *means* of admonishing a child. In another of our TAT stories, the death of a parent is followed by responsible reform, hard work and success. For example, these are story summaries elicited by a differing variety of cards:

> W, age 16 (Card J7M)[6]   DDA-scold *KD-death RA-work* AA-persist.   A son, scolded by his father, later, the father dies; then the son works hard and becomes successful.
> M, age 39 (Card J5)[7]   RC-wrong RB-duty NDB-welfare *KD-ill-die RA-reform* AA-persist.   A mother worries about her delinquent son, becomes sick, and dies; the son reforms himself and becomes successful.

Emphasis on hard work and success after the death of parents clearly suggests some expiatory meaning related to the moral masochistic attitude of the mother. The mother's moral responsibility is also suggested by other stories, such as a mother being scolded by a father when the child does something wrong, or a mother (not the father) being hurt when the child does not behave well. The feeling experienced by the child when he realizes, consciously or unconsciously, that he has hurt his mother is guilt – because guilt is generated when one hurts the object of one's love. The natural ambivalence arising from living under close parental control supplies sufficient unconscious intent to hurt to make the guilt mechanism operative.

In the same context, if one fails to achieve, there is no way to atone. One is lost. The only thing left is to hurt oneself, to extinguish oneself – the one whose existence has been hurting one's parents and who now can do nothing for them. Suicide as an answer is shown in several stories. In many tests administered in the United States, and elsewhere, to various ethnic groups I have never had suicide narratives related to failure or social transgression:

> M, age 57 (Card 3BM, original Murray card)   A girl fails an examination, kills herself.

Among many Japanese people a feeling of guilt very often underlies the strong achievement drive and aspiration toward success achieved with a strong sense of social conformity. If this hypothesis is accepted, then it can easily be understood that the death of a parent – that is, the symbolic culmination of the parent's being hurt following some bad conduct of a child – evokes in the child a feeling of guilt strong enough to bring him or her back from delinquent behavior and to drive one toward hard work and success or maternal dedication. A need to conform to social directives to protect the family is what underlies the TAT theme of parental death and the child's reform found in a number of Japanese.

Internalized guilt related to performance and social or political compliance

Past TAT material such as the above taken from Niiike village in 1954, combined with other evidence (De Vos, 1960) suggested to us how deeply imbued traditional attitudes, including guilt, were prevalent in the Japanese of that period. Such feelings were aroused when there was failure in the performance of expected role behavior. There was little pronounced guilt directed toward physical expression of sexuality *per se*; rather, sexuality was related to guilt indirectly through a possible loss of control which would interfere with prescribed life goals.

The definitions of proper role behavior become more and more exacting as the child grows and comes into increasing contact with others as a representative of the family. As such, one learns to be more and more diplomatic and to contain and suppress impulses and feelings that would be disruptive in social relations and that would put one at a disadvantage. One does not bring a system of moral absolutes into relations with others any more than does a diplomat who negotiates for the advantage of one's country. The Japanese learned to be sensitive to 'face' and protocol and to be equally sensitive to the feelings of others.

One learns to keep personal feelings to oneself as a family representative. It would be fallacious to assume, therefore, that the Japanese is without much sense of guilt, just as it would be to assume that a career diplomat has no personal sense of guilt. The fact that so much of Japanese conscious life is concerned with a system of social sanctions helps to disguise the underlying guilt system operative within. This system is well-disguised not only from the Western observer but also from the Japanese themselves. The Westerner, under the tutelage of Christianity, has learned to 'universalize' aggressive and other impulses and feel guilt in regard to them in general terms. The modern Japanese is moving toward such an attitude, but remains affected by the traditional moral structure based on the family system, or, in expanded form, to conformity to social authority.

In studying the Japanese, whether in contemporary Japan itself or as ethnic minorities abroad, it is helpful, therefore, to try to understand the nature of an inherited and perpetuated pattern of conformist internalization of an ego ideal defined in terms of maintaining proper social role behavior.

Respect for social authority and minority status among Koreans in Japan and the United States

The Korean minority in Japan has experienced strong discrimination. They are manifestly ambivalent about being governed by standards and proscriptions to which they are considered implicitly, if not overtly, 'innately inferior' to Japanese, and therefore assumed not to be capable of adhering to. Animosity and resentment over discrimination, in one sense, frees the individual from assuming the internalized standards of the majority. A dilemma of identity for a Korean in Japan is whether he or she should attempt to meet the social obligations assumed by ordinary Japanese.

As is well-evident in Japanese statistics on crime and delinquency, for many Koreans, maintaining a Korean identity entails a socially antagonistic posture that condones illegal or deviant marginal activity as well as political protest.[8] Alternatively, to 'pass' by posing as 'Japanese' is to accept as valid the deprecatory attitudes directed toward Koreans including one's secret self. The individual is caught in a dilemma of integrity: one is caught by possible conscious or unconscious prejudices internalized as part of living in the larger society. Frequently the resolution of such a conflict is to resist 'passing' as Japanese, because to pass implies acceptance of Japanese negative judgments about one's own people and their past.

To remain 'Korean' has the possible advantages of avoiding civil responsibility. In an ethnically pluralistic society, an individual may retain his minority status to avoid assuming certain obligations that are part of the role expectations of the majority. Conversely, one would expect some individuals from the majority to 'drop out', identifying with a supposedly freer minority to indulge in behavioral patterns ordinarily forbidden. In the relationship of minority Koreans and Japanese, this latter move is not often made. A few Japanese, however, do identify themselves as Koreans. To be considered 'tough', some Yakuza or gangster types use Korean speech mannerisms. Occasionally, some lower-class Japanese prefer to live in Korean or Burakumin ghettos because they favor such a lifestyle to living among their own group and its restrictive responsibilities. We found that such outsiders are tolerated in some instances, and rejected in others. Koreans are usually as suspicious of any outsider as are black Americans of any 'white' who seeks to gain acceptance in a black ghetto.

The maintenance of a Korean identity in Japan invariably implies some conflict regarding responsibility and guilt. If the individual has introjected a negative self-image, there may be more internal conflict about ordinary ethical standards. Assuming the same moral, ethical and social obligations as the majority Japanese may be distasteful or burdensome to many Koreans. Conversely, the avoidance of responsibility may at times be made easier through blaming the negative attitudes of the majority for one's avoidance of any form of responsible social commitment to society in general.

Using the TAT, among other methods, we have been comparing with ordinary Japanese, Korean minority members in Japan, and Korean immigrants to the USA over two decades. Here I report TAT evidence to three Murray cards; Card 1, the boy with the violin, Card 17 a card depicting a man either climbing or descending a rope, and Card 7BM, a picture of a younger man and an older man with their heads together. These cards, among others, illustrate the dramatic attitudinal differences in future-time-oriented stories, and stories of mentorship received from a legitimate authority.

Card 1: ambition vs incapacity

Koreans in Japan and the USA show striking contrasts in future-time orientation. Card 1 evokes, for samples generally, a percentage of stories related to achievement motivation projected into the future. Koreans from Japan are less likely to resolve their stories with a self-motivated positive view of the future. In contrast, of the 50 Korean immigrants sampled in Los Angeles, 25 gave stories of eventual success compared with the Japanese Korean sample from Kyoto and Osaka of 31 who gave *only two* such stories (Figure 14.1).

Parental pressure appears as an element in the stories comprising 42 per cent of the Japanese Korean sample. In only two of these 13 stories was there a positive compliance. Parental pressure also appeared in 32 per cent of the Los Angeles sample, in which five of 16 were resolved positively. Overall, 87 per cent of the Osaka-Kyoto sample gave stories with no resolution or with negative outcomes, compared with 36 per cent among the American Koreans. The Koreans in Japan do not give the stories found among the majority Japanese who worry about incompetence but persist until they

Groups	Los Angeles	Japan
Total Cases	50	31
Themes 1. Questions of motivation and competence	**29**	**14**
Percentage of Total Sample	58%	45%
Positive outcome	**25** (50%)	**2** (6%)
Negative: unresolved ambivalence or unresolved outcome	**4** (8%)	**12** (39%)
Themes 2. Questions of Parental Pressure	**16**	**13**
Percentage of Total Sample	32%	42%
Positive: complies and continues positively	**5** (10%)	**2** (6%)
Negative or unresolved	**11** (22%)	**11** (35%)
Themes 3. Other	**5**	**4**
Percentage of Total Sample	10%	13%
Total unresolved and negative results	**36%**	**87%**

Figure 14.1   Summary comparison of Card 1: Los Angeles Koreans and Korean Japanese.

accomplish. However, the Confucian-influenced Koreans coming directly from Korea to the United States give stories similar to those of the majority Japanese. For example, in the Los Angeles sample we obtained such stories as the following:

LA. Female age 22: AA-self CC-artist ESB-shame AA-persist   The boy hopes to be a good violinist. Today he played the violin badly before his violin teacher. He would practice the violin harder. He will eventually be a good violinist.

Concern with competence in 26 per cent of the stories results in overcoming incompetence and eventual mastery in all but two of the Los Angeles stories. Competence is the single most prevalent theme dealing with personal motivation. In brief, the fantasies elicited on Card 1 give evidence that the Korean immigrants, by and large, maintain a very positive internalized attitude about the possibilities of achievement. They seem very aware of a necessity to have a strong will to overcome individual weaknesses and disabilities in attaining a long-range goal. Contrast this with these illustrative stories from the Koreans in Japan:

J.K. Male, 26: NSA-edified CC-Failure PB-anger   He was receiving a violin lesson from a tutor. As he could not make a good sound, however, he was deeply annoyed, and then, ... that is all.

J.K. Male, 25: NSA-reward CB-able KB-illness   He was bought and given a violin. But he does not know how to play the violin, so he is watching the instrument. He is worrying if he will become a violinist. I wonder if he has a toothache. That's all.

Card 17 Kinesthetic Confidence

Card 17 is another symbolic measure of achievement concerns. There is a kinesthetic response to this card that results in the individual on the rope either being perceived as climbing up, resting, or climbing down. This card can be used as an indication of a relative amount of spontaneous vitality and upward surge projected spontaneously by particular individuals. The content elicited is also symbolic of attitudes of self confidence, the awareness of performance before an audience or concern in some instances with possible illegal or sexual activities.

Expressions of confidence and vitality betoken interest in active accomplishment By and large the Korean American stories are highly imaginative compared to some other samples that I have studied. Out of the 50 stories, most of those sampled in Los Angeles see activity of an active energetic nature. Their stories are manifestly more positively toned than those gathered from Koreans in Japan. Both samples uncharacteristics for the Japanese, are apt to depict more illegal or dysfunctional activity. This reaches 37 per cent in the minority Koreans in Japan.

There is direct contrast between the LA and the Korean residents in Japan in the tone of the stories dealing with these stories of performance or sports-like activity. Examples from Los Angeles:

KLA m, 21: OB-body *CA-able* CA-test PB-dislike   He is an acrobat. He climbs up the rope. He seems to be an old man but he is healthy. He is a veteran acrobat. He is full of confidence in climbing on the rope. He is looking at somebody. He has a slight feeling of repugnance for his job but he will climb to the end of the rope.

KLA f, 29: CA-test *AA-self* PA-nature   He climbs the rope. He must be climbing up a mountain. Maybe he will go to the top of the mountain easily. He is a person who enjoys mountaineering. He enjoys rock climbing.

In contrast to the American Koreans with a very vital positive tone, the Japanese Koreans give stories in which the performer is malformed, or is clownish in a depreciated way.

KJ m, 25: *ESC-abase-s* ESA-approve OB-body PA-joy   Should I look at picture lengthwise or crosswise? He is playing a fool. His face is playing a fool. He is playing as a show, for a show booth. He is masculine. This is more cheerful one than the other pictures. I don't mind if he is naked or not. This is the most masculine and cheerful picture.

Groups	Los Angeles	Japan
Total Cases	50	27

Themes 1. **Climbing**	**35**	**14**
Percentage of Total Sample	70%	53%

climbing positive tone	**20** (40%)	**3** (12%)
climbing, performing, ambigous tone	**5** (10%)	**5** (19%)
performing, but with negative tone	**2** (4%)	**6** (22%)
climbing for unsanctioned activity	**8** (16%)	**2** (7%)

Themes 2. **Escaping, climbing down or falling**	**13**	**10**
Percentage of Total Sample	26%	37%

escaping from prison, etc.	2	4
unsuccessful escape (recapture by police, etc.)	5	0
falls in escape from hell	0	2
running away, mad	4	1
Accident, falls into alcoholism	0	1
falls to death (in circus 1)	2	1
self destruction in elevator shaft	0	1

Themes 3. **Other**	**2**	**3**
Percentage of Total Sample	4%	12%

Figure 14.2 Summary comparison of Card 17: Los Angeles Koreans and Korean Japanese.

KJ f, 20: KD-defect *ESC–abase-s* OB-body CA-defect   This reminds me of a hunchback of Notre Dame. He may be a clown in a circus. Is he naked? He may wear a tight wear. He is very masculine. He seems to be opposed against the law of gravity. This is the poorest picture that I've seen.

Attitudes toward authority: Card 7

Authority relationships also influence adult adaptation in minority communities. Card 7 depicts an older and a younger man in conversation. The Japanese in Japan most often interpret it as reflecting mentorship, an older man such as a company president advising or encouraging a younger man. Among the Koreans there are, in contrast, many stories of conspiracy and plotting (48 per cent in the LA group and 55 per cent in Japanese Koreans). Compared with majority Japanese, relatively less attention is given to the age and status differential of the two figures. In Japanese Issei immigrants (De Vos and Kim, 1993), 94 per cent depicted compliant attitudes as did 68 per cent of Nisei. In 28 per cent of the American Nisei, however, there was rebellion, assertion of autonomy, or status-equivalent relationships. Only one Issei gave such a story. In majority Japanese in Japan, age disparity also remained central to the story (De Vos, 1973).

In the LA Koreans, an age-status differential still appears in 52 per cent of their stories. However, in strong contrast, in the present sample of contemporary Koreans in Japan only in 16 per cent is respect for age or differential status a consideration expressed in the story themes. In contrast to the LA sample who see positive younger–older situations in 24 per cent of all their stories, the Japanese minority sample gave only four such stories(13 per cent). One notes that, overall, the Koreans in Japan are much less mindful of status differentials than are the Koreans in LA. The Koreans in Japan are more negatively tuned than any previous sample collected. Only eight of their 31 stories (25 per cent) have a positive quality (see Figure 14.3)

Distrust is normative in both Korean groups. In LA, in half of these older–younger situations (13), there are thoughts of possible conspiracy. In 11 of the remaining stories without attention to age there are other negative themes, either about politicians, businessmen, criminals or simply friends, a total of 48 per cent of their stories. The propensity to be politically or socially distrustful is heavily present in both samples. The problems of distrust toward authority, even evident in those coming to the United States, is compounded in Japanese Koreans by a bleak

Groups	Los Angeles	Japan
Total Cases	50	31
1. **Younger- Older: Cooperate, Advice, Mentorship**	**12**	**4**
Positive or autonomous	24%	13%
2. **Mutual Cooperation or Conflict**	**10**	**8**
no status difference	20%	26%
cooperative or positive exchanges	8	4
dispute or negative exchange	2	4
3. **Conspiracy: Evil or Negative Activity**	**13**	**1**
Status difference. (older-younger)	26%	3%
4. **Conspiracy and Evil Activity**	**11**	**16**
no status differences	22%	52%
5. **Other**	**3**	**2**
Percentage of Total Sample	6%	6%

Figure 14.3 Summary comparison of Card 7: Los Angeles Koreans and Korean Japanese.

conviction that the future holds no hope. There is hope for success only if you curry favor with someone who is corrupt, as is suggested in the following:

> KJ f, 25: *MTC-plot* DSA-soothe   They seem to be doing something evil. They are directors of a company or politicians. This older man is saying, 'How is that business going? You have to manage successfully by using a bribe.' So, younger one answers, 'Yes, sir. I'll do it skillfully.' This older man is talking calmly, this younger man (points to the right) is carefully listening to him. He is trying desperately to gain his favor.

Contrast these stories with the more positive tone of the LA stories:

> KLA f, 23: DDA-author *MTA-task* CA-present AA-peer   They are discussing business. The person on the left is the other man's boss. The topic they are discussing is about the sales strategy of the company. The plan which will be produced from their discussion will be successful because they seem to be very bright men.

Longitudinal comparisons

Glimpses into the perception of political authority or guidance

The TAT can sometimes provide an early indication of changes in cultural patterns. For example, over the years, I have found an increasing cynicism toward the political figures appearing on Card 7BM. In Japanese youth in the 1950s, this picture of a younger man and an older man with their heads together elicited almost invariably a normative theme about paternal or employer mentorship by a nurturing older figure of a younger man with a problem. Age differences were an important concern in creating such a story. Business executives or political figures, when they occasionally appeared, were seen in a positive light. In Korean groups, however, as we noted, whether taken in Korea, Japan or the USA (De Vos and Kim, 1993), age differences and mentoring of the young by their elders were of less concern than the suspicion of possible negative activities. Political distrust was apparent in a not infrequently given theme of two politicians or businessmen involved in some questionable scheme.

In a more recent sample of 900 majority Japanese high-school students from Japan (Vaughn, 1988), increasing political cynicism is found reflected in similar stories appearing about plotting politicians. Age-graded mentorship is also a slowly diminishing theme in this new generation of youth. These portents suggest a long range diminution of trust in government. The behavioral signs are beginning to appear in the new generation of modern Japanese.

Longitudinal comparison of internalized social directives revealed on Card 1

The Confucian heritage of a past trust in government seems to be slipping away in the modern state. However, internalized achievement motives as part of early family socialization, are still quite evident as evoked in responses to Card 1, a boy looking at a violin.

American and Japanese styles of achievement concerns evoked by Card 1, can numerically be clustered into two major areas: First, narratives of self-initiated activities, either with positive or to-be-resolved motivation; and second, stories of a youth's reaction to having the task of playing the violin assigned to him. In Caudill's initial 1950s sample[9], 93 per cent of the stories of Issei immigrants were about self-motivation, and 7 per cent had the task assigned. In the Nisei, 62 per cent were self-oriented, whereas 38 per cent had the task assigned. The American middle class were concerned with self-motivation in 75 per cent of their stories, compared with 35 per cent of a lower-class sample that saw 65 per cent of their stories as task-assigned. My own initial studies with the TAT in Japan evoked stories that resembled those given by the Issei.

Unresolved attitudes about parental pressure to perform appeared characteristically in many majority American protocols from the first results reported by Caudill (Caudill and De Vos, 1956) on testing conducted in the late 1940s. Connor's TAT samples from the 1970s picked up much more reluctance to initiate or to perform an assigned task. Connor (1977) recorded only 24 per cent achievement among white college students at California State University at Sacramento in the early 1970s, a period of rebellious unrest throughout the United States. There was a marked contrast from Caudill's earlier middle-class sample wherein initial reluctance to take on the task was resolved in the direction of ultimate conformity. More recently, in Connor's middle-class sample of the late 1980s subjects saw self initiated positive achievement in 10 per cent of their stories and resolutions toward achievement after initially reluctant motivation in another 30 per cent. Achievement, initially compliant to please others, accounted for 11 per cent of the responses, while still in 31 per cent of the stories the youth rebelled and refused to take on the task.

Among Japanese Americans there has remained more concern with achievement motivation. Connor's Japanese American sample was comprised for the most part of third-generation or 'Sansei'. Fifteen per cent reported positive achievement themes, and 29 per cent noted reluctant achievement themes. Note that 27 per cent still stated that they would comply and practice to please someone else, while 20 per cent gave themes of rebellion, a rise in this category. The Japanese norms are slowly approaching those of majority white Americans, but still remain somewhat more compliant or achievement oriented.

Continuity of Confucian family morality and achievement motivation in Brazil

American–Brazilian differences in Japanese ethnic minorities

In Brazil we followed up on our research on the cultural continuity of the Japanese. From the turn of the century on, Japanese were migrating in large numbers into South America, principally Brazil. We found that the Japanese Brazilians, living in their own communities as a separate subgroup, continue to show on psychological tests as well as in interviews the continuing effects of internalizing a past Confucian family heritage. They fail to reflect the more negative social attitudes found among many other Brazilian ethnic subgroups.

In the 1990s in Brazil, they were still more apt to express the same attitudes toward work or toward social responsibility found earlier among the Japanese American migrants tested in the United States. As we have just noted, these attitudes have persisted from the test reports of the late 1940s by Caudill into the following generations of Japanese Americans reported in Connor's college-level research in the 1970s and 1980s (Connor, 1977; Connor and De Vos, 1989) and that of Vaughn's (1988) Japanese high-school samples obtained in the 1980s. The evidence of some cultural continuity in respect to achievement motivation among those growing up in a Japanese family, whether in Japan, the United States or Brazil, is strongly supported. However, while Japanese Americans share an overall American theme about feeling undue parental pressure to succeed in 47 per cent of their cases, there is less evidence of this theme in Japanese Brazilians. Some acculturative differences in this respect are noticeable comparing the two samples.

In Japanese Brazilians, 10 per cent expressed awareness of parental pressure compared with the 14 per cent of such stories of the Japanese high school samples in Japan, and an overall 60 per cent of stories of parental pressure given by the American high-school youth tested by Vaughn. In other Brazilian samples, such parental pressure related to an achievement theme appeared in only 5 per cent of the other ethnic subgroups. These overall Brazilian results about sensitivity to parental pressure to succeed at a task are therefore in direct contrast with the parental pressure portrayed by American youth, including Japanese Americans.

In the context of self-motivated achievement, in 50 responses to Card 1 given by Japanese Brazilians, most (34, or 68 per cent) were solely about achievement (13) and/or a concern with acquiring competence (21). In most of these stories there is optimism. As in similar stories found in Japan, hard work overcomes possible inadequacy in accomplishing the task of learning the violin. This was very close to the 75 per cent of such stories reported in Vaughn's recent sample from Japan which covered the same categories.

When expressing concerns with questionable ability, other Brazilian ethnic groups were more pessimistic; in 10 out of 12 (of the overall total of stories given to Card 1), 14 per cent were in this category and over 80 per cent of these stories were not completed or ended in failure. While some ambivalence about motives occurred with some frequency among the Japanese (17 per cent), it was found more rarely in the other Brazilian samples (9 per cent). There is also, with the exception of the Japanese, a sex difference in the distribution of positive and negative stories, with the Brazilian teenage women showing the most pessimism or helplessness about competence or achievement throughout the cards administered.

Discussion and speculation the role of the primary family in social-self identity within multiethnic populations

This presentation partially had the purpose of demonstrating the usefulness of a test device such as the TAT to elicit responses that directly or indirectly reflect social attitudes of either a conforming or deviant nature. In the cards selected illustratively from our various research data with Japanese and other groups in Brazil and elsewhere, we did not aim directly to elicit attitudes with any specific political or social import, but in what we have presented it should be obvious that whereas family life was the most immediate preoccupation, economic, social and political implications are also forthcoming interpretively when we consider the nature of psychological internalization as it generally influences social conformity or deviancy.

The family as matrix of internalization

It is through what happens in the birth family that social experiences can be reflected quite variously through the prisms of selves formed differently by ethnicity or class membership and the heritage in which one is born. The norms for different groups continue to be different.

What is internalized as part of the self does selectively distort how one sees the future. McClelland's perception of how achievement motivation works is correct in stressing that some individuated-self concerns directed toward future purpose will result, in a statistical sense, in a higher rate of economic and social accomplishment than that possible for those who more readily see a negative economic or social destiny, or are internally preoccupied with a sense of deprivation or neglect. Private projections of either a positive or negative nature are both selective, and hence can be seen as distortions influenced by internalized personal inclinations. These inclinations result in different forms of social or political behavior.

There are very evident and continuing ethnic characteristics which are found to be statistically prevalent in Japanese and other Asian ethnic minorities in the Americas. Concern with self-motivated achievement, gaining competence and adequacy through hard work, remains interwoven

with other attitudes. Family cohesion remains operative, as does the existence of community networks, whatever the enveloping society in which
they find themselves.

Forms of ethnic or social continuity related to social authority

Generationally considered, cultural continuities such as a Confucian heritage can be socially adaptive, as our work with the Japanese illustrates, or
they can be problematic given an inheritance of being socially oppressed in
a class or caste structure. Oscar Lewis forcefully challenged us to consider
the relative incidence of dysfunctional ethnic families prevalent in some
communities, as a semi-autonomous, continuing, 'culture' of poverty. He
documented by intensive interviews such dysfunctional family patterns
operative among the ex-peons of Mexico (Lewis, 1961), and the Puerto
Rican immigrants in New York (Lewis, 1969). Such experiences were not
conducive to developing effective, mature levels of social action.

We can argue semantically whether any social segment by itself can constitute an independently operative 'culture', but we cannot dismiss, as has
been done glibly by many, the force of generational continuity deforming
the perceptions and anticipations of the life-course of those trapped in an
underclass. From our foregoing materials from the United States, Japan and
Brazil, it should be evident how fantasy, even that of high school adolescents, differentially reflects not only personal issues but continuities from
past into future social attitudes. The past, in some deformation, lives on in
the present and influences perceptions of the future. That is the nature of
'cultural' or ethnic continuity.

For a 'culture' to change the specific institutions directly concerned with
the basic socialization of the next generation, the intimate family and
youthful peer interaction must be altered. As we have noted in respect to
the Japanese migration into the Americas, family patterning as a formative
institution resists, to some degree at least and for some considerable time,
changes in technology or political institutions, or the migration of ethnic
groups from one society into another. There is to be observed what I term a
'psychological lag' (De Vos, 1973, 13–19, 107–8) between what is occurring
in the society at large and what persists psychologically in the family
matrix and the immediate social community. In situations of social discrimination or degradation it takes more than one generation to have the
negative effects internalized, and it takes more than one generation to have
them ameliorated

It is through what constitutes the birth family that social experiences,
seemingly shared by all in a modern state, can be reflected quite variously
through the prisms of selves formed differently by ethnic or class-belonging
and the particular heritage in which one is born. The norms for different
groups continue to be different. Early self-confidence is integral with later
social status or the readiness to internalize forms of social conformity or to

express, even in a self-defeating rather than ameliorative way, socially-defiant antagonistic or alienated behavior.

Note

1. Internalization remains pivotal to any study of moral development. Conceptualized as 'superego' it is central to the psychoanalytic study of the human personality (see for example Schafer, 1968), and what the individual experiences 'internalized social constraint'.
2. In the state of California the Japanese American youth in the 1960s had 1/80th the delinquency rate of the majority population (De Vos, 1973, chapter IX)
3. This section is excerpted from De Vos (1960), and De Vos (1973), chapter 5.
4. Card J6GF is a picture of an older man leaning over a couch on which a younger woman is seated.
5. Card 18GF is a picture of an older woman either strangling or caressing the neck of another figure turned away from the viewer.
6. Card J7M portrays an older man seen discussing something with a younger man in the foreground.
7. Card J5 depicts an older woman who has just opened a door and is looking within.
8. One must note that at one point in the 1960s (De Vos and Wagatsuma, 1966) we found that Korean youth had seven times the delinquency rate of the majority Japanese.
9. See De Vos (1973), p. 231.

References

Caudill, W. and G. De Vos (1956) 'Achievement, Culture and Personality: The Case of the Japanese Americans', *American Anthropologist*, vol. 58(6), pp. 1102–26.

Connor, J. (1977) *Tradition and Change in Three Generations of Japanese Americans*, Chicago: Nelson Hall.

Connor, J. W. and G. A. De Vos (1989) 'Cultural Influences on Achievement Motivation and Orientation Toward Work in Japanese and American Youth', in D. Stern and D. Eichorn (eds.), *Adolescence and Work: Influence of Social Structure, Labor Markets, and Culture*, Hillsdale, N. J.: Lawrence Erlbaum Associates, pp. 291–326.

De Vos, G. (1960) 'The Relation of Guilt Toward Parents to Achievement and Arranged Marriage Among the Japanese', *Psychiatry*, vol. 23(3), pp. 287–301.

——— (1973) *Socialization for Achievement: Essays on the Cultural Psychology of the Japanese*, Berkeley: University of California Press.

——— (1975) 'Apprenticeship and Paternalism: Psychocultural Continuities Underlying Japanese Social Organization', in E. Vogel (ed.), *Modern Japanese Organization and Decision Making*, Berkeley: University of California Press.

——— (1983) 'Adaptive Conflict and Adjustive Coping: Psychocultural Approaches to Ethnic Identity', in T. Sarbin and K. E. Scheibe (eds.), *Studies in Social Identity*, New York: Praeger, pp. 204–30.

——— (1992) *Social Cohesion and Alienation: Minorities in The United States and Japan*, Boulder Col.: Westview Press.

——— (1993a) 'Problems with Achievement, Alienation, and Authority in Korean Minorities in The United States and Japan', in K. K. Lee and W. Slote (eds.) *Overseas Koreans in the Global Context*, Seoul: Association for the Study of Koreans Abroad, pp. 145–80.

——— (1993b) 'A Cross Cultural Perspective: The Japanese Family as a Unit in Moral Socialization', in P. Cowan, J. Filed, D. Hansen, M. Scolnick and G. Swanson (eds.), *Family, Self, and Society: Towards a New Agenda for Family Research*, Hillsdale N.J.: Lawrence Erlbaum Associates.

——— (1993c) 'The Rites of Pleasure: The Religion, Morality and Aesthetics of Bodily Propriety', in I. Dosamantes (ed.), *Body Image in Cultural Context: Interdisciplinary Essays*, Los Angeles: DMT publications, pp. 35–63.

——— (1996) 'Internalized Achievement or External Authority: Some Cultural Comparisons of Responses to TAT Card 1', in Ir. B. Weiner (ed.), *Rorschachiana XXI Yearbook of the International Rorschach Society*, Göttingen: Hogrefe & Huber.

——— (1997) 'Heritage of Exploitation: A Brief TAT Report on South Brazilian Youth', *Political Psychology*, vol. 18 no. 2, June, pp. 437–74.

——— (ND) *Narrative Analysis Cross-Culturally: The Self as Revealed in the Thematic Apperception Test* (in preparation for publication)

De Vos, George and Kwang-Kyu Lee (1981) 'Attitude Toward Authority: Dilemma of Ex-Colonial Society', in Changsoo Lee, ed. *Modernization of Korea and the Impact of the West*, Los Angeles: University of Southern California, pp. 150–62.

De Vos, G. and Eun-Young Kim (1993) 'Koreans in Japan: Problems with Achievement, Alienation Authority', in Ivan Light and Parminder Bhachu (eds.) *California Immigrants in World Perspective*, New Brunswick NJ: Transaction Books.

De Vos, G. and Hiroshi Wagatsuma (1966) *Japan's Invisible Race: Caste in Culture and Personality*, Berkeley: University of California Press.

Dore, R. P. (1965) 'The Legacy of Tokugawa Education', in *Changing Japanese Attitudes Toward Modernization*. Marius Jansen (ed.) Princeton, New Jersey: Princeton University Press.

Erikson, Erik H. (1950) *Childhood and Society*, New York: W.W. Norton.

Fauconnet, P. (1920) 'La Responsabilité', *Etude de Sociologie*, Paris: Librararie Felix Alcan.

Lee, Changsoo and George De Vos (1981) *Koreans in Japan: Ethnic Conflict and Accommodation*, Berkeley: University of California Press.

Merton, R. C. (1964) *Social Theory and Social Structure* (Revised Edition), London: The Free Press of Glencoe,

Ogbu, J. (1978) *Minority Education and Caste: The American System in Cross-Cultural Perspective*. New York: Academic Press.

Piaget, Jean (1932) *The Moral Judgment of Children*, London: Routledge and Kegan Paul.

Schafer, Roy (1968) *Aspects of Internalization*, N.Y.: International Universities Press.

Slote Walter and De Vos, George (eds.) (1998) *Confucianism and the Family in an Interdisciplinary, Comparative Context*, Albany: State University of New York Press.

Vaughn, Curtis (1988) *Cognitive Independence, Social Independence and Achievement Orientation: A Comparison of Japanese and U.S. Students, Dissertation*, Dept. of Education, University of California at Berkeley.

15
Multicultural Policy and Social Psychology: The Canadian Experience

J. W. Berry and Rudolf Kalin

Introduction

In this chapter, we examine the relationships between national culture in Canada and the social policy of multiculturalism. We investigate attitudes and identities that are associated with this policy, and their links to ethnicity. We thus seek to portray comparatively, ways in which national culture, social policy and ethnicity intersect within the emerging field of cross-cultural political psychology.

Multiculturalism as social fact

Virtually all countries in the world are culturally plural. In the case of Canada, since the time of confederation in 1867 when 91 per cent of Canada's population was of French (31 per cent) or British (60 per cent) origin, there has been constant change in the ethnic composition of the country's population. In the most recent census (1991), 29 per cent were of British, 24 per cent of French, and 27 per cent of other than British or French origin; the balance (22 per cent) were various combinations of these three origins. This 'other' category has increased steadily in size, and has changed in ethnic composition since 1867; initially it consisted of large numbers of people of Western and Northern European origin; these were followed by those of Eastern and Southern European origin, and for the past 25 years by those not of European origin, particularly from East and South Asia, the West Indies and Latin America. In 1995, over 65 per cent of the 200 000 immigrants to Canada came from outside Europe. This changing pattern of migration has made the Canadian population even more diverse, particularly with respect to 'racial' composition. Of course, the Aboriginal population has had a continuous presence; it is now increasing rapidly due to a fertility rate that is more than double that of others in Canada. All of these changes have increased the need for public policies that seek to accommodate diverse populations in all their varieties – cultural, linguistic, 'racial' and immigration status.

Multiculturalism as public policy

The plural Canadian society came about largely on its own, without any help from public policy or programs. Indeed, many observers consider that it came about *in spite of* the implicit (and sometimes explicit) policy of Anglo conformity, or assimilation to British culture. However, by 1956 the federal government's view was that assimilation had not worked anywhere in the contemporary world, and that it was impracticable as a general policy. As an alternative to assimilation, in 1971 the prime minister announced a policy of multiculturalism. The key sections were:

A policy of multiculturalism within a bilingual framework commends itself to the Government as the most suitable means of assuring the cultural freedom of Canadians. Such a policy should help to break down discriminatory attitudes and cultural jealousies. National unity, if it is to mean anything in the deeply personal sense, must be founded on confidence in one's own individual identity; out of this can grow respect for that of others and a willingness to share ideas, attitudes and assumptions. A vigorous policy of multiculturalism will help create this initial confidence. It can form the base of a society which is based on fair play for all. The Government will support and encourage the development of the various cultures and ethnic groups that give structure and vitality to our society. They will be encouraged to share their cultural expression and values with other Canadians and so contribute to a richer life for all. (Government of Canada, 1971)

In a social psychological analysis (Berry, 1984), four elements of the policy were identified. First, it is clear that the policy wishes to avoid assimilation by encouraging ethnic groups to maintain and develop themselves as distinctive groups within Canadian society; this element we may term 'group development' (and is sometimes referred to as the 'cultural' emphasis in the policy). Second, a fundamental purpose of the policy is to increase intergroup harmony and the mutual acceptance of all groups which maintain and develop themselves; (that is, to 'break down discriminatory attitudes and cultural jealousies'); this we term 'group acceptance'. Third, the policy argues that group development by itself is not sufficient to lead to group acceptance; 'intergroup contact and sharing' is also required (and is sometimes referred to as the 'social' emphasis). Fourth, full participation by groups cannot be achieved if some common language is not learned; thus the 'learning of official languages' is also encouraged by the policy. In addition to identifying these four elements, some relationships among them are suggested in the policy. For example, the *multicultural assumption* proposes that 'confidence in one's identity' is a basis for tolerance; and the *contact hypothesis* is asserted, such that contact and sharing are assumed also to be a basis for tolerance.

Attitudes towards both the social fact and the policy of multiculturalism can be objects of research. Other aspects may also be important psychological phenomena in culturally plural societies, including a sense of identity and attachment to the national society and to one's own group or region.

What pattern of attitudes and identities would be required in order to maintain a multicultural society in which all groups find ways to live together? In our view, there needs to be general support for multiculturalism, including acceptance of various aspects and consequences of the policy, and of cultural diversity as a valuable resource for a society. Second, there should be overall low levels of intolerance or prejudice in the population. Third, there should be generally positive mutual attitudes among the various ethnocultural groups that constitute the society. And fourth, there needs to be a degree of attachment to the larger Canadian society, but without derogation of its constituent ethnocultural groups. These four elements constitute a conceptualization of tolerance that is appropriate to our time and place (Berry and Kalin, 1995).

An earlier national survey of multicultural and ethnic attitudes (Berry, Kalin and Taylor, 1977) provided a fairly comprehensive account of the distribution of ethnic and multicultural attitudes, and their demographic and attitudinal correlates; a recent overview (Kalin and Berry, 1994) has brought this account up to 1990. Other studies by Breton, Isajiw, Kalbach and Reitz (1990), Bourhis (1994), and Sniderman, Northrup, Fletcher, Russell and Tetlock (1993), as well as more popular analyses (for example Richler, 1992) have also addressed these issues. Generally, attitudes in the Canadian population have been found to be moderately supportive of multiculturalism; ethnocentrism and prejudice are moderately low, and attitudes towards various ethnic and racial groups are variable but usually positive. For example, in 1974 more than twice as many supported the policy than opposed it; and this was also the case for the Multicultural Ideology scale (see Table 15.2 below). Scores on a scale of ethnocentrism were below the mid-point (3.4 on a 7-point scale), and attitudes towards most ethnic groups were in the positive range (Berry *et al.*, 1977). This moderately positive picture, of course, may be due in part to some degree of socially desirable responding.

However, there are important group variations to this general picture. First, there is some indication that multiculturalism is viewed more positively, and levels of ethnocentrism are lower, among those of British and 'other ethnic' backgrounds, as compared with those of the French background. One interpretation of this difference has been in terms of the perceived cultural threat to the French language and culture that multiculturalism (and immigration) may pose for francophones (Berry *et al.*, 1977; Bourhis, 1987; Lambert and Curtis, 1983; Bolduc and Fortin, 1990). This perceived threat may undermine the confidence or sense of security identified in the policy as a prerequisite for tolerance. This threat is likely rooted in a series of historical and modern phenomena: the military conquest of the French by the British forces (in the 1760s); the attempts to assimilate the French to British language and culture ('Angloconformity'); the differential access to education, and to economic resources (now largely eliminated); and the continuing minority demographic position of the French in Canada (who are now less than 25 per cent). The move to redefine Canada as a 'multicultural' (rather than a 'bicultural') society, along with high immigration from non-French-speaking countries, all combine, in the view of some, to pose a threat to the survival and vitality of the French language and culture in Canada.

Second, attitudes towards specific ethnic and racial groups have also been found to vary. Those of Western and Northern European background are generally evaluated positively, followed by those of Eastern and Southern European background, and then by those not of European background (Berry *et al.*, 1977; Pineo, 1977).

The rest of this chapter presents an overview of results from the 1991 national survey, and considers changes since the 1974 survey. More detailed results can be found in a series of publications (Berry and Kalin, 1995; Kalin, 1996; Kalin and Berry, 1995).

National survey research

The survey instrument was designed by the Department of Multiculturalism and Citizenship, and the Angus Reid Group, partly based on a draft instrument prepared by the present authors. The final instrument consisted of 130 opinion statements, three ethnic identity questions and 22 demographic questions. They were grouped in various ways, separating attitudes into beliefs, knowledge, perceptions, evaluations and self-characterizations. English and French language versions were prepared.

Sample

In all, 3325 individuals responded to these questions. This total consisted of a 'national sample' of 2500 adults (aged 18 and over), and an 'oversample' in Montreal, Toronto and Vancouver to ensure a sample of 500 in each city.

The survey was carried out in late June and July 1991, using a random telephone dialling procedure. This procedure generates telephone numbers by census divisions so that the selected sample can represent the Canadian population. A quota system ensured proportionate representation of regions and males and females. The response rate (based upon the number of completed interviews, as compared with households contacted) was 15.5 per cent. In most essential respects (age, gender and region) the sample is representative of the Canadian population over the age of 18. The only demographic features that differ from the population are education, with better educated individuals being overrepresented in the sample; and income, with wealthier persons being overrepresented. However, the generally good representation of the sample provides assurance that findings are moderately generalizable.

Scale development

Rather than working with responses to individual questions, it was a goal of the study to create psychological scales that met psychometric criteria of reliability and validity, and that provided some continuity with scales developed in the earlier survey (Berry *et al.*, 1977). From the array of questions used in the survey (responded to on a 7-point scale), we identified those that represented a number of core social psychological constructs. This initial theoretical clustering was checked by various empirical analyses (internal consistency of items in a scale, factor analysis of items, convergent and discriminant analyses and scale intercorrelations). The result was the creation of five scales that met these criteria. Generally, the five intended scales were constructed with adequate internal consistency (alphas ranging from .69 to .84), with item-total correlations ranging from +.19 to +.68, and with items correlating more highly with their intended scale than with other scale scores. The first three scales are similar to those used in the 1974 survey, and permit some limited comparison between the two surveys. Following is a short description of the nature and content of these scales.

Program attitudes

This scale measures the degree of support *vs* opposition to nine 'possible elements of federal multiculturalism policy'. All are phrased in a positive direction and so there may be an acquiescence response set problem. Two examples are supporting or opposing 'Ensuring that organizations and institutions reflect and respect the cultural and racial diversity of Canadians', and 'Developing materials for all school systems in Canada to teach children and teachers about other cultures and ways of life'.

Perceived consequences of multiculturalism

This scale measures what people feel 'could happen in Canada as a result of multiculturalism policy'. There are ten items in the scale, made up of five positive and five negative consequences; the scale is thus balanced. A high score indicates a perception of positive consequences. Two examples are agreeing or disagreeing that multiculturalism policy will 'Provide greater equality of opportunity for all groups in Canada', and 'Cause greater conflict between groups of different origins' (reversed).

Multicultural ideology

This scale assesses support for having a culturally diverse society in Canada, in which ethnocultural groups maintain and share their cultures with others. There are ten items, with five in a negative direction (hence it is a balanced scale). Of these negative five items, two advocate 'assimilation' ideology, one advocates 'segregation', and two claim that diversity 'weakens unity'. Two examples are supporting or opposing the view that 'Recognizing that cultural and racial diversity is a fundamental characteristic of Canadian society', and agreeing or disagreeing that 'The unity of this country is weakened by Canadians of different ethnic and cultural backgrounds sticking to their old ways' (reversed).

Tolerance

This scale is made up of nine items that assess one's willingness to accept individuals or groups that are culturally or racially different from oneself. There are four items phrased positively (that is, indicating tolerance) and five items phrased negatively (that is, indicating prejudice). Thus the scale is nearly balanced. A high score is indicative of tolerance. Two examples are agreeing or disagreeing that 'It is a bad idea for people of different races to marry one another' (reversed), and 'Recent immigrants should have as much say about the future of Canada as people who were born and raised here'.

Canadianism

This scale measures one's sense of attachment and commitment to Canada. It has eight items (six are positive, one is negative, and one is responded to on a 4-point scale, but converted for scoring purposes to seven points). It is thus not a balanced scale. Two examples are agreeing or disagreeing that 'I am proud to be a Canadian Citizen', and 'I feel less committed to Canada than I did a few years ago' (reversed).

Comfort ratings for various ethnic and immigrant groups

Respondents indicated (on 7-point scales) how comfortable they would feel being around individuals from various groups. Comfort ratings were made twice for each target group, first thinking of group members as immigrants to Canada, and second thinking of them as having been born and raised in Canada. These comfort ratings, taken as indicative of attitudes towards immigrant and ethnic groups, were expressed for British, French, Italian, Ukrainian, German, Jewish, Portuguese, Chinese, Native Canadian Indians (as an ethnic group only), West Indian Blacks, Arabs, Muslims, Indo-Pakistanis and Sikhs.

Comfort ratings for the various ethnic and immigrant groups were analysed in two ways: 7-point scale raw scores and standardized scores. Analyses revealed that the raw comfort ratings yielded very high means, with even the least preferred group, Sikhs, receiving a mean of 4.8 out of 7 as 'immigrants', and 5.3 as 'ethnic'. These high ratings may, in part, have been due to response sets, such as social desirability, or positivity bias. In order to minimize such response sets, the comfort ratings were also standardized within each particular respondent. Standardization was accomplished by taking the average rating given by a respondent to all 14 groups and subtracting that average from the comfort rating given to a particular group. Positive standardized comfort ratings therefore indicate above average comfort levels, or a positive preference, within a respondent for a particular group. Negative ratings indicate that the group is relatively less preferred than average.

Self-identity

There were three questions used to assess self-identity. The first asked, 'To which ethnic or cultural groups(s) did your ancestors belong?' (If Canadian mentioned, probe: 'Other than Canadian, to which ethnic or cultural group(s) did your ancestors belong'?). All responses were recorded, and were tracked as first mention, second mention, and later mention. In a second question, respondents were told, 'People may describe themselves in a number of ways. If you had to choose one, generally speaking, do you think of yourself as: (1) First origin reported (in the first question, e.g., Dutch), (2) First origin–Canadian (e.g., Dutch–Canadian), (3) Second origin, if reported (e.g., Italian), (4) Second origin–Canadian (e.g., Italian–Canadian), (5) A Province of residence (e.g., Manitoban), (6) A Canadian, (7) Other (coded as missing in subsequent analyses)'. All seven choices were read out by the interviewer before respondents gave their choice.

From this question respondents were placed in the following identity categories: (1) 'Canadian', if they selected the Canadian alternative; (2) 'British–Canadian', if they assigned themselves a hyphenated identity in terms of their first or second origin and that origin was British; (3) 'French Canadian', if they picked a hyphenated identity in terms of first or second origin, and that origin was French; (4) 'Provincial', if they described themselves in terms of a province; (5) 'Other Ethnic–Canadian', if they selected a hyphenated identity in terms of their first or second origin, and that origin was other than French or British; (6) Other National, if they described themselves in terms of their first or second origin without qualifying it with Canadian. Canadian and Provincial can be regarded as civic identities while British–Canadian, French–Canadian, other Ethnic Canadian and other National qualify as ethnic identities.

In a third question, respondents were asked, 'Using a 7-point scale where 1 is very weak and 7 is very strong, how strongly do you identify with being …' Each of the first six options were read out again to the respondents. This third question was used to assess the strength of each of the identities.

Demographic variables

Two demographic variables were employed in the present analyses: Region of Residence and Ethnic Origin. For region of residence, Québec was distinguished from the rest of Canada. This division (Québec/Rest of Canada) is now a conventional one in Canadian social research. It is based on the view of Québec as a 'distinct society' within Canada, with French as its official language, an established set of public policies and institutions of its own, and its use of the Civil Code (rather than British Common Law) in non-criminal legal matters. Thus the variable of 'region' is far more than a simple geographic place, and carries a complex set of historical, political and cultural attributes. However, it is not coextensive with ethnicity or language: there are significant French-speaking populations living outside Québec, as well as non-French populations living inside Québec.

Ethnic origin was ascertained from the first question noted above that served as a lead in to self-identity ('To which ethnic or cultural group(s) did your ancestors belong?'). If more than one origin was offered, the first mentioned was used to categorize respondents into one of three groupings, namely, British (an aggregation of English, Irish, Scottish and Welsh), French (including French, Québécois, Franco-Ontarian, Franco-Manitoban, and Acadian), and Other Ethnic (respondents who were not of British or French origin). Respondents of mixed ethnic origin were categorized according that first mentioned.

Attitudes towards multiculturalism policy

In the 1974 and 1991 surveys, two scales were used to examine public attitudes towards the policy. While the content of each scale changed somewhat to reflect contemporary issues, the core constructs remained the same: what is the acceptance of various programs associated with the policy (Program Attitudes); and what will be the consequences of the policy (Perceived Consequences)? Although strict comparisons are not possible with the whole scale, since some items changed, limited comparisons are possible. Table 15.1 presents the means and distributions of the two scales, and the common items.

For both scale scores, the means and distributions are positive in 1974 and 1991, and are more positive in 1991 than 1974. There is thus general support in the population, and increasing support, for the policy. One specific item in the Program Attitudes scale, ('funding festivals') received *less* support in 1991 (contrary to the overall scale score), but for the two common items in the Perceived Consequences scale, both received more support in 1991 (consistent with the overall scale score).

Attitudes towards diversity

The Multicultural Ideology scale is a measure of general acceptance of cultural diversity. The descriptive statistics for the scale for 1974 and 1991 are also presented in Table 15.1, along with those for some common items. The statistical results for the Tolerance scale, used only in 1991, are also

Table 15.1 Descriptive statistics for five multicultural attitudes in 1974 and 1991 surveys

		1974 distribution						1991 distribution				
Scale	N	Mean	Sd	% opp	% neut	% supp	N	Mean	Sd	% opp	% neut	% supp
1 Program Attitudes	1830	4.71	1.4	25.2	6.2	68.6	3322	5.95	1.0	5.1	1.1	93.8
Item												
'Fund festivals'		5.79	1.6	9.1	8.6	82.3		4.70	2.1	25.6	16.4	59.9
2 Perceived Consequences	1827	4.52	1.5	32.4	6.6	61.0	3293	4.97	1.2	17.7	3.4	78.8
Items												
'Destroy Canadian Way' (R)		3.43	2.2	53.7	14.9	31.5		2.60	1.9	68.1	13.8	18.1
'Enrich Canada Culture'		4.84	2.0	22.0	16.2	61.9		5.60	1.7	11.0	11.4	77.6
3 Multicultural Ideology	1835	4.51	1.2	32.2	3.9	63.9	3313	4.59	1.2	27.3	3.4	69.3
Items												
'Forget background' (R)		3.05	2.1	61.6	12.3	26.1		3.10	2.3	55.1	13.0	31.9
'Tackle new problems'		4.65	1.9	23.1	24.4	52.5		5.10	1.7	14.3	20.5	65.2
'Unity weakened' (R)		3.68	2.1	47.0	16.8	35.7		3.90	2.1	41.6	16.0	42.5
'Keep culture to themselves' (R)		4.30	2.3	38.0	13.1	48.9		3.80	2.2	45.0	16.1	38.9
4 Tolerance			Not used				3316	5.37	1.0	8.8	2.3	88.9
5 Canadianism			Not used				3317	5.56	1.0	8.4	1.1	90.5

Note: Means and distributions of reversed items are presented in original direction; they were reverse scored for inclusion in the total scale score.

shown in Table 15.1. For both scales, attitudes are positive, and for the Multicultural Ideology scale, there is a modest increase between 1974 and 1991 in the mean and in percentage support (from 63.9 per cent to 69.3 per cent support). There were changes in all four common items: on two reversed items, agreement was higher (that is, attitudes were less in favour of multiculturalism), but on the other two items, attitudes were more in favour in 1991.

Scores on the Canadianism scale are also shown in Table 15.1, but will be described in relation to Identities (below).

Variations by ethnic origin and region

The possibility that these attitudes vary by ethnic origin and region of residence of respondents was examined. Table 15.2 shows the means on the scales in 1991 broken down by ethnic origin of the respondent (British, French, other) and region (living in Québec, outside Québec), and presents the analysis of variance. For the first four attitude scales there are no differences due to ethnic origin; however there is a regional effect for Tolerance and interactions for Program Attitudes and Multicultural Ideology. These different patterns require different explanations. For Tolerance, it may be that where intergroup relations are generally contentious (for example in Québec) all groups are relatively less tolerant. For Program Attitudes and Multicultural Ideology, a kind of 'self-interest' seems to account for the distribution: where people are advantaged by policies and programs supporting multiculturalism (for example British and others inside Québec; French outside Québec) support is high; but where the cultural position of one's group may be threatened by such pluralist policies (for example French in Québec), support for diversity is lower.

Attitudes towards ethnic groups

Respondents indicated their degree of comfort being around persons of selected ethnic backgrounds. Figure 15.1 shows these 'comfort levels' according to the ethnic origin of the respondents. In the national sample there are three important aspects. First, while comfort levels were generally high, not all groups receive the same ratings. There is a hierarchy of acceptance in which British- through to Aboriginal-Canadians are evaluated more positively than other groups (5.5 or higher on the 7-point scale). Second, while there are no differences between British- and Other-origin ratings, ratings given by French-origin respondents are noticeably less positive (approximately one scale point below the British and others). A third observation is that those groups that are generally less positively rated tend to receive relatively less positive ratings by French-origin respondents. These patterns are similar to those found within Québec by Joly (1996), who used

Table 15.2   Attitude scale means by ethnic origin, inside and outside Québec, (1991 survey)

| | Ethnic origin | | | | | |
	British	French	Other	F Origin	F Region	F Interaction
N in Québec[a]	109	564	146			
N outside Québec	1298	187	897			
Programme Attitudes				0.84	2.35	7.00**
In Québec	6.15	5.99	6.10			
Outside Québec	5.88	6.18	5.92			
Perceived Consequences				0.34	0.78	2.88
In Québec	5.12	5.00	5.11			
Outside Québec	4.90	5.15	5.01			
Multicultural Ideology				2.60	2.00	9.94**
In Québec	4.68	4.35	4.80			
Outside Québec	4.59	4.81	4.69			
Tolerance				0.77	11.63**	1.43
In Québec	5.34	5.16	5.29			
Outside Québec	5.43	5.46	5.44			
Canadianism				25.24**	79.82**	25.20**
In Québec	5.66	4.80	5.41			
Outside Québec	5.78	5.76	5.72			
Security				0.93	16.66***	2.93*
In Québec	4.90	4.58	5.02			
Outside Québec	5.19	5.36	5.26			

Notes:

* < 0.01

** < 0.001

[a]N given is for total sample. Individual analyses Ns will vary.

[b]Minimum difference required for any pair of means to be significant by Scheffé test at alpha = 0.01; All analyses are weighted by respondent weight.

MANOVA: Wilks' Lambda $F(10)$ for Origin = 8.24, p < 0.0001
Wilks' Lambda $F(5)$ for Region = 25.95, p < 0.0001
Wilks' Lambda $F(10)$ for Interaction = 6.77, p < 0.0001

Source: Berry and Kalin (1995), table 3.

the same 'comfort-level' question with two representative samples, one in Montréal, and one in the rest of the Province.

The overall high level of 'comfort' may indicate that intergroup attitudes really are very positive, or that some degree of desirable responding is present. Taking these comfort levels at their face value, it is clear that respondents do make *differential* ratings. This has resulted in a clear hierarchy of acceptance,

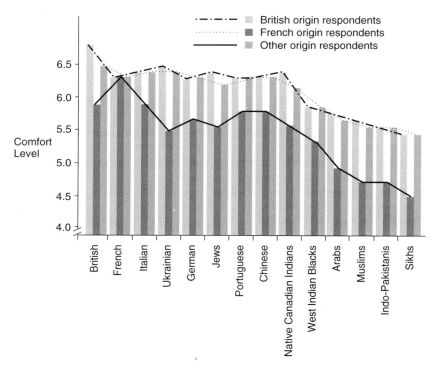

Figure 15.1   Mean comfort levels with ethnic groups, by ethnic origin of respondents in the national sample (1991 survey).

but its interpretation is not entirely clear. One possibility is that prejudice (in particular, racism) accounts for these ratings. However, it should be noted here that Chinese-Canadians and Native-Canadians are generally as highly rated as those of European background; thus, a simple *racism* interpretation is not generally valid. Other explanations include: *familiarity* with various groups, with those groups who are less numerous and not as long-established in Canada being rated less positively; and *similarity*, with those whose cultural origins are less similar to the dominant (European-based) population being rated less positively. These two basic explanatory concepts have widespread support in the social psychology of intergroup relations.

Ethnic and civic identities

The third area of interest is how people identify themselves. The 1991 survey had three questions dealing with self-identity: an ethnic *origin* question (similar to the 1991 census question); an *identity* question (how respondents usually thought of themselves), with various ethnic options provided, based on answers to the first (origin) question, along with regional and national options (for example 'Québécois', 'Canadian'); and a *strength* of identification (on a 7-point scale) analysed for three identities ('Canadian/Canadien'; provincial; ethnic). Related to these identity questions, was a scale of *Canadianism* attempting to assess a sense of attachment and commitment to Canada.

Responses to the identity questions are presented in Table 15.3 according to respondents' ethnic origin for both the 1974 and 1991 surveys, and in Table 15.4, according to ethnic origin and region for the 1991 survey (Kalin and Berry, 1995). In both the 1974 and 1991 surveys (Table 15.3) the most frequent identity was 'Canadian/Canadien'; however, this was more the case among British- and Other-origin, than among French-origin, respondents. Among the latter, the most frequent identity in 1974 was 'Canadien-Français' (47 per cent), but this mostly shifted to a provincial (largely 'Québécois') identity in 1991 (47 per cent), and somewhat less to a 'Canadien' identity (32 per cent). 'Other Ethnic' identities were the third most frequent, but declined from 1974 to 1991 (28 per cent to 20 per cent).

For the 1991 survey (Table 15.4), this national pattern breaks down according to region of residence and ethnic origin. Most clearly, the 'Canadian/Canadien' identity is lower in Québec than outside (28 per cent vs 76 per cent), even for those (the British origin respondents) who claim it most frequently (82 per cent outside vs 55 per cent inside Québec). It is least frequent among those of French origin in Québec (21 per cent), while their most common identity is Provincial (Québécois at 59 per cent). The Provincial identity is claimed by those of British and Other origins more often inside Québec (26 per cent and 30 per cent respectively) than respondents outside Québec (7 per cent and 6 per cent respectively). This general

Table 15.3 Self-identity (in per cent) of respondents in two national surveys by ethnic origin

| | Ethnic origin | | | | | | | |
| | MAS 74 | | | | MAS 91 | | | |
Identity	Total	British	French	Other ethnic	Total	British	French	Other ethnic
Canadian/Canadien	59	80	26	59	64	80	32	65
British-Canadian	7	13	3	3	2	6	0	0
Canadien-Français	15	3	47	3	4	1	16	0
Provincial	7	1	22	1	19	9	47	9
Other Ethnic-Canadian	8	0	0	28	7	1	1	20
Other National	3	2	2	5	4	3	4	5
N =	1810	708	376	541	3276	1392	746	1027

Source: Kalin and Berry (1995), table 1.

Table 15.4   Self-identity (in per cent) by ethnic origin, inside and outside Québec (1991 survey)

Identity	Total	Ethnic origin		
		British	French	Other
Outside Québec				
Canadian/Canadien	76	82	65	70
Province	7	7	10	6
'Ethnic'	16	10	25	24
Inside Québec				
Canadian/Canadien	28	55	21	34
Province (Québécois)	49	26	59	30
'Ethnic'	23	19	20	36

differential pattern is similar when broken down by language of interview; however, in this case, a Provincial (Québécois) identity is claimed by only 7 per cent of those taking the interview in English in Québec, compared to 57 per cent of those taking the interview in French. This suggests that the 'Québécois' identity is strongly linked to French language preference, even more than to one's ethnic origin.

There appears to be no important variation in strength of identification as 'Canadian'/ 'Canadien' outside Québec (range 6.6 to 6.8 on a 7-point scale; see Table 15.5). However, respondents in Québec of French origin had a lower strength rating for this identity (4.9), combined with a higher strength rating for a 'Provincial' (that is, 'Québécois') identity (6.3). Those of British and Other origins had somewhat lower strengths of identity as Québécois (5.5 and 5.3).

Table 15.5   Mean strength of identification with three self-identities by region and ethnic origin (1991 survey)

Identity	Ethnic origin		
	British	French	Other
Outside Québec			
Canadian/Canadien	6.8	6.6	6.6
Province	5.0	5.0	5.1
'Ethnic'	3.7	4.4	4.2
Inside Québec			
Canadian/Canadien	6.1	4.9	5.7
Provincial (Québécois)	5.5	6.3	5.3
'Ethnic'	4.1	5.1	4.6

When these identities are related to the ethnic and multicultural attitudes within the three ethnic self-identity categories, some variations do appear (see table 6 in Kalin and Berry, 1995). For British-origin respondents, those with a 'Provincial' identity were lower than those with other identities on Tolerance (but not on Multicultural Ideology). The reverse was true for French-origin respondents, those with a 'Provincial' identity were lower than those with other identities on Multicultural Ideology (but not on Tolerance). As one might expect, among Other-origin Canadians, those with an 'Ethnic' identity were most supportive of a Multicultural Ideology, while those with a 'Provincial' Identity were least Tolerant. Most importantly, there is no evidence that those who identify as 'Canadian' are less supportive of diversity.

Canadianism

Mean scores on this scale were presented in Table 15.2 (and are shown in Figure 15.2) by ethnic origin and region. Unlike scores for Multicultural Ideology and Tolerance, scores on Canadianism vary significantly by ethnic origin and region, and in their interaction. All three features are evidently due to the lower score on the scale among French-origin respondents living in Québec (4.80). It is clear that a sense of attachment to Canada is lower among respondents in Québec, especially among those of French origin. When these scale scores are related to the three identity categories, a common and significant pattern appears in all three ethnic-origin groups: those with a 'Provincial' identity score lower on Canadianism, and (not surprisingly) those with a 'Canadian' identity score higher. And for British- and Other-origin groups, those with an 'Ethnic' identity do not score lower on the Canadianism scale, indicating that the 'hyphenated identity' is no threat to one's attachment to Canada.

Security

An attempt was made to assess respondents' 'confidence' or Security in order to evaluate the Multiculturalism Assumption. In the 1974 study, a two-item scale was employed, but only one item was retained in the 1991 survey: 'If more people from various backgrounds come to Canada, then Canadians (Québécois' for French language interviews in Québec) will lose their identity'. This item is considered to be an indicator of one's sense of security in the face of increased cultural diversity.

The means of security were presented in Table 15.2, broken down by ethnic origin and region (these means are presented in Figure 15.3). There is no effect of ethnic origin, but there is a regional effect, and an inter-action. Those living outside Québec feel more secure than those inside Québec; for the analysis by ethnic origin, those of French origin feel less secure (especially in Québec, according to the interaction); and for the

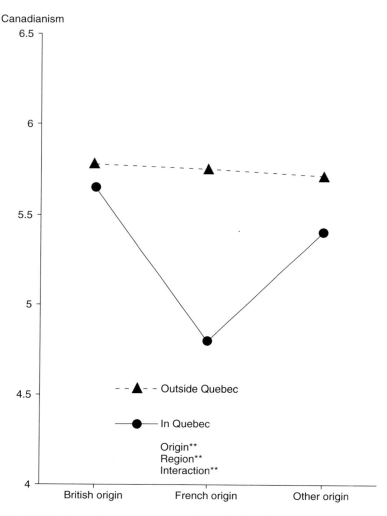

Figure 15.2   Distribution of mean scores on Canadianism, by ethnic origin and region of residence of respondents (1991 survey).

analysis by identity, those living in Québec and those with a Provincial identity (Québécois) feel less secure than others. When correlations are examined between individuals' scores on security, there is a clear pattern of support for the Multicultural Assumption: within all subsamples (that is, inside and outside Québec, broken down by ethnic origin and language of interview) there is a significant positive correlation between Security and scores on Multicultural Ideology and Tolerance. These coefficients range

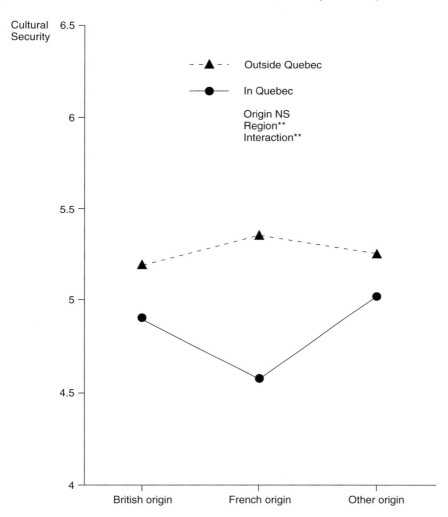

Figure 15.3   Distribution of mean scores on security, by ethnic origin and region of residence of respondents (1991 survey).

from .53 to .65 for those of British origin, .45 to .57 for those of French origin, and .45 to .49 for those of other origins.

Discussion and conclusions

In the case of Canadian multiculturalism, public policy appears to flow from the present day recognition that Canada was culturally plural from the outset, and is increasingly so. Despite initial (and some continuing) attempts at assimilation (mainly to British culture, often termed Angloconformity) public policy has now been brought into conformity with social and cultural reality. The policy recognizes and advocates the desirability of diversity. This policy response chosen by Canada is not inevitable, witness other culturally diverse societies' attempts to achieve cultural homogeneity (for example France, Germany) in the face of increasing diversity. It is to Canada's credit (and to those of other societies, such as Australia and Sweden) that such a match has been sought, and to some extent achieved.

Do one's ethnic origin and region matter when it comes to one's ethnic attitudes and identities? Clearly, the evidence presented here indicates that they do. However, the pattern is complex; simple assertions about the importance of one or another factor cannot be supported. For example, our findings do not indicate that being of French origin, or living in Québec (or the two combined) account for the pattern of differences in ethnic attitudes (see for example Richler, 1992; Sniderman *et al.*, 1993). Depending on which attitude is examined, it is sometimes one, or both, or their interaction that accounts for differences. However, there is a common theme: wherever there is relatively less support for multiculturalism, it is among those of French origin living in Québec; it is not among those of British or other ethnic origins living outside Québec.

Perhaps the most significant feature of the identity data is the 'redistribution' of identity among those of French origin between 1974 and 1991 (Table 15.3). While there was a slight increase in identity as 'Canadian' (from 26 per cent to 32 per cent) the major shift was a cross-over between 'Canadien-Français' (16 per cent) and a 'Provincial' identity (47 per cent) in 1991. When only Québec French respondents are considered, the Provincial (that is, 'Québécois') identity rises to 59 per cent. It is not known to what extent there is correspondence between those of French origin who identity as 'Québécois' and those who voted for separation in the 1995 referendum; however, the percentage so voting is almost exactly the same as those claiming a Québécois identity.

With respect to identity, the often repeated claim (for example Balthazar, 1995) that the Québécois identity is in essence a pluralistic 'civic' or 'territorial' identity, one not limited to a single (that is, French) origin, is not fully supported by our data (see Table 15.4). On the one hand, twice as many respondents in Québec of French origin claim a Québécois identity than those of British or other origins; on the other hand, those of other origins in Québec are about evenly divided between a Canadian, Québécois and an 'ethnic' identity. And when examined by language; only a handful (7 per cent) of those taking the interview in English profess to be Québécois (compared to 57 per cent of those interviewed in French). Hence, the 'Québécois' identity is primarily claimed by those of French origin and language preference. It is clear that the transition from an 'ethnic' to a 'civic' meaning of the Québécois identity has not been completed (as noted by Breton, 1988), and possibly is only just underway.

Beyond our own data, the general measures of tolerance and acceptance of others, and the attitudes toward specific groups found by Joly (1996) in a survey in Québec tend to support our conclusions. In the general measure of prejudice (made up of 35 attitude items), those of French mother tongue were more prejudiced than those of English or other mother tongues. And on the attitudes towards specific groups there is remarkable correspondence with our own findings. It is thus not possible to say that this pattern of attitudes derives from research carried out by unsympathetic (or even biased) researchers from Ontario(!), or that our data (1991) are out of date. As recently as a year ago, and in research carried out by the Government of Québec, our earlier results are supported.

What does this differential pattern of attitudes mean? As we noted earlier, 'region' is a convenient term to cover a host of interrelated and shared events and experiences inside and (to some extent) outside Québec. Similarly, 'ethnic origin' and 'mother tongue' are labels for a set of historical and contemporary social phenomena. When we use these categories, we are not dealing simply with a geographical space, or demographic descent line from some original settler group, but with a complex set of experiences that have come to define a people with a sense of themselves as a 'distinct society'.

In 1977, we proposed that the critical psychological variable needed to relate these experiences to this pattern of attitudes is rooted in the 'multiculturalism assumption', that is in one's sense of *cultural security*. This too is a complex, including a linguistic (and possibly some economic) component. The core idea, contained in the 1971 multiculturalism policy is that confidence is one's identity is the foundation for positive intergroup relations; threats and challenges, conversely, undermine this confidence (see also Berry, 1984; Kalin and Berry, 1994; Brown, 1995; Gudykunst and Bond, 1997).

While not including a full-scale assessment of such a sense of security in the present study, we were able to gain access to it through one survey question. The results reported in Table 15.2 (by ethnic origin and region) for this security measure clearly parallel this attitude pattern. And at the individual difference level, the security measure correlates significantly with the general attitudes (multicultural ideology and tolerance) inside and outside Québec, and in British-, French- and other-origin samples.

Turning to the relationship between public policy and individual behaviour, we have seen that program attitudes and perceived consequences of multiculturalism are generally positive; and, where it can be judged, there appears to be increasing acceptance. If multicultural ideology is also considered as a policy-related attitude, this claim for policy support is reinforced. Overall, in 1991 the percentage of the sample indicating support ranged between 69 and 94 per cent, depending on the scale, up from 64 per cent and 69 per cent in 1974. That these three scales can be considered together is indicated by their high mutual intercorrelations (ranging between .51 and .58 in 1974, and .55 and .66 in 1991; Berry and Kalin, 1995). Of course, there are some variations in these attitudes; and they appear to vary in a way that resembles ethnic attitudes and identities. One's ethnicity and region, probably rooted in one's sense of cultural security, may account for these variations.

What conditions will bring about the necessary sense of security for *all* groups in Canada that is necessary for a more positive intergroup climate? First, we have to stop threatening each other: some contemporary political rhetoric is clearly viewed as threatening by large numbers of people in Canada, both inside and outside Québec. Proposals to 'separate' from Canada by a proportion (approximately 50 per cent) of Québec residents is seen by them as exercising a democratic right, but is seen by others (both inside and outside Québec) as breaking up their country; and attempts to limit that democratic right (for example by seeking a supreme court ruling on the legality of separation) is seen as a threat to their freedom for self-determination. Conversely, the proposition that if Canada can be divided, so too can Québec (following separation), is viewed as a further threat by many (probably the vast majority of Québécois). These threats and counter threats clearly do not provide the sense of security that is a precondition for mutual tolerance. Undoubtedly, there are those on both sides of the issue who recognize this fact, and exploit such threats to create greater intolerance, which may well serve as a vehicle for achieving the goal of separation.

Second, given the results of analyses carried out by Kalin (1996) and Kalin and Berry (1982) on contact and ethnic attitudes, there is a need for improved vehicles for mutual familiarity, ones that are both voluntary and at equal status. In these analyses, there is evidence that for most groups in contact, there is a positive relationship between the percentage presence of specific ethnic groups in one's neighbourhood, and comfort levels with members of that group. This relationship held, not only for attitudes towards British and French, but also for many other groups (for example Italians, Germans, Portuguese and Arabs). However, no relationships were found with respect to comfort levels with Indo-Pakistanis, Chinese, West Indians and Native Indians). In keeping with these findings, Berry *et al.* (1977) found consistent positive relationships between ratings of familiarity with a particular ethnic group, and the overall evaluation of that group. Thus, there appears to be a consistent body of evidence in Canada to support the increased contact between groups as a way to enhance mutual acceptance. This conclusion clearly supports the 'social' (contact and sharing) emphasis in the policy.

These conditions require political action, but such political action is possible only when attitudes in the population are supportive. Our reading of the current survey data is that attitudes are (still) sufficiently positive to take such action. That British- and French-origin peoples serve as a positive reference group for each other is encouraging, and provides hope for peaceful relationships in the future, no matter what the political outcomes.

The policy of multiculturalism was intended to provide a sense of security for all cultural groups in Canada: in essence, it asserted that it is just fine to be culturally different, and sought to find ways to avoid such difference serving as a basis for exclusion. This view of the existence and likely persistence of social and cultural distinctiveness is a realistic one, that is well-founded in social psychological research (see for example Tajfel, 1978). Our reading of the various findings is that the policy is achieving its goals among the great majority of the Canadian population. Ironically, the largest single cultural group (French) may still feel relatively more threatened than more secure as a result of the policy and its various programs. However, mutual attitudes remain positive on average, and may yet be sufficient to hold the country together.

References

Almond, G. and S. Verba (1963) *The Civic Culture*, Princeton: Princeton University Press.

Balthazar, L. (1995) 'The Dynamics of Multi-ethnicity in French-speaking Québec: Towards a New Citizenship', *Nationalism and Ethnic Politics*, vol. 1, pp. 82–95.

Berry, J. W. (1984) 'Multiculturalism Policy in Canada: a Social Psychological Analysis', *Canadian Journal of Behavioural Science*, vol. 16, pp. 353–70.

Berry, J. W. and R. Kalin (1995) 'Multicultural and Ethnic Attitudes in Canada: an Overview of the 1991 National Survey', *Canadian Journal of Behavioural Science*, vol. 27, pp. 301–20.

Berry, J. W., R. Kalin and D. Taylor (1977) *Multiculturalism and Ethnic Attitudes in Canada*, Ottawa: Supply and Services Canada.

Bourhis, R. (1994) 'Ethnic and Language Attitudes in Québec', in J. W. Berry and J. Laponce (eds.), *Ethnicity and Culture in Canada: The Research Landscape*, Toronto: University of Toronto Press (pp. 322–60).

Breton, R. (1988) 'From Ethnic to Civic Nationalism: English Canada and Québec', *Ethnic and Racial Studies*, vol. 11, pp. 85–102.

Breton, R., W. Isajiw, W. Kalbach and J. Reitz (1990) *Ethnic Identity and Equality*, Toronto: University of Toronto Press.

Brown, R. J. (1995) *Prejudice: Its Social Psychology*, Oxford: Blackwell.

Government of Canada (1971) Statement to the House of Commons by Prime Minister P. E. Trudeau.

Gudykunst, W. and M. Bond (1997) 'Intergroup Relations Across Cultures', in J. W. Berry et al. (eds.), *Handbook of Cross-Cultural Psychology: Vol. 3, Social Behavior and Applications*, Boston: Allyn and Bacon (pp. 119–62).

Joly, J. (1996) *Sondage d'opinion publique québécoise sur l'immigration et les relations interculturelles*, Québec: Gouvernement du Québec (Ministère des Relations avec les citoyens et de l'immigration).

Kalin, R. (1996) 'Ethnic Attitudes as a Function of Ethnic Presence', *Canadian Journal of Behavioural Science*, vol. 28, pp. 171–9.

Kalin R. and J. W. Berry (1982) 'The Social Ecology of Ethnic Attitudes in Canada', *Canadian Journal of Behavioural Science*, vol. 14, pp. 97–109.

Kalin R. and J. W. Berry (1995) 'Ethnic and Civic Self-identity in Canada: Analyses of the 1974 and 1991 National Surveys', *Canadian Ethnic Studies*, vol. 27, pp. 1–15.

Kalin R. and J. W. Berry (1994) 'Ethnic and Multicultural Attitudes', in J. W. Berry and J. Laponce (ed.) *Ethnicity and Culture in Canada: The Research Landscape*, Toronto: University of Toronto Press (pp. 293–321).

Pineo, P. (1977) 'The Social Standing of Ethnic and Racial Groupings in Canada', *Canadian Review of Sociology and Anthropology*, vol. 14, pp. 147–57.

Richler, M. (1992) *Oh Canada! Oh Québec!*, Toronto: Penguin.

Sniderman, P., D. Northrup, J. Fletcher, P. Russell and P. Tetlock (1993) 'Psychological and Cultural Foundations of Prejudice: the Case of Anti-Semitism in Québec', *Canadian Review of Sociology and Anthropology*, vol. 30, pp. 242–70.

16
American Character and National Identity: The Dilemmas of Cultural Diversity

Stanley A. Renshon

'It is really potentially a great thing for America that we are becoming so multi-ethnic...But it's also potentially a powder keg of problems and heart break and division and loss. And how we handle it will determine, really, – that single question may be the biggest determination of what we look like fifty years from now and what the children of that age will have to look forward to.'

William J. Clinton, 11 April 1997[1]

'Can we define what it means to be an American, not just in terms of the hyphen showing our ethnic origins, but in terms of our primary allegiance to the values that America stands for and values we really live by?'

William J. Clinton, 14 June 1997[2]

Fueled in part by enormous, unprecedented numbers of new immigrants in this century, the United States is becoming dramatically more diverse – racially, ethnically and culturally. At the same time, the stability of American political and normative culture has been challenged in recent decades by an assertive expansion of individual and group rights, acerbic debates regarding the legitimacy and limits of these claims, and a preference on the part of national political leaders to finesse rather than engage these controversies. Freed by the end of the cold war from a need to focus on external enemies, the country appears at a crossroads.

Race relations have in many ways improved, yet paradoxically worsened. Immigrants are idealized by some, even as high levels of immigration are greeted with suspicion and apprehension by many others. Definitions of the family and relations between men and women, at home and in the workplace, have dramatically changed, but a question remains as to whether they have improved. In short, while America is undeniably more diverse than at any time in its history, Americans appear more fragmented, alienated and polarized. Advocates of diversity have given more attention to pressing and expanding their claims than to the psychological requirements necessary to build a consensus that would support and sustain them. Critics of diversity have yet to explain how to satisfactorily accommodate the reality of diversity and its opportunities, without recourse to traditional hegemony.

Moderating and working through the increasingly pointed demands of both groups is perhaps the fundamental domestic issue facing American society. Success is by no means assured. Divisive issues such as affirmative action, abortion rights, English as our primary language, homosexual marriage, the apparent conflict between merit and equality, and many more matters of heated contemporary debate raise important questions, political and psychological. They also raise profound questions of national psychology and identity. Is it inevitable that cultural, psychological and political diversity lead to a fragmented and thus dysfunctional national identity? Can it be avoided, and if so, how?

Some (Isbister, 1996, 1998; Maharidge, 1996), applaud these developments. They view the decline of key American cultural traditions, and especially its 'dominant elites', as a necessary step in developing a less 'hegemonic', more democratic society. Others (Schlesinger, 1992; Miller, 1998) are much less certain. They see an America whose central traditions, many of which in their view are critical to supporting a free democratic society, in danger of being lost – perhaps past the point of recovery. These two views frame a debate with the most profound consequences for the country. What does it mean to be an American? Given enormous diversity, what, if anything, binds us together as a country? What will happen to the psychological elements that have been essential to our country's history and development – a commitment to pragmatic excellence, achievement, mobility and the ambition that underlies them?

At the same time, these questions raise issues of substantial relevance for the culturally framed study of political psychology. What is culture, and its role in psychological and identity development? What is identity, and what, exactly, is the relationship between individual and national identity? Is there any relationship between national identity and national character? Is one more central to contemporary issues of diversity in America, or do both play important roles? These large questions cannot be wholly resolved here. However, we can hope to illuminate some of the conceptual issues involved and, as well, begin to build a framework through which we can clarify the psychological relationships between American national identity and psychology on one hand, and contemporary issues of diversity on the other. With that as a basis, it may be possible to discern whether the questions raised here at the outset are amenable to answers, and if so, what shape they might take.

The riddle of American psychology and identity

In 1783, the Frenchman Creveceour (1997, 43–44) famously asked, 'What, then, is the American, this new man?' His answer was that 'he is either a European, or a descendent of a European';[3] however, most of all he is, 'an American, who, leaving behind all his ancient prejudices and manners receives new ones from the new mode of life he has embraced, the new government he obeys, and the new rank that he holds.' The key to this transformation, Creveceour thought, was this 'new mode of life'. Where in Europe these families had no economic or social standing or hope to acquire it, here they did. *Ubi panis ibi patria*, he quotes as the motto of the new immigrants and sums up its transition thus: 'From involuntary idle-ness, servile dependence, penury, and useless labor, he has passed to toils of a very different nature, rewarded by ample subsistence – This is an American' ([1783] 1997, 44–45).

The key then to this 'new man', the American, was opportunity and mobility, both economic and political. Freed from the steel ceilings of social class and the accidents of heredity, this new man was able to pursue his labors and his destiny, on 'the basis of nature and *self interest*'. And, as he put it, 'can it want a stronger allurement?' ([1783] 1997, 44, emphasis in original). Creveceour's observations are notable for another, less remarked upon, reason. They anticipate by almost two hundred years Eric Erikson's psychocultural formulation of the intersection between identity and culture. 'No ego can develop outside of social processes which offer work-able prototypes and roles' (Erikson, 1963, 412). Or, as Hoover (1975, 122) put it in his examination of the implications of Erikson's theories for the politics of identity, 'culture largely determines the materials available for identity formation.'

Creveceour was not the only observer to draw an early link between a new American identity and the circumstances of a 'new mode of life'. In 1893, Frederick Jackson Turner asserted that the frontier was not only the engine of American social development, but of American character. Moreover, he saw it as, 'the line of most rapid and effective Americanization.' Why? Part of his answer lay in the 'perennial rebirth', 'fluidity', and 'opportunity' asso-ciated with it. But equally important, he argued, was the effect of this envir-onment on habits and patterns that the newly-arrived brought with them:

> The wilderness masters the colonist. It finds him a European in dress, industry, tools, modes of travel, and thought. It takes him from the railway car and puts him in the birch canoe. It stripes off the garments of civilization and arrays him in the hunting shirt and moccasin. It puts him in a long cabin of the Cherokee and Iroquois... Before long, he has gone to planting Indian corn and plowing with a sharp stick... In short, the frontier is at first too strong for the man. He must accept the conditions it

furnishes, or perish... Little by little he transforms the wilderness, but the outcome is not the old Europe... *The fact is that here is a new product that is American...*[4]

Appreciating the relationship between self and circumstance in the development of identity is helpful. However, it frames our focus without answering our questions. Consider: What is identity? The most famous and widely-employed theory, Erikson's (1968), tells us more about its development – his eight stages, than what it is. In one place (1968, 211) he defines ego identity as 'that which consists of role images'. Shortly thereafter, he defines self-identity as what 'emerges from experiences in which temporarily confused selves are successfully reintegrated into an ensemble of roles which also secure social recognition'. Elsewhere (1980, 160), he defines the term as, 'the more or less actually obtained, but forever to be revised, sense of the self within social reality'.

If this sounds somewhat vague, it is. Erikson himself recognized its ambiguity, commenting, 'I have tried out the term identity...in many different connotations...Identity in its vaguest sense suggests...much of what has been called the self by a variety of workers.' Hoover (1975, 116), Erikson's explicator, sums up identity as the sense of 'who we are which emerges from a mutual recognition of self and others'. This is fine as far as it goes, but the difficulty is that it doesn't go far enough. It provides no guidance, for example, in gauging the relative contributions of occupational, ethnic, racial, religious and national identities to the development and consolidation of a personal identity. Nor does it tell us very much about the process through which people balance, much less integrate, 'coherent individuation' and 'of being on the way to becoming what other people, at their kindest, take one to be' (Erikson, 1963, 35). Small wonder that Robert Coles has characterized the term as 'the purist of cliches'.[5]

Perhaps it is. Still, it is a concept with enormous psychological and political resonance worldwide. The aspiration to freely develop personal and national aspirations is not restricted to those who have been puzzled by Erikson.

In search of American national character and identity – three perspectives

Since its beginnings as a country, Americans (and those interested in them) have made a virtual cottage industry of trying to understand themselves (Wilkinson, 1988, 1). He (1988, 9–12) identifies two reasons for this.[6] One he calls 'psychology writ large', the other American intellectualism. The first is a reflection of the fact that as a large robust country, America produces more of everything, including analyses of itself. The second, and in my view more useful framing of the possible reasons for such interest, lie in the nature of the country. He argues that, it reflects a need for Americans to master, at least cognitively, the political and social anxieties generated by a diverse, dynamic country whose people, culture and experiences defy neat categories. As a result, in the two centuries since Creveceour first asked his famous question, there have been no shortage of answers. Foreign visitors,[7] anthropologists (Mead, 1943; Gorer, 1948; Hsu, 1972), psychologists (Wachtel, 1983), social writers/commentators (Whyte, 1963; Lerner, 1957), historians (Commager, 1959; Potter, 1954), sociologists (Lipset, 1963; Inkeles, 1997a,b),[8] and psychoanalysts (Erikson, 1964)[9] have all provided perspectives on what this new man is, the American.

The answers to his question, not surprisingly, have been diverse; as have the methods used to obtain them. Why expect that the distinctive backgrounds, intellectual and experiential, that distinguish, say, a de Tocqueville from an Erikson, or a Creveceour from a Lipset, might result in an identitical core list of what it means to be an American. Moreover, there is no theoretical reason to expect that the core elements of what it means to be an American would remain static through the enormous and profound changes that have shaped this country during its two hundred plus years of experience. Indeed, if one is persuaded by the basic insight of the culture and personality school, (see Chapter 1 and the analysis that follows here on pp. 292–5), the opposite is more theoretically accurate (cf., Potter, 1954, 62–3). Does an examination of American history suggest that some elements of national psychology or identity have endured? Are they reconcognized by scholars of diverse perspectives, thus adding to our confidence in their existence and possible relevance?[10] In a word, yes. And, they provide a point of departure for addressing the critical questions already raised about their contemporary viability and future usefulness[11] as a basis for organizing a diverse society.

American character traits

Before examining what, if anything, lies at core of the multiple and changing views of what it means to be an American it is well to draw some basic distinctions. The first are among terms which are often used as if they were, but are not, synonymous; sometimes in the same book. So, for example, Wilkinson's (1988) book is titled, *The Pursuit of American Character*, but one soon encounters the following (p. 3): 'By "social character" or 'American social character" [these two terms apparently being interchangeable and synonymous with the plain old *American Character* of the title], I mean those traits of individual personality or attitude that the population shows more frequently or in different ways than other, compared populations do.'

Numerous questions immediately arise. Why is social used as an adjective to modify character? Is not character a term with an intrapsychic referent? And, if that is true, isn't social character unconnected to 'private' (internal) character elements an oxymoron? Are 'traits of personality', and 'traits of attitude' equivalent, and are either or both synonymous with character? They are not so considered in the psychology literature.[12] Many searches for American 'character, social or otherwise, have borrowed the term, but not the theoretical foundations that support and ought to accompany it. A trait is simply a personal(ity) element that is sufficiently anchored in an individual's psychology, through rewarded function and experience, to become a characteristic response to diverse circumstances. Assuming it is present, it ordinarily tells us something, but not much. Indeed, torn from its cultural and psychological contexts, a single trait tells us very little.

That is one reason the trait approach to national character has a long but troubled history. At one time, Bulgarians were noted for their 'plodding endurance and taciturn energy', Italians for their 'aesthetic aptitude', and Serbs for their 'warm poetic temperament' (sic).[13] Even if it were true, would it tell us very much? Not really, unless we were willing to make the implausible assumption that everything of importance about a particular national psychology could be summed up in one trait. Moreover, as Potter (1954, 12) points out, trait theorists sometimes confound categories. Americans are thought to be optimistic (a trait of temperament), productive (a trait of character or behavior?), and prone to joining organized groups (a behavioral tendency derived presumably from an underlying psychological trait).[14] Wilkinson (1988, 71–4) finds the content of American character in its fears, not its traits. In the tension between individualism and community (see also Lipset, 1954, 101–39), he posits four historically persistent and not always conscious concerns that define American character: of dependency, of selfishness, of social and personal entropy, and the falling away from past virtue and promise.

However national character traits are defined, their use presumes their presence. How are we to tell if 'American traits', however defined, show up 'more frequently or in different ways than other compared populations do'.[15] Consider the American emphasis on achievement that observers as historically and professionally diverse as de Tocqueville, Mead, Gorer, Lipset and McCleland have emphasized. Would the overall level of, or focus on, achievement in this country, assuming we had valid measures of these items, be significantly higher than in, say, Japan, Hong Kong or Germany? Assuming valid translation of the term for crosscultural comparability, would it even be higher than those 'less developed' countries where life is hard, and making ends meet is a full-time concern? It seems unlikely.

There is finally, the confusion that can easily develop between a national character trait(s) and its possible origins in, or association with, other categorical groupings organized along political, ethnic, religious or class lines. For example Americans, Potter (1954, 18) notes, 'are said to be competitive, materialistic, and comfort loving'. But aren't these also the characteristics of the American middle class, proportionally one of the largest in the world? So, is nation being confounded with class, or is the former legitimately considered a reflection writ large of the latter?

American character: creed and values

Many lists of American traits are really descriptions of the values or beliefs by which Americans do, or aspire to, live. Such elements are not merely abstract embodiments of national ideals, although they certain are that to some extent. Rather, they serve as a moral and behavioral compass which helps to organize the energies of individuals. They operate also as principles that can, and are, invoked by organizations and institutions waging political and social struggles on behalf of often divergent understandings of the benefits or accommodations which individuals or groups have a 'right' to expect.

The fact that neither always abide by them or that some are not even capable of doing so, does not lessen their power. Gunnar Myrdal (1964 [1944]) commenting on American race relations underscored the discrepancy between the American creed – a commitment to equality – and the actual conditions of Americans of African descent in the country. He pinned his hopes for the future on the inability of Americans to continue to tolerate these discrepancies. So did leaders of the civil-rights movement. When movement leaders chose to march in Bull Conner's racist town, they counted on his harsh response and larger American discomfort at seeing any group of peaceful demonstrators attacked by dogs and high-pressure water hoses (Heifetz, 1996). And, they were proved correct in doing so.

There is another, less-appreciated way in which values and the ideals they incorporate influence the interplay between American culture and psychology. Their internalization, by individuals, groups and institutions have consequences. As will become clearer in the following section families, and that means here parents, who internalize the American values of achievement in relation to mobility, shape their childrens' experiences (and thus their psychologies) in ways consistent with their understanding of how best to achieve and actualize those values. To the extent that children of parents with those commitments share them, their psychologies are shaped by their own choices in pursuit of these values as well. Of the many accessible developmental paths in societies in which wide choice is available and valued, the internalization of values provide direction, and limits. The pursuit of values, therefore, is an engine of motivation that orients individuals and groups toward a particular set of experiences. And, in doing so, it facilitates the development of particular patterns of interior psychology.

A number of these same values and ideals have repeatedly been noted over time. Creveceour noted the fundamentally liberating role of opportunity on ambition. One hundred and forty-five years later the psychoanalyst

Karen Horney (1938) made that fact the center of her analysis of the 'neurotic personality of our time'.[16] In 1893, Fredrick Jackson Turner noted our pragmatism and self-reliance, required values for frontier living. Seventy-nine years later the psychological anthropologist Francis L. K. Hsu wrote (1972, 248, italics in original):

> What we need to see is that the contradictory American 'values' noted by sociologists, psychologists and historians are but manifestations of one core value. The American core value in question is *self-*reliance...

In 1848, de Tocqueville pointed out the volatile mix of private acquisitiveness and public egalitarianism.[17] One hundred and six years later, Lipset (1954, 110–22) was arguing that, far from having changed toward 'other-directedness' as Riesman (1950) had suggested, Americans were still trying to reconcile achievement and equality on one hand, and conformity and individualism on the other. It would be an unusual analysis of American values, in any period, that did not include or allude to those just noted. However, many such lists aspired to comprehensiveness and, as a consequence, produced mixed results. Thus Coleman's (1940, 498) early list of 'American traits' included a belief and faith in democracy, equality, freedom, associational activity, individual freedom, disregard of law-direct action, local government, practicality, prosperity, puritanism, religion and conformity. Hsu (1972, 242) notes the list is contradictory (democracy and disregard of law?), and no attempt is made to reconcile apparent contradictory values (for example, equality and freedom). To this one might add the question of why 'local government', to name just one oddity in the list, appears to carry the same weight as democracy and equality. Some years later Cuber and Harper (1948, 369) shortened that list but added their own curious values to the first rank (for example, monogamous marriage and science).

None of these lists attempted to weigh the relative significance of the items included. Those that did (Williams, 1951, 441) distinguished different kinds, or levels, of value orientations.[18] However, aside from providing a range of value categories into which every conceivable aspect of a culture might be placed, even these hierarchical lists provide little help in determining which are more central and which more peripheral to a culture. Nor do they provide any theoretical guidance of how, if at all, the different value categories are related to each other, or what relationship, if any, they have to 'American psychology'. So, in the end, lists of 'American values' may be just that, and not theories of either American identity or psychology.

Psychocultural perspective on American national character

The observations of early visitors and observers were not informed by any theoretical understanding of either character or culture. Those did not become available until the development of the 'culture and personality' school, and its legacy – national character studies (see Chapter 1). The key insight of this school was the interrelationship of the social values that characterized a culture, the reflection of these values in culture's primary institutions, and the net effect of both on the psychology and development of those who grew up within its confines. For Mead (1942; see also Gorer, 1948) a major key to understanding American character was in its emphasis on success – a double reflection on mobility. Americans could, were expected to, and expected themselves to, make every effort to take advantage of the opportunities enshrined as cultural ideals and which for many, though not all, were actual fact. Success was measured by mobility – the distance between start and finish, or, in a word, achievement.

Following Freud, 'culture and personality' theorists saw the family as the primary institution of American cultural and psychological preparation. It both prepared children for the culture into which they were born and, in doing so, reflected in themselves the internalization of the culture's predominant values. Unfortunately, American culture provides no specific formulas as to how this might be accomplished other than general admonitions to work hard, do your best, and so on. So, mobility has been, and remains, infused with anxiety (the exact point made by de Tocqueville 89 years earlier). This leads, according to Horney (1937, 14–33), to 'compulsive competitiveness', and its emotional siblings, interpersonal aggressiveness and hostility. At the same time, the competitive life is a lonely one. Intimacy and competition are difficult to reconcile, a point also made by de Tocqueville 89 years earlier. Horney notes that competition and conflict are accompanied by fear – of failure and of others. These fears weaken self-esteem and, as a result, the 'neurotic' craves love.

These patterns are fueled, in part, by parents' concerns for their children's success. As a result, parents tend to reward their children's performance, not their existence. Given these circumstances, it is difficult for children to develop an inner anchor for their own self-identities. Rather they are oriented in substantial part towards others – their parents, their peers or their teachers – who provide them with conditional cues of their success. In short, as more than a decade before David Riesman brought the phrase 'other-directed' into our analytic vocabularies, anthropologists (Mead)[19] and psychoanalysts (Horney) belonging to the 'culture and personality' school observed and documented the same feature in the unfolding circumstances of the interplay between American culture and psychology. Whether this reflected a turn from individualism, or one further reflection of it, is a key question which I will take up on the following section.

One of the key insights of early visitors to America was the extent to which the physical and psychological circumstances in which settlers found themselves shaped responses that were necessary for success. These, in turn, were instrumental in shaping the development of a particular American psychology. That interplay between external circumstances and the development and maintenance of patterns of interior psychology was, as noted, a foundation of the 'culture and personality' school. So, the question naturally arises: If circumstances change, will patterns of American psychology do so as well? The social scientist most associated with the affirmative answer to this profound question is Riesman (with N. Glazer and R. Denny 1950, with N. Glazer, 1951; see also Whyte, 1956). Yet, as noted above, Mead and Horney had laid the theoretical basis for expecting some conformity in American psychology two decades earlier.[20] Moreover, that tendency was in fact part of early observations of this country and its people. Bryce (1912, quoted in Almond, 1960, 35–6, italics mine) observing the power of 'majority opinion' wrote that

> absolute, unquestioned and invoked to decide every question...Out of the dogma that the views of the majority must prevail...grows up another...that the majority is always right... *Thus, out of mingled feelings that the multitude, because it will prevail, must be right, there grows a self-distrust...a disposition to fall into line, to acquiesce in the dominant opinion, to submit thought as well as action to encompassing powers of the numbers.*

It is often not appreciated that Riesman's 'other-directed' and 'inner directed' are two of three forms of *conformity*. In Riesman's theory, the 'inner-directed' person has simply internalized general social precepts in a society in which population and economic changes have made learning detailed social customs ('tradition directed' psychologies) too complex and cumbersome to individually teach and maintain. Such persons, of course, stand against elements of the community, but the point was that he wasn't often required to do so. Internalizing the generalized standards of a community worked well, but only if those standards were relatively stable. If not, the skill most needed, and rewarded, was the ability to ascertain just what standards were expected, and adapt accordingly. Riesman's postwar America was a society characterized by large-scale social and economic changes. It was also one in which these changes coincided with the development of large-scale social institutions in which efficient performance depended on teamwork. In such circumstances, being 'other-directed' was an economic asset, as well as a socially-valued skill and personality trait.

It is not as great a psychological distance, as it might seem at first, from Riesman's other-directed character to Lasch's (1979) culture of narcissism. In Riesman's 'other-directed' character the extensive veneer of sociability became a well-refined tool for 'making it'. Achievement was still paramount, and competition continues unabated, but now success is achieved in group settings by fitting in, not by self-reliance. Autonomous thinking, or an independent sense of personal values and ideals to which one is able and willing to give primacy, or at least fidelity, generally a minority position historically, becomes a cause for others' concern, not admiration. Small wonder that Arthur Miller's Willy Loman proved a more accurate fictional representative of his time than Ayn Rand's Ned Roark.

The lack of any firmly-established internal psychological compass makes people vulnerable to the temptations of increasing abundance and repeated messages that delayed consumption is unnecessary and perhaps even odd. In the past, Lasch noted, the American penchant for self-improvement had been associated with achieving something solid and lasting. However, in an age which promised 'you could have it all', or advised you to 'be all that you can be', and with some professional psychologists touting 'self-actualization' as the north star of psychological development, enticing images of endless and easy satisfaction trumped the hard work of building a satisfying life.[21] Consumption might well fuel an economy, but an increasing emphasis on 'self-fulfillment'[22] did not quiet increasing feelings of emptiness, isolation, and dissatisfaction.

Lasch, writing in the aftermath of the 'me' and 'now' generations,[23] viewed American private and public life as increasingly dominated by ambitiously aggressive and self-centered individuals, in what one might characterize as a culture of selfish individualism. Riesman (1980) agreed, and while finding evidence of narcissistic elements elsewhere in American history, nonetheless thought that what was different now was the public acceptance and even 'approval' of clearly 'self-serving conduct'. It is not so far from Riesman's 1980 observation to the extraordinarily high approval ratings, primarily related to a booming economy, of an impeached and disgraced president.[24]

American identity and psychology: a psychocultural amalgam

We are now in a better position to take up the questions with which we began this essay. Let us begin with the question of national identity. One concern growing out of issues of diversity is whether the concept of assimilation has been damaged as an ideal and practice with a corresponding loss in the sense of a national American identity (Glazer, 1993). This is no idle question when the latest census figures show that the number of immigrants living in the United States has almost tripled since 1970, rising from 9.6 million to 26.3 million today and far outpacing the growth of the native-born population (Escobar, 1999). Yet, in spite of its centrality, that question is in some respects, peripheral to an even more fundamental question: Just what is the nature of the culture to which we want immigrants to assimilate? Salins (1997, 2–8) has argued the matter would be resolved if immigrants would just continue to learn English, abide by the work ethic, and take pride in American identity, believing in America's liberal democratic and egalitarian principles.

If only it was that simple. Rumbaut (1997, 937–8) reports the results of a large multiyear survey of 80000 students in the San Diego Unified School district. He reports that on a number of measures, 'there is a negative association between length of time of residence in the U.S. and second generation [immigrant] status with both GPA [Grade Point Average] and educational aspirations.' Some insight into how this happens is made clearer by looking at the number of hours viewing tv. In multivariate analysis, it is the single best predictor of GPA (less of the former translates to more [higher] of the latter). No doubt more television watching is not what advocates of assimilation have in mind, but it is an aspect of what is happening. Portes and Zhou (1994, 20–1, 26–7) report that among Haitians in Florida and Hispanics in a Californian community, physical proximity to cultural and political 'adversarial groups' often resulted in immigrant children dropping their educational aspirations in order not to appear to be 'acting white'.

Nor is 'pride in American identity', even if it includes beliefs in democracy and equality, of much use as a criterion unless one knows just what that means. True, Lipset is right when he calls attention to the historical persistence of these ideals. However, Riesman and Lasch are also correct in pointing out that the old ideals have changed. How can both be right?

A basic flaw of the values ideals approach to American national identity is not that values don't carry much actual behavioral or psychological weight. They do. However, most advocates of this approach have never really addressed the issue of how the highly abstract ideals they find embedded in American history and culture actually serve as a framework for psychological development and behavior at the level of the actual lives that people lead. Some theorists of American values discuss them as if they were independent and unitary – the ideal of democracy, the ideal of equality, and so on. Others, have focused on conflict between values, a commitment to achievement for example, being at odds with a commitment to equality. However, it seems more useful to focus on *clusters* of national ideas if, as in the United States, this focus can be substantively supported. Viewed not as discrete isolated entities, but as integrated cultural packages, it would then be easy to distinguish one national cultural cluster 'package' from another. It would also be easier to understand how such packages can both remain constant and change. And, finally, it would be possible to more easily discern how a particular national psychology or 'character' might develop in relation to a particular 'package' of national ideals.

National cultural clusters

What then is a *National Cultural Cluster*? It is quite simply a specific set of a country's core cultural value ideals. The origins of American national culture clusters can be traced to the twin motivations behind the establishment of the first colonies, economic and social *opportunity* on the one hand, and religious and political *freedom* on the other. Yet, while it is accurate to single out these values as primary motives, it would be an error to view them as isolated and discrete ends in themselves.

Freedom and opportunity came together in a particular way in the religious colonies, but in quite another in those searching for economic advancement, not religious freedom. Moreover, in neither was freedom or opportunity an isolated, absolute value. In case of religious freedom it was embedded in a community context, and in the case of economic opportunity it coexisted with a strong belief in public social and political equality. In short, both freedoms (economic and political) were embedded in communities. Both religious and economically-based freedom seekers confronted the issue finding ways to live with others whose interests and motivations differed.

The third major value ideal that defines the American culture cluster grew out of the circumstances in which the other two were played out – a land rich in promise but short, at first, in the ordinary and routine. The physical realities of frontier conditions required a psychology of courage, independence and self-reliance from those living there. However, these people were not hermits. After all, Natty Bumpo (Hawk-eye) had Uncas and his father Chingachgook, and even that image icon of righteous individualism, the Lone Ranger had Tonto. Here we can see the third major continuum of the set that forms the American Culture Cluster – that of *independence/self-reliance* and *interdependence*. So, we can now distinguish the following three core elements of the American culture cluster:

- freedom for self-ambition ↔ communities of others
- achievement-excellence ↔ social/political equality
- independence/self-reliance ↔ dependency

National culture clusters, then, are defined by the unique composite of specific value ideals central to a society, the relationship of these cluster elements to each other, and the range and specific location on each of the core value-ideal continuums. No society has a monopoly on any particular ideal or value. For example, most societies must grapple with the dilemmas of interpersonal dependence and independence. However, a society which prizes independence and couples that with an emphasis on personal and political freedom will develop quite differently than one in which community is given precedence over both.

American culture clusters and national psychology – the role of culture codes

National culture clusters tell us what a society says it values. Yet cultures serious about what they value embed them in their institutions and practices. Their political, educational and family institutions are charged with the responsibility of translating these abstract precepts – equality, freedom, and so on – into rules and understandings which can serve as a reliable guide to living in that society. Put another way, every culture must provide mechanisms for translating its ideals into real life. The understandings of how to translate these abstractions into concrete life-rules, I term *culture codes*. These codes tell a culture's members how to bridge the gap between ideals and practice. They are not 'scripts', which reflect more precise rules of behavior and sequence. Rather, they are embodied, not always formally, in a culture's institutions. And, they are also embedded in a culture's 'folk knowledge' or cultural narratives – a term which covers stories constructed for a culture's purpose.

Consider the continuum of achievement/excellence ⟷ social/political equality. How can a society honor both excellence in achievement and equality? Equality of opportunity is one answer, separating the sphere of achievement from the sphere equality expected in normal social discourse is another. But cultural codes tell us more than how to understand, and resolve, the dilemmas that might appear in a culture's organizing ideals. They also provide culture's proscriptions for how to achieve its goals. Want to succeed? Put your shoulder to the wheel, or your nose to the grindstone. However, if at first you don't succeed, try, try again. And remember, the early bird gets the worm.

It is, I think, easily seen that changes in the national core cultural values are not likely to take place at the level of the elements themselves. Thus, in this respect Lipset is correct. However, change, sometimes profound change, can and does occur at the level of cultural codes that guide practice and institutions. Riesman and Lasch are correct as well. It is also quite clear that national core culture values and codes both reflect and facilitate patterns of national psychology. Consider just one of a highly complex set of relations among the core American culture elements and historical changes in their related cultural codes. As noted, early observers were united in the observation that 'this new man', the American, was motivated by the desire to do what had not been possible in his country of origin. That was to make use of talents in the service of ambitions to improve the material (and social) circumstances of life.

A primary goal of achievement was to acquire wealth, and the social and political freedom to do so was what made it possible. But, at the same time, no man was deemed better than any other – the ethic of 'democratic egalitarianism' (Lipset, 1954, 123). And, there was no real standard of achievement's success, but wealth. In those circumstances, opportunity was bound to lead to competition and anxiety, as both de Tocqueville and Horney emphasized. Lipset (1954, 113) argues that there is ample historical evidence of 'other-directedness' which, following the lead of then contemporary commentators, he attributes to the lack of a formal American class structure. According to this theory, having no agreed upon standards by which to judge their place, Americans were forever turning their attention outward. In short, their status anxiety made them anxious and 'other directed'.

However, the observations of observers is not by itself direct evidence that status insecurity is at the root of whatever turn toward others might be evident. While status anxiety *might* lead to conformity, it can as easily lead to its opposite. Acute status anxiety coupled with intense competition for both success *and* status might lead one to try to distinguish oneself from others, not be part of the group. Or, we might ask why men used to making their own way, by their own means, might wish to be accepted by others with whom they might well be in competition, at any price. Moreover, there remains the problem why in a country devoid of widely accepted status symbols, except for wealth and its display, wealth itself did not qualify as more than enough indication that one had succeeded. It certainly must have for those who subscribed to the Protestant ethic.

The choice of course is not between material and structure changes in the circumstances of competition as Riesman argued, or the unchanging conflict between equality and achievement and the resulting conformity that Lipset emphasizes. Even assuming the causal link which Lipset argues between value conflict and conformity, there is no reason why changes in 'material' circumstances wouldn't bring a corresponding change in the nature of the relation among the three. It represents a real change of psychological circumstances when increasing financial security and the mass production of an increasingly large number of symbols of success become more widely available though most strata of American society. How do you tell where you stand in Levitttown? You keep up with the Jones', but you don't want to stand out or stand apart.

On the other hand, the achievement ethic of the 1960s was quite different. 'Tune in, turn on, drop out' is an invitation to withdraw from traditional cultural codes surrounding achievement. From that vantage point, achievement is certainly not measured by the accumulation of wealth, but of inner 'peace' and understanding. The realization of one's own unique internal blueprint is the goal and self-enlightenment is the means. Conformity to 'conventional' values or views is seen as absolutely antithetical to achieving self-realization. Cole Porter's signature composition, 'Anything Goes', seems an apt theme song for a cultural movement in which 'do your own thing', and 'let it all hang out' are taken as essential cultural cues.

Finally, surveying Americans at a time of economic insecurity, Yankelovich (1981, 163–218) found us increasingly turning away from fusion of relentless ambition for mobility and the work ethic that had been part of American culture for centuries.[25] Following the lead of de Tocqueville, Turner, Erikson and Riesman he finds cultural values responsive to structural circumstance. He (1981, xviii–xix) views the turn inward as a response to diminished economic opportunities and expectations yet he

also sees in it a new effort to resolve the dilemmas raised by a firm commitment to ambitious self-advancement in a context of stagnant mobility. In
these circumstances, the 'rat race' seems less attractive than the ambiguous,
but still ambitious phase, 'self-fulfillment'.

Paradoxically and 'emphatically', Yankelovich (1981, xviii) does not see
self-fulfillment as the middle classes' version of counter-cultural narcissism.
Although, he does note that in its more extreme forms, 'the new rules
simply turn the old ones on their head, and in place of the old self-denial
ethic [delay of gratification], we find people who refuse to deny anything
to themselves-not out of bottomless appetite, but on the strange moral
principle that "I have a duty to myself"'.

How are the duties to oneself reconciled, if they are, with the traditional
American commitment to community and interpersonal ideals and values?
Easily. Self-fulfillment, being an entirely personal matter, requires those
who pursue it to simply adapt the cultural code: 'Live and let live.' Or as
Yankelovich (1981, 88) notes,

> Traditional concepts of right and wrong have been replaced by norms of
> 'harmful,' or 'harmless', If one's action are not seen as penalizing others,
> even if they are 'wrong' from the perspective of traditional morality,
> they no longer meet much opposition.

Unlike, the 1960s in which 'counterculture' adherents dismissed 'traditional' values as bourgeois and confining, the new ethic is summed up by
what has become almost an eleventh commandment, 'Thou shall not
judge.' The 'non-judgmentalism of middle class Americans' in matters of
religion, family and other personal values emerges as the major finding of
Wolfe's (1998) in-depth interviews with Americans across the country. He
attributes it to an emphasis on pragmatism rather than values in making
tough personal decisions, a reluctance to second guess the tough choices of
other people, and ambivalence or confusion as the 'default' position moral
position.[26]

Needless to say, a strong ethic of self-fulfillment coupled with the view
that whatever I or anyone else does, which doesn't directly harm anyone
else, is alright 'often collides violently with traditional rules, creating a
national battle of cultural norms' (Yankelovich, 1981, 5). Almost two
decades later, it is clearer that America's cultural wars are indeed that, but
also so much more.

One, or more, American cultures and psychology?

America's basic cultural ideals and values, like those of any country, are
embedded and embodied in institutional norms and practices. Institutions
primarily led, made up of, or responsive to individuals with 'counter-

cultural,' or 'self-fulfillment' ideals and values will operate very differently than those with a more traditional focus. Moreover, they also operate very differently than those with a *unified* set of value missions and practices. Here is the core dilemma of Western democratic multicultural societies. They got to their present state of political, economic and social development by providing abundant opportunities for mobility. They leveraged personal ambitions as a tool to transform individuals' social and economic circumstances, and in the process they helped develop and reinforce psychological elements which were consistent with what most considered 'success'. They were an emphasis on consistency, hard work, delay of immediate gratification, and considering the consequences of one's actions or inactions.

These are, of course, the characteristics of the 'Protestant ethic'. However, over time, this ethic became divorced from its religious origins. Successive waves of immigrants – Irish, Hispanic, Asian – not all of them Protestant by any means, found a place by accepting and building on what then truly became a national American cultural element. In fostering these values in the home, at school and in occupational networks such groups not only reinforced this 'traditional' American cultural element, and the codes that supported it, but furthered the psychology that sustained it. It is in this direct way that National cultural cluster elements and national psychology are related.

Five contemporary American cultural clusters and their associated psychologies

It seems quite clear that almost all the elements of the American cultural cluster have been altered by challenges to the understandings of what these terms mean, how they are to be accomplished, and how much weight is to be given to one or another element. Freedom for self-interest, for example, which traditionally had to be reconciled with the values of community, must do so to a substantially smaller degree when the most weight is accorded to 'doing your own thing'. Independence and the tendency to stand apart from others has traditionally had to be reconciled with the pleasures of attachment, and hence the possibility of conformity. However, independence and self-reliance rest on a strong sense of personal identity and confidence in the personal skills that support them. Therefore, when occupational identity trumps its intra-psychic foundation, and success in the former rests on 'good interpersonal skills', individuals are more vulnerable to the evaluations and value views of others. And, of course, the view that getting all that you want, when you want it, is the definition of a fully-realized life, leaves little room to worry about others except as they further or impede your desires.

Finally, these changes can be seen in the cultural ideal of achievement and the cultural code of excellence and persistent hard work to refine it.

Traditionally, this ideal had to be reconciled with the value of social and political equality. As noted, this tension was addressed by making achievement and the assumption of equality somewhat independent of each other. One did not need to achieve in order to be accounted public equality. Nor did public equality require fast runners to race slowly, or smart businessmen to lose money.

De Tocqueville and others worried that the tendency to value equality over excellence would lead to mediocrity. Some modern critics equate any focus on excellence with 'elitism', however, in truth, as Lipset (1963) points out, there has always been a tension between those willing and able to reach excellence and high achievement in their pursuits and the push to make every one equal. Contemporary resolution of these issues has become more complex and conflictual in a society in which 'live and let live' and 'Thou shalt not judge' vie for primacy in the cultural code. If every life-style has equal value and weight, how can we not accord parity to any person of group's choices? If 'self-fulfillment' is the goal of achievement, of what use are traditional concerns with, and measurement of, excellence? And on what basis do we deny anyone the fruits of social equality when they fail to measure up to constructed, and thus 'artificial', standards. Questions like these lead to the paradox of 'social promotion' policies in many major American school systems which pass children onto the next grade who cannot read, write or do math at anywhere near their grade level. At the same time, presidents assert that we must do everything possible to insure that American children receive educations second to none.

If every disparity between individuals or groups is suspect, how can we object to decades of government-sponsored programs which reward group membership as much or more than performance? If the full weight of vast federal, state and local resources is placed behind mandated results rather than developing opportunity, isn't that just a new and more democratic definition of opportunity? These and thousands of similar questions are at the heart of America's culture wars. However, that war is not solely a fight between 'left' and 'right', or 'liberals' and 'conservatives'. As our analysis suggests, there are at least five different groups in American society which are united or separated by their understanding of the relative weight to be given to each of the elements in the American cultural cluster and to their accompanying cultural codes:

- There are *traditional achievers* whose cultural value views would be roughly consistent with an emphasis on freedom defined as self-interest in the pursuit of excellence and achievement. As a group they are highly competitive, supportive of traditional culture codes that define ambition and success, and able to join up with others in pursuit of their social, economic and political self-interest.

- *Conforming achievers* are those with some commitment to traditional norms of accomplishment, but who see the vehicle of their success as their skills with others. Not likely to value standing out or standing alone, their motto for achievement (to get along, go along) parallels their stance toward contentious cultural issues (live and let live,)
- *Self-fulfillment achievers* value accomplishment in principle, but only if it directly and immediately provides tangible personal benefit. Whether that comes in the form of self-enlightenment or self-aggrandizement, the motives are similar. In terms of contentious political or social issues, they are either tolerant or contemptuous. The first often reflects the wish to be left alone to pursue their own interests without having to make judgments which might lead others to judge them ('judge not least ye be judged'). The second comes from a supreme confidence in one's own views and values and a corresponding downgrading of those who don't agree.
- *Cultural dissenters* may be either high or low achievers. They are found in the highest levels of some professions as well as at the bottom of the social ladder. These seemingly disparate groups are united by the view that current cultural values and codes must be substantially modified, if not replaced. The more cerebral of them are convinced that freedom for self-interest is antithetical to community, excellence in achievement subversive of equality, and independent self-reliance a mask for selfishness. The less intellectually-inclined simply have no patience, aptitude or hope to succeed as this culture has traditionally been structured, but want the enjoyment of its benefits nonetheless. They have strong convictions about all these matters. Paradoxically, while very tolerant of claims for parity and even primacy of many counter-culture initiatives, this cultural flexibility, like that of some self-fulfillment achievers, is not easily extended to those with whom they disagree.
- Finally, there are the *principled individualists*. It is made up of people with a commitment to pursuing excellence in their achievements but within a context of understanding that others and community count. They are capable of being self-reliant, but can as easily be comfortable with attachment and commitment, though on their own terms. They can stand apart from others if they have to, move against them if they must, and so are not overly reliant on, or separate from, others. In matters of judgment they come to their own views and are willing to stand on them, even if it means standing out or standing apart. They are probably, the smallest American cultural group.

American culture and psychology: fragmentation or a new synthesis?

Space precludes a detailed consideration of the ways in which each of these five groups approach the major cultural and social issues noted at the start of this chapter. However, the basic nature of the dilemma of diversity should be quite clear. American multicultural democracy is that it is populated by groups with very different understandings (codes) of the major values that have historically served to integrate divergent ethnic groups. What is different now is the existence and institutionalization of organizations which are culturally 'oppositional', as well as the placement of 'cultural dissidents' in major leadership roles in what have formerly been 'traditional' institutions.

Therefore, institutions are not only the targets of different views of how America should culturally proceed, they are also a source of the very same tensions. It means that the country is split not only by political, but more basically by cultural and psychological cleavages. These are related to, but not wholly congruent with, generational sources of value change.

'Traditional achievers' are a potential source of support for traditional cultural values, if they can take time out from the pursuit of their own self-interest. 'Conforming', and 'self-fulfillment achievers' have combined a commitment to 'do your own thing' with a 'live and let live' philosophy. As a result they are hardly stalwart defenders of traditional values, or indeed anything that might prove controversial. In the meantime, those with strong conviction about reversing traditional American value clusters have the benefit of their certainty, and others' timidity and self-preoccupation. Only the 'principled individualists' have the strength of conviction and the capacity to take unpopular cultural stands in defense of some traditions. However, they are used to being individual not movement voices.

Abraham Lincoln, speaking to the prospect of a country 'half free and half slave', famously said, 'a country divided against itself cannot stand'. He was, of course, referring as much to American culture as to its politics. Whether his insight proves prophetic has become a very troubling contemporary question.

*I am grateful to George De Vos, Jack Diggins and William Runyan for their comments on earlier drafts of this paper.

Notes

1. William J. Clinton (1997) 'Remarks and Question and Answer Session with the American Society of Newspaper Editors', 11 April 1997, *Weekly Compilation of Presidential Documents*, April 14, 33:15, 509.
2. William J. Clinton (1997) 'Remarks at the University of California at San Diego Commencement Ceremony', 14 June 1997, *Weekly Compilation of Presidential Documents*, June 23, 33:25, 877.
3. Creveceour's question and its answer, 'has probably been quoted more than any other in the history of immigration' (Gleason, 1980, 31). The reason, Glazer (1993, 22) remarks, is that it appears to celebrate America's diversity and its role in forging a new national identity. Yet, modern sensibilities alert us to the fact that Indians, women, Hispanics, Asian Americans and blacks are not included in this understanding.

4. The above quotes are all taken from Turner's original presentation, *The Significance of the Frontier in American History* ([1893] 1996, chapter 1, emphasis added). Similarly, Erikson (1963, 293) views the frontier as 'the decisive influence which served to establish in the American identity the extreme polarization which characterizes it.' Here he is referring to the need to prepare children to live in the community life which was taking root, but also to be able to take the physical hardships of homesteading on the frontiers. Potter (1954, 68) makes use of the term frontier in a more psychological sense, and relates it to consumption and abundance.

5. Quoted in Gilles (1994, 3). See also Gleason (1983) and Handler (1994).

6. Wilkinson mentions, but does not agree with, what seems the most likely explanation of this national self-concern, namely that as a country of immigrants we are more likely to be concerned with who we are as a nation, and how the many can become one (cf., Potter, 1954).

7. Citations for the views of foreign visitors are found in Lipset (1963) and Inkeles (1997). These include Creveceour ([1783] 1997) de Tocqueville ([1848] 1998), Martineau (1837), Berger (1943), Brooks (1908), and Bryce (1912). Lipset uses the observations of Martineau and Bryce to suggest that the elements of 'other-directedness' emphasized by Riesman (1950) and Whyte (1956) were in fact present in the earliest periods of American history. However, Inkeles (1997, 164) notes that many foreign observers reached contradictory conclusions about 'this new man, the American'.

8. See his chapters 'Continuity and Change in American National Character', and 'National Character Revisited' in Inkeles (1997), 161–92 and 359–84 respectively.

9. See his 'Reflections on American Identity' in Erikson (1963), 285–325.

10. A similar argument for this criteria of relevance is made by Almond (1954, 47).

11. As Sowell (1994, 4–6) points out, the effectiveness of a particular cultural element or elements can only be judged in relationship to their purpose(s) and effects. We are, he notes, understandably repulsed at the idea of labeling any peoples or culture 'superior', or 'inferior'. Yet, he also underscores a paradox contained in a wholesale reluctance to make any judgments: some cultural elements do work better.

12. There, the term character is understood as a related set of psychological elements with long developmental histories which form the foundations of, and operate across, personality structures. As Baudry (1989, 656) puts it, 'Our concept of character is made necessary because we find in individuals reoccurring clusters of traits with a consistency suggesting that some underlying principles, govern the selection, ordering, and relations of these traits to one another.' Thus, Fenichel's (1945, 463–540) early formulation of 'compulsive character' was built on the clinical findings that orderliness, stubbornness and parsimony were dynamically united by the anxiety caused by the fear of loss of control.

    Attitudes can best be described as stable orientations toward object classes. One has an opinion about the Gulf or Korean war, but an attitude toward war itself (cf., Bem (1970, 14 or Fishbein and Ajzan, 1975, 336). And, Greenstein's (1969, 23) lament about the large number of diverse formulations of 'personality' awaiting political scientists, and others, hoping to make use of the concept is correct. However, it is extremely rare to equate attitude with personalty. The 'functional theory' of attitudes (Smith, 1968) does, but in such an abstract way that it is virtually content free.

    For these reasons, equating character with personality, or worse, attitude, is a categorical mistake. The psychological force, durability and behavioral significance of the former is not matched by the latter.

13. Carleton H. J. Hayes cited in Potter (1954, 12–13). Potter refers to this approach as 'a cabinet of curiosities.'

14. Of course, there is no reason why any 'national character', to the extent it exists, cannot consist of different kinds of psychological elements. What is necessary, however, is some recognition that the elements are not dynamically or functionally equivalent. Moreover, some attention to the psychological connections between, or among, them would also seem a necessary theoretical undertaking.

15. Wilkinson suggests that any discussion of 'American traits' be undertaken in comparison only to their appearance, or lack thereof, in other equivalent populations. He suggests (1988, 3) the comparison standard be with people in 'other modern industrial countries'. But this is rarely, if ever, done.

16. Horney's book entitled, *The Neurotic Personality of Our Time*, is a reflection on American culture and psychology, more generally, than it is a work focused on 'clinical populations'.

17. For de Tocqueville, they both sprang from the same source, the anxiety brought on by unrestrained competitiveness. To this he might well have added the volatile psychological paradox of Americans' conscientious adherence to public (and political) equality, even while devoting themselves wholeheartedly, some would say relentlessly, to their own self-interest primarily reflected in the pursuit of the accumulation of wealth and the social standing that accompanied it. In a similar vain, Hsu (1972, 245–9, 251) argues that the ideal of unlimited equality and self-reliance, and the inability to psychologically measure up to its demands, results in a tendency to embrace its opposite, in this case conformity.

18. For example, his list includes: 'quasi-values' such as material comforts; 'instrumental' values such as power, work and efficiency; 'universalistic values of the Western tradition' such as rationalism, justice freedom, universalistic ethics (?) and values of individual personality; and finally 'particularistic, segmental, or localistic' values.

     For a somewhat different approach to values as resolving 'basic human problems' to which solutions must be found, see Kluckhohn (1953, 246). In her analysis, these problems include: the basic nature of man, man's relation to nature, time orientations, valued personality types, and the relationship of men to each other.

     There are numerous other approaches to values. For example Rokeach (1979) distinguishes between instrumental and terminal values, that is, those you aspire to get to, and those that help you do so.

19. A second key element of Mead's analysis, the fact of being a 'nation of immigrants', also reinforced conformity. Many 'third generation' children of immigrants, she argued, turned their backs on their traditions of origin. As a result, parental authority was downgraded at the expense of those persons and institutions which provided much sought after cues for 'fitting in'. In short, the desire to belong coupled with a lack of reliable parental guides of how to do it, lead outward and elsewhere.

20. Potter (1962) argued for two American egalitarian traditions, one which stressed equal opportunity, the other in public domains where, regardless of measures of social standing, people expected to receive equal social deference. The latter encouraged sensitivity to others and thus an element of 'other-directedness'.

21. The best book on the seductive psychology of the image and the public's role in encouraging it is still Boorstin (1987).

22. Yankelovich's national opinion data on the growing emphasis on self-fulfillment in American culture led him (1981, xix) to conclude that, 'it was not a by-product of affluence, or a shift in the national character toward narcissism, [but

rather] a search for a new American philosophy of life.' Of course, 'philosophies of life' are themselves reflections of values and psychology and, as noted, helped to facilitate the very psychologies that will buttress them.

Optimistically, he saw (1981, 259–60) Americans growing 'less self-absorbed and more prepared to take a first step toward an ethic of commitment'. However, he also noted that the development of such an ethic would require direct support from 'the larger society – political leadership, the mass media, institutional leadership (business, education, labor, artists and scientists, the intellectual community', in short, for the most part all the groups caught up in the ethic of relentless self-interest. Small wonder that seventeen years later, Nicholas Lehmann (1998, 38) writing in the *New York Times Sunday Magazine* lamented a new consensus which 'represents an embrace of...one-way libertarianism: the average citizen has no obligation to the country, but the government has a very serious obligation to that citizen.'

23. Interestingly, as early as the 1940s psychoanalysts began reported treating persons who 'appeared on casual inspection as successful members of the community, as able lawyers, executives, and physicians, [but] they did not, it seems, succeed in the sense of finding satisfaction or fulfillment in their accomplishments.' Cleckely, among the first to notice this group, entitled his study *The Mask of Sanity* (1976) reflecting the then anomalous finding that there were persons who appeared to be functioning well, even very well on a surface, conventional level, but who were seen on closer clinical observation to have areas of deep psychological disturbance which manifested itself in unstable behavior. Among the symptoms of those who would be later classified as 'narcissistic' was a surface adherence to conventional moral norms, coupled with a willingness to exploit others and circumstances for the own benefit. Guilt (Riesman's other-directed superego) seemed largely inoperative.

24. An analysis of President William Clinton's high public approval ratings in the aftermath of the revelations that led to his impeachment are found in Renshon (1998).

25. For example, he reports (1981, 38–9) data that in the mid-1960s, 72 per cent of college students agreed that 'hard work always pays off'. By the early 1970s, this figure had dropped to 40 per cent. These findings were paralleled in adults, for whom, between the late 1960s and the late 1970s the percentage of adults agreeing with that aphorism fell from 58 to 43 per cent.

26. There is an important distinction to be drawn between being slow to judgments, and being adverse to making them. Why Americans now seem more adverse than slow is a question left unanswered by Wolfe, but is nonetheless critical in understanding the public's response to the dilemmas of diversity being fought out around them.

References

Almond, G. A. (1960) *The American People and Foreign Policy*, New York: Preager.

Baudry, F. (1989) 'Character, Character Type, and Character Organization', *Journal of the American Psychoanalytic Association*, vol. 32, pp. 455–77.

Bell, Daniel (1996) *The Cultural Contradictions of Capitalism. 20th Anniversary Edition*, New York: Basic Books.

Bem, D. J. (1970) *Beliefs, Attitudes and Human Affairs*, Belmont, Cal.: Brooks/Cole.

Berger, M. (1943) *The British Traveler in America, 1836–1860*, New York: Columbia University Press.

Boorstin, D. J. (1987 [1961]) *The Image*, New York: Vintage.

Brooks, J. G (1908) *As Others See Us*, New York: Macmillan.

Bryce, J. (1912) *The American Commonwealth*, New York: Macmillan.

Cleckely, Wm. ([1941] 1976) *The Mask of Sanity,* 5th edn, St Louis, Mo.: C. V. Mosby.

Coleman, L. (1941) 'What is American: A Study of Alleged Social Traits', *Social Forces*, vol. 19, p. 4.

Commager, H. S. (1959) *The American Mind: An Interpretation of American Thought*, New Haven, Ct.: Yale University Press.

Cuber, J. F. and R. A. Harper (1948) *Problems of American Society: Values in Conflict*, New York: Henry Holt.

De Creveceour, J. H. St. John ([1783] 1997) [Susan Manning, editor]. *Letters from an American Farmer*, New York: Oxford.

de Tocqueville, A. De. ([1848] 1998) [translated by G. Lawrence, edited by J. P. Mayer] *Democracy in America*, New York: Harper.

Erikson, E. H. (1963) *Childhood and Society,* 2nd edn, revised, New York: Norton.

Erikson, E. H. (1968) *Identity: Youth and Crisis*, New York: Norton.

Erikson, E. H. (1980) *Identity and the Life Cycle*, New York: Norton.

Escobar G. (1999) 'Immigrants' Ranks Tripled In 29 Years,' *The Washington Post*, January 9; Page A01.

Fenichel, O. (1945) *The Psychoanalytic Theory of Neurosis*, New York: Norton.

Fishbein, M. and I. Ajzen. (1975) *Belief, Attitude, Intention and Behavior: An introduction to Theory and Research*, Reading, Ma.: Addison-Wesley.

Gilles, J. R. (1994) 'Introduction,' in J. R. Giles (ed.) *Commemorations: The Politics of National Identity*, (pp. 3–24). Princeton: Princeton

Gorer, G. (1948) *The American People: A Study in National Character*, New York: Norton.

Glazer, N. (1993) 'Is Assimilation Dead?,' *The Annals of the American Academy of Political Science*, 530: 122–136.

Gleason, P. (1980) 'American Identity and Americanization,' in A. Arlov and S. Thernstrom (eds) *Harvard Encyclopedia of American Ethnic Groups*, (pp. 31–38). Cambridge: Harvard University Press.

Greenstein, F. (1969) *Personality and Politics: Problems of Evidence, Inference, and Conceptualization*, Princeton, N.J.: Princeton University Press.

Handler, R. (1994) 'Is Identity A Useful Concept?' in J. R. Giles (ed.) *Commemorations: The Politics of National Identity*, (pp. 27–40). Princeton: Princeton University Press.

Heifetz, R. (1996) *Leadership Without Easy Answers*, Cambridge, Ma: Harvard University Press.

Hoover, K. (1975) *The Politics of Identity*, Urbana: The University of Illinois Press.

Horney, K. (1937) *The Neurotic Personality of Our Time*, New York: Norton.

Hsu, F. K. H. (1972) 'American Core Values and National Character,' in F. L. K. Hsu (ed.) *Psychological Anthropology* (pp. 242–262). Cambridge, Ma: Schenkman Publishing.

Inkeles, A. (1997) *National Character: A Psycho-social Perspective*, New Brunswick, N.J.: Transaction.

Isbister, J. (1996) *The Immigration Debate: Remaking America*, New York: Kurnarian Press.

Isbister, J. (1998) 'Is America to White?,' in E. Sandman (compiler) *What, then is the American, this new man?* (pp. 25–32). Washington, D.C., Center of Immigration Studies.

Kluckhohn. F. and Strodtbeck (1961) *Variations in Value Orientations*, Evanston, I11.: Row Petterson and Co.

Kluckholn, F. (1953) 'Dominant and Variant Value Orientations,' in C. Kluckholn and H. Murray (eds.) *Personality in Nature, Society and Culture* (pp. 342–357). New York: Knopf.

Lasch, C. (1979) *The Culture of Narcissism: American Life in an Age of Diminishing Expectations*, New York: Basic books.

Lehmann, N. (1998) 'The New American Consensus: Government of, by, and for the Comfortable,' *The New York Times Sunday Magazine*, November 1, pp. 37–42, 68–70.

Lerner, M. (1957) *America as a Civilization*, New York: Simon and Shuster.

Lipset, S. M. (1963) *The First New Nation*, New York: Basic Books.

Maharidge, D. (1996) *The Coming White Minority: California's Eruptions and America's Future*, New York: Times Books.

Martineau, H. (1837) *Society in America*, New York: Saunders and Otlay.

Mead, M. (1942) *And Keep Your Powder Dry*, New York: Morrow.

Miller, J. J. (1998) *The Unmaking of Americans: How Multiculturalism Has Undermined America's Assimilation Ethic*, New York: Free Press.

Myrdal, G. ([1944] 1964) *An American Dilemma*, New York: Harper and Row.

Potter, D. (1962) 'The Quest for the National Character,' in John Higgam (ed.) *The Reconstruction of American History*, New York: Harper.

Potter, D. M. (1954) *People of Plenty: Economic Abundance and the American Character*, Chicago: University of Chicago Press.

Portes, A. and M. Zhou. (1994) 'Should Immigrants Assimilate?, '*The Public Interest*, 11:6, 18–33.

Renshon, S. (1998) *The Psychological Assessment of Presidential Candidates*, New York: Routledge.

Riesman, D., with N. Glazer and R. Denny. (1950) *The Lonely Crowd: A Study of the Changing American Character*, New Haven, Ct.: Yale University Press.

Riesman, D., with N. Glazer. (1951) *Faces in the Crowd: Individual Studies in Character and Politics*, New Haven, Ct.: Yale University Press.

Riesman, D. (1980) 'Egocentrism: Is the American Character Changing?,' *Encounter*, 55 (August–September): 19–28.

Rokeach, M. (ed.) (1979) *Understanding Human Values. Individual and Societal*, New York: Free Press.

Rumbaut, R. (1997) 'Assimilation and Its Discontents: Between Rhetoric and Reality,' *International Migration Review*, 31:4.

Salins, P. (1997) *Assimilation, American Style*, New York: Basic Books.

Schelsinger, A., Jr. (1992) *The Disuniting of America: Reflections on A Multicultural Society*, New York. Norton.

Skerry, P. (1988) 'Do We Really Want Immigrants to Assimilate?,' in E. Sandman (compiler) *What, Then is the American, this New Man?* (pp. 37–46). Washington, D.C.: Center of Immigration Studies.

Smith M. B. (1968) 'A Map for the Analysis of Personality and Politics,' *Journal of Social Issues*, 24:15–28.

Sowell, T. (1993) *Race and Culture: A World View*, New York: Basic Books.

Turner, F. J. ([1893] 1996) *The Frontier in American History*, New York: Dover.

Wachtel, P. (1983) *The Poverty of Affluence*, New York: Basic Books.

Whyte, W. H. Jr. (1956) *The Organizational Man*, New York: Simon and Shuster.

Wilkinson, R. (1988) *The Pursuit of American Character*, New York: Harper and Row.

Williams, R. M. (1951) *American Society: A Sociological Interpretation*, New York: Knopf.

Wolfe, A. (1998) *One Nation, After All*, New York: Viking, 1998.
Yankelovich, D. (1981) *New Rules: Searching for Self-fulfillment in a World Turned Upside Down*, New York: Random House.

Index

Aboriginal peoples, 263, 267
abortion, 112
accountability, 50, 55
achievement motivation, 243, 246, 247, 249, 251, 253, 257, 258, 259, 260
achievement versus equality, 289, 301–2
Adorno, T. *et al.*, 90, 98, 109, 110, 115, 117, 124
African Americans, 245
Afro-Brazilians, 259
aggression, 159, 162–5; control of, 161, 167–8, 170, 173; humiliation as, 172
alienation, 242, 243, 244
Almond, Gabriel, 24, 28
Altemeyer, B., 91–3, 94, 96, 97, 98, 99, 109, 110, 115, 117, 120, 124
amae (indulgent love), 74, 185–6
American, meaning of being an, 286; national identity and, 286
American national character, 288–95; abundance and, 294–5; achievement and, 290, 294, 301; ethnicity and 291; conformity and, 294; culture of narcissism and, 294–5, 300; equality and, 292; faith in democracy and 292, 296; fears and 288–9; importance of community and, 294; mobility and, 293; other directedness and, 292–3; pragmatism and, 292; self-reliance and, 292; social character and 289; traits and, 289–91
American national identity, 288, 295; assimilation and, 295; founding basis of, 296–7; and historical change, 289, 296
American values, 286, 291–2; attempt to weight, 293; behavior and, 291–2; beliefs and 291; equality and, 301; ideals and, 292, 295, 296; institutions and, 300–1; instrumental and terminal, 293; relationship to American character,

294; relationship to each other, 293; unitary, 296; value cluster and, 296
American voter: attitudes of, 194–5
Angloconformity, 264, 266, 280
anomie, 119, 242, 262
anthropology: and culture concept of, 24; methodology of, 26–7
anti-minority prejudice, 99–103
antidemocratic, 111, 117
Arab–Israeli conflict, 132
Aristotle, 18
armed conflict, 121
assassination, 136, 143, 264
assimilation: dilemmas of, 296
attitudes, 265, 267
attitudinal variables, 123
Aum Shinrikyo (Supreme Truth) cult, 197
authoritarian: actions, 110; aggression, 110–12, 124; attitudes, 108, 111, 115–17, 121–3, 125; beliefs, 112; character, 117; conventionalism, 109, 124; dictatorship, 113; government, 115, 124, 125; hierarchy, 110–12; ideas, 109, 110; organization, 110; personality, 90–3, 108, 117, 196–7; reactions, 115; regimes, 109–11, 123–5; social attitudes, 93–4; state(s), 111, 113, 118; submission, 110–12, 124
authoritarianism, 108–11, 117, 119–21, 124
authority, 35–6, 115, 117, 121, 186
authority ranking, 50
authority relations, 115, 117, 121, 205–7, 211–13
authority structures, 118
awase ('to adopt oneself to the other person, particularly to the guest'), 186

Balinese cockfighting, 26
Balthazar, L., 280

311

Basic law, 140–1
Befu, Haruhiro, 191, 193 293
Bell, Daniel, 11
Benedict, Ruth, 3, 6, 24, 25, 185
benevolent authoritarianism, 139
'benevolent leader', 195
Berry, J. W., 264, 265, 266, 267, 277,
    281, 282
biased elections, 121–3
Billig, M., 79, 110
blame, *see* policy-makers' tactics to
    avoid blame
Boas, Franz, 24
Bonta, B., 104
boundary definition and maintenance,
    38, 42, 68–9, 149–50
Broek, A. van den, 217, 218, 219
Brooker, P., 109
Bucci, W., 173–4, 180
buckpassing, 86
Buddhism, 207–8
Bulgaria, 219–20, 224, 226–27, 230
burakumin (descendants of former
    outcasts), 192

Canadianism, 268, 277
capital punishment, 112
causal accounts (vs. normative
    accounts), 202, 214
causal model, 121–3
causal relationships, 124
Central and Eastern Europe, *see* Eastern
    Europe
censorship, 112
change, 201–3
Chagnon, N. A., 79
charisma, 74
China, 207
chosen trauma and chosen glory, 150–1
civil liberties, 111
civil rights, 109, 124
Clinton, William, J., 285
cognitive schema, 89
cognitive style, 120
Cohen, Abner, 41–2
Cohen, Raymond, 148
collectivism, 119, 124
Cold War period, 192, 194
Comaroff, Jean, 26
Communism, 109

Communist, 110, 117, 118
Communist regimes, change of life
    circumstances after collapse of,
    231–2, 234–5; impact of living
    under (adaptation to,) 217–24,
    227–8, 230, 234–5; political
    education in, 218
commensurability, *see*
    incommensurability
communal sharing, 50
comparison, *see* incommensurability
compartmentalizing, 50, 57
community, 35, 36
communication, 74, 77
concealment, 100
conflict among values, 52; *see also*
    tradeoffs
conflict, 36; and culture, 36; external,
    39; internal, 39; redefinition, 146
Confucian heritage, 246, 247
Confucian traditions, 139
Confucianism, 207–8
communication, 184–6
competition and anxiety, 298
competition and loneliness, 293
competitive-jungle worldview, 97, 99,
    107
concurrent validity, 113
conflict, 192
'conflict model', 192
constitutive incommensurability, 49
constitutive rules, 47–8
consumption and loneliness, 295
conformity and anxiety, 289–98
conforming achievers, 303
consensus, 184, 189, 191
'consensus model', 192
consciousness, 175, 179–80; political,
    160, 172, 178–9; and the
    Unconscious, 160, 167, 175–8,
    179–80; *see* also Unconscious
contact, 264, 282
cooperative-harmony worldview, 97,
    99
core authoritarianism, 109
cousin marriage, 118
Crevecoeur, J. H., 287, 289, 291
crosscultural equivalence, 132
crosscultural research in Japan, 118–26:
    amae (indulgent love) and, 120;

anomie and, 119; charisma and, 119; communication and, 119, 120; Diet members and 123, 125; *haragei* ('the art of the abdomen') and, 120; 'heart to heart communication,' or empathic understanding) and, 120; harmony and, 119, 125; homogeneous society and, 118; *honne* ('the real intention') and, 124; identity and, 119; ideology, 119; *ishin-denshin* ('traditional mental telepathy,' *machiai seiji* ('behind-the-scene politics') and, 125; *misshitsu seiji* ('political decision made behind closed doors') and, 125; national character (Japanese) and, 118; *nemawashi* ('trimming of a tree's roots prior to its being transplanted') and, 120; Political: Leader and, 121; Socialization and, 119; *tatemae* ('formal truth') and, 124; Western society and, 120, 121; xenophobia and, 119

crosscultural studies 193, 196–7

crosscultural techniques: distinctive methods for cross-cultural political psychology research, 67; diverse theoretical perspectives and, 66–7

crosscutting ties, 35, 147

crossnational, 117, 124, 125

Crystal, D. S., 229

cultural anthropology: mixed legacy for political psychology, 3–4; non-judgmental nature of, 4

cultural causes, 116, 117

cultural change 48, 51, 58–9, 229–30

cultural codes, 297–300

cultural constitutive rules, 47

cultural dissenters, 303

cultural domains, *see* domains of sociality

cultural factors, 116, 120, 124

cultural goal schema, 96–7, 104

cultural institutions and conflict, 304

cultural nationalism, 183

cultural presuppositions, 47, 48

cultural relativism, 245

cultural socialization, 97–9

cultural truths, 5

cultural values, 94–5, 117, 121

cultural variables, 115, 123, 125

cultural worldview, 96–7

culturally constituted elements, 34, 70

culture: adaptive functions of, 6; and authority, 42; 'basic personality' and, 7–8; and change, 71; and communication, 42; concept of, 20–3, 33–4, 43, 70, 72; consequences of, 5–6, 10; critical theory and, 7; and decision-making, 42; definition of groups, 38; and discipline, 42; and distinctiveness, 41–2; and elites, 78; the how does culture work problem, 71–3; the humanities, 25; and identity, 68–9, 71; and ideology, 42; and layers of meaning, 79; and mobilization, 41–2, 73, 151; and organization, 41–2; and peacemaking, 152–3; and political prioritization, 34–5; as a political resource, 41–3; and politics, 33, 67, 71; popularity of concept, 20–1, 26; and power inequalities, 78–9; quantitative and qualitative approaches to, 23; rational choice theory and, 29; and religion, 42–3; subjective character of, 21–2; as a system of meaning, 34, 37, 72; the unit of analysis problem, 68–9; and values 217, 219–21; the within-culture variance problem 69–70

culture free, 125

culture and personality, 89, 289, 293: 'civilized' vs. 'primitive' definition of, 3; controversial nature of, 10–11; development of, 4–5; early psychoanalytic views of, 2–3; feelings, categories and, 5–6; functionalist views of, 5; as human product, 4; identity and, 18–19; immigration and, 11; intercultural contact and, 6; judgements of, 12–13; as learned understanding, 5–6; ordinary social practices and, 8; policy and, 9; poverty and, 7; regulation of expression and 6; social change and 6; theoretical use of in WWII, 7; unconscious and, 5; view of, 5

culture and political psychology: cognition and, 13; early studies of 4; group dynamics as basis for the study of, 14; historical experiences and, 12–13; multi-cultural, multi-ethnic states and, 11, 13; multiple identities and, 12–13; personality as culture writ large, 3–4; political culture and, 12; state authoritarianism and 15; values in relation to, 13–15
culture and psychological identity, 286
culture wars, 41, 285–6, 300, 302, 304
cultures of honor, 104
cultures of prejudice, 104
Czechia (Czech Republic) 219, 224, 226

Daimyo, 212
D'Andrade, R., 40, 43, 70, 72, 95–6
dangerous world belief, 96, 101
Dangerous World Scale, 101
de Tocqueville, A., 302
decision-makers' strategies to avoid blame, 50, 59, 61–3; buckpassing, 50; compartmentalizing, 50; concealment, 61–2; decision avoidance, 62; demagoguery, 63; obfuscation of tradeoffs, 50, 61–2; spheres of justice, 86
decision-making, 189–91
decision-making by a group, 51, 54–5
democracy, 108, 111, 116, 118
democracy, In Eastern Europe 230–1, 235
Deng Xiaoping, 138
Dependence, 185–6; *see also amae*
delay of gratification, 301
Deutsch, Karl, 20
developing countries, 119
deviancy: political, 242; social, 242
dictatorship(s), 109–11, 124
Diet (Japan's National Parliament) 188, 197
Diet members, 77, 78, 196–7
differentiating societies, 39
discriminant validity, 113
distributive injustice, 132
distributive justice, 129, 137
diversity, 265, 270; and political leadership, 285; and divisive social issues, 285–6

dogmatism, 109, 117
Doi, Takeo, 185–6, 210–11
domains of sociality, 47, 48, 50
Duckitt, J., 120

Eastern Europe: comparisons with Western Europe 218, 224–34; democracy in, 230–1, 235; economic level in, 219–20, 228, 232, 234–5; life circumstances after collapse of communism in, 231–2, 234–5; life under communist regimes in 217–24, 229, 234; religion in 219, 228–29; values in, 217–35
economic development, 115, 116, 119–21, 123–5
economic insecurity, 299–300
economic situation, 115, 120
education, 115, 120, 121
educational attainment, 120, 122–4
educational development, 116, 119–21
egalitarianism, 136
elections, 111, 121
emotions, 162; anger, 159–60, 162, 168, 172; cultural emotion schemas, 159, 163, 167, 168, 171, 173–5; desire, 159, 162, 164, 167–8; emotion stories, 159, 161, 162, 164–5, 167–70, 173, 175, 180; envy, 169; in folktales, 162, 164–5, 175, 178; *see also* aggression, inequality
endogamous, 118
endowment effect, 56
enryo ('social reserve'), 185
ethnic conflict: and culture, 146–53; and ethnic cleansing, 149; and boundary maintenance, 148–9; and interpretations, 148
ethnic groups, 266: attitudes toward, 216, 268, 271, 272; origin, 266, 272–80
ethnicity, 241
ethnocentric biases, 125
ethnocentrism, 73, 153, 153, 265
Equal Employment Opportunity Law (EEOL), 209
equality matching 50
erabi ('selective'), 186
Erikson, Erik, 25, 288

exogamous, 118
extended family, 118

F scale, 90
family, 117, 118
family attitudes, 117
family and internalization, 259, 260, 261
family practices, 115, 117
family structure, 117, 118, 121, 123
family system, 121
family traditions, 115, 117
fascism, 109, 119
feudal family structures, 118
fuehrer principle, 110
France: political learning in, 195
Frankfurter Schule, 117
free elections, 121
Freedom House, 115, 116, 120
Fromm, E., 109, 115, 117
Freud, S., 176–7

Gay, Peter, 24
Geertz, Clifford, 26, 34, 35, 40, 44n, 152
gender gap, 120, 121, 123
generalizing societies, 39
Georgia, 219–20, 224, 226
global, 123, 125
Goldstein, K. and Blackman, S., 115, 120
Green Party, 53
Greenfeld, Liah, 20
grid-group analysis, 84
gross national product, 120–3
group: group dynamism, 189; 'group
    model', 192; 'group orientation',
    187, 188, 193
guilt culture, 185
Gurr, Ted Robert, 146

Haeri, S., 205
haragei ('the art of the abdomen'), 75, 184
harmony, 74, 78, 184, 187, 189, 192
hierarchical culture, 115, 116, 118, 119,
    121–3
hierarchical societies, 119
Hitler, Adolf, 97
Hobbes, 241
Hofstede, G., 95, 115, 117–19
homogeneity, 185
homogenous society, 73–4
homosexuality, 112

honne ('the real intention'), 77, 185
Horkheimer, M., *et al.*, 115, 117
Horney, Karen, 292
Horowitz, Donald, 149
human rights, 108, 109, 115, 124, 125
human rights bodies, 112
Hungary 217, 219, 224, 226, 231–4
Huntington, Samuel, 6–8, 147, 148

identification: dynamics of, 37; objects
    of, 37; vagueness of definition of,
    288–9
identity, 74, 187, 193, 269, 280, 288–90:
    civic, 274–7; definition of, 36–7,
    288; ethnic, 274–7; external social
    processes and, 287; individual and
    collective, 37; multiple, 69
ideology, 51, 52–4, 60, 74, 109–12, 194
'Ie' (Japanese household), 212
Ike, Nobutaka, 187–8
imitation, 48
immigration and diversity, 285–6
implementation paradigms, prototypes,
    and rules, 51, 53–4
incest taboo, 118
incommensurability, 49
individual-group disparities, 302
individualism, 119, 287
individualism-collectivism, 128–9, 132
individualistic cultures, 119
inequality, 159, 171; and authority, 159;
    and dependence, 168, 170, 171,
    178; and humiliation, 160, 161,
    169, 171–3, 179; and retaliation,
    168–70, 172–3, 179
Inglehart, R., 228, 230–1
integrative complexity, 54
interactional justice, 130
intercultural communications, 148
interests, 33, 34, 40, 147
internalization, 291
internalized constraint, 242
interpretations, *see* psychocultural
    interpretations
Intifada, 135–6
Iran: gender, 203–5; *'hejab'* (veil), 204–5;
    modernization, 205; everyday social
    practices, 205; temporary marriage,
    205
Iraq, 136

ishin-denshin ('traditional mental telepathy,' 'heart to heart communication,' or empathic understanding), 74, 184
Israeli–Egyptian relations, 148
Israeli–Palestinian conflict, 146, 150, 153–4
Italy, politicians in, 196–7

Japan, 73–8, 182–200
Japanese: as an American minority, 242, 244; as a Brazilian minority, 258, 259; Burakumin, 245; Connor's college-level research and, 258; constitution, 191; delinquency patterns, 245; Diet, 211; education, 208–9; family and group responsibility, 248; gender, 207–11; guilt, 248; mentorship, 259; political: candidates, 188, competence, 188, culture, 193, cynicism, 195–6, efficacy, 196, leadership, 196–7, party identification, 194, party system, 194, socialization, 195; politics, 210–11; race, 184; role behavior, 249; *sarariman*, 212; Shogun, 212; social obligation, *giri-ninjo*, 247; Vaugn's high school level research, 258; voter, 187, 194–5
Joint Declaration, 139–41

Kabashima, Ikuo, 194
Kaifu, Toshiki 191
Kameda, A., 209
Kelman, Herbert, 153–4
Kluckholm, Clyde, 7, 24
Kohak, E., 222
Koreans in Japan: 245, 261; deviancy, 251; discrimination, 251
Kosovo, 51, 150
kuuki ('air', 'mood' or 'atmosphere'), 185, 189–91

labor unions, 112
Lasch, Christopher, 24, 295
Lasswell, Harold, 24
leadership, 23, 187–8
leadership principle, 110

learning cultural paradigms, 48
left-wing authoritarianism, 117
Leighton, Alexander, 24
Leites, Nathan, 8, 24
liberalism, 53
libertarianism, 53
Lincoln, Abraham, 304
Lipset, S. M., 290, 298, 302
Loman, Willy, 295
Lu Ping, 140

machiai seiji ('behind-the-scene politics'), 78
machismo, 104
male dominance, 120
Margaret Thatcher, 138
market pricing, 50
Marx, 242
Marxism, 53
Maslow, A. H., 219
maturational levels, 242
maximizing utility, 58
McClelland, D. C., 202
Mead, Margaret, 3, 24, 25
Meiji era, 208
Meiji restoration, 191
Meloen, J., 112, 113, 117, 120
Mexican Americans, 245
micro–macro problem, 20
Middlebrook, K. J., 203
military conflict, 121–3
Minami, Hiroshi, 183
minorities, 192
minority group adaptation, 244
minority status, 241
misshitsu seiji ('political decision made behind closed doors'), 78
Moghaddam F. M., 201–3, 229
'Mommy track', 210
Moor, R. de, 217, 218, 219
moral authority, 241
moral evaluations, 48, 58, 59–61; *see also* trade-offs; taboo trade-offs
moral exclusion, 135
motivational goal, 95–7
motives: attribution of, 39–40
multi-causal model, 116
multicultural assumption, 264; ideology, 267, 270, 277; policy, 264

multiculturalism, 301
multidisciplinary, 125
multiple loyalties, 35

Nakane, Chie, 187
national character (Japanese), 74, 183,
184, 192: *nemawashi* ('trimming of a
tree's roots prior to its being
transplanted'), 74, 189;
nihonbunkaron ('discussions of
Japanese culture'), 183; *nihonjinron*
('discussions of the Japanese' or
'theorizing on the Japanese'), 183,
184, 185, 187, 188, 191, 192, 193;
nihonkyosetsu ('theorizing on
Japaneseness'), 183; *nihonron*
('discussions on Japan'), 183;
nihonshakairon ('discussions of
Japanese society'), 183; *oyabun-
kobun* (boss-employee or master
follower), 187
national character traits, 290; and social
class, 291
national core culture, 298
national cultural clusters, 296–7, 301
National Front (UK), 79
national identity, relationship of
national character to, 287, 295–6;
frontier hypothesis and, 287
national unity, 264
nationalist ideology, 109
Nazism, 109
nemawashi ('trimming of a tree's roots
prior to its being transplanted'), 74
Neumann, F., 115
new American man, 287–8; ambition
and 432; immigration and, 287,
mobility and 288; opportunity and,
287–8
Nigerian civil war and reconciliation,
152
non-western cultures, 125
Northern Ireland, 43, 150, 151, 152
not culture free, 125
nuclear family, 118

obedience, 110
observation as mechanism for learning a
culture, 48; *see also* methods in
crosscultural political psychology

observers' reactions to taboo trade-offs,
see taboo trade-offs
Ogbu, J., adaptation theory of voluntary
and involuntary migrants, 243
operational codes and culture, 8
opposition parties and politicians, 63–4
opportunity and ambition, 291
Oslo Accords, 132, 134

patriarchal family structures, 118
Patten, 140–2
Peterson, S. R., 206–7
Poland 217, 219, 224, 226, 231–4
policy-makers' tactics to avoid blame,
see decision-makers' strategies
political: demonstration, 192–3;
leadership, 188; personalized
channels, 187–8
political culture, 108–11, 124; concept
of, 24; crosscultural studies of 8–10;
revival of concept, 27 operation
code of the politburo as example of,
8; value approach to, 9
political education (political teaching),
218, 230
political factors, 116
political ideology, *see* ideology
political leader, 75
political prioritization and culture,
34–5
political psychology, 125
political psychology and culture, 3
political rights, 109
political science and psychology, 18–20
political system, 116, 121
political system: impact on personal
values, 217, 219–20, 227–28, 230,
234–5; in Eastern Europe 218–20,
223, 230–2, 234–5
post-materialism, 119
power distance, 119, 129–30, 131–2,
134, 137, 139
PP-MAD scale, 96, 99
Pratto, F., 91–2
precedents, *see* implementation
paradigms, prototypes and rules
principled individualists, 303
prisoners of conscience, 112
procedural injustice, 133
procedural justice, 130, 139,

projective tests, 79; *a priori* judgements, 80; rapport, 82; scoring, 80; validity, 80
propaganda, 109
Protestant Ethic, 301
prototypes, *see* implementation paradigms, prototypes and rules
psychocultural interpretations, 33, 147, 150–1; and dispositions, 147; the dynamics of, 37; and ethnic conflict, 147, 150–1; frameworks for, 39–40
psychological factors, 116
psychological lag, 246
Putnam, Robert, 28, 229

Qing government, 137

race, 263
rational choice theory, 40, 43; and culture, 29
Redfield, Robert, 24
region: and cultural mobilization, 42–3; origin, 270, 272–80
relational models and relational theory, 48, 50–61; *see also* authority ranking, communal sharing, domains of sociality, equality matching, ideology, market pricing, taboo trade-offs
Reich, W., 109, 117
relationships, 56–7
religion in Europe, 218, 228–9
repression of opposition, 112
retributive injustice, 134–5
retributive justice, 130–1, 134, 141
Richler, M., 280
right-wing authoritarianism, 117
ringisei ('a system of referential inquiry about a superior's intentions'), 189
rituals and symbols of identity, 146
Rokeach, M.,109, 117
Rorschach, 79; collaborative fieldwork, 81
Ross, M. H., 96, 98, 104
Russia, 219–20, 224–25, 226–27
RWA scale, 91–2, 93–4, 96, 99, 101, 103

Sahlin, Marshall, 27
Sapir, Edward, 24

Schaffner, B., 115, 117
schema, 89
Schwartz, S. H., 94–5, 217–20, 224–25
Scott, James, 26, 172
SDO scale, 91–2, 93, 94, 96, 97, 99, 101, 103
security, 264, 277, 281, 282
security–autonomy goal-schema, 96
self-fulfilment, 300–1
self-interest versus community, 301
sempai-kohai (senior-junior), 187
shame (shame culture), 185
sharia, 130
Shils, E., 117
Sidanius, J., 91–2, 96
Sino–British conflict, 137
Simpson, M., 120
Slovakia, 217, 219, 224, 226, 231–4
Slovenia, 219, 224, 226
Sniderman, P., 280
social class, 241
social conformity, 98, 101, 103
social deviancy, 241
social Dominance Orientation, 91–2
social identity, 241
Social reducton theory, 202–3, 213
socialization, 74
socio-economic development, 116
socio-political attitudes, 93–4
soto ('outside'), 185
South Africa, 104–5, 150, 152
spheres of justice, 50; *see also* domains, incommensurability
'spiral of silence' theory, 191
Spiro, Melford, 34, 70
Spouse selection, 118
Sri Lanka, 151, 152
state authoritarianism, 108, 109, 111–17, 120–5
State Authoritarianism Index, 112–15, 118–21
state terror, 113
status anxiety and conformity, 299
Stern, D., 173–4
Stoller, R., 172–3, 178
Stone, W., *et al.*, 117
strikes, 193
submissiveness, 186
substance and method, 66
suppression, 112

suppression of criticism, 112
suppression of opposition, 112

taboo trade-offs, 47–64; definition, 49;
    no criterion for, 52; observers'
    responses, 50, 59–61; permissibility,
    50; responses to, 59–64; trade-offs;
    violations, 50
Tajfel, H., 283
tatemae ('formal truth'), 77, 185
techniques: as method for clarification
    of advantages and limits, 66; in
    relation to more systematic and
    reliable analyses, 66
terror, 110, 111, 113, 124
terrorism, 134–6, 143
Thematic Apperception Test (TAT), 79,
    246; differences among Brazilians,
    258, 259; interpersonal concerns,
    80; Korean results, 251–7;
    longitudinal comparisons of
    Japanese, 257; longitudinal use, 82;
    modification, 80; normative
    themes, 80
threat-control culture, 98
threat-control goal-schema, 96
Todd, E., 115, 117, 118
Tokugawa era, 208
tolerance, 265, 268, 277, 281
totalitarianism, 118
toughmindedness, 99, 101, 103
trade-offs, 47–64; cognitive
    incommensurability, 49; economic
    theory, 48–9; implicit, 58–9; moral
    limits to, 49; resistance to, 49; taboo
    trade-offs; utility maximization, 58
trade unions, 112
traditional achievers, 302, 304
traditional family structure, 116, 117,
    122, 123
traits: and interior psychology, 290–1;
    temperament and, 291
Treaty of Nanking, 137
Tsujimura, Akira, 184–5
Turner, Frederick Jackson, 287, 292
type of government, 116, 122

uchi ('inside'), 185
Unconscious, 160, 175, 179–80;
    political, 175–8; projection, 160,

177–8; repression, 161, 174–5,
    176–8, 179–80; schema, 160, 162,
    167, 175
undemocratic rule, 109
United Kingdom: political learning, 195;
    views on political leaders, 195
United Nations Peace Cooperation Bill,
    191–2
United States: children's attitudes
    toward leaders in, 195; gender and
    politics, 213–14; new sexism, 213;
    political protest in, 193; relations
    with Japan, 147, 184; voters'
    behavior in, 194–5, 196

value clusters, 296–7; cultural codes
    and, 297–8; definition of, 296;
    freedom and opportunity as, 297;
    national cultural cluster and, 297
values, 50–1, 55–6, 62: acclimation
    218–22, 230, 234; change of
    218–19, 224, 229–34; compensation
    219, 222–23, 227, 230; cross-
    national study of 217–18, 220–21,
    224–29, 231–4; cultural, 217–21,
    233–5; impact of adaptation to life
    circumstances on 218–24, 227–31,
    234–5; in Eastern Europe, 217–19,
    221–35; impact of economic level
    on (economic development), 220,
    228, 234–5; impact of
    indoctrination on (political
    education, political teaching), 218,
    224, 229; impact of political system
    on (political atmosphere), 217,
    219–20, 230, 234–5; impact of
    religion on, 228, 235; in Western
    compared to Eastern Europe,
    218–19, 224–26, 228–30, 232–4
Vanhanen, T., 125
Verba, Sidney, 28
vertical society, 184, 185
Volkan, Vamik, 150–1, 152

war, 121
West (Western culture), 182–5, 188,
    193–6
Western countries, 119
Western cultures, 125

Western Europe: comparisons with
    Eastern Europe 224, 225–35
Western society, 75–6
Western standards, 125
Wiggershaus, R., 117
Whiting, Beatrice, 72
world map, 113, 114

worldview, 34, 36, 43, 69, 96–7, 98, 101,
    104, 150

xenophobia, 74

Yamamoto, Shichiei, 189–90
Yanomamo, 79